Surviving Field Research

In recent decades there has been increasing attention to mass atrocities such as genocide, war crimes, crimes against humanity and other gross human rights violations. At the same time, there has been a vast increase in the number of academics and researchers seeking to analyse the causes of, and offer practical responses to, these atrocities. Yet there remains insufficient discussion of the practical and ethical challenges surrounding research into serious abuses, and dealing with vulnerable populations.

The aim of this multi-edited volume is to guide researchers in identifying and addressing challenges in conducting qualitative research in difficult circumstances, such as conducting research in autocratic or uncooperative regimes, with governmental or non-governmental officials, and perhaps most importantly, with reluctant respondents such as victims of genocide or war criminals. The volume proceeds in five substantive sections, each addressing a different challenge of conducting field research in conflict scenarios:

- Ethics
- Access
- Veracity
- Security
- Identity, objectivity, behaviour

This important and necessary text will be vital reading for students, scholars and researchers in the areas of research methods, international relations, anthropology and human rights. It will also be of keen interest to policy practitioners and especially relevant for those working in the regions of Africa, Latin America, and Asia.

Chandra Lekha Sriram is Professor of Human Rights and Founder of the Centre on Human Rights in Conflict at the University of East London, UK.

John C. King is scholar-in-residence at the American University, USA.

Julie A. Mertus is Professor and Co-Director of the MA program in Ethics, Peace and Global Affairs at the American University, USA.

Olga Martin-Ortega is Senior Research Fellow at the Centre on Human Rights in Conflict at the University of East London, UK.

Johanna Herman is Research Fellow at the Centre on Human Rights in Conflict at the University of East London, UK.

Research on civil war and peacebuilding has grown substantially in the past decade, but there is as yet little guidance for those willing to go to the field in the special conditions of conflict zones. This volume of case studies provides a wealth of ethnographic information about what to expect and extremely useful advice from those who have done it. Practitioners as well as students will find it immensely welcome.

Susan L. Woodward,
The Graduate Center, City University of New York, USA

The contributors to this imaginative book confront head on the daunting obstacles of field research in 'difficult' places to produce a sensitive guide to the ethics and responsibilities that attend such work.

The academic world is quite aware of the challenges and predicaments of conducting field research in difficult, often violent environments and it needs this well informed guide and advice of noted scholars. The chapters in this book capture well some of the most important considerations for researchers who work in societies where one's research subjects face threats of reprisals, the burdens of government surveillance, and the personal difficulties posed by divided communities.

This sensitive guide to the ethical and practical issues that accompany the conduct of field research in conflict and post-conflict settings (Rwanda, Guatemala, for example) is an absolute must for those who care about the safety and well being of those among whom they work. Each chapter is truthful and honest, and is based upon the authors' deep grasps of the scholar's craft.

Gracefully written, this collection of the reflections of remarkably talented scholars, should make a major impact on thinking about the responsibilities of the field researcher in situations where their questions and conclusions can pose threats to the subjects of their research and to themselves.

William Reno, Associate Professor & Director of Graduate Studies,
Department of Political Science, Northwestern University, USA

Surviving Field Research
Working in violent and difficult situations

Edited by
Chandra Lekha Sriram, John C. King,
Julie A. Mertus, Olga Martin-Ortega,
Johanna Herman

LONDON AND NEW YORK

First published 2009
by Routledge
2 Park Square Milton Park Abingdon Oxon OX14 4RN

Simultaneously published in the USA and Canada
by Routledge
270 Madison Avenue, New York, NY 10016

Routledge is an imprint of the Taylor & Francis Group, an informa business.

© 2009 Chandra Lekha Sriram, John C. King, Julie A. Mertus, Olga Martin-Ortega, Johanna Herman selection and editorial matter; individual contributors, their contributions

Typeset in Times New Roman by
Taylor & Francis Books
Printed and bound in Great Britain by
CPI Antony Rowe, Chippenham, Wiltshire

All rights reserved. No part of this book may be reprinted or reproduced or utilised in any form or by any electronic, mechanical, or other means, now known or hereafter invented, including photocopying and recording, or in any information storage or retrieval system, without permission in writing from the publishers.

British Library Cataloguing in Publication Data
A catalogue record for this book is available from the British Library

Library of Congress Cataloging in Publication Data
Surviving field research : working in violent and difficult situations / edited by Chandra Lekha Sriram ... [et al.].
  p. cm.
Includes bibliographical references and index.
  1. Social conflict–Research. 2. Ethnic conflict–Research. 3. Violence–Research. I. Sriram, Chandra Lekha, 1971-
    HM1121.S87 2009
    303.6072–dc22
                    2008054934

ISBN10: 0-415-48934-2 (hbk)
ISBN10: 0-415-48935-0 (pbk)
ISBN10: 0-203-87527-3 (ebk)

ISBN13: 978-0-415-48934-8 (hbk)
ISBN13: 978-0-415-48935-5 (pbk)
ISBN13: 978-0-203-87527-8 (ebk)

Contents

About the contributors   vii
Acknowledgments   x

1 Introduction: Surviving field research   1
JULIE MERTUS

2 Demystifying field research   8
JOHN C. KING

PART 1
Ethics   19

3 Exceeding scholarly responsibility: IRBs and political constraints   21
JUDY HEMMING

4 Methods and ethics with research teams and NGOs: Comparing experiences across the border of Rwanda and Democratic Republic of Congo   38
ELIZABETH LEVY PALUCK

5 Maintenance of standards of protection during writeup and publication   57
CHANDRA LEKHA SRIRAM

PART 2
Access   69

6 Got trust? The challenge of gaining access in conflict zones   71
JULIE NORMAN

7 From cell phones to coffee: Issues of access in Egypt and Lebanon   91
COURTNEY RADSCH

8 'That is not what we authorised you to do … ': Access and
government interference in highly politicised research environments
SUSAN M. THOMSON   108

PART 3
Veracity   125

9 Researching repellent groups: Some methodological considerations
on how to represent militants, radicals, and other belligerents   127
CAROLYN GALLAHER

10 Interpreting truth and lies in stories of conflict and violence   147
LEE ANN FUJII

PART 4
Security   163

11 Maintenance of personal security: ethical and operational issues   165
JULIE MERTUS

12 Impact on research of security-seeking behaviour   177
AMY ROSS

PART 5
Identity, objectivity, behaviour   189

13 Fieldwork, objectivity, and the academic enterprise   191
MARIE-JOËLLE ZAHAR

14 Dilemmas of self-representation and conduct in the field   213
STEPHEN BROWN

15 There and back: Surviving research in violent and
difficult situations   227
OLGA MARTIN-ORTEGA AND JOHANNA HERMAN

Selected Sources   242
Index   256

About the contributors

Stephen Brown is Associate Professor of Political Science at the University of Ottawa (Canada). His main research interests are foreign aid, democratization, political violence, conflict prevention and peacebuilding, mainly in relation to Sub-Saharan Africa.

Lee Ann Fujii is Assistant Professor of Political Science and International Affairs at George Washington University. She is also Program Coordinator for the politics cohort of the Women's Leadership Program. Her most recent book is *Killing Neighbors: Webs of Violence in Rwanda* (Cornell University Press, 2009).

Carolyn Gallaher is an associate professor at American University. Her research focuses on right-wing politics in the US and abroad. Her first book, *On the Fault Line: Race, Class and the American Patriot Movement*, examined the militia phenomenon of the 1990s. Her recent book, *After the Peace: Loyalist Paramilitaries in Post-Accord Northern Ireland* examines paramilitary activity in a post-conflict setting.

Judy Hemming is a research scholar in the International Relations Program, School of Social Sciences at the Australian National University. She has conducted extensive fieldwork on sex trafficking and sex work in Southeast Asia and the Pacific and has several publications relating to this area.

Johanna Herman is a Research Fellow on the Centre on Human Rights in Conflict, an interdisciplinary centre aimed at developing knowledge about the relationship between human rights and conflict (www.uel.ac.uk/chrc). Her research interests include peacebuilding, transitional justice and human rights.

John C. King is scholar-in-residence in the School of International Service at American University. He focuses his research primarily on investigating determinants of disrespect for personal human integrity rights and on methodological innovation in both quantitative and qualitative research designs.

viii *About the contributors*

Julie A. Mertus is Professor and Co-Director of the MA program in Ethics, Peace and Global Affairs at American University. Her books include *Bait and Switch: Human Rights and U.S. Foreign Policy* (Routledge, 2004); *Human Rights and Conflict* (United States Institute of Peace, 2006) (editor, with Jeffrey Helsing); and *Kosovo: How Myths and Truths Started a War* (University of California Press, 1999).

Julie M. Norman has a Ph.D. in International Relations from American University, with concentrations in Peace and Conflict Resolution and Human Rights. She is currently working on a book on Palestinian nonviolent resistance during the second *intifada*, based on her dissertation research.

Olga Martin-Ortega is Senior Research Fellow at the Centre on Human Rights in Conflict in the University of East London. She received her Ph.D. in Law at the University of Jaen (Spain). She conducts research in the areas of business and human rights, post-conflict reconstruction and transitional justice. Her lastest monograph is *Empresas Multinacionales y Derechos Humanos en Derecho Internacional* (Bosch, 2008).

Elizabeth Levy Paluck received her Ph.D. in Social Psychology from Yale University. Her research focuses on the role of mass media and dialogue for prejudice and conflict reduction. She is an Assistant Professor at Princeton University's Psychology Department and the Woodrow Wilson School of International and Public Affairs.

Courtney Radsch is a Ph.D. candidate at American University in Washington DC whose research focuses on media in the Arab world. Her dissertation is about cyberactivism in Egypt. She is also Associate Editor and Senior Journalist for AlArabiya.net and is currently based in Dubai.

Amy Ross is Associate Professor of Geography at the University of Georgia, and affiliate faculty for the Institute of Women's Studies and Latin American Studies Program. Her research examines transformations in power and space through the effort to achieve justice and accountability in the wake of mass atrocity. She has researched truth commissions and international courts in Latin America, Africa and Europe.

Chandra Lekha Sriram is Chair of Human Rights in the University of East London School of Law and Director of the Centre on Human Rights in Conflict (www.uel.ac.uk/chrc). She conducts research on human rights, conflict prevention, and peacebuilding. Her most recent book is *Peace as governance: Power-sharing, armed groups, and contemporary peace negotiations* (Palgrave, 2008).

Susan M. Thomson is a doctoral candidate in political science at Dalhousie University in Halifax, Canada. Her dissertation research focuses on the lived experiences of ordinary Rwandans with the post-genocide policy of national unity and reconciliation. She will pursue post-doctoral research at the University of Ottawa from 2009.

Marie-Joëlle Zahar is Associate Professor of Political Science at the Université de Montréal. Her research focuses on militia politics and the dynamics of violence in civil wars and conflict resolution. She recently co-edited *Intra-State Conflict, Governments and Security: Dilemmas of Deterrence and Assurance* with Stephen Saideman (Routledge, 2008).

Acknowledgments

A project of this size and nature is necessarily collaborative, and the five editors are grateful for support from their own institutions, as well as a range of individuals who contributed to the development of this project. These include participants at a roundtable convened on the topic at the International Studies Association annual conference in 2007 in Chicago. The editors would also like to thank the fine editorial staff at Routledge for their hard work on the manuscript.

Chandra Lekha Sriram, Olga Martin-Ortega, and Johanna Herman, the editors based at the Centre on Human Rights in Conflict in the University of East London School of Law (www.uel.ac.uk/chrc), would like to express their sincere gratitude to the ongoing institutional support from the university to the Centre. We would also like to express our particular gratitude to Fiona Fairweather, dean of the School of Law, for her active support to us, which facilitates our work on a daily basis. Finally, our management team within the school, and our international advisory group, provide us with vital guidance in our work.

Julie Mertus and John C. King would like to thank Dean Louis Goodman, Acting Provost Ivy Broder and Provost Scott Bass for their support of human rights research and, in particular for their backing of the American University Human Rights Council (www.american.edu/humanrights) and their encouragement of human rights research on campus. Julie would also like to thank Janet Lord and Carole O'Leary for their assistance with this project. Julie acknowledges with great appreciation the influence of her former colleagues at Human Rights Watch, especially the pioneering field work of Jeri Laber. John C. King would also like to thank his wife Marylyn for always making her brilliant mind available to him and for her gracious soul. He thanks his two college-age daughters, Natalie and Julie, for the countless joys they've brought and continue to bring to his life. He also acknowledges and thanks Xiaoyan Gao for her expert research assistance.

The editors would also like to express their thanks in advance to two pledges of support which will facilitate the dissemination of the final book. First, we would like to thank Rachel Kerr, of King's College London (KCL) and the coordinator for the British branch of Women in International

Security (B-WIIS), for committing to host a launch at KCL with B-WIIS publicity. Second, we would like to thank Dimitri Neos, Executive Director, Center for International Relations, (http://www.ia-forum.org/About/) for his pledge of a generous donation to help off-set costs for editors' participation in the launch. Last, but certainly not least, we would like to thank your editor at Routledge, Heidi Bagtazo, and her colleague Lucy Dunne.

1 Introduction: Surviving field research

Julie A. Mertus

Why this book?

In recent decades there has been increasing media attention to mass atrocities such as genocide, war crimes, crimes against humanity, and other gross human rights violations. At the same time, there has been a vast increase in the number of academics and researchers seeking to analyze the causes of, and offer practical responses to, these atrocities. Yet there remains insufficient discussion of the practical and ethical challenges surrounding research into serious abuses where researchers operate under difficult circumstances and deal with vulnerable populations. Respect for and protection of interlocutors and researchers and the challenges of assessing the veracity of information gathered in research in conflict areas are issues that arise with greater frequency in academic field research, yet rarely arise as a central topic of scholarly study.

That the ethical issues surrounding human rights fieldwork receive scant attention in existing literature on qualitative research is deeply troubling. Without a set of materials acknowledging and examining these issues, university professors face great difficulty in adequately preparing their students embarking on qualitative studies that bring them into conflict areas and in conflict with vulnerable populations. In the absence of academic analysis and debate on these important issues, field researchers act without the benefit of the knowledge and experiences of their colleagues and, thus, continually find themselves reinventing the wheel. The stress of determining effective research strategies in the field on a case-by-case basis, under pressure, in isolation and without considered connection to praxis, weighs heavily on researchers and their subjects, underlying possibilities for short- and long-term fruitful collaboration.

With this book we seek to help researchers identify and address challenges in conducting qualitative research in difficult circumstances; circumstances such as in autocratic or uncooperative regimes and with governmental or non-governmental officials and, perhaps most importantly, with reluctant respondents such as victims of genocide, or (on the other side of the coin) war criminals. How do we gain authentic information and generate credible

2 *Introduction: Surviving field research*

knowledge from research in difficult places and from difficult audiences? Can we do this? Are there practical and ethical solutions to the challenges and barriers often put before us? In this way we strive to inform on-going debate about responsible scholarship, and seek to inform not just students and scholars, but also policymakers engaged in research in difficult situations.

Where did this collaboration arise?

This volume is a direct response of university professors to the need for more timely and complete teaching materials for courses in qualitative research. A continual topic of concern, discussed each year after year in academic circles, the question of qualitative research in difficult circumstances made its way onto the agenda of the 2007 annual meeting of the International Studies Association. The enthusiastic response to the panel and discussion at that meeting led directly to the present collaboration between two research hubs on both sides of the Atlantic: the Centre on Human Rights in Conflict (London)[1] under its Director Professor Chandra Lekha Sriram and researchers Olga Martin and Johanna Herman, and the American University Human Rights Council,[2] under its Director Professor Julie Mertus and Professor John C. King (Washington, DC). The resulting collaboration has proven to be far richer and much more significant than the sum of its parts.

Who should read this book?

This book has been crafted to address the needs of three audiences:

For university instructors and students: The volume will be ideal for use in M.A. and Ph.D. research methodology classes (required in most programs), and for qualitative research courses or field research courses in anthropology, international relations and political science. In addition, the text will address a void in the literature available for students of human rights, a burgeoning field on many university campuses. Students of applied ethics will also be attracted to this text.

For researchers: This text will be an ideal guide for all researchers concerned with conducting ethical field research in conflict areas. While it will be of particular use to those newly engaged in fieldwork, the discussions across a range of practical, ethical, and social dilemmas that are often encountered in the field will be of interest to even the most seasoned researcher.

For practitioners: The wide range of practitioners who will turn to this volume include both governmental and non-governmental employees engaged directly in fieldwork in conflict areas and indirectly through the training of others.

How is the book designed?

The volume proceeds in five substantive sections, each addressing a different challenge of conducting field research in conflict scenarios: 1) ethics; 2) access; 3) veracity; 4) security; and 5) identity. All five of these challenges can have a substantial impact on the behaviour of the researcher and on their ability to carry out their research as planned. The authors address these challenges with reference to their own field experiences, whenever possible, providing context for the application of concepts that at first appear in the abstract.

Part 1: Ethics

The book opens with discussions of unanticipated ethical concerns often raised by field research in difficult and often hostile settings. Can we be ethical researchers? Specifically, how do we manage relationships where we ask personal questions about experiences and feelings from individuals who may continue to be targets of the state and, thus, be at considerable personal risk in interacting with us? How do we present our research and information from our interviewees after the fact? Can we meet these issues and be ethical?

The success of field researchers is determined in large part by their ability to develop trust with local counterparts. The unions researchers form in the field are critical pathways through which perceptions are formed, and thus, can significantly enhance or hinder the process of building credible knowledge in all sorts of ways. Contact with researchers, however, often poses significant risks to respondents, and these risks are magnified in conflict settings. This section explores how tradeoffs are made between the imperative of researchers to extract data from subjects and the interests of persons at risk.

Judy Hemming, for example in Chapter 3, reminds us that the political dimension of academic field research is often played out in the academic setting before research review boards. Intervention by these institutional structures, Hemming warns, may undermine academic responsibility and threaten academic freedom. Using her own experience researching Thai women sex workers as an illustration, she explains how the power invested by the university in its research ethics committee can be flexed through questioning the worthiness of the research project. Hemming explains how, in her case, the research review board was effectively trying to stifle research into sex workers and industries because it was itself a captive of stereotypes that the research pointed to as part of the problem.

In Chapter 4, Elizabeth Levy Paluck focuses on direct challenge of conducting survey research in conflict settings, suggesting that this well-accepted method may raise more complex ethical questions than originally meets the eye. In Chapter 5, Chandra Lekha Sriram examines the maintenance of standards of protection during write-up and publication, identifying, among other issues, the concerns raised by the increased culture of sharing draft

4   Introduction: Surviving field research

documents with colleagues via e-mail or on the Internet. While certainly not exhaustive in their scope, taken together the Hemming, Paluck and Sriram chapters serve to shed light on some of the most pressing ethical concerns facing contemporary researchers today.

Part 2: Access

The second section of this book explores a matter of great importance to all researchers planning work among vulnerable populations in conflict settings: the question of gaining access to research subjects. Julie Norman, writing in Chapter 6, introduces the concept of trust, suggesting it as a crucial element for gaining access to potential research participants. Informed by her own fieldwork in the Occupied Palestinian Territories, she examines the close connection between a state's willingness to trust a researcher and the researcher accesses to the field, and to particular researchers within that field. In so doing, Norman also identifies a link between the willingness of collectives and individuals to place their trust in the researcher and the researcher's ability to reach certain research subjects. Norman concludes her chapter with specific recommendations for overcoming some of these challenges of building trust.

The discussion of trust is expanded and refracted through a more anthropological lens by Courtney Radsch (Chapter 7). Building on her extensive fieldwork in Egypt and Lebanon, Radsch looks at the role of culture and politics in shaping the feasibility and practicality of fieldwork. In some cultures, she suggests human contacts are vitally important: research begins and ends with a cup of tea. Radsch explains how in her case studies *wasta*, loosely translated as 'connections', and *isnad*, the 'tracing of a chain of witnesses as a criterion of veracity', are especially important for a researcher making initial contacts for a project and for building the kind of trust and credibility required to pursue an interview or participant observation.

The many ways in which researcher access may still be restricted is taken up in greater detail by Susan Thomson in Chapter 8. Referring to her own experiences in post-genocide Rwanda, Thomson considers three points of entry to the field where access can be complicated: 1) the host government and government-approved local partners; 2) the social spaces and sites where both access to potential informants and participant observation is possible and appropriate; and 3) individuals who may be unwilling or unable to speak due to their position of marginality or vulnerability. Among its contributions to the larger discussion, Thomson's chapter serves to alert researchers to the sensitivities of interacting with and interviewing individuals who are emotionally traumatized by their experiences of political violence.

Part 3: Veracity

Once researchers solve accessibility issues, they encounter the question of veracity or, most often, lack of veracity. Researchers confront all sorts of barriers to authentic information, including: multiple subjective perspectives and intentionally misleading statements. In her contribution to this volume, Lee Ann Fuji (Chapter 10) suggests ways to recognize and address the mistruths that may arise. Sorting data into two tidy groups – 'truths' and 'untruths' – is both impossible and undesirable in some settings. That a research subject provides information that is exaggerated or untrue does not negate the importance of the data gathered from that subject. Misleading statements from informants are data within and of themselves. However, researchers may use untrue data differently from other data. For example, racist speech may be used to demonstrate the state of mind of respondents and the context in which they act. As Fuji demonstrates, for many reasons the need to identify untruths and to evaluate them adequately remains strong.

Carole Gallaher (Chapter 9) highlights one type of respondent prone to mistruths, a population she terms 'repellent' – that is, groups that promulgate an ideology that promotes dominating other groups in society. Gallaher explains that researching such subjects challenges the predominant qualitative research models, in particular, the IRB model and the 'critical model'. These models focus on the protection of vulnerable subjects, with little or no attention to the protection of researchers. A major concern of researchers studying repellant populations is their (the researcher's) own safety, however. Another contrast between the IRB model and research on repellant populations is that the IRB model assumes empathy between researchers and their informants, yet such empathy rarely exists for those doing research on repellent groups. Woven throughout Gallaher's discussion are concrete suggestions for addressing these and other needs of researchers that currently go beyond traditional research models.

Part 4: Security

The questions Gallaher raises about the need to safeguard researcher security are addressed further in Part 4, where Julie Mertus and Amy Ross suggest an emerging agenda for improving the operationalization of security for fieldwork. In Chapter 11, Julie Mertus explores the kinds of threats to personal security that many researchers working in difficult scenarios encounter and examines the ethical issues presented by efforts to guard against such risks. Academic researchers would do well to follow the lessons learned from practitioners, Mertus contends. Human rights practitioners, for example, generally are better trained on security matters than are academic human rights researchers, and practitioners. She identifies three specific training programs on human rights and humanitarian fieldworkers as useful case studies for exploring a range of security concerns.

Ross (Chapter 12) further develops the security section with a study on the impact on research of security seeking behaviour. She discusses the intersections, contradictions and potentially dangerous collisions between research and security. She considers: How does looking after one's own security

6 *Introduction: Surviving field research*

influence both the research collection process and the security of others? As researchers in conflict zones, what rights (if any) do we have to working within life-rafts of relative safety amidst a sea of suffering? When is the data important enough to justify the disruptive presence a researcher can have on people in a conflict zone? How does one make these kinds of assessments? Drawing from this researcher's experiences (primarily in Guatemala and Uganda) the chapter probes how paying attention to security dialectically impacts the knowledge-production process in conflict zones.

Part 5: Identity, objectivity, behaviour

Marie-Joelle Zahar offers a cautionary note for researchers. In Chapter 3, she examines the ways in which scholarly and disciplinary biases can undermine our objectivity in the field, blinkering our research as it shapes our perceptions of the situations we encounter on the ground. Specifically, she argues that the state-centric nature of the discipline of international relations can undermine attempts to engage and interpret non-state actors, particularly the study of non-state armed groups. Drawing upon her own experiences of research into militias in Bosnia and Lebanon, she demonstrates how such biases, and a false presumption of objectivity derived from the comfort of disciplinary 'scientific' language, can restrict the scope of enquiry and of possible solutions.

Just as a false presumption of objectivity may influence – and, at times even derail – research, so can issues of self-representation. When asked about personal issues that may reveal a controversial answer, how should the researcher respond? To what extent does the researcher's personal conduct matter when in the field but in an 'off duty' mode? Using examples drawn in part from the author's own experiences, Brown (Chapter 14) addresses a series of professional and personal dilemmas upon which other researchers may wish to reflect before being placed in similar situations. What one reveals in a seemingly innocent or private context can circulate, at times inaccurately, and do harm to one's research relationships and even one's sense of security. Examples include cohabitation or having children out of wedlock; being gay, lesbian or bisexual; or belonging to a specific religious group or being an atheist. Dissimulation or lying about these issues may avoid problems, but raise other ethical concerns which Brown invites readers to consider.

Conclusion

Although the authors in this volume do not claim to settle all of the practical, ethical, and social challenges researchers can face in difficult situations, they hope to shed light on some of the main problems that often arise in the field. In this spirit, John King in Chapter 2 weaves together many of the authors' experiences in a further attempt to help demystify fieldwork. Among the characterizations he develops is the *dramaturgical metaphor*. He argues that this theoretical framework helps the reader to systematically compare countless decisions, tactics, and strategies devised by authors in their attempts to solve a range of unforeseen challenges encountered in the field. Field research is never static. The context in which fieldwork is conducted is subject to many forces that continually transform it, presenting new challenges and opportunities. At the same time, all of the characters are continually developing and changing, including the researcher. The editors of this book hope that it will help prepare researchers for the unknown and offer guidance on the way.

Notes

1 The Centre on Human Rights in Conflict is an interdisciplinary research centre promoting policy-relevant research and events aimed at developing greater knowledge about the relationship between human rights and conflict. Details of the Centre and its work can be found at http://www.uel.ac.uk/chrc/index.htm.
2 The American University Human Rights Council is an umbrella organization that brings together all of the many human rights activities at American University, promoting the integration of human rights issues throughout the curriculum through a small grants program and by other direct forms of support. See http://american.edu/humanrights.

2 Demystifying field research
John C. King

Introduction

It is clear from the experiences discussed by authors in this volume that all too often researchers are left to their own innate sensibilities, talents, and skills to identify and resolve a range of ethical, social, and political challenges that inevitably arise in the field. Challenges and dilemmas that, if not recognized and managed effectively, particularly in the difficult, unstable, and dangerous contexts explored in this book, can at the minimum threaten the validity of one's data and at the maximum threaten the personal security and well-being of the respondents, their families, the researcher, and members of her or his research team. Of course, researchers can and do look to published codes of ethics and behaviour from professional organizations for guidance and can and do seek direction from home Institutional Review Boards (IRBs) for solutions, but that advice almost always falls short in helping the researcher successfully navigate unanticipated ethical, social, and political challenges in the field. This is because the codes and the boards have narrow mandates to protect the researched from the researcher (e.g. guarantees of free consent, guarantees of anonymity, and so forth) and offer little toward guidance for the researcher beyond that.[1] The richness of experiences documented here in this volume shows there is a lot more to navigate beyond guarantees of free consent and so forth.

What then, if anything, can be done to prepare the researcher to successfully resolve unanticipated dilemmas and challenges in the field and particularly in difficult and dangerous fields? Can the decisions, tactics, and strategies recorded by the talented group of researchers in this volume help in demystifying field research? Can their experiences be systematically characterized and, in this way, help to guide others in successfully navigating their own unanticipated challenges in the field? There is little doubt that many in the social sciences would argue that each researcher is unique and that each research context has its own unique challenges and, therefore, any attempts at systematizing such disparate experiences as documented here is based on a false premise and is a fruitless waste of time. I disagree. I begin by characterizing the decisions from a group of the authors as illustrative of successful (and not so successful) management of the *dramaturgical* in the field. And from there I develop other characterizations that, taken together, help to systematically show how these authors' experiences help in demystifying fieldwork.

The dramaturgical metaphor

The word *dramaturgical* is a technical term that defines the art of the theatre particularly the writing and management of the craft or techniques of dramatic composition. The person at the centre who creates the dramatic composition and who is ultimately responsible for directing all of the activities to make the vision come to life is the playwright. This can be a metaphor for thinking about research design and for carrying it out where the composition, the vision of the artist is the fieldwork and the director, the manager is the researcher himself or herself.[2] And as any playwright will tell you, there inevitably will be glitches along the way and she or he must adjust to them successfully or suffer the consequences. Thus, when a researcher is in the field, their play and their particular role as playwright is in progress and good management of the techniques of production, including managing unanticipated dilemmas, challenges, and developments determines to a large extent the success or failure in carrying out the research vision and developing new knowledge.

The *dramaturgical metaphor,* thus, provides an analytical framework from which to compare decisions, tactics, and strategies devised by authors in the field. When Elizabeth Levy Paluck (Chapter 4), for example, was strictly prohibited by authorities in post-conflict Rwanda from asking specifics about ethnic group interactions among the Hutus, Tutsi, and Twa (a key and necessary focus in her planned research), she faced a series of unanticipated ethical dilemmas. Should she put herself and her indigenous research team at risk of arrest and likely abuse and danger by ignoring the authorities' official denials of lingering ethnic conflict and continue with her research as planned or should she alter her research quest fundamentally to focus on a low-risk government approved topic? Or should she just abandon research in Rwanda altogether? Her solution was not to give up on her original quest, but rather to quickly change her tactics to use non-threatening code words in her team's interactions with indigenous respondents. Questions concerned with the extent of ethnic group interactions became questions concerned with interactions between 'people'. This tactic worked for her. She later relied on expert help from trusted indigenous assistants who knew the cultural and geographic context well enough to sort through the obliquely coded references to 'people' in the data and to use them to identify patterns in ethnic group interactions within the region. This task also posed a serious ethical dilemma, this time for her research crew. It was well-known among the indigenous that anyone trafficking in ideas and/or documented knowledge of ethnic-based conflict where none existed officially could expect to be punished severely. Paluck was willing to take that risk herself but she could not in good conscience put her assistants at risk. Her solution was to make sure everyone on her staff was fully aware of the risks involved and then to accept his or her help with the coding strictly on a volunteer and confidential basis.

These examples are a small testimony to all the decisions, tactics, and strategies Paluck devised to facilitate her fieldwork. There were many other unanticipated challenges and dilemmas along the way. And they are illustrative of a pattern she set in her work (i.e. in her play) from the outset and carried through to the end. That pattern was to take charge in the field to devise tactics that ensured the performance went forward with careful attention not to explicitly violate rules prescribed by the Rwandan post-conflict regime, no matter how seemingly misplaced they were, and with careful attention not to violate her own professional ethical standards regarding the security and well-being of her respondents, her staff, her sponsoring NGOs, and herself. Similarly, Lee Ann Fujii (Chapter 10) took charge of her fieldwork and adjusted her research tactics to particular conditions on the ground. She quickly recognized, for example, that inhabitants from the two rural communities in Rwanda who became the focus of her fieldwork systematically evaded speaking about the true conditions of their post-1994 life histories and instead exaggerated and/or embellished their facts with misleading stories, evasions, silences, and rumours. This was an unanticipated development. Instead of challenging each of the respondents' lack of veracity on grounds of what she (Fujii) knew to be true and to be false and, thereby, risk alienating her respondents, she recognized value in their needs to account for their post-conflict life stories in these ways. Consequently she successfully shifted her research design (her 'play') and her tactics in management of it to assemble what she calls 'meta' data that helps reveal full contours of this personal need shared by so many in post-conflict rural Rwanda.

Smooth stage management of all details was more elusive for others. Carole Gallaher's fieldwork (Chapter 9), her 'play', focused on interacting with truly repellent right-wing groups – the Kentucky State Militia (KSM) and the Loyalist paramilitaries in Northern Ireland. Her quest was to successfully approach and probe for a nuanced understanding of the assumptions driving their behaviour. Both groups were potentially dangerous and difficult to access. In Susan Thomson's research, her 'stage' (Chapter 8) focused on understanding how ordinary Rwandans in 2006 made sense of the 1994 genocide. In Gallaher's case, some of the personal pragmatic challenges she had to navigate were: 1) how to discipline her emotions such that she could cope with the processes of probing into the hearts and minds of people whose views run so diametrically counter to her own; 2) how to refrain from challenging and/or trying to dissuade them by argument; 3) how to maintain personal poise and transparency at all times in order to avoid provoking any individual(s) into suspicion, defensiveness, or any situation into danger; and, 4) how to prevent herself from being perceived by anyone inside or outside the groups as empowering their views or their causes. Thomson's unanticipated pragmatic challenge was essentially to conduct her research smoothly under conditions of suspicious officials and consequent heavy-handed surveillance by them throughout her time in the field.

There were relative breakdowns in the dramaturgical processes in both of these cases which are instructive by example. The breakdown for Gallaher came when she was asked to appear as an interviewer on a public access television programme produced by a militia member. At stake was the ethical question of whether she should risk even the slightest perception of giving respectability to the group by her status as a university professor. Consultation with her university IRB officer as to how she might best manage and resolve this dilemma was not helpful, as the officer's only real concern was making sure that the informant's participation was properly protected. Not certain as to how to respond in a way that would not compromise the access and rapport she had worked hard to develop with the group, she finally decided to take a calculated risk and consented to the broadcast. Her regret was immediate. It came from a strong feeling that she did indeed inadvertently give a perception of legitimacy to the group by her presence; a perception of legitimacy magnified even more by her self-described quiet probing interview style. In dramaturgical terms, her stage management of this part of her play broke down and that led to an obvious regrettable consequence for her – a misperception of her motives in agreeing to participate. In hindsight, a solution would have been to negotiate every parameter of her participation, including freedom to make disclaimers about her motives.

The breakdown for Thomson was precipitated by a seemingly innocent humane gesture that cascaded into increased suspicion and surveillance of her activities by local officials and demands from them that she be 're-educated' in official Rwandan policy. The humane gesture consisted of her touching the shoulder and offering her personal empathy to a Rwandan woman one day who was obviously in emotional pain over the displaced remains of her husband (a Hutu) who had been killed in the 1994 genocide. What Thomson did not know is that that particular Hutu husband was the one who had killed the husband of her very next interviewee. The interviewee responded with intense suspicion toward Thomson upon hearing the news that she had touched her 'enemy', a response that had far-reaching personal and methodological consequences for Thomson. With her innocent decision to reach out to offer personal empathy to a bereaved (Hutu) widow, she inadvertently angered and alienated others in the area, an area where intense personal, ethnic animosities lingered. The alienated apparently spoke about her in unfavourable terms to her paired Rwandan partner, who in turn, likely passed those perceptions on to local governmental officials. In the end, the 'suspicion thicket' was next to impossible to resolve once it gained a life of its own and was the primary source that led to a breakdown in her fieldwork. Thomson cut short what was originally intended to be a one-year stay by clandestinely leaving the country after six months.

Full-time stage management in the field is never easy. Stephen Brown's essay (Chapter 14) points out just how difficult it is to balance one's private and public lives while in the field, particularly during long-term engagements and particularly if one is not married or with a partner. Researchers get lonely. They get tired. They seek refuge at times from the daily work and pressures in the field and sometimes need to just unwind with trusted confides behind closed doors so to speak – to be 'off-duty'. But as he points out, and following the dramaturgical metaphor, it is next to impossible to completely separate the public from the private selves. Everything about the researcher and what she or he does while in the field can complement or undermine the data gathering processes. There is no way around it.

Digital networking, file sharing, and making trust in difficult settings

Everyone knows that digital technologies have made the world a smaller place than it was just a few years ago. And researchers, in particular, know that the new technologies are a boon and a great asset in gathering, managing, and communicating data easily from the field and dealing with it in post-field settings. But, where there are up sides to their uses, there can also be down sides and lessons can be gathered from the experiences. Courtney Radsch (Chapter 7), for example, details the ins and outs of gaining access to journalists and bloggers in Egypt and Lebanon through her attention to cultural and/or ethical mores applied to modern digital technologies during her recent fieldwork in those countries. Chandra Lekha Sriram (Chapter 5) cautions readers about ethical dilemmas (among other concerns) that can arise from the modern 'culture of research', which often entails dissemination of draft papers through websites.

For Radsch, gaining access to professional journalists and influential bloggers in Egypt and Lebanon, to the extent that she did and in the short amount of time that she did it, was no easy feat. As Julie Norman (Chapter 6) demonstrates in her work, gaining access to her particular targeted respondents in the Occupied Palestinian Territory took a lot of time and a lot of careful attention to nuance in the micro-level steps of building trust; the building of trust both between herself and the Palestinians who were her principal focus and between herself and the Israeli 'gatekeeper' officials who potentially could and did block access easily and frequently. Radsch works to gain access to her cases in a different way.

As with many, if not most, people everywhere, and especially among the younger generations, Egyptians and Lebanese use cell phones and computers as part of their daily lives and, as Radsch shows, they have discovered that networking and communication in some of the newest venues – Facebook and Twitter – are powerful tools that can create an underground culture where individuals can speak about and debate political conditions, events, and policies in ways that they would be prohibited from doing openly in public. As she documents, the key to access to the digital underground cultures in Egypt and Lebanon, and by extension in other countries, is to be attuned to cultural specifics, just as Norman did with her more traditional approach in the Palestinian Occupied Territories. In the particular cases of Egypt and Lebanon, Radsch learned quickly that two Arabic social traditions – *wasta* and *isnad* – determine to a large extent who will, and who will not, gain access into the interior lives of people, including access into the interior lives of journalists and bloggers. *Wasta* refers simply to referencing a person (or two) that the person you are trying to gain access to know. *Isnad* is more substantive. It refers to carefully establishing your veracity with a stranger through (roughly speaking) name dropping. That is, to create linkage through known persons to the stranger of interest (sort of like detailing membership in an extended family) to establish your credibility with the stranger. Skilfully navigating these social/cultural traditions via digital technology, Radsch gained access to the underground digital networks in Egypt and Lebanon and enthusiastically built her own community of cell phone and Facebook contacts among journalist and bloggers relatively rapidly; a network that she can access anytime, anywhere as a resource for information, data, and research.

On the other hand, a modern culture of research facilitated by easy communication through the Internet and cell phones can lead to serious unanticipated ethical problems, particularly in post-research, pre-publication scenarios. What do we do when, in our enthusiasm to communicate with and share new information with colleagues, we post early drafts of our work on our personal webpage and/or on a professional organization's webpage and inadvertently leave identifying confidential information about informants in our footnotes or in other forms of the manuscript? As we know a webpage can reach a much wider audience than publishing an article in a professional journal and, once posted, damage has been done. As Sriram (Chapter 5) illustrates, this happens too often. The consequences for the informants and researcher can be far reaching and very serious, particularly when the research context was dangerous for both. One obvious consequence, of course, is that the researcher has violated the first rule of ethics – to guarantee the anonymity and personal security of informants. This breach in professional ethical standards could damage the researcher's reputation among peers and close hard-won paths to access to the field, but those concerns pale in light of putting informants' personal and familial security at risk of loss of livelihood, imprisonment, and other forms of punishment at the minimum and death at the maximum. As Sriram points out, the solution, of course, is to be very vigilant about checking our post-research rough drafts and data before sharing them digitally with friends and colleagues via the Internet or via any other forms of modern technology.

Likewise what do researchers do when a prospective publisher of one's work demands to see and file one's original anonymized interviews as verification of the work and as a firm prerequisite to publication? Sriram shows through personal experience how a seemingly reasonable request can quickly turn into an ethical dilemma. On the one hand, the journal has a reputation to protect and editors need copies of original data, including actual names of respondents, to validate the research. But on the other hand, the researcher is ethically bound to protect the anonymity of all participants in the research and a refusal to share that information risks a strong likelihood that the new knowledge will not be published. The question thus quickly becomes to what extent should the researcher trust assurances by editors that the information will be safely locked in a filing cabinet and never released to anyone? Maybe in the older days of paper copies this ethical issue would have been small, but in our modern times of electronic copies of things and easy transference of information, the issue is large and not easily resolved. In Sriram's case it was paper copies they wanted, but the point remains valid. These are just a couple of the concerns brought forward by Sriram that modern researchers must learn to think through carefully, particularly when conducting field research in difficult and dangerous settings.

IRB or not to be

Judy Hemming (Chapter 3) demonstrates that not all unanticipated social, political, and/or ethical thickets arise in the context of fieldwork itself. Sometimes they arise at the home gatekeeper stage, namely at the Institutional Review Board (IRB) stage, and they can be difficult to navigate to say the least. As detailed more subtly by her and other authors in this volume, IRBs were created during the decades following World War II in the wake of many egregious examples of work by field and clinical researchers who were shown to have from little to no consideration of ethical protections toward those they researched. More particularly, IRBs emerged rapidly as an essential part of Western university research life during the latter part of the 1970s and 1980s after national governments began to respond to perceived lapses in ethical judgments by many researchers in many different contexts.[3] The operable response by national governments was to link their grant monies for research to the creation of site-specific internal review boards mandated to oversee good ethics in research. The particular mechanism relied on to make evaluations of good ethics is the familiar *risk versus benefit* analysis whereby any proposed research project and its processes are to be scrutinized closely by the site-specific board (or its principal officer) to gauge the extent of harm that might come to either the researcher or to the researched or both. If the research proposal and/or its processes are judged to not be up to the standards of good ethics prescribed by the board, the proposal will be renegotiated with the author(s) or rejected outright and university affiliation will not be allowed.

In theory, the IRB initiative is a good solution where there was none not long ago and I believe it is needed for that reason alone. But as a practical matter the IRB initiative is not without problems, as many of the authors testify here. The problem most consistently cited is that IRBs are typically narrowly focused on protecting the integrity of the researched as a political and ethical norm to the relative exclusion of any protections of the researcher. Other complaints are that to a lesser extent, but nevertheless to an extent, IRBs are too preoccupied with legal liabilities that might result from failure to protect the researched adequately and, IRBs are more preoccupied with approving 'safe' research that might enhance the status and reputation of their particular institutions than they are with taking chances on perceived risky research.

Hemming's particular experiences in seeking official approval from her home IRB, the Australia's Group of Eight (GO8) Human Research Ethics Committee,[4] demonstrates that the approval process is not easy. In fact, she shows that negotiating with her home IRB was a very exhausting and trying experience, akin to walking through a field of political landmines where it is difficult to find safe passage [my analogy]. This comes through in a number of ways in her bid or conducting fieldwork on the life experiences of sex workers in Thailand. First, her board members objected to her characterization of most female sex workers in Bangkok as semi-autonomous, independent and alert business women who are not victims of sex traffickers. She presented evidence, based on earlier pilot fieldwork, that it was quite the contrary: female Thai sex workers are largely in control of their own destinies and have chosen sex work for any number of reasons, including for economic reasons.

Despite evidence to the contrary, at least some members of the board preferred the characterization that prevails in much of the dialogue in the sex trafficking literature that all sex workers in Thailand are victims in need of paternalist protection. With this rigid framing of the issue in at least some of the board members' minds, Hemming had to endure a series of difficult e-mail negotiations with the board where they objected to her proposed research vision overall, objected to her proposed protocol in accessing and interviewing the sex workers in particular, and implicitly threatened to not allow her research to go forward under the auspices of the university's name. And to make matters worse, she suspected that a second dynamic was also at work within the board – a political dynamic that had more to do with enhancing the university's reputation relative to other universities than it had to do with supporting new 'exotic' research. In particular, that dynamic was a strong preference among at least some board members for more acceptable, safe proposals focused on topics such as 'healthy aging', 'dementia and aging', and 'health in the Asia Pacific': topics that would more likely win, from the IRB's point of view, outside funding and lead to more aggregate publications quickly for the university than an exotic proposal focused on understanding life experiences of female sex workers in Thailand.

Hemming's experiences with her home IRB demonstrate that successfully navigating through a politicized IRB can be a frustrating and trying experience, but one that a researcher must be prepared and willing to do in order to protect the integrity of one's research quest and to secure approval for it. Her

16 *Demystifying field research*

difficult interactions with her board members culminated in a face-to-face meeting with the entire board where she finally gained approval to proceed.

Saving the security of the person

Fieldwork, particularly fieldwork in dangerous contexts, always raises concerns about security of the person, be it security of the researcher him or herself or of the researched or of both. As I've mentioned, several authors in this volume point out that the balance of attention by IRBs and professional organizations has been primarily on protecting the security of the researched to the relative absence of attention to protecting the security of the researcher. Julie Mertus in Chapter 11 proposes ways to close this gap. She advances a comprehensive set of practical procedures researchers can do to devise their own individualized 'security of person risk assessment' before entering the field. Amy Ross in Chapter 12 addresses a different security concern. She identifies how the lack of security of person within a population can affect every aspect of a scholar's research plans and processes after entering the field. In dramaturgical terms, Mertus emphasizes exhaustive pre-field preparation as a way to manage part of her production (her 'play'), whereas, Ross emphasizes recognizing and dealing with complex security fear-based barriers to the unspeakable within respondents as a way to direct part of her 'play'. The work of both helps to demystify field research.

How might a researcher go about developing an individualized 'security of person risk assessment' before entering the field? How might a researcher penetrate fear-based psychological barriers once she or he is in the field? Mertus calls on researchers to look closely at both internal and external factors of a given country as part of one's pre-entry research. For example, one needs to ask what is the country's record in protecting human rights? What about its level and character of street crime? Is there a history of ethnic and/or political fractional conflicts? Or of external war? Who are the players? These are but a few of the many questions one ought to answer before entering the field. She also recommends, and I agree, that academic researchers and institutions would do well to look to the Office of the United Nations Security Operations (UNSECOORD) for explicit guidance in country-specific security matters for field staffers.[5]

Ross argues that penetrating fear-based psychological barriers to speaking about the unspeakable is almost impossible in countries that have lost the security of the person. How does the researcher penetrate profound silences about personal injury, about loss of loved one(s), and about the giving of misinformation about perpetrators in these countries? As she shows, even when a return to a rule of law has been declared and truth commissions have been created, as in the case of post-civil war Guatemala, victims can be so traumatized by their experiences that coherent descriptions from them are most often too emotionally taxing and difficult to convey to anyone, much less to an academic researcher. Ross makes a compelling case that such conditions in contexts of prolonged insecurity of self can and do undermine a researcher's work in important ways: from constructing a sample, to collecting data, to interpreting meaning from data, and to making one's research relevant to victims and to others. And as she argues, there are no easy solutions for the researcher in these cases. Guarantees of free consent and of protections from the researcher turn into small concerns to people who have endured a profound loss of the security of the person. Mertus and Ross both analyze the challenges in ways that go beyond prescribed IRB mandates and published professional codes of ethics. As such, both make compelling arguments for more attention to be paid to the security of the person in the field.

Conclusions

I began this chapter with the question what, if anything, can be done to help demystify for others the countless decisions, tactics, and strategies researchers have to make (most often intuitively) to successfully cope with and resolve a range of unanticipated ethical, social, and political challenges that are sure to arise in the field? The answer is found in the experiences of the authors themselves. Their narratives are the data from which to interpret and learn from. The fact that their experiences are with difficult and dangerous settings brings their 'examples by experience' even more into relief. I characterized these data, these narratives, into categories to help facilitate the demystification process.

Notes

1 For example, the American Political Science Association's code of ethics is found at http://www.apsanet.org/section_513.cfm. Likewise, the (British) Economic and Social Research Council's codes are available at http://www.esrcsocietytoday.ac.uk/ESRCInfoCentre/Images/ESRC_Re_Ethics_Frame_tcm6-11291.pdf. The Australian National Statement on Ethical Conduct in Research Involving Humans is available at <http://www.nhmrc.gov.au/publications. A statement prescribing ethical commitments by human rights professionals is outlined at http://www.humanrightsprofessionals.org/images/statement%20of%20ethical%20commitments_nov%2028%202007_website.pdf. The School of International Service's link to American University's IRB prescriptions is http://www.american.edu/sis/irb/index.htm
2 Erving Goffman developed the dramaturgical metaphor as a theoretical framework to unlock complex, multi-layered human interactions in his 1959 seminal book *The Presentation of Self* (New York: Doubleday, 1959). A. Paul Hare and Herbert H. Blumberg expanded his work in their important 1988 *Dramaturgical Analysis of Social Interaction* (New York: Praeger, 1988). And, more recently, Bruce L. Berg applied the metaphor in his 2006 text *Qualitative Research Methods for the Social Sciences* (Boston: Allyn and Bacon, 2006).
3 Examples include the notorious Tuskegee Syphilis experiments conducted in the US during the 1930s; the infamous obedience – compliance experiments by Stanley Milgram in the early 1960s; the gamma globulin experiments also during the 1960s at the New York state Willowbrook school for 'mentally defective' children; Philip Zimbardo's famous 1971 'Stanford Prison' experiment; and Laud Humphrey's

1970 'tearoom trade' study of anonymous homosexual behaviour among men who outwardly presented a heterosexual identity. All of the research designs and methods were determined to have ethical problems.
4 Hemming clarifies on page 7 in Chapter 3 that her Human Research Ethics Committee was composed of several academics, a clinical psychologist, university executives, and laypeople, including a minister of religion. This composition was mandated in the 1997 Australian national government's *Statement and Guidelines on Research Practice*.
5 http://www.google.com/search?hl=en&client=firefox-a&rls=org.mozilla:en-US:official&hs=KQM&q=UNSECOORD&start=10&sa=N

Part 1
Ethics

3 Exceeding scholarly responsibility: IRBs and political constraints

Judy Hemming

Introduction

Many pitfalls befall researchers who scrutinize topics such as prostitution and/or sex trafficking.[1] Among the difficulties encountered is the issue that there is no formula to follow that will indicate whether someone has or has not been trafficked, exploited, and/or coerced into prostitution or, is a voluntary participant,[2] contrary to the claims made by Donna Hughes.[3] What overshadows those difficulties is the experience of gaining clearance from my institutions' Ethics Committee.[4] These latter difficulties are the focus of this chapter.

As I present in this chapter some of the difficulties and complexities encountered albeit, from a limited perspective, these hurdles relate specifically to my application for ethical clearance from one of Australia's Group of Eight (Go8)[5] University's Human Research Ethics Committee (HREC/IRB). During the process, I discovered that although my research project had been accepted on one level through admission to the Ph.D. programme by the university's prescribed body – Postgraduate Studies – there was another 'gatekeeper' who had the potential power to withhold ethical clearance from me and my wherewithal to carry out my own fieldwork in order to collect original data.

The aim of this chapter is to demonstrate that despite the normative rhetoric of 'risk factor' used by the IRB, which emphasises its 'duty of care toward and, integrity of' the researcher and their research participant[s], its real concern lay in the fact that the committee's unease was skewed toward protecting the university's public reputation. I argue that this is a result of political wind-of-change within the university system.[6] With the rise of the neoliberal university, research needs to be either of innovative marketability/ grant income value or of public policy feasibility in order to legitimate an instrumental measurement for it to be valued.[7]

The concept of stereotyping underpins my analysis of the IRB's approach. Michael Pickering argues that stereotyping embeds 'the ideological construction of social groups' as a form of social control and although an imprecise representation, it permits the existing power structure to remain stable.[8] He argues further that 'othering' and stereotyping are one the same. 'Othering' is a means to deny history, yet, symbolically it establishes an identity dependent on 'difference'. In arguing this, Pickering utilizes Simone de Beauvoir's work, in particular, to show that gender is also 'othered'.[9] To embrace Pickering's work, is to acknowledge stereotyping occurs 'in all sorts of discourse … ', but it also emphasises the point that it operates 'as a means of placing, and attempting to fix in place, other people or cultures from a particular and privileged perspective'. Intertwined throughout my claims of stereotyping is the notion of the power élite: a concept developed by C. Wright Mills in 1968.[10] In other words, the power élite is comprised of different levels. Those who make national decisions, and then there are those who act as 'captains' for that top level. It is the 'captains' to whom I am referring; and as they contemplate and make their decisions in their realm of power, they do so, only after taking into consideration the power élite.[11] In my own work the scholarly dominant prostitution/sex trafficking discourse has been hijacked by anti-prostitution authors (i.e. the elite group) constructing a political representation for sex workers as victims of sexual exploitation and violence – in need of paternalistic rescuing because they lack the capability to overcome sexual exploitation. Moreover, I argue that this attitude is very prevalent toward those women from developing nations.[12] Such a constructed stereotypical gives support to the paradigm behind *all* Thai sex workers' identity. In other words, throughout the ethics clearance journey, what became apparent and problematical for my research proposal was: 1) the committee's stereotypical understanding of the Thai sex worker and industry, whether separately or in concert, plus, 2) the projects' research value. This resulted in the committee's hesitancy to grant ethics permission.

In the pages that follow, I will deal with a brief description of the basics of who, the why and how of my participants plus the methodology of my research. Along with this, I will explain how I arrived at the need to do ethnographic research. Then, I will outline differing aspects of the IRB at this particular Australian university. In that section, I will explain the fundamentals such as, who comprises the committee, why it was established, its specific legal and institutional mandate. Following on from this, I will discuss the conflict that ensued and, finally, the resolution.

Sex workers in Thailand: the research context

The research participants for this project were randomly chosen, initially, from open beer and expatriate bars in the greater Bangkok area. Random in the sense that when I sat in these bars and, if, served and/or did not receive 'overly' hostile looks or if the body language from workers, owners or clientele was not intimidating, I considered them as a research site. I eventually settled on two sites: one an open beer bar in Patpong and, the other, an expatriate bar in the Nana District. Each of the participants were individually approached by me, but only after I gained permission to conduct my research from the bar owners. A further criterion was that the women had a proficiency in English. After my initial discussions with many of the women, it became clear that my research site needed to be expanded. This I did, to Singapore, where I sought out participants from the illegal sex trade.

All of the women participants were Thai and whilst there was a mixture of rural and urban locations, for the most part, those women who were from the rural regions of Thailand were from the north. However, two did come from Southern Thailand and both of these women worked in the expatriate bar. The significance of the latter was that these women had easier access into Malaysia for their occupationally (working) holidays. After a period of time all the participants' 'lived experiences' emerged and it was interesting to find out how many of these women actually were 'trafficked' into the sex industry, in some form or another.[13] Regardless of the fact that these women would be considered victims of international trafficking, they did not desire this label. On an individual level these women 'chose to work in the international sex trade' and their choice was not based in poverty but motivated adventure and life betterment.

Among the multifaceted identities these women possess, some identified themselves as mothers, whereas others were single women earning a substantial income, which was not possible to do in other sectors of the Thai informal economy. Many had previously worked in factories or other aspects of the hospitality industry. Whereas for others they had been teachers or worked in other professions yet, notwithstanding their differing educational standards, their monthly wage was comparable to a new graduate with a 'pass' degree and they had the ability to earn far more. They knew the international and national political identity articulated them as, 'poor, rural and exploited women'. Briefly, it was amusing at times to watch how these women were able to 'exploit' the customer by utilizing this 'imposed' representation. However, none of the interviewees perceived themselves as a victim; they considered themselves as nothing less than a worker.

Contrary to the assumptions in much of the existing literature and discourse surrounding the Thai sex industry, these women had autonomy. Of course, there are the differing working conditions between the different genres of bars but, nonetheless, the capability for each of the women to negotiate with customers and/or bar owners was very evident. One demonstration of autonomy is the combination of their living arrangements. Some lived by themselves in an apartment complex whilst others shared with either workmates, friends or partners. Each day these women went off to work just like any other Thai worker, except that their workday was an afternoon shift; hence, arriving at work either by cab, scooter or train, but again this was as diverse as any other aspect of their individual lives.

Another aspect of autonomy is that the women are able to choose their own clients. In the bars, men would order their drinks from the woman and then once poured she would serve it to them. Sometimes, she will 'hang around the male' other times the worker will simply deliver the drink and then go and sit elsewhere, either to talk with her co-workers or other customers. Alternatively, the customer might ask her to sit with him, if he sees her intention to leave. He will then offer to buy her a drink or play pool. Always, she is in the position to accept or reject. The bar's requirement is for business to be kept constant. This means that if one worker does not like the customer generally another will sidle up next to him. Once again, this is just another expression of the diversity, but also complexity, found amongst the workers.

Research methodology

My initial research question led me to employ an ethnographic perspective, which included whether the social, economic and political realms affect Thai women's employment choices. And, if so, how or why and to what extent? Previous research gives the impression that most researchers had an agenda in which they *needed* the research to support. Among the agenda items were economic factors forcing the women's entry whilst, in some feminist work, patriarchal power relations was dominant. However, Cleo Odzer[14] and Erik Cohen,[15] among others, have explored the complexities of the industry, and come to different conclusions and demonstrated varying degrees of competency. Nonetheless, I thought there were other issues that needed extrapolating. I wanted interviews to be more along a conversational mode rather than specific questions on a survey form in order to learn from the women and not be the one who had all the answers. I wanted to regard my research participants as more than 'subjects'. My goal was to have their voice come through my work. This required an expenditure of both time and energy observing, interviewing formally and informally associates, experts and informants. From the many stories and experiences reported to me, I then discovered sex trafficking was an essential component of the theme. This would not have occurred had I gone into the bars with a set of *a priori* survey questions.

The IRB[16]

It was post-World War II when an awareness of the need for ethical codes became apparent. Amid the uncovered Nazi medical experiments at the Nuremberg Trials, the Stanford Prison Experiment (1971 – Philip Zimbardo), and Stanley Milgram's 'obedience/compliance' experiment (1961), apart from the earlier horrendous medical research conducted in the 1930s known as the Tuskegee Syphilis Study, all were determined to have ethical problems. In Australia, the *National Health and Medical Research Council* (NHMRC) took responsibility to develop and write a code of ethics for researchers and subsequently, produced the *National Statement on Ethical Conduct in Research Involving Humans* (NSECRIH). This statement was tabled into federal parliamentary law in 1999. Furthermore, a Joint NHMRC/AVCC (Australian Vice Chancellors Committee) Statement and Guidelines on Research Practice (1997) was created to provide assistance to institutions in developing their own procedures and guidelines of a comprehensive framework.[17] Under this statement, any researcher involving human participation was required to gain ethical clearance as a precautionary measure against abuse and rights violations for research participants. Thus, a responsibility for each research institution extends from the public to professional practice and public policy. Each institution expects its researchers to be 'committed to high standards of professional ethical conduct' and protectors of the truth.[18]

With the new 'managerial governance' view, research was to be a quantitative instrument for universities and government to define 'institutional prestige and income'.[19] That is, university research became a managed project in the newly enforced economic system requiring the filtration of projects for specific input and output outcomes. Content is not what is necessarily strived for; instead, what pleases the managers is the 'applied, useful and bureaucratically popular topics'.[20] In many instances, this demanded the erosion of, what Seumas Miller describes as, academic autonomy[21] but, more sadly, the duty of the academic was eroded. Academics have a 'community duty' to inquire freely in the pursuit of truth, despite the opposition faced because of others' goals, interests, including the national interest.

Those given the position within the Australian IRB to safeguard these broad principles comprise several academics, a clinic psychologist, university executives plus laypeople including a minister of religion. This mandated composition is from specific criteria formulated within the Statement and Guidelines.[22] There are basic ethical principles which this collective group needs to enforce: however, an essential value is the 'integrity of researchers', which includes a commitment to 'contributing to the knowledge' of the discipline, 'pursuit and protection of truth' and, the methodology which is to be 'appropriate to the discipline and honesty'. Furthermore, the Belmont Report requires the following conditions be exemplified: respect for persons, maximization of possible benefits and minimization possible harms, and protection of justice regarding who benefits from the research.[23] In part, to ensure this happens, the HERC puts the supervisors of candidates in a position of responsibility to ensure further research honesty from the research data.[24]

The conflict: an IRB exceeding its scholarly responsibility?

The IRB expressed concern over my protocol because it did not seem to think the merits or benefits outweighed the alleged risks. Under Section 1.13 'Research Merit and Safety' of the NHMRC

> [e]very research proposal must demonstrate that the research is justifiable in terms of its potential contribution to knowledge and is based on a thorough study of current literature as well as prior observation, approved previous studies, and where relevant, laboratory and animal studies.[25]

To restate: their concern lay in the fact that any new and/or significant knowledge would be forthcoming from studying the Thai sex industry and/or the sex worker. At the time of my application, the ethics committee was of the opinion there were too many research applications on this topic. To my knowledge and, which was confirmed in an interview with a committee member, there were two other 'similar' proposals: one was looking at human rights issues in relationship to Thai female sex workers and, the second, a case study on the Cambodian sex industry/workers. The IRB took measures to divert and/or block both applicants delving into prostitution.[26] Both of these application protocols took considerable time to be processed and, needed, not only revision of the topic but also a 'roundtable meeting' with the IRB. The former protocol was disallowed, or more to the point, the committee made it financially impossible for the researcher to undertake the research, hence, the applicant changed focus. The latter altered the proposed methodology. Meanwhile, a further accusation was that the power both researchers would exert over the research participants outweighed the benefits of their research.

Hence, a summary of the committee's concerns outlined in their assessment of *my* protocol application follows. The risk factor – did the overall interview process impinge on the welfare and safety of the women, in relationship to the bar owners and the 'pimps'? Subsequently, it was suggested I do my interviewing away from the bar, to overcome this risk. Meanwhile, other concerns were: what did I mean by the term 'informants'; how would I establish the age of the respective woman;[27] and where did I intend to keep the codes such as, the participants' correct names, pseudonyms and consent forms? In turn, this brought up questions of the extent of literacy attained by the sex workers: were the women illiterate? Moreover, the women were perceived as economically dependent on the male customer. Consistent with these concerns, which had the overall potential to scuttle the whole project was whether the balance between the benefits/risks to me and the research participants *warranted* my involvement. In addition, was this research going to bring about new and significant knowledge on the subject matter? And, lastly, the already mentioned research methodology – ethnography. In the face of the NSECRIH Statement and Guidelines, these concerns seemed quite rational but nonetheless, they underpinned concerns about IRB stereotyping. This became apparent when several of the members raised concerns over consent forms, the security of the identifiers and codes. These issues had been addressed in the application but, somehow, these documents had been overlooked.

Risk versus merits of the research

Due to the nature and subject matter of my research, I was acutely aware that there were numerous potential ethical issues, hence, my initial research 'scouting' trip. The IRB indicated its primary concern was related to the overall merit of my research, albeit, this concern stemmed more from the 'alleged' off-handed manner in which I addressed the apparent dangers the committee thought loomed for both the participants and/or me. I received an e-mail to alert me to this fact:

> Your protocol is one of several that have recently come to the committee that are causing considerable concern because of an insufficient appreciation of possible dangers, both to the researcher and to the participants ... The University has a duty of care to its students and it would be unethical not to address this issue.[28]

Regardless that the sex workers' activities centred on committing an illegal act – prostitution – the committee did not flag this. Prostitution, in Thailand, is deemed illegal under the *Prostitution Act 1960*. The IRB's specific concerns though, did centre on perceived inadequate consideration of adverse reactions toward the women not only from their employers, but also, from their 'pimps'. I had not addressed these issues. The concern was raised because the committee thought in the event that I interviewed workers in their workplace this would cause strained relationships between the pimps, bar owners and customer since they would be included in the process. This concern had not been included as a topic of discussion in any of the existing literature or, uncovered on my 'scouting trip' to Thailand. So framed, the ethics committee's suggestion was that to overcome this possible risk, I should conduct my interviews with the women away from their workplace. Since I was proposing to do ethnographic research, suffice to say, this proposed change would have in part negated, or at least, jeopardized my accepted presence in the bars to do any observations of the workers in their natural work habitat. Adhering to this suggestion would have negated my ability to listen to the vital 'everyday' conversations between the participants, informants and customers, which could highlight the individuals' worldview. For instance, how could I determine the coercion factor or whether she did have choice in her selection of customers, as I suspected?[29] In practice, this was important because the dominant discourse argues women would not voluntarily enter prostitution and if therefore, they are working in the industry, they are controlled.[30]

Another hesitation that I had with interviewing the women away from their workplace was contrary to the committee's perspective. I proposed that if the women were at risk from 'their' pimps, 'johns' or employers, but chose to speak to me away from the bar, it could suggest to an observer that the women were trying to hide their contact with me. This could have subsequent repercussions if it got back to their pimps or employers, compared to carrying the conversations out openly in the bar.

Notwithstanding this, the IRB seemed to be unwavering in its adherence to the NSECRIH document regarding 'Research Merit and Safety, Section: 1.14';[31] and this reinforced the stereotyping issue, rather than them professionally critiquing the protocol. This disquiet became more conclusive as I reassessed their concerns through e-mail correspondence. Persistently, I was asked to revisit concerns that I had already readdressed, but to no satisfaction. Eventually, it came to the point where I had to attend a face-to-face roundtable conference with the ethics committee.[32] This was brought about because the IRB continually thought my 'response seems not to acknowledge the possible ramifications adequately'.[33] Again, my disquiet loomed because the only literature that mentioned the danger women faced from pimps was from the radical feminist and abolitionist authors. Others such as Marc Askew or Thomas M. Steinfatt, who had spent time examining the Thai sex industry, did not see it that way.[34]

Mounting concern continued even after I had explained the experience and situation which I knew to be true (at least 'my' truth) – that there were no pimps for the women who I intended to study. Moreover, the IRB repeatedly dismissed the validity of my responses by returning to the assumed existence of mamasans. ' ... the police may be involved, and there are still the mamasans. The real issue is that there may be people controlling the women.'[35] The mamasan's job in open beer bars unlike brothels or other genres, entails keeping track on which woman was 'bought out' and, who was left in the bar or alternatively, on holiday or sick. The mamasan was able to keep track particularly in respect to who had been bought out because she took the 'bar fine'. In addition, she noted the departure time and which venue the woman was going to. Above all, the mamasans' job was to ensure there were enough available women in the bar. Given what I knew to be facts 'on the ground', I was suspicious that the members of the IRB were engaging in stereotyping of the sex workers.

As previously mentioned, the purpose of my earlier 'scouting trip' – was to try to negate as many unexpected situations as possible. My strategy to eliminate some of the risk factors, as laid out in my research protocol, was the anticipated type of accommodation. In addition, I had contacts with academics and NGO workers who knew the 'lay of the land' so to speak and there was an agreement reached via e-mail contact that I would utilize their knowledge and wisdom. With due respect, this strategy was pre-planned not only for myself, but also for the women that I may have inadvertently put at risk.

To contextualize further my claim of stereotyping, I will briefly discuss my proposed question list, the economic dependency and consent procedure issues raised by the IRB, juxtaposed with the risks and merits. In my initial protocol, which I submitted as an Appendix, I developed two lists of proposed questions: one for the women themselves and the second for informants such as NGO worker, family or academics. I became disturbed when the committee asked if I had submitted the required question list. This was troubling because I could only surmise the protocol was not read thoroughly. Nevertheless, whilst I had loosely put together some questions, including one on marriage, the type of research I was proposing lent itself to initiating a

Exceeding scholarly responsibility: IRBs and political constraints 29

conversation and listening to people's life stories rather than a formal interview style. Yet the response was:

> [T]he committee felt that the last question re marriage to a Thai or a foreigner was invasive. It presupposed too that they were not married already. Also, although sex work might form part of their duties, no questions about their sex work were included, which seemed a curious omission.[36]

It would be wrong to underestimate the potential damage caused to research participants by inappropriate questions. I agree with Linda Shopes' assertion that, '[t]here's a real difference in the nature of the harm done between not being treated for syphilis as in Tuskegee, and asking someone a blundering, embarrassing question'.[37]

Moving to another condition advanced by the IRB, the notion that I should 'pay' the woman participant given they 'may be in an economically dependent situation', not surprisingly, I was not prepared to pay for the interview time with these women. To begin with, I would not have sufficient research funds to accommodate this suggestion; although, I had no problem buying the women drinks or snacks. I even played pool with some of them, which was another means for them to earn extra cash. As long as the customer spent money, the women economically benefited for their efforts of 'friendship' and 'attentiveness'. Further, I did not want to subject my data to unnecessary scrutiny because I had paid the interviewees. Suffice to say, the women were very good at extorting money from *vulnerable* male customers by living up to the politically constructed stereotypical image. Therefore, by telling woes such as 'my brother is sick in the village' or 'my father cannot work and needs an operation', extra money was typically forthcoming. So, with all due respect, I was not going to subject my research data to 'stereotypical answers' let alone to the other perspective which entails unrestricted agency (rational action theory) because my data could fall prey to women thinking I am paying for information and the money would stop if their answers did not 'please the researcher'. The IRB based its thoughts in a taken-for-granted assumption that these women were economically dependent because of their presumed poverty and the subsequent entrapment in prostitution and yet, this was a false premise. In the case of my participants, each one received a retainer 'wage' (6,000bt per month) of which they were able, if they chose to, increase that amount through negotiated sexual servicing, holidays or shopping expedients with customers. I knew this through reading employment signs often displayed in windows, plus from conversations that I had had with bar workers on my previous trip to Thailand. Even without these observations, I would have clung tightly to my reasoning, as I believed it to be foundationally sound.

A matter of consent

Finally, I wish to mention the 'consent forms'. Although the committee initially *overlooked* my submitted (and translated forms), they eventually approved the use of them. Before locating them in my application, the question asked of me was: '[A]re these women illiterate?' Sadly, I thought this demonstrated a further unfounded assumption. Thailand has the highest literacy rate for any Southeast Asian country. The NSECRIH[38] insists on consent to be obtained by the researcher prior to conducting the research, however, consent forms are not a regulation but one implied by the IRB. According to the NSECRIH there are many forms of consent. Yet, producing consent forms in a research environment not only invites but also prolongs any risk element. I decided the argument for my ethnocentric imposed requirement for signed consent forms needed shelving. Thereby, I accepted Val Braithwaite's argument that the '[s]ocial context plays a very large role in both communicating the voluntary nature of participation and in assuring participants that they can withdraw at any time'.[39] Furthermore, it is Braithwaite's belief, and one that I support, that it is the social situation which dissuades power relations. When the participant understands the researcher has no authority, no coercive power to chastise or capability to insist on their cooperation then there is voluntary participation. My capability to insist on women's participation was nil because of the 'good will' extended to me by the bar owners to utilize their facility to conduct the research. Their 'condition' was for me to be 'invisible' so as not to disrupt or threaten business.

The irony is that whilst past researchers may have invoked their power over research subjects and, as I was to find out personally, Thai women are not the 'meek and passive' persons much of the literature portrays. Thai women are just like other women the world over; some are demure and quiet whilst others are more rambunctious and outgoing. Furthermore, this assumption of 'power over' is intellectually bereft. Yet, many sex workers are not inclined to allow themselves to be placed in a powerless position unless it benefits them. Especially, when it comes to speaking with a researcher, as I was to discover, the women and the owners only *permitted* me as a researcher to conduct my research in their place – after laying down the ground rules – *they* were not to be coerced into any study. Again, they had had so many people studying them they knew I was in *their* social space. This then gave them the power.

A question of reputation

In keeping with my suspicion of stereotyping on the part of the IRB, I argue, the committee further exceeded its *true academic* authority in the sense it placed the public reputation of the university above protecting the integrity of the researcher and researched by politicizing of the research. The NHMRC 'Media Releases 2002'[40] indicates what the researchable topics were and who received research grants for that period. Among those topics funded in 2002 were, 'healthy aging', 'obesity', 'skin cancer', 'dementia and aging', 'health in Asia Pacific', 'a review of university funding', and 'animal organ transplants'. I draw on this document to give an overview of what appeared to be 'acceptable research' for 2002. Juxtaposed with the current environment of the modern university it has become an awkward marriage between adhering to NHMRC's regulations paralleled with the seemingly politically motivated attacks on the institution including the 'new' CEO management style with the push for public/private cooperation to fund research.[41]

Furthermore, this Go8 University consistently competes in research output, to retain its reputation as one of the 'world's great research institutions'.[42] This competition is nationwide of course, because of the scarce resource of government funding. Performance indicators are among the criteria to achieve and maintain this reputation. As part of this university's Strategic Plan for 1995–2004 to maintain its world ranking, the university concluded all research and education must be related to public policy and national issues. Thai prostitution really did not fit these criteria.

Under Section 2.13 of the NHMRC, the IRB are able to 'approve, require amendment of, or reject a research proposal on ethical grounds whereby, the IRB must record decisions in writing and should include reasons for rejection'.[43] Admissible reasons for rejection or amendment are outlined in Section 1 of the NHMRC. Under 'Principles of Ethical Conduct' the researcher is to show ' ... respect for persons which is expressed as regard for their welfare, rights, beliefs, perceptions, customs and cultural heritage, both individual and collective, of persons involved in research'. In addition, 'the ethical principle of beneficence' is to 'minimise risks of harm or discomfort to participants in research projects'. As well, the precedence of the protocol design must 'ensure respect for the dignity and well being of the participants ... over the expected benefits to knowledge'. In addition, no group should be subjected to more research than any other.[44] Meanwhile, Jeffrey Brainard explained, 'social-science and humanities scholars complain that they are being unnecessarily burdened by a system of supervision that was primarily designed to prevent abuses of patients involved in medical studies – where a poorly designed survey could result in serious harm or even death'.[45] Ultimately, however, the basic necessity for the protocol's ethical acceptability is the researcher's skill, experience and the [social] scientific quality of the proposal.[46]

Also under the benefits of research, the NHMRC clearly specifies that research involving humans is advantageous for society because it illuminates social well being, dysfunction, and disease. In addition, this type of research opportunity 'provides the education of Australian students and researchers [which] should not be underestimated'.[47]

Throughout my protocol application and dealings with the IRB I endeavoured to meet all criteria. Yet, due to the reforms instituted throughout Australia's universities since the Dawkins Report it appears the managerial persona is the most soul-destroying apparatus when it comes to freedom in research. The philosophical explanation behind the apparent corporatisation and privatisation of the university is to assist the economy, build national interest, lessen waste in research funding, and bring accountability. Seumas Miller argues, the current trend is for both university staff and the general public to embrace the 'myth' that the modern (Australian) university needs to be privatised and corporatised. This is so this 'public' institution can 'become more competitive and better able to contribute to the growth of the economy'.[48] As a result of this, I judge, no matter how you look at it, it really is an attack on the traditional conception of the university and driven by neoclassical economics.

Furthermore, Miller states that alongside this assumption is a new rhetoric, which espouses the 'bureaucratisation' of the higher education section involving different requirements for data collection as well as the fact that research money is getting harder to obtain hence, the need for 'second-guessing political agendas'.[49] Universities now compete for the scarce research monies, which leads to the other criteria for a successful university – publications. New knowledge is 'applied' and tied to research quantum which is a measure for government funding which in turn becomes an indicator of a given university's academic standing in research relative to others.[50] Acknowledgment of successful research in the university only comes when it generates quantum and relevant publications.[51] This includes PhD dissertations, since for early-career researchers seeking academic positions, and in some instances, positions with the Public Service, the expectation is the applicant must have a substantial publication record plus the ability to attract 'outside' money.

Subsequently, research is managed. How? It is not by taking away the total autonomy of the researcher but through 'systems and mechanisms based on "steering from a distance".'[52] Marginson argues now that the creativeness or the inquisitive researcher is considered as the 'other' and hence, needs to be brought back into the 'corporate fold'. Overall by 'managing' research through the IRB, the university is able to ensure its international competitiveness through marketing its ability to gain government and private funding, research quantum and publications. Hence, in the scheme of seeking status, the reputation of the university is intact if 'acceptable' research is undertaken.

The resolution

As previously mentioned it became obvious, by both parties, that a face-to-face meeting was necessary. During the roundtable conference, which was finally suggested by the IRB chairperson, in an attempt to finalize my ethics approval, I was asked many questions. Fortunately, I had spent time during 2002 in Thailand and my trip became my reference point in answering many of those questions. What emerged was an assumption which could have eviscerated my proposed research and to my way of thinking, the sex workers themselves. The 'taken-for-granted' assumption presented by the committee was that women sex workers performed their services on the clients in a room, which had mattresses strewn around on the floor. In other words, when the women reported for work, they would enter a room and just lay on a bed, awaiting clients. According to a member of the committee, my interviewing the women in this environment would cause the women to be distracted and, thereby, the customers not liking this distraction may become violent, to the women as well as me. I am not discounting that such an environment exists in the Thai sex industry, but the point that I am trying to make throughout this chapter is that there are different levels in all sex industries which need to be recognised. As such the taken-for-granted assumptions or stereotyping negated the complexities and diversity which I have addressed previously. However, I was able to quickly dispel such notions with a more accurate description of the bar workers employment environment, or at least, the workers I intended to interview. Again, it was at this point that my resolve to obtain ethics approval was paramount. New knowledge would only emerge in an environment where discussion and debate was allowed. The dominant discourse did not seem to permit this and such a conjecture only highlighted the necessity for this meeting.

Furthermore, I was not naïve of the corruption that was rampant in Thailand. To inform and prepare myself for this research project, I was familiar with the literature stating police and politicians were often cooperating with bar owners.[53] As mentioned previously, I was not comfortable with this situation but reasoned that by obtaining a research visa this risk could be minimised. The potential that bar owners or anyone would alert those in authority of my presence and purpose of being 'in country' was a possibility, but with the correct paper work, harm minimisation could be exercised hence, further protecting the workers. In Thailand, a foreign researcher is required to have their research approved by the appropriate government department – the National Thai Research Council. Nevertheless, by the time my ethics approval was given, I did not have time for this process as it takes a significant amount of time due to the bureaucratic procedures.

Putting this aside, I was able to spend time with the IRB explaining my perspective on the question list. This issue was subsequently resolved when they realized from my input that my questions would lead rather than direct the conversation. Additionally, the issue concerning my consent forms, despite the mix up, had been resolved prior to the roundtable conference, however, I raised the subject of usage and, in the end, the IRB seemed nebulous of their use. The committee members told me I could determine whether consent forms were necessary 'on site'. The decision to both query the usage of them and raise it at the meeting was not taken lightly but, after reading up on the use of signed consent forms I was convinced by authors such as Will van den Hoonaard[54] and Braithwaite,[55] of how highly contestable this issue was, despite the guidelines.

Invoking my sociological professionalism, I rethought the imposed use of consent forms. I reasoned in my own mind that if I presented a bar worker with a form to write her name on and, then sign it, that would be more inflammatory and harmful than just sitting down and talking. Instead, I handed out my university business card to all who consented to be a participant.[56] That would not only allow me to retain some anonymity, amidst a bar full of Western males and Thai women but it definitely helped the interviewees. If pressured to use consent forms, the image of me walking discreetly into a bar with an armful of forms or even just unpacking my backpack on the counter, then scrambling to find a pen conjured up an uncomfortable image. The trouble with me attempting to get signatures from each of the participants is, for what 'Charbonneau describes as the cornerstone of all Western ethical codes', that its only purpose is to meet a public requirement which for all intent and purpose is not adequately structured around the social sciences or humanities style of research. Furthermore, drawing from van den Hoonaard's argument it is especially inappropriate for ethnographical research as it takes away the natural anonymity.[57]

In keeping with this, and through reflection over the risk concerns, my thoughts were resolved on the already presented premise – that the IRB was more focused on maintaining the stereotypical image toward the sex worker. Plus, it became apparent that the true academic community, once recognized for its contribution to society via its bold and brilliant research visions, had been changed fundamentally through the Dawkins Reform. The end result appears to be that a university's current reputation is driven more by economic prowess and success than by contributions to society; an economic prowess and success overseen by a bureaucratic, corporatist structure.

Conclusion

I have made the claim that the concept that underpinned the concerns of the ethics committee was its stereotyping of Thai sex workers. Both historic and contemporary IRBs are charged with protecting researchers and participants alike, as well as assessing the merit of the research project. They are the vanguard to not repeating the previous atrocities and mistakes by safeguarding against inflections on unsuspecting research participants from unscrupulous researchers. Yet, was the IRB causing its own inflection? There was doubt as to whether a representation was to be permitted to challenge the dominant discourse, despite the research of Murray, Odzer or Cohen, for example, that shows a different reality. Stereotyping negates the complexities and diversity of, in this case, a social group. The committee seemed to be pushing for a homogenized group, not only for the sex workers themselves but also for researchers.

Different research methodologies produce different knowledge. Thereby, yes, the IRB has a responsibility to point out the risks pertaining to the chosen research methodology but, not be paternalistic nor to 'politicise' the project. Helping the researcher manage the risks is the goal, not to use them to stop or insinuate that there are no merits in doing the research project. A stereotypical image helped form the dominant discourse and, in this instance, permits the powerful to maintain and/or reproduce an inaccurate image of the Thai sex work. The powerful do not require an accurate image as much as the powerless do.

Notes

1 My research on sex workers does not include child prostitution and hence, this chapter does not deal with this topic at all.
2 See Denise Brennan, Guri Tyldum and Anette Brunovskis's work in the Special Edition of *International Migration*, vol. 43 (2005), pp. 35–54:17–34.
3 Donna Hughes, 'Hiding in Plain Sight' A Practical Guide to Identifying Victims of Trafficking in the U.S. (2003), available at <http://www.uri.edu/artsci/wms/Hughes/hiding_in_plain_sight.pdf > , accessed 3 January 2004.
4 Also known as an Institution Review Board (IRB) and, herein will be referred to as IRB.
5 Go8 is a lobby group for eight Australian leading tertiary institutions. This group was established informally in 1994 by a network of vice-chancellors and formally incorporated in 1999. For a full account of Go8 see also Simon Marginson and Mark Considine, *The Enterprise University Power, Governance and Reinvention in Australia* (Victoria, Australia: Cambridge University Press, 2000).
6 Marginson and Considine, *The Enterprise University*, p. 30, see also John Molony, 'Australian universities today', in Tony Coady (ed.), *Why Universities Matter* (St Leonards, Australia: Allen & Unwin, 2000) pp. 72–84; Simon Marginson, 'Research as a managed economy: the costs', in Tony Coady (ed.), *Why Universities Matter* (St Leonards, Australia: Allen & Unwin, 2000) pp. 186–213.
7 See Marginson and Considine, *The Enterprise University*, pp. 136–174.
8 Michael Pickering, *Stereotyping The Politics of Representation* (New York: Palgrave, 2001).
9 Pickering, *Stereotyping*, pp. 47–78.
10 C. Wright Mills, *The Power Elite* (New York: Oxford University Press, 1968).
11 Mills, *The Power Elite*, pp. 18, 290.
12 Alison Murray, *Pink Fitts* (Victoria: Monash University Press, 2001) p. 87.
13 I use the working definitions in the United States *Victims of Trafficking and Violence Protection Act of 2000* (Public Law 1006–1386): Sec. 103 which outlines the definitions. SEX TRAFFICKING means, 'the recruitment, harbouring, transportation, provision, or obtaining of a person for the purpose of a commercial sex act'. Meanwhile, commercial sex act is, 'any sex act on account of which anything of value is given to or received by any person'.
14 Cleo Odzer, *Patpong Sisters: An American Women's View of the Bangkok Sex World* (New York: Blue Moon Books, 1994).
15 Erik Cohen, *Thai Tourism Hill Tribes, Islands and Open-Ended Prostitution Collected Papers, Studies in Contemporary Thailand No 4*, (Thailand: White Lotus Press, 1996).
16 Some of the information below reflects what is available on this particular Go8 university's internal website. To therefore, protect its good name I have omitted the url. Furthermore, the IRB was formed in 1986.
17 Joint NHMRC/AVCC Statement and Guidelines on Research Practice (1997), available at <http://www.nhmrc.gov.au/funding/policy/researchprac.htm>, accessed 16 April 2008.
18 Joint NHMRC/AVCC Statement and Guidelines on Research Practice (1997), available at <http://www.nhmrc.gov/funding/policy/researchprac.htm>, accessed 16 April 2008.

19 Marginson and Considine, *The Enterprise University*, p. 133.
20 Marginson and Considine, *The Enterprise University*, p. 135.
21 Seumas Miller, 'Academic autonomy', in Tony Coady (ed.), *Why Universities Matter* (St Leonards, Australia: Allen & Unwin, 2000), pp. 110–131.
22 National Statement on Ethical Conduct in Research Involving Humans (1999), available at <http://www.nhmrc.gov.au/publications>, accessed 30 June 2004.
23 National Statement pp. 3–4; See also Statement and Guidelines on Research Practice (1997). Important: under this section there is no specific understanding for the Humanities or Social Sciences.
24 Statement and Guidelines on Research Practice (1997), p. 3.
25 NHMRC, p. 13.
26 Confidential interview with member of the IRB, 29 June 2004.
27 This question relates to the dominant discourse that categorizes women and children consistently and where many researchers use the two terms as synonymous. It reinforces the notion that many women in the sex industry are perceived to be underage. The IRB thought I would encounter underage women and thereby, I would not be able to do the research. However, eighteen years old is a Western construct of what constitutes a legal age to perform commercial sexual activities.
28 Committee Secretary, Research Ethics Officer, e-mail 2 October 2002.
29 By this I mean many of the interviewed women had the choice of whether to just talk and accept drinks from a client or play a game of pool with him and decide not to be 'bought out' from the bar. Usually this means, to either go back to his accommodation for the night – sex work – escort him to do his shopping whereby she acts as his interpreter or haggler. Many women liked to do the shopping because often that meant the 'client' bought them a nice dinner. Also it had the potential, if they worked it, to be asked to go on a holiday with the client.
30 Kathleen Barry, *Female Sexual Slavery* (New York: Avon Books, 1984); Donna Hughes, 'Men Create the Demand, Women Are the Supply', *feminista!*, vol. 4, no. 3 (2000), pp. 1–6, available at <http:///www.feminista.com/archiviews/v4n3/hughes.html> , accessed 10 January 2005; Janice Raymond, '10 Reasons for Not Legalizing Prostitution', *The Coalition Against Trafficking in Women*, (15 September 2003), available at <http://action.web.ca/home/catw/readingroom.shtml?x=32972&AA_EX_Session=7578 > , accessed 14 July 2004.
31 NSECRIH, p. 13.
32 I attended this meeting with my supervisor and advisory panel, in conjunction with a Departmental Honours Programme academic representative. The meeting took place on 22nd November 2002 at 4pm in the Chancellery Tower at ANU. My protocol was first submitted on 30th August and finally approval was granted 4th December 2002.
33 Committee Secretary, e-mail 30 October 2002.
34 Marc Askew, 'City of Women, City of Foreign Men: Working Spaces and Re-Working Identitites Among Female Sex Workers in Bangkok's Tourist Zone', *Singaporean Journal of Tropical Geography*, vol. 2, no. 2 (1998), pp. 130–150; Thomas M. Steinfatt, *Working at the Bar Sex Work and Health Communication in Thailand* (Westport, Connecticut: London: Ablex Publishing, 2002).
35 Committee Secretary, e-mail 30 October 2002.
36 Committee Secretary, e-mail 2 October 2002 also, 30 October 2002.
37 Jeffrey Brainard, 'The wrong rules for social sciences', *The Chronicle of Higher Education* (9 March 2001), p. A22, available at, <http://proquest.umi.com/pqdweb?Did=000000069316752&Fmt=3&Deli=1&Mtd=1&Idx=7&Sid=o&RQT=309&LDid=000000070601773&LSid=7&L=1>, accessed 3 July 2005.
38 NSECRIH, Principle 1, Section 1.7 p.12–13.
39 This is a quote from an unpublished discussion paper written by Val Braithwaite after her own encounter with the same Go8 IRB. The author circulated a paper

which addresses four central issues relating to doing quality research and maintaining high ethical standards. Braithwaite's central argument is that the ethics committee should support the researcher to manage the risks involved rather than take on the role to prevent risks. By preventing risks, it creates armchair theorists and research is about taking risks. It is not their role to prevent risk because this leads to impediments which stop controversial research. Interference moves from protection to being political (Braithwaithe n.a. p.2).
40 Media Releases 2002 (Australian Government: National Health and Medical Research Council), available at, <http://www.nhmrc.gov.au/news/media/rel102/index.htm> , accessed 16 April 2008.
41 Tony Coady, 'Universities and the ideals of inquiry', in Tony Coady (ed.), *Why Universities Matter* (St Leonards, Australia: Allen & Unwin, 2000), pp. 3–25.
42 The Go8 university has a website available on http://www.dest.gov.au/archive. However, this url is incomplete so as to keep the university's confidentiality.
43 NHMRC, p. 17.
44 NHMRC, p. 11.
45 Brainard, *The wrong rules for social science?* p. A21.
46 NHMRC, p. 5.
47 NHMRC, p. 9–10.
48 Seumas Miller, 'Academic Autonomy', in Tony Coady (ed.), *Why Universities Matter* (St Leonards, Australia: Allen & Unwin, 2000), p. 111.
49 Miller, 'Academic Autonomy', p. 115.
50 Marginson and Considine, *The Enterprise University*, p. 212.
51 Marginson and Considine, *The Enterprise University*, p. 140.
52 Simon Marginson, 'Research as a managed economy: the costs', in Tony Coady (ed.), *Why Universities Matter* (St Leonards, Australia: Allen & Unwin, 2000), p. 193.
53 See Pasuk Phongpaichit, Sangsit Phiriyarangsan, and Nualnoi Treerat, Guns, Girls, Gambling, Ganja: Thailand's Illegal Economy and Public Policy (Chiang Mai, Thailand: Silkworm Books, 1998), pp. 6–7.
54 Will C. van den Hoonaard, 'Is research-ethics review a moral panic', *The Canadian Review of Sociology and Anthropology (Revue canadienne de sociologie et d'anthropologie)*, 38, 1 (February 2001), pp. 1–7, available at, <http://proquest.umi.com/pqdweb?Did=000000071379715&Fmt=3&Deli=1&Mtd=1&idx=8&Sid=O&RQT=309&LDid=000000072996661&LSid=8&L=1> , accessed 3 July 2005.
55 Braithwaite, unpublished paper.
56 My business card is like all cards: it has the university's official emblem in the corner; my name, the department and school in which I am located; the university's address; my position (Ph.D. candidate); phone and facsimile numbers, and e-mail address.
57 van den Hoonaard, 'Is research-ethics review a moral panic?', p. 4.

4 Methods and ethics with research teams and NGOs: Comparing experiences across the border of Rwanda and Democratic Republic of Congo

*Elizabeth Levy Paluck**

Rwanda, May 2005

I sat in an immaculate office in the Rwandan capital Kigali with a bureaucrat who crossed out words on my questionnaire with a black bic pen. 'Your research team cannot ask about "ethnic groups".' He dug the pen into the paper. I sighed inwardly, although this was the expected response. I wasn't an independent researcher who could slip under government radar – I was working with a registered NGO. 'Then, could I use the word "group", in general?' I felt confident my participants would understand group to mean ethnic. 'No', the bureaucrat shook his head. You can't use the word *group*. I started to fidget. I was supposed to research ethnic relations without using the word 'ethnic' or 'group'. 'What word do you suggest, then?' He tapped his pen against my questionnaire. 'Perhaps, "people". For example in question number 15, "I would be willing to allow my daughter to marry *people*?".'

Later that day my Rwandan research assistant spoke in low consoling tones. 'We will write "people" and say "people", but as we explain the question, participants will understand what we mean. Everyone speaks in code here.' Recent arrests of Rwandan researchers working for an international organization weighed on my mind. 'But if this code is so easy to understand, what is the difference – aren't our researchers still at risk for discussing ethnicity?' He shrugged. 'Our participants know us, so I don't think there will be a problem. And I don't think we have another choice.'

Democratic Republic of Congo, July 2007

In an office tucked under palm trees north of Goma, DRC, I squeezed onto a narrow wooden bench with ten researchers and one driver to face the mayor's desk. '*Karibu,* welcome', the mayor smiled at us. I explained that we were evaluating an NGO-produced radio programme about community relations, and I presented him with our *ordres de mission*. He nodded and started to sign and pass them back to us. 'Many people will be grateful that an NGO is showing interest in our situation. You are invited to work in the neighbourhood where I live.' I explained that our choice of neighbourhoods and people was random. He smiled a bit regretfully and turned to a faded hand-painted map on the wall. 'I should update you on the security situation. You should not go farther than these neighbourhoods here, because outside there has been some fighting.'

Back in our vehicle, we reviewed which languages we would probably use that day – Swahili, Kinyarwanda, Mashi, French for the 'intellectuals'. Discussions about language provoked the chronic good-natured teasing between the researchers about their different accents and origins. I assigned two to the local radio station to interview participants we had invited via radio broadcast. All 20 had arrived by foot early that morning. Just as everyone dispersed and I had settled into my own work, I received a text message from the head of our NGO. 'Attack 9km from your location. Evacuate immediately with the convoy waiting at Presbyterian lodge.' My research assistant broke the news to the participants waiting at the radio station. 'Please stay', a few entreated. 'Be brave. This happens all the time ... ' But within an hour we had contacted the rest of our researchers using hired motos and cell phones and were riding back to Goma in 4×4s while our participants walked home.

Introduction

This chapter is about conducting fieldwork with teams of researchers and with non-governmental organizations (NGOs). Drawing on four years of experience directing field experiments with NGO programmes and research teams in Rwanda and the Democratic Republic of Congo (DRC), I focus on the methodological and ethical decisions involved in this work. In both countries I conducted national (Rwanda) and sub-national (DRC) field experiments, gathering quantitative and qualitative evidence to measure the impact of NGO-produced radio programmes aimed at increasing constructive political dissent and community collective action.[1] As anticipated by many other discussions of research methodology and ethics, my methodological techniques and ethical concerns were shaped by the differing political and social environments of Rwanda and the DRC – differing levels of violence, state control, and population fractionalization.

Less frequently do textbooks and research reports discuss the way context shapes methodological and ethical issues with specific reference to research teams (such as data collection assistants, surveyors, or enumerators) and to partnering or sponsoring organizations (e.g., non-governmental organizations). My research relationship with research teams and NGOs, and their relationship with participants and other local actors, had a profound impact on the kinds of data I was able to collect and how I interpreted those data. Typically, methodological and ethical discussions focus on the role of the principal investigator and her relationship to the research participants: for example, they discuss challenges in obtaining access to communities, boundaries of researcher–participant relationships, and concerns about participant confidentiality and protection.[2] This chapter seeks to explain how work with research teams and NGOs raises different methodological and ethical issues that are neglected at a significant cost.

The social sciences boast a long tradition of using large teams of researchers to compile significant datasets to be used by academics, governments and organizations. Social scientists interested in social, political, health and economic interventions (particularly in conflict or post-conflict areas where NGOs are concentrated) also evaluate NGO programmes or affiliate with NGOs for logistical and security support or for access to local populations. Yet documentation of this research process largely keeps research teams and organizations invisible: they are the 'ghosts in the machine', to borrow Ryle's (1949) phrase. To date, there has been little discussion of how collaboration might affect research methods and ethics. I argue that when the data collection process is invisible, analytic opportunities, data problems, and appropriate contextualization are often lost.

The fundamental goal of this chapter is to shed light on the process of working with research teams and NGOs. Some of the observations I use from my own research projects in conflict and post-conflict contexts may prove particular to those settings and research questions, but it is likely that many can be generalized to various challenging fieldwork settings and across disciplinary lines. Initiating a wider discussion on this topic among other researchers who collaborate with research teams and organizations will further illuminate unexplored conditions of collaborative research.

I exploit variation on either side of the Rwanda–DRC border to show how fieldwork context significantly affects methodological and ethical decisions particular to collaborative research. Differing levels of violence, state control and population fractionalization in either country affected my decisions about, for example, how I identified the research project, who I hired for the research team, how I handled day to day debriefing methods, and how I managed my obligations to my partner organization. Researchers working in different contexts and in different times may confirm or dispute the importance of these contextual elements and contribute others. More systematic analysis of these issues will help researchers to anticipate how their methods and ethics will be shaped by research collaboration in various field contexts, and will improve the quality of research design, data, and analysis.

The rest of this chapter proceeds as follows: for necessary background, I briefly describe my research projects, and I define and describe levels of violence, state control and population fractionalization in Rwanda and DRC during the time of my work with research teams and non-governmental organizations. I analyze how differing levels of these three factors on either side of the Rwanda–DRC border affected critical methodological and ethical concerns pertaining to my research collaborations. I conclude with recommendations for research planning, training and reporting on collaborative research projects in fieldwork conditions generally and challenging conditions in specific.

Background: Research project and context

Research project

In both Rwanda and the DRC, I evaluated the impact of 'entertainment education' radio programmes aimed at changing citizens' beliefs and perceived norms with respect to violence, community and authority, and at promoting actual dissent, collective action and tolerance.[3] I conducted these studies first as my dissertation research, and then after my Ph.D. had been awarded. The same regional NGO (La Benevolencija) produced both programmes, and in both countries I utilized a randomized field experimental design, collecting quantitative and qualitative evidence with teams of local researchers. I led these teams in the field with the assistance of a permanent research assistant who worked with me from the start of the project to its finish, who helped me with logistics, planning and research team leadership, and who generally served as a cultural interlocutor.

Rwanda. In each of 14 communities representing salient identity groups across Rwanda, I randomly selected a stratified sample of 40 adults for a total sample of 560. After matching the most similar communities into pairs, I randomly assigned one within each pair to listen to the 'reconciliation' radio programme and the other to a different entertainment-education radio programme addressing health behaviours. The same set of researchers visited each community and played the randomly-assigned radio programme on a cassette player to each community's participant group (in Rwanda, people typically listen to the radio in groups).

After one year, my research assistant and I led a team of 15 Rwandan research assistants to each site, collecting data using quantitative surveys, open-ended focus groups, interviews with families and community members, and observations of participant behaviour.[4] I returned the next year to follow up with the same participants.

Democratic Republic of Congo. In the eastern Kivu region of DRC, I studied the impact of a radio talk show that was broadcast after a Congolese entertainment-education soap opera (created by the same regional NGO), aimed at community building. The talk show encouraged listeners to discuss the soap opera topics with friends and family, and featured listeners' letters about previous episodes. I identified non-overlapping broadcast areas in the Kivu region and randomly assigned some areas to broadcast only the radio soap opera, and others to receive the soap opera followed by the talk show.[5]

After one year of broadcasting, I took two different research teams into the field (one for North and one for South Kivu) to measure outcomes in a random sample of residents in each broadcast area. We conducted over nine hundred quantitative and open-ended interviews, and measured a behavioural response at the end of each interview.

Research context

Below I identify and define the three contextual dimensions along which variation in Rwanda and the DRC most affected my methods and ethical decisions with these research teams and NGO bureaus. They are 1) violence, 2) state control, and 3) population fragmentation.

Violence. I define physically violent acts as those targeted at certain genders or class groups (e.g., rape, killing or capture of young men or boys, attacking prosperous families), at political individuals or groups (e.g., assassinating political party members) or ethnicities (e.g., killing people identified with one ethnic group, displacing regional 'non-natives'). Civilians, militia, the state, or international actors may commit such violence.

Rwanda from 2004–7 experienced relatively low levels of violence, thanks to the security established by its powerful and well-organized government. However, the threat of violence for rural citizens was often implicit in their denouncements of witnesses and of local judges in the community courts set up to try genocidal crimes, and in state intimidation of journalists and human rights activists. Lending weight to this implicit threat were extrajudicial killings of community court witnesses (by citizens and unknown actors) including killings of suspects detained by the government.[6]

On the other hand, during the two years in which I worked in the Kivu region of the Democratic Republic of Congo (2006–7), the region was experiencing 'one of the world's worst humanitarian crises' (ICG, 2005; 2007). Physical violence against civilians and between various armed groups in the region caused thousands of deaths and tens of thousands of displaced people, all despite the presence of the largest and most expensive mission of United Nations (UN) peacekeepers in the world.

State control. By state control I mean the level of state presence and surveillance in local (fieldwork) contexts and in the operations of independent organizations and researchers working in the country. This includes the state's control of the movement, speech and general privileges of organizations, researchers (citizens and foreigners), and citizens who become research assistants and participants. Others have defined state control in more operational terms, such as the 'probability that a certain event or class of events will not occur within a defined area within a defined period of time'.[7] My more general definition serves my present purposes, which are to evaluate how the state affects the behaviour and concerns of research teams (who are usually citizens of the state), and of the NGO.

By any definition the state in Rwanda is visible and powerful at all levels; Rwanda's president Kagame was elected in 2003 with 95% of the vote, and his government retains tight control on speech, economic (particularly agricultural) activity and other freedoms.[8] Rwanda is effectively a one-party state; journalists practice self-censorship to avoid official sanction, and the current constitution bans speech about ethnicity as 'divisionist', a charge that is applied liberally to opponents of the state. I needed four months of sustained in-country work to obtain research permissions to work at 14 research sites from each relevant national ministry, governor, mayor, all the way down to each *nyumbakumi* (the local person responsible for a group of ten houses).

The DRC, on the other hand, recently held its second-ever presidential elections in 2006, ending a transitional government installed by the United Nations after several bloody years of war. The government has a tenuous grasp on the eastern Kivu region in particular, where armed groups refused to integrate into the national army and preyed upon the local population during my fieldwork. The population of eastern Kivu views their government as corrupt and inept (a fair accusation of a country that cannot account for a quarter of its national budget) and in many interviews research participants asked, 'why did we bother to vote?' reflecting their realization of the government's unwillingness or inability to improve their situation.

Population fractionalization. Social scientists frequently use the number and proportions of identity groups in a population to predict that country's economic and political development, quality of governance, and the like.[9] The way in which a population is divided into ethnic, religious, linguistic, or regional groups also matters for methods and ethics of research, particularly when the project employs teams of local researchers and works with local organizations that are situated in certain regions and focus on certain populations. Just as some researchers have demonstrated the need to identify locally meaningful cleavages in measures of population fractionalization,[10] only some out of all 'official' group cleavages may be significant for a collaborative research project. Significant population fractionalization (i.e., many groups, or a few disproportionately-sized groups) may compel NGOs to tailor their work to different groups' agendas. Research team members in the field may conduct their work differently or relate to various participants in different ways because of the salience of their own and the participants' identity.

In Rwanda, population fractionalization is much greater than the Hutu and Tutsi distinction rent by the genocide; in addition to the Batwa, a small (pygmy) minority group, Rwandans are divided into regional groups, historical diaspora groups (e.g., 'caseloads' of refugees across time, returnees from Congo, Uganda, and Burundi, Rwandans who 'never left'), and class groups.[11] Much post-conflict NGO and research activity focuses on the Hutu–Tutsi divide, but public discussion of this identity distinction is muted by the official government stance that there are *no* distinct identity groups in Rwanda. Underneath is a less salient but very sensitive distinction between Tutsis who survived the genocide and those who were living outside the country at that time, as well as regional groups representing the historical seats of power for different political parties, all recognizable by accent (Rwanda's *lingua franca* is Kinyarwanda).

Identity groups are more numerous and openly acknowledged in the Democratic Republic of Congo. DRC is home to approximately 250 ethnic groups and 700 languages and dialects. In the eastern Kivu region we used five different languages to conduct interviews, and recorded self-identification with over 20 ethnic groups. No government narrative discourages identification with an identity group; open identification with certain ethnic or pan-ethnic ('Bantu') identities has drawn the lines of battle for many years in the east. Different groups claim rights to citizenship, land and grievances against other groups and countries (specifically Rwanda).

The level of violence, state control and population fractionalization repeatedly affected my methodological and ethical decisions during fieldwork in Rwanda and DRC. I specifically examine issues of *identification* (e.g., of the research project as part of or separate from the NGO; of researchers themselves), *security* (e.g., psychological and physical safety of the research team; the security of the NGO's legal standing), and *expertise exchange* (e.g., my relationship to the NGO and the research team, the feedback I invited from each).

Methodological and ethical issues

Identification

In Rwanda and in DRC I made different decisions about identifying the research project as collaborative with or separate from the NGO, about which identities to include on the research teams, and about how to observe participants' identity or ask them to self-identify.

Identifying the research project. Investigators have an ethical obligation to identify the research project with enough clarity and detail for people to make a fully informed decision about whether they would like to participate. This obligation is often in tension with the need to avoid communicating the investigator's ideological or political leanings or general hopes for study findings. Working with a partner organization often accentuates this tension because organizations often have a widely known, or even misinterpreted, ideological orientation. I found that the level of state control in Rwanda and violence in DRC led to different decisions about how to identify the research project to people so as to secure their consensual, willing participation.

In Rwanda, I hoped to disassociate the research project from my partner NGO because of the close association between NGOs and the government in local settings. I introduced the project to our participants as an independent study that I, an American student, was conducting about the 'media and social life' in Rwanda. Although I did not hide that I was interested in evaluating the NGO's radio programmes, I emphasized my identity and goals as a student of Rwanda when I first met with each group of participants.

This separation helped to address my concern that a clear connection between the research and the NGO would invite 'correct' responding from participants who would assume (correctly) that the NGO (and any government officials associated with the NGO) would desire positive answers with respect to their mission of ethnic reconciliation and trauma healing. It did seem that participants identified me primarily as a student – at one site in the west of the country, the participant group would sombrely greet me by asking 'are you getting good grades?'

In DRC, violence guided my decision to take cover in a trusted identity, namely that of an NGO. Identifying the research with an NGO won the trust of our participants and contributed to the safety of my research team. Violence in eastern DRC has fostered mistrust in the international community (represented by the UN peacekeeping mission) among Congolese, who accuse the UN of disregarding citizens' welfare and creating more problems. My study participants had no reason to trust an American student or university, but they did associate NGOs with humanitarian aid that was a positive force for civilians.

My discovery of the importance of NGO identification in DRC is best illustrated by my initial struggle against the use of NGO t-shirts. Most NGOs produce t-shirts emblazoned with their logo, and the t-shirt of my NGO partner was colourful and eye-catching, advertising the radio show's name and broadcast schedule. I was alarmed on the first day of our fieldwork when the research team turned up wearing the t-shirts, which my research assistant had distributed. I saw them as bright flags reminding our participants of a rich organization's desire for them to know about this radio programme concerned with peace and community. However, one of my researchers protested, '*Les tricots nous protègent*' (the t-shirts protect us). Indeed, later that day a man started harassing one researcher who had approached him for an interview. He was demanding to know her 'real motives' until another passerby noticed the scene and exclaimed: 'Oh, another person from that NGO! They are everywhere!' The t-shirts gave credibility to my researchers' claims that they were from an NGO doing research, not spying or hustling for money as was common in some of the rougher *quartiers* where we worked.

Identity of researchers. Research participants use researchers' physical appearance, accent, mannerisms and multilingual abilities to identify them with certain ethnic, regional and even political groups. It is an important methodological and even ethical consideration to compose a research team that will invite the confidence and frankness of the whole range of participants in the sample. The collection of identities on a research team can also make them more or less likely to be perceived by participants as biased, foreign, or unfriendly, which would hamper their ability to work, risk the NGO's reputation, and in some cases put the researchers in danger. Levels of violence, state control and population fractionalization in each country affected the considerations I used when hiring a research team that could reflect important identities in the research population.

In Rwanda, to arrive at a rural community with a disproportionate number of Tutsi researchers would have clearly associated the project with the real and perceived Tutsi dominance in the government (in some rural areas more than 90 per cent of the population was Hutu). However, seeking an ethnically representative team is often not a straightforward task – and in Rwanda especially, it was illegal to ask candidates about their ethnicity or to self-identify on their résumé or in conversation. Moreover, I needed a team that would be *perceived* as balanced – self-identification was not the only thing that mattered. Like most places in the world, ethnic misclassification in Rwanda is rampant.

With the help of my primary Rwandan research assistants I assembled a research team by guessing ethnic identification based on applicants' appearance, self-reported birthplace and current residence, and education. I grossly underestimated the importance of accent and dialect when hiring my first research team. Many of the Tutsi researchers I hired were born or had lived for a long time as a refugee outside of Rwanda. They had different accents and sometimes mingled their mother tongue with neighbouring languages, which were immediate signals of ethnicity, geography and class to our research participants. The accents sometimes provoked laughter from participants during our customary group greetings at the start of each research day, and according to the researchers, made it more challenging to establish rapport (which points to the need to pad the beginning of an interview with benign conversational items).

With this lesson, and with the great variety of groups and languages in eastern DRC, I sought ethnic and linguistic diversity on my research team, which was not as difficult to identify. Following an employment test (which required applicants to describe how they would respond to various research dilemmas), we asked applicants about their background, and they often volunteered ethnic and regional identity readily: 'I'm a Mubembe from Uvira'. My Congolese research assistant also asked questions in a variety of languages, to be sure that our research team would be able to collectively handle the wide variety of languages *and* regional dialects. In a few cases, I had to use linguistic identity as the deciding factor between two candidates.

Levels of violence in each country also affected the gender balance on each of my research teams. While in Rwanda I was able to find equal numbers of female researchers for my team, in the DRC I was able to hire only two qualified women candidates (out of a team of 20 total researchers). In the midst of high levels of physical violence, women lose out the most in educational and professional opportunities (although certainly other cultural and political factors were at play).

Besides a general ethical objection to gender inequity in hiring, I worried that the overrepresentation of males on the team would bias participants' responses, particularly those related to violence (which often means sexual violence for women of this region). There is a great deal of motivation for women to remain silent about sexual violence, particularly in DRC, because it is considered the woman's fault and a personal shame. However, we noted in Rwanda that women participants *chose* to speak with male researchers just as often as they chose female researchers (we allowed a choice of interviewers when several were available at the same time).

In DRC participants could not select their interviewer since researchers worked separately when randomly approaching individuals. In this context I could empirically test whether there was differential reporting to male and female researchers about gender-sensitive topics. I found to my surprise that female participants discussed their experience of rape just as often with the male researchers as the female researchers. The only factor that seemed to influence whether rape was mentioned was the quality of the interview – whether the researcher reported that there was a good rapport, something which varied for each individual researcher. This finding supports some researchers' observations that interviews are often more open when the participant feels 'different' in some way from the researcher (whether according to gender, ethnicity, class, etc.). Some hypotheses about why this might be so are that the interviewer is treated more like an outsider who must be educated, or because there is less suspicion or self-comparison than there is between two 'insiders'.[12]

Identification of participants. Decisions about how to compose a representative sample and how to compose questions about participants' identity shift under differing conditions of violence, state control and population fractionalization. In both Rwanda and DRC, sampling a range of identity and age groups that my research assistant, partner NGO, and I projected to be affected by the radio programme was difficult for different reasons. My university's committee for the protection of human subjects did not approve of my proposal to conduct research in the prisons in Rwanda because of the strict government control over which prisoners were allowed to participate. My partner NGO was not willing to drop this aspect of the research design, so I conducted research in the prisons for the NGO in a purely 'consultative' role and was prevented from reporting on data from the prisons in an academic setting. In DRC, I was unable to collect data in two regions where our radio programme was broadcast because of recurring violence in those areas, and even in areas where we could travel, our research was often delayed or cut short by short outbursts of local violence.[13]

Despite obstacles presented by the level of state control in Rwanda and by the threat of violence in DRC, I found ways to ask about the identity of participants in both countries using different kinds of compromises. Asking about participants' identity in Rwanda was illegal (technically termed 'divisionist'). I was concerned for the safety of the research team – three weeks prior to the start of our fieldwork several Rwandan researchers working for an international organization were arrested for conducting research perceived as divisionist. My partner NGO risked being penalized or even expelled from the country for violation of this law.

I was able to get a global estimate of the ethnic makeup of my Rwandan sample by extrapolating from historical data in the regions where I was working. However, to attain an individual measure of ethnic identification, I asked two Rwandan colleagues who had been visiting each research community for one year prior (as part of the research design) to help me identify the ethnicity of each participant from our lists. The researchers marked a '1, 2 or 3' next to each participant's name to correspond with Hutu, Tutsi or Twa, using the information collected in the survey on each person's birthplace, movement during the genocide and afterward (e.g., which refugee camps they stayed in), current address, and their personal recollections of the participant. I paid them for this task before we began, and I emphasized that they could take the money and opt out of the work. In all honesty I knew that I could not erase all coercive elements from the fact that I, the employer, was asking them to do a job for me that was illegal. In the end I used the ethnic information only for my own purposes, to reassure myself there were no predictable global ethnic differences in the results (there were not). If I had found differences, I would have quarantined them for a number of years.

In DRC, the weak to non-existent government regulation in DRC meant that I did not submit my questionnaire to any government officials. The permissions process was limited to two hours – one for contacting the relevant local official to say the team would come to the area, and a second for visiting the office and asking him or her to sign our *ordres de mission* (letters from the head of our NGO stating our authorization and purpose). However, ethnically targeted violence made participants suspicious of questions about ethnicity.

'Kabila' (Swahili for ethnicity) was the fourth item on our questionnaire. The research team and I decided on a way to soften this question by taking advantage of the ethnic diversity in the general region. 'I don't live here' researchers would begin, 'could you tell me which ethnic groups live in this area?' Ninety-nine per cent of the time this was sufficient to induce the participant to identify their own ethnicity, perhaps by saying 'there's the Nande, and then also the Hunde, like me ... '

Security

Concerns about security encompass both physical and psychological security of the research team and the partner NGO. The difficult nature of fieldwork was exacerbated by varying levels of violence, state surveillance and antagonistic identity groups in the population. In both countries I learned methods to ensure the psychological health and physical security of the research team. High levels of state control and surveillance in Rwanda compelled me to take special measures with respect to appropriate speech (and appropriate silence), to ensure the safety of the NGO's reputation; in DRC I had to adjust to security procedures within the NGO system established in response to violence.

Physical and psychological security of research team. In both Rwanda and DRC, each researcher conducted an average of four interviews per day, with interviews lasting seventy-five minutes in Rwanda and two hours in DRC. In the rural areas where we primarily worked, it was rarely feasible to eat or drink during the day, on the one hand because there was not much available to buy, but more importantly because it was unethical to eat in front of most participants, whose level of poverty or distance from home meant they too had nothing. On top of these difficult conditions was the interview itself, which covered topics like prejudice, memories of violence and trauma. Although committees for the protection of human subjects rarely inquire about the well being of research teams, I was just as often concerned about the psychological and physical security of the research team as I was about the participants.

These conditions made me acutely aware of the importance of team morale building and relaxation at the end of a long day (during and after a meal). A common research design is to scatter researchers to cover each area individually over a longer period of time, but I believe that the solidarity achieved by working together as a team unit in one area was a distinct advantage. In both Rwanda and DRC, the research teams lived and ate together in the same tiny rural lodgings, and evenings after a day of interviewing were punctuated by a great deal of laughter and storytelling. The threat of violence outside our rooms in DRC made togetherness mandatory – no one wandered outside after dark. I encouraged researchers in DRC to use their general observation notebooks for writing personal reactions to the research as well, in the interest of defusing their stress.

During evenings over meals and afterward, I held back from asking a great deal about the events of the day. I reserved such questions for the period at the end of each workday when I spoke with each researcher about his or her completed interview records. However, listening to the broad-ranging evening conversations were often just as educative for me as were formal discussions about the project. After dinner when people retired to their rooms, I would return to mine and read through as many interviews as possible, so as to point out blank spaces or unclear notes, and to write down follow-up questions the next morning.

Differences in the security measures I took in Rwanda and DRC sprung from differing levels of state control and of violence. In Rwanda, I was sure to inform, re-inform, and remain on good terms with authorities in the area so that my researchers could be confident moving around and asking questions without trouble. More than once I was obliged to leave an interesting focus group or conversation in order to speak with a curious member of the local police or military forces who had wandered onto our site. In DRC I took many routine physical security precautions such as buying all of my researchers 'minutes' for their cell phones to keep in touch, carrying a satellite phone, and asking researchers to meet up and walk back to our hotel together at the end of the day. I adopted security suggestions from my research team, who knew the areas well. I avoided some security procedures recommended by foreigners when possible, for example travelling with the international peacekeeping force, because of the local population's intense dislike of them. Instead we were able to travel safely in convoys with other NGOs.

Security of NGO. To a certain extent, conducting fieldwork with an NGO transforms an independent researcher into an NGO representative. Respecting the security of my partner NGO's standing in each country involved careful attention to the state in Rwanda and to patterns of violence in DRC.

In Rwanda the challenge was to ensure that the research team and I did nothing to jeopardize the NGO's standing with the government. This included methodological adjustments such as avoiding contentious or controversial questions in our questionnaire, controversial comments when in the field, and for me personally, refraining from overt critiques of the government in my own academic writing or speech. A researcher from my team even warned me that I should not keep company (i.e., have dinner or be seen) with known critics of the government when living in the capital. (I did not always follow this advice, after weighing the small chance that the NGO would be penalized against the benefit I derived from gathering different perspectives.)

In DRC the greater concern was following the NGO's rules of physical security, which protected the team but also in many ways limited the research. The rules were frustrating when they delayed or prevented research, and it became important not to lose sight of the importance of security as violence became normalized. Complicating this issue was that occasionally the security rules of the NGO contradicted the instincts of my research team. While I was obligated to follow NGO rules, I also trusted the wisdom of the researchers, who knew the milieu extremely well. I walked a delicate line in which I respectfully tried to serve as a representative of my team's judgments to the NGO while also cooperating with their final judgments. In the end, it was usually the case that the NGO took good precautions and that I had no choice but to cooperate if I wanted to continue my work.

Expertise exchange

Research collaborations are built on expectations of the exchange of expertise, which shifted under the different conditions of violence, state control and population fractionaliztion in Rwanda and DRC. Below I specifically discuss conditions that shaped my invitation of the feedback and interpretation from the NGO and my research teams and other issues that arise in maintaining a respectful and productive research relationship.

Feedback. I relied on the research teams in both countries to a great extent for initial feedback on the research questionnaire and for ongoing feedback on the research process. Every research training session that I held in Rwanda and in DRC doubled as a chance for me to expose my questionnaire to a group of local experts (the researchers).

No one in Rwanda was better than my researchers at advising me on how much our participants felt constrained by government surveillance and at alerting me to nuanced signs of trust or suspicion. After the first pretest in Rwanda, the team agreed during a roundtable discussion that answers were routinely superficial for one particular question – *Would you share a beer with a person from 'another group'?* (A standard social scientific question of social distance). One researcher suggested a simple but crucial variation on the question: *Would you share a beer with a person from the 'other group,' if the bottle was not opened in your presence?* This variation touched upon the deep cultural suspicion of poisoning, and participant responses took an interesting and dramatic turn after we changed the question. I would not have been brave enough to break out of this standardized question had it not been for the insistence of the researchers and their own familiarity with the limits of public discourse in that context.

In DRC, I doubled the amount of time allotted to the research team training sessions to accommodate the long and lively discussions about the composition and translation of interview questions. Most of this discussion resulted from the researchers' knowledge of the great diversity among participants – their different languages, dialects and customs. An example is our hours-long debate over the choice of material for a behavioural measure – would we give participants beans, rice, sugar, or salt to test their willingness to aid other ethnic groups (by asking them to give some proportion of the food)? Beans were judged to be too common in the north, rice too precious in all rural areas and unethical to ask for a donation; sugar was suggested, but since it was a luxury item we finally agreed that salt was the best measurement tool – essential and thus meaningful.

Inviting interpretation. I usually review my interpretations of the data with members of the research team. In Rwanda I limited these discussions so as to protect researchers from government interest in our findings. I worked on data analysis primarily with one researcher who had only joined the team for the final post-test. Because he was not individually familiar with each participant, he was relieved of a certain amount of responsibility in the case that the authorities contacted him for specific information (they never contacted the researcher, although they did contact me). In DRC I did not hesitate to discuss the data, because we were not closely monitored by powerful political groups.

Relationship with researchers. Researchers from countries like Rwanda and DRC are often looking for an educational experience as well as references for their next job, which are difficult to come by in both countries (due to chronic instability this problem is even more pronounced in the DRC). Sometimes I felt as though I was cheating the researchers of a full educational experience because of my need to keep them 'blind' to hypotheses, and I never seemed to have the time or funds to hold an additional training session after we had finished the project.

In both countries, I tried to help researchers continue to find jobs; I designed certificates of research assistance and I continue to write recommendation letters to potential future employers. I gave the researchers an option to be listed on my website, and all of them chose visibility to my colleagues, who might also hire them over anonymity. The research is relatively short-term and never pays enough for the researchers to survive with their big families, and I am constantly aware of this in the field when I see researchers skimp on the dinners they buy in order to save money for people back home. On this point, I recommend making at least one meal part of the standard salary or *per diem*. Research supervisors should be constantly aware of the tradeoff their employees often make between sharing their earnings and maintaining their present well being.

Relationship with the NGO. For the privilege and opportunity to conduct research on an NGO's programme, I often felt I owed the NGO the help they requested with extra jobs like writing questionnaires for other programmes and statistical consulting. I tried to stay away from advising about substantive issues that would affect the programme I was evaluating. I have always felt one ethical obligation in particular, which is to write a non-academic report aimed at the NGO's donors. I believe it is unfair to give the NGO an academic report that will not be read by donors or by other NGOs, although I have observed this to be common practice with many other NGO-academic relationships.

Occasionally an NGO's needs conflict with my own academic research ethics. One situation arose in Rwanda when a high-ranking government minister called the NGO, stating that he had some questions for me about the community where the research team had worked that week. He specifically wanted to know how community members had responded to my questions about their local genocide trials (*gacaca*). I told the NGO administrators that I would not reveal my data to this minister, that I was bound to confidentiality as an ethical obligation to my participants. Understandably worried about souring their relationship with the government, the NGO administration asked me if there was a way to share averaged or masked data. I knew even group-level data would put my participants at risk because it would be easy for the government to find out who had participated in the study. Fortunately in this case, I was able to avoid a confrontation by postponing meetings with the minister until the subject dropped.

On a more banal point, most NGOs are not prepared to handle the sudden spike in demand for logistical support created by a research project and the accompanying research team. A collaborating researcher should be prepared to act as a logistician, accountant, mediator, shopper, and even chauffeur – all roles that I assumed in order to realize the fieldwork plans. I learned NGO organizational language and procedures – foreign words like *proforma* and *ordre de mission*, acronyms like MOU and TOR – and mastered dozens of forms, contracts and banking regulations. I was often called on to intervene in salary negotiations and advances for my researchers, discussions about car drivers and mechanical problems and office politics. This kind of work is perhaps more stressful in a society that is also violent or politically repressive, but the work is similar within all field offices – office, manual, and all other types of labour distract from research. It is part and parcel with working on large-scale collaborative projects.

Conclusion

Research collaborations with teams of interviewers and partner organizations have long been important to social scientific investigation. However, methodological and ethical considerations that arise in these collaborations – e.g., those pertaining to identity, security, and expertise exchange – are often overlooked. Demonstrating how collaborative research in different field contexts gives rise to different research strategies reveals the centrality of the collaborative relationship to research design and analysis. In my own research, varying levels of violence, state control and population fractionalization on either side of the Rwanda–DRC border brought methodological and ethical issues of research collaboration to the fore.

Heretofore experience with the stakes of collaborative research has not been systematically analyzed in the interest of guiding or teaching research design and analysis. The absence of discussion is arguably most damaging for researchers in conflict and post-conflict settings where the methodological and ethical stakes are high and where collaborative projects are common. The unique contribution of this chapter is to make visible these issues of research collaboration and to stimulate systematic thinking about how these methodological and ethical issues are affected by the research context.

No matter the type of overarching research logic (e.g., field experiment, case study) or kind of data collected (e.g., quantitative survey, qualitative focus group), decisions about the role of research teams and organizational partners bear on the quality of data collected and the interpretation of those data. Many of these points may sound familiar to qualitative researchers who are practiced in analyzing the interaction of the social scientist and her participants. For quantitative researchers, the thrust of this chapter is relatively more novel but equally important – instances from my own mixed quantitative and qualitative fieldwork demonstrate there is just as much room for interpretation in the collection and analysis of quantitative field data as qualitative.

I have drawn from my research experience with small regional non-governmental partner organizations, but I believe many of the same issues arise with larger international non-governmental organizations. One important question is how the methodological and ethical issues change when researchers work with governments as their 'partner organization'. In this case, state control carries a whole new meaning for research teams – it can facilitate or limit their work to a much greater extent than I described here. Future discussions of collaborative fieldwork could productively address this kind of collaboration.

Recommendations

Depending on their own research questions and locales, researchers may be able to use some of the specific descriptions of my own research choices as recommendations for their work. The most universally applicable recommendations of this chapter are, of course, to remain aware of the methodological and ethical issues of collaborative fieldwork and to communicate these issues in research reports and to people new to fieldwork.

With respect to the operative issues of fieldwork, I would add two specific recommendations: one, to appreciate the value of a primary local research assistant (or research team leader), and two, to maintain a presence in the field. My first recommendation stems from the vital role played by my primary research assistants in both Rwanda and DRC. I was fortunate to have the capacity to hire long-term research assistants who facilitated countless interactions for me and who worked closely with me to understand and to shape my methodological and ethical decisions. If hiring a long-term research assistant is not feasible, I suggest at the very least that one research team member be designated as the team leader. I found it important to have assistance managing the data collection from a person who was intimately familiar with the geography of our research sites and with the citizens who were our research participants and our research team colleagues.

My second specific recommendation, to maintain a presence in the field, is important for obvious reasons provided throughout the chapter. All of my observations and subsequent critical decisions about methods and ethics with respect to my fieldwork partners came from my intimate engagement with all aspects of the field research. I argue that the principal investigator should always be present to monitor the research team and to work with the partner organization on the ground, no matter what kind of data needs collecting. An instructive example comes from a household consumption survey conducted in DRC a few years prior to my own research. The research team hired for this project spent one month with the same few families in remote villages, measuring and recording every item of their income and consumption down to a gram of salt. Because families were not paid for their participation, researchers were forced to give them a little money from their own pocket as incentive to continue (researchers were not paid if the surveys were returned incomplete). These small donations, as well as the food offered to the researchers while they stayed with the family in the household, shaped the results of the study, but there was no way for the researchers to report this to the investigators back in the capital, Kinshasa. Thus, even the most 'straightforward' data collection of weights and numbers is heavily influenced by social relations, which are neglected at a significant cost.

The corresponding recommendation of this chapter is to describe and analyse methodological and ethical quandaries and decisions when writing and teaching about fieldwork. In the body or appendix of their research reports, researchers should report problems and decisions taken with respect to their fieldwork collaborators, and how they believe these decisions affected their data quality and interpretation. Increasingly, research journals are allowing researchers to publish extra materials online, so notes on special considerations for methods and ethics with fieldwork partnerships would be appropriate for such online addenda. The more that these discussions appear in print, the more available they will be for social science students who are preparing to do fieldwork. Ultimately, open communication about these issues will recognize research teams and partner organizations for what they are – not 'ghosts in the machine', but centrally important research collaborators. This recognition is not only long overdue, it is critical to the quality of research produced by these collaborations, and to the design of future research projects.

Notes

* Melani Cammett, John Gerring, Christopher Muller, Lee Ann Fujii and Elisabeth Jean Wood provided excellent comments on earlier drafts. The Weatherhead Center for International Affairs at Harvard University supported the author while writing this chapter.
1 Elizabeth Levy Paluck, 'Reducing intergroup prejudice and conflict using the media: A field experiment in Rwanda', *Journal of Personality and Social Psychology* (forthcoming); Elizabeth Levy Paluck and Donald P. Green, 'Deference, dissent, and dispute resolution: An experimental intervention using mass media to change norms and behavior in Rwanda', Working Paper, Harvard University, 2008.
2 Annette Lareau and Jeffrey Shultz. *Journeys Through Ethnography: Realistic Accounts of Fieldwork* (Boulder: Westview Press, 1996); Lyn Lofland, John Lofland, David Snow and Leon Anderson, *Analyzing Social Settings*, 4th edition (Belmont: Wadsworth Publishing Company, 2006); Herbert Rubin and Irene S. Rubin, *Qualitative Interviewing: The Art of Hearing Data* (London: Sage Publications, 2005); Elisabeth Wood, 'The Ethical Challenges of Field Research in Conflict Zones', *Qualitative Sociology*, vol. 29, no. 3 (2006), pp. 307–341.
3 Levy Paluck, 'Reducing intergroup prejudice and conflict using the media' and Levy Paluck and Green 'Deference, dissent, and dispute resolution'.
4 Levy Paluck, 'Reducing intergroup prejudice and conflict using the media'.
5 Elizabeth Levy Paluck, 'Is it better not to talk? A field experiment on talk radio and ethnic relations in Eastern Democratic Republic of Congo', Working paper, Harvard University, 2007.
6 Human Rights Watch, *Killings in Eastern Rwanda*, No 1 (January 2007). Lars Waldorf, 'Mass Justice for Mass Atrocity: Rethinking Local Justice as Transitional Justice', *Temple Law Review,* 79:1 (2006).
7 Race (1973) cited in Stathis Kalyvas, *The Logic of Violence in Civil War* (Cambridge: Cambridge University Press, 2006) p. 210.
8 E. Zorbas, *Reconciliation in Post-genocide Rwanda: Discourse and Practice*, Dissertation submitted to London School of Economics 2007; Human Rights Watch, *Killings in Eastern Rwanda;* International Crisis Group, C*onsensual Democracy In Post-Genocide Rwanda. Evaluating the March 2001 District Elections*, Africa Report No. 34 (2001).
9 Paul Collier, 'The Political Economy of Ethnicity.' Paper prepared for the Annual World Bank Conference on Development Economics, Washington DC, April 20–21, 1998; Ibrahim Elbadawi and Nicholas Sambanis, 'How Much War Will We See? Estimating the Incidence of Civil War in 161 Countries, 1960–99', *Journal of Conflict Resolution* 46 (June): 307–334 (2002); Daniel Posner, 'Measuring Ethnic Fractionalization in Africa', *American Journal of Political Science* 48:4 (October 2004), pp. 849–863.
10 Posner, 'Measuring Ethic Fractionalization in Africa'.
11 An Ansoms, 'Striving for growth, bypassing the poor: A critical review of Rwanda's rural sector policies'. *Journal of Modern African Studies,* 46:1 (2008), pp. 1–32.

12 Herbert Rubin and Irene S. Rubin, *Qualitative Interviewing: The Art of Hearing Data* (London: Sage Publications, 2005), p. 88.
13 This violence caused the displacement of thousands of people, with an indirect impact on our research – some displaced people were not living in places where we had broadcast the same radio programme, which confounded our experimental treatment.

5 Maintenance of standards of protection during writeup and publication

Chandra Lekha Sriram

Introduction

While all scholars understand that it is necessary to conform to ethical standards prior to conducting research as well as during the conduct of research, the standards may begin to slip or may face particular challenges once the research has been completed. This chapter will examine some examples of ways in which post-research activities that may violate ethical rules and may put some of the researchers' interlocutors or interviewees at risk. This may particularly be the case because of the increased culture of sharing draft documents with colleagues via e-mail or on the Internet. In such situations, researchers may forget to, or incompletely, redact the names of individuals whose comments have yet to be cleared. Yet the individuals are no less placed at risk for having their name or general identity circulated in such a fashion than they are having their name cited in a final published document. Similarly risks may arise where the process of publication requires or seeks to require that the author reveal the names of his or her sources. Law journals in particular insist upon provision of such information, even though they insist that they will only hold it in their files and will not share it with any individuals. Nonetheless, maintenance of anonymity and confidentiality remains important throughout the process, particularly where informants are at risk. This chapter will discuss the dilemmas that may confront authors in seeking to maintain protection of both the identity and security of their interlocutors, whilst still engaging in collaborative sharing of academic ideas and information. The chapter proceeds through the presentation of three incidents with clear ethical implications, and one with more complex implications for academic independence, involving the author's own experiences as well as upon the experiences of other scholars whose names will not be noted in this chapter. I argue that there is a need for greater attention and caution in general in the post-interview, prepublication stages. There is also potentially a greater need for consideration of ethical obligations beyond those owed directly to one's interlocutors, which may include research assistants and other collaborators as well as interviewees, to individuals such as their relatives and colleagues with whom one may have had no direct contact.

Confidentiality, clearance and ethics

The rationale for offering interviewees confidentiality, and for clearing their comments where they do agree to attribution, have been covered generally in earlier chapters. So too have the professional ethical requirements for such precautions. I treat as the baseline professional ethics requirements the Economic and Social Research Council's *Research Ethics Framework* because I am based in the UK, but the American Political Science Association similarly regulates the ethics of research dealing with 'human subjects'.[1] The framework requires identification of potential risks, both physical and mental, to research subjects, that participation of research subjects is to be voluntary and with informed consent, and that confidentiality and anonymity are to be respected unless participants have consented to disclosure, and that harm to participants must be avoided.[2]

This framework offers guidance and procedures for ethical research in the social sciences generally. However, it is well worth reaffirming the particular importance of these precautions in the context of what we have termed 'difficult situations'. The ESRC framework even notes that ethical review should be proportionate to the potential risk, given that some research, particularly that involving secondary data, will be low-risk, while that involving primary data will necessitate greater scrutiny.[3] While interviewees in all situations, as human subjects, deserve the protections that professional ethics require, individuals living and working in situations of armed conflict, state repression, and gross human rights violations are clearly at particular risk. This is the case whether these individuals are outsiders temporarily working there – as humanitarian aid workers, donors, members of UN missions, human rights monitors – but may be particularly important where the persons in question are from the society of study, and are likely to remain in the location, or involved with the local politics, for some time to come. This is not to say that foreigners deserve less ethical protection, for this is certainly not the case. Rather, it is to note that because local interlocutors are likely to be less mobile than internationals, they may need extra protection. However, such interlocutors should not be treated paternalistically – most are well aware of the risks they face in their daily work as politicians, human rights advocates, and civil society leaders, or for their status as members of the opposition, ex-combatants, and so on. They are also aware of any risks in voicing their opinions, particularly opposition to a local elite or *status quo*, and choose to do so precisely because they want to draw attention to a situation that they perceive as unjust. Ethical regulations do not preclude presenting those statements with appropriate clearance, even if they generate risks. And indeed, it may be at odds not only with the demands of our interlocutors, but also our goals as scholars, advocates, and advisers on policy to overly limit our reporting from 'difficult situations'. Nonetheless, the demands of collegiality, particularly in the age of Internet communications and postings, may generate new risks. These demands are discussed next, while the perils of 'oversharing' are discussed in my third 'incident'. The fourth incident discusses the challenges posed by interlocutors who seek to manipulate research findings during the clearance phase.

Collegiality and draft-sharing

I have suggested that the culture and demands of collegiality, draft sharing, and web posting may generate peculiar risks that may potentially be at odds with ethical protections, and that scholars may need to exercise extra care in their treatment of pre-publication drafts. We increasingly e-mail draft papers to colleagues around the world or post them on professional association websites (such as that of the International Studies Association) in advance of annual conferences, through journal submission/pre-print sites such as Expresso Preprint and bepress legal series, and on our own websites.[4] There is not only nothing inherently wrong with this practice: it is part of the research and academic culture of exchanging ideas, papers, and comments that can enrich the final output. Sharing of drafts also often helps to enhance policy recommendations; I have routinely been given draft documents by donors and other actors for comment, which often have drawn on incompletely anonymized sources. The goal, of course, is to improve knowledge, and in many cases also to improve policy and action. The valid goals of such improvements, however, can only be sought within the parameters of clear ethical obligations.[5]

The professional ethical requirements will always come first, of course, but there may well be grey areas. These may include situations where attribution or citation has been approved, but the larger context or argument may put interlocutors at risk, particularly if the author's own argument can be attributed by some (if wrongly) to certain interviewees. Politically motivated or biased readers may flatly misinterpret quoted statements, or the author's own interpretation of them. These are always risks, but there may be greater risks in the post-research, pre-publication stages, where drafts are often rough and ambiguous. Hasty writing and editing may mean, even, that attribution is publicized before the text is approved. Finally, as I discuss in the fourth of four incidents, informants may seek to manipulate the final text as part of a clearance process, creating new dilemmas for the researcher.

Incident 1: Posthumous clearance

Tragically, the first incident is not an unusual situation for researchers in difficult situations: the determination of how to manage interview material from a deceased interviewee, often one who has died through violent means.

In February 1999, I conducted dissertation research in Sri Lanka where I examined the use of commissions of inquiry into disappearances in the context of the ongoing internal armed conflict between the government and the Liberation Tigers of Tamil Eelam (LTTE). The primary focus of my research, part of a broader project on transitional justice and accountability mechanisms in conflict and post-conflict situations, was primarily on these commissions of inquiry. However, the research took place in the context of, and also examined, the broader movement for constitutional reform and a degree of devolution in the North, as part of the effort to promote a peace settlement. Many moderate Tamils and Sinhalese supported devolution and constitutional reform, but Sinhalese hardliners adamantly opposed both, as did the LTTE, which argued that it fell short of a homeland with full autonomy. The LTTE particularly targeted moderate Tamil politicians, including members of the Tamil United Liberation Front and others who were engaged in mainstream politics, including parliamentarians. The LTTE condemned moderate Tamils as traitors to the Tamil cause, and had assassinated several, often through suicide bombing.

While in Sri Lanka, I had an extensive discussion with Dr Neelan Tiruchelvam, one such moderate politician. A champion of constitutional reform and the peace process, Dr Tiruchelvam was also a TULF member of parliament, as well as the founder of the International Centre for Ethnic Studies (ICES), an interdisciplinary think tank, advocacy centre, and research library on conflict and conflict resolution, in Colombo. He was also a champion of other civil society groups promoting peace in the country and was a chief drafter of the government's devolution plan, making him a particular target.[6]

Dr Tiruchelvam spoke openly about the prospects for devolution, for peace in the country and encouraged me to engage with various NGOs. He invited me to speak at ICES (intentionally focused on Argentina and El Salvador rather than the current Sri Lankan situation) as part of his ongoing campaign to promote more open, informed dialogue about peace processes generally.[7] As with all of my interviewees, I provided him with the option of full anonymity, citation with only a general reference to him by type of position (i.e. parliamentarian, Tamil parliamentarian, or other characterization of his choice) or citation by name subject to clearance. Dr Tiruchelvam kindly indicated that he would be happy to be cited with clearance to maximize the utility of my interview with him. He was also quite generous with his time and support, helping me to make contacts with other experts and politicians.

Following my field research, I returned to the US to complete the writeup of my research in Sri Lanka, and to finalize the remainder of my thesis. As agreed with interviewees, I either anonymized or cleared all citations by e-mail, phone and regular mail. I provided each of them with draft sections of the relevant chapter, carefully excluding references to any other interviewees within those sections, and providing enough context for each person to not only approve or amend direct reference to his/her statements, but to assess my general representation/interpretation, or mode of contextualizing those statements. In early July I received a brief e-mail from Dr Tiruchelvam indicating that he was looking over my text and would send any specific changes shortly, but that overall it looked fine. Later that month he was assassinated by an LTTE suicide bomber.[8]

As someone who had met him and experienced his kindness and generosity, and as someone genuinely hoping to see a peaceful resolution to the conflict in Sri Lanka, I was devastated. His assassination was certainly an inhumane act to a very humane person, and a devastating blow to efforts in the peace process. As a scholar, my feelings were no less pained, but were more complex. Should I, could I, cite to his interviews? He had offered such detailed, and thoughtful, comments that in one sense it seemed to me to be a terrible shame not to include them in my discussions. However, he had not given final cleared comments or altered text; he had only given a general positive indication, subject to final review. To whom did my obligation of clearance now flow? Had it expired with his tragic death? Or did I owe a measure of caution to his surviving family members and to those who had worked with him? Did I 'owe' anyone an accounting of his comments, for the sake of knowledge and scholarship? These were not easy questions to think about, much less actually answer, particularly in the absence of strong guidance, whether in the form of clear professional regulations or from other researchers who had faced similar dilemmas.

Ideally, a scholar in this position would conduct a risk analysis, considering the likelihood that their research would be read by someone who might deliberately choose to misinterpret and/or mischaracterize the interaction, considering the types of responses such a person might undertake, and the possible targets. However, this involves a great deal of speculation about the access of potential LTTE extremists to such publications, about their interest in responding with violence, and about their access to potential targets, all of which are difficult to quantify. I could only attempt to weigh the risks in absence of any clear evidence, but with a clear understanding of the worst possible consequences that could be inflicted. In light of what I did not know (but what was reasonable to fear) about what might befall other members of his family or colleagues should I attribute statements to him, I decided to err on the side of caution – believing that any misinterpretation of comments attributed to Dr Tiruchelvam by me could lead to reprisals. Instead, my dissertation, and the book and articles that resulted from it, refer to his support and generosity, but not to the substance of our discussions.[9] I felt that in these circumstances, it was preferable to drop reference to our discussions, even if it meant the loss of the opportunity to sharing information with scholars and policymakers which might have been of some import.

Incident 2: Can filing breach confidentiality?

Following the brutal war in Sierra Leone where some 75,000 people were killed, thousands more displaced, and where widespread rape and mutilation and extensive use of child soldiers were ordinary, a peace agreement was finally reached in 1999. The Lomé Peace Accord enshrined a blanket amnesty for all parties to the conflict, including the notorious rebel group the Revolutionary United Front (RUF) and government fighters who often colluded with them. It also established a Truth and Reconciliation Commission (TRC). However, shortly after the accord, the RUF defected and returned to fighting, which was only terminated with outside assistance, most notably from the United Kingdom. During the fighting, RUF leader Foday Sankoh was captured, generating discussions about how to deal not only with him, but with a range of perpetrators regardless of the previous amnesty. At the request of the government of Sierra Leone, the United Nations Security Council authorized the creation of the Special Court for Sierra Leone (SCSL) by bilateral agreement between the UN and the Sierra Leone government. It began to hear substantive cases once the procedural and jurisdictional issues were resolved in the summer of 2004. I travelled to Freetown to examine the reception of the court by broad swathes of Sierra Leonean society: civil society organizations, ex-combatants, and members of the bar, as well as the relationship of the SCSL to broader attempts to (re)build peace, infrastructure, and the rule of law in that devastated country.

In the context of a country just emerging from conflict, all discussions of legal accountability and personal blame for atrocities committed during the war were extremely fraught. Many recently demobilized fighters were, not surprisingly, worried about indictment and arrest by the court, and often feared the TRC for similar reasons. Many in civil society, even among human rights groups, viewed the SCSL with suspicion, as an outside imposition or even 'spaceship'.[10] And a range of people questioned how it could be the case that the RUF, and members of the Civil Defence Forces (CDF), could be prosecuted, while members of the government who worked with and relied upon the CDF, were not to be. Feelings ran high over the prosecution of CDF 'heroes', and rumours were rife that there would be attempts to free CDF leader Sam Hinga Norman from custody. In such an environment, while internationals tended to voice strong support for accountability and the Court generally, and its specific measures, locals were more circumspect. Their caution was perhaps further encouraged by the political firestorm surrounding the unsealing of the indictment of former Liberian president, Charles Taylor, who went into exile in Nigeria, but left many in the region fearful that he could return to politics.[11]

In the light of this charged situation, securing interviews, as well as frank opinions, proved a bit of a challenge, but I had many very sharp interlocutors. Those who were willing to speak most openly about the more politicized aspects of accountability, and in particular, were willing to question the government, generally preferred to speak on condition of anonymity, or at the very most with a generic reference such as 'NGO representative, Freetown'. I accommodated this request in the written documents emerging from the research and, of course, cleared each attributed statement in the same manner recounted above. The resultant book chapter and articles included anonymized attribution wherever it was requested.[12]

However, while my final publications fully complied with the strictures of anonymity, I faced a challenge in seeking to publish my findings in one law journal. For an article in the *Fordham International Law Journal*, I was asked to provide non-anonymized interview notes to substantiate the article, not least because so many of my interviewees had requested anonymity. Certainly, law reviews in the United States do generally require a great deal of substantiation of sources and materials not easily found in libraries or online. Indeed, the law journal in question also requested photocopies of many newspaper articles I cited, but because I had only my handwritten notes, was sceptical of the validity of these articles as sources. Before my handwritten notes were deemed acceptable, I had to explain that newspapers for the time periods of interest were not available online and the limited availability of electricity in Sierra Leone rendered photocopying nearly impossible. With reference to anonymized interviews, however, they were unable to compromise. I explained in some detail the ethical concerns raised with sharing details of interviewees, and tried to highlight the particular issues that often arise in interviewing people in post-conflict and conflict-affected countries. While sympathetic, the journal's editors could not waive their scholarly standards. It appeared from our correspondence that the problems I raised were relatively novel to the editors, whose authors in general (although the research methods of many authors were already changing) had drawn upon published opinions and archival material more than field research. They could however promise me that the files would be locked in the journal filing cabinet, would not actually be read by staff, and would therefore have the same level of security as if they were in my own filing cabinet. This guarantee was in line with the guidance from the ESRC, requiring that data must not be transferred outside the European Economic Area unless the data can be subjected to the same degree of control; here one could be satisfied that it was, as it was to be held within locked files in a locked office at a reputable law school based in New York.[13]

Here, my post-research dilemma was both similar to, and distinct from, that presented in the previous example. I felt the same obligation, ethical, professional, and personal, to the interviewees and to the maintenance of their anonymity and security. At the same time I felt a responsibility and desire to share with the scholarly and policy communities some important observations and lessons arising from those discussions. For me, the balance of risks and security issues were distinct. The interviewees had had the opportunity to review the text. Further, no attribution to them was to be publicized, and I was reassured that the filing with the journal would be no different than maintaining those same files in my own office. Indeed, those files were undoubtedly safer than they had been while I was in Sierra Leone, in a room with no safe and which was accessible by a range of guesthouse staff. The files remain confidential, but I remain concerned that this is right at the ethical margins, if within the rules. I would note that for scholars who have obtained ethics approval from their universities to obtain verbal rather than written consent, as Julie Norman's contribution to this volume indicates that she did, publishers who require this additional paper trail of written consent and notes may limit publication options.

Incident 3: Premature web publication with attribution

The third incident involves a colleague at another institution, who will not be named, but is by no means an unusual story. I have chosen to omit the specifics of the country of research as well, so as to maintain anonymity. The colleague in question engages in research in a range of post-conflict situations, commenting upon the appropriateness of interventions by external actors, particularly international NGOs. These observations draw heavily upon in-country interviews with both local experts and internationals, which are cited in the footnotes. He proceeds with research following appropriate ethical standards, including confirming the wishes of interviewees regarding attribution, anonymity and so forth. He takes careful account of these requests, and subsequently clears any statements as necessary through interviewees. Final publications with statements not for attribution are so noted. The concern therefore is not that the colleague in question is wilfully or negligently violating professional research ethics.

Rather, the concern arises because the culture of research-sharing can lead to early drafts, with incomplete anonymization being shared. In the instance in question, the colleague himself drew my attention by asking for comments to a research paper he had posted on his own website, based on fieldwork in a country emerging from conflict with a significant international presence, both military and development actors. No individuals were intentionally cited by name without prior clearance. However, in several instances, footnotes in the document referred to persons by job titles so precise that they could only refer at most to one or two individuals in that locale, followed by 'not for attribution'.[14] When I raised this issue with the colleague in question, his response was that he would have a look, but that there was no cause for concern because it was just posted on a website, the evident implication being that cleanup would be necessary and take place at the publication stage.

Clearly, a number of potential risks arise from this set of events and discussion. The first is that documents posted on websites or sent via e-mail may be subject to less ethical scrutiny by otherwise scrupulous authors than those published in academic journals or books. Yet material available on the Internet, or transmitted electronically through e-mail, has a potentially much wider audience than academic publications. Indeed by its very nature it is impossible to predict who might download it or receive it as a forwarded attachment. Thus there is potentially cause for greater, rather than lesser caution, or at least the same degree of caution, with respect to such writing. Otherwise, individuals who sought and received assurances of anonymity in final publications may be 'outed' in working drafts. This has of course always been a risk in the context of collegiality and draft-sharing, but the speed and accessibility of information technology magnifies the risk.

Maintenance of standards of protection during writeup and publication 65

Technology may also generate a separate risk, which authors and their interlocutors may be unable to control: documents fully cleared through interviewees may be misused and misinterpreted in highly politicized situations. Again this is not a new risk, but one made easier with access to the web, particularly when documents and arguments may then be quoted out of context, or incompletely, to make a political or partisan point. This may again be exacerbated where drafts posted on the web or e-mailed for comments have not been thoroughly edited and thus have ambiguities that are easily exploited. This may particularly be the case where multiple interviewees are cited for complex, overlapping propositions and readers may erroneously (wilfully or not) attribute them to the wrong person. Complete clearance processes help to eliminate some potential for misreading, although certainly do not eliminate all of it.

The need to engage in thorough clearance is illustrated by my own experience. In a draft chapter drawing on my field research in Sudan in 2006, I erroneously bundled two claims by two distinct people into a discussion and footnote about Riek Machar, the current vice-president of the government of Southern Sudan. I cleared the same text and footnote through both interlocutors, in each case excluding reference to the other in so doing. One returned the text with no changes, while the other spotted a significant interpretive error. I was in this instance quite relieved that I had not shared the draft with colleagues prior to completing clearance.[15] This experience should stand as a stark warning to scholars not to circulate drafts or post them prior to full clearance, to avoid potentially dangerous misstatements or misinterpretations.[16]

Incident 4: Post-interview clearance and academic integrity

A distinct challenge may arise in the post-fieldwork phase, which is generated in part by adherence to ethical standards and procedures, but with the potential to bias the final written product even if the researcher exercises careful judgment. This may occur in situations in which the interviewees attempt, at the clearance stage, to influence not just the researcher's judgment and analysis, but the text of the written work in ways that the preponderance of the evidence simply cannot support. When I was conducting research on peace negotiations and power-sharing in Kilinochchi, the seat of the self-proclaimed LTTE government, in 2005, I interviewed a range of 'officials', from the putative minister of justice to a number of judges on LTTE courts as well as several officials, including the head of the LTTE human rights secretariat. Not surprisingly, all of these sought to convince me of the rectitude of the LTTE cause and fight, the legitimacy of the parallel government which had been in place for a decade, and to their own commitment to the rule of law and human rights. Clearly, the challenge of assessing statements of individuals with evident agendas is not unusual in such fieldwork, and is well addressed in chapters by Carole Gallaher and Lee Ann Fujii elsewhere in this volume on veracity. I may also have been subjected to additional pressure to agree with the LTTE officials because of my Tamil (albeit Indian Tamil) name, raising the question of perceived identity, also discussed elsewhere in the chapter by Marie-Joelle Zahar in this volume. For my purposes here, however, of most note was not what was said or not said during the interviews, but what happened once I sought to clear the comments made during the interviews.

When I sought to clear this text, I was presented, perhaps not surprisingly, with additional pressure and suggestions for new text. The spokeswoman I had spoken with, for example, wanted me to say more about predations by the Sri Lankan army, which had not been raised in the interview. I was able to evade this by emphasizing that I had, drawing upon neutral sources such as the Sri Lankan Monitoring Mission, offered data on the behaviour of Sri Lankan forces. However, the comments from the human rights secretariat went well beyond this. In response my standard clearance request, where I presented statements made in interviews with surrounding text for context, I was e-mailed a massive rewrite of text that amounted to LTTE propaganda. Despite several attempts by e-mail to clarify whether the original text could be cleared, or whether all citation should be removed if I was not to use the rewrite, I was unable to elicit a direct answer. Instead I was provided with the same propagandistic text, with further embellishments within e-mails. It became evident that I would not be able to negotiate a compromise.

Clearly, as a scholar I faced a quandary. I could not and would not allow an academic work to be captured by propaganda, particularly by statements I found to be untrue based on other interviews and evidence. I could also not, ethically, include uncleared references to the interviews as I had conducted them. Yet of course I wanted the final work to capture the range of views and actors I had engaged with. In the end, I made the only ethical and professional choice I felt comfortable with, which was to remove reference to the content of the interview altogether from the published chapter on Sri Lanka in my book on peace negotiations.[17]

Concluding thoughts

All researchers engaged in fieldwork involving human subjects in 'difficult situations' should be aware of the basic requirements of professional research ethics. These requirements clearly involve how one engages with interviewees in the field, how one maintains confidentiality of materials during fieldwork, and how one treats interviews during publication. A critical issue is the way in which both what is said during interviews and the identity of interviewees is managed, vetted, and concealed as necessary. In difficult research situations, maintenance of ethical standards is particularly crucial as individuals may well have put themselves at significant risk to provide the raw material for our books, articles, and indeed our careers. We should not be cavalier in our treatment of them. However, I have argued that a number of unanticipated complications may emerge post-research, and prior to or during the publication process, for which the rules are not always clear. These are related in part to the very impetus that motivates many of us to conduct such research – a desire to reveal the truth of a particular situation, analyze it as accurately as possible, and often to make recommendations to improve the situation. This urge may be very much in line with that of our interlocutors. We must also exercise caution in how we utilize the material we generate in difficult settings. Thus for example, while we may have no direct obligation to deceased interviewees not to cite their comments (particularly if, say, they have indicated general or specific approval), it is likely best to exercise caution where we suspect that certain attributions may imperil their families or colleagues. Similarly, we may wish to reflect whether we have struck the right balance between anonymization and knowledge dissemination where we provide our files to a publisher, albeit on the promise of anonymity and security. And we may need to be especially cautious in disseminating early drafts where rapid drafting or lack of careful editing may enable identification of anonymized sources or dangerous misinterpretation. Finally, completed work may suffer from the necessary exclusion of uncleared material, where interlocutors attempt to alter the content not only of their own interview, but of the author's analysis in the clearance process.

Notes

1 Economic and Social Research Council, *Research Ethics Framework* (not dated) at http://www.esrcsocietytoday.ac.uk/ESRCInfoCentre/Images/ESRC_Re_Ethics_-Frame_tcm6–11291.pdf; American Political Science Association, *A Guide to Professional Ethics in Political Science* (Second edition, revised 1998, reprinted 2004), available at http://www.apsanet.org/imgtest/ethicsguideweb.pdf.
2 ESRC, *Research Ethics Framework*, pp. 1–2, 21–22.
3 Ibid., p. 2.
4 Details of Expresso and bepress can be found at: http://law.bepress.com/expresso/eps/.
5 The particular challenges of research linked to activist or policy goals, going beyond the standard strictures of Institutional Review Boards, have been well articulated by those engaged in Participatory Action Research. See for example Caitlin Cahill, 'Repositioning Ethical Commitments: Participatory Action Research as a Relational Praxis of Social Change', *ACMS: An International E-Journal for Critical Geographies* vol. 6, no. 3 (2007), pp. 360–373.
6 The devolution plan under development would have involved greater regional autonomy, particularly in the North.
7 Links to publications both by and about Dr Tiruchelvam can be found on the website of the Neelam Tiruchelvam Trust, at http://www.neelan.org/publication.asp.
8 'Sri Lanka: Tamil politician assassinated' (29 July 1999) at http://news.bbc.co.uk/2/hi/south_asia/406644.stm.
9 Chandra Lekha Sriram, *Confronting past human rights violations: justice vs. peace in times of transition* (London: Frank Cass, 2004); Sriram, 'Dilemmas of accountability: politics, the military, and commissions of inquiry during an ongoing civil war: the Sri Lankan case', *Civil Wars* vol. 5, no. 2 (Summer 2002), pp. 96–121.

10 Tom Perriello and Marieke Wierda, 'The Special Court for Sierra Leone Under Scrutiny' (March 2006), at http://www.ictj.org/static/Prosecutions/Sierra.study.pdf, p. 2, describes the critique of Sierra Leoneans who have viewed the SCSL as a 'spaceship phenomenon'.
11 'Liberia Leader Defiant to the End' (11 August 2003), at http://news.bbc.co.uk/1/hi/world/africa/3140417.stm, reports him saying 'God willing, I'll be back'.
12 Chandra Lekha Sriram, 'Wrong-sizing international justice? The hybrid tribunal in Sierra Leone', *Fordham International Law Journal* vol. 29, no. 3 (2006); Sriram, 'Revolutions in Accountability: New Approaches to Past Abuses', *American University International Law Review* vol. 19, no. 2 (2004); Sriram, *Globalizing justice for mass atrocities: A revolution in accountability* (London: Routledge, 2005).
13 ESRC, *Research Ethics Framework* p. 18.
14 For the sake of anonymity I will not reproduce the citation or indicate the offices in question, but imagine a footnote reading 'Head of X office, Y province, not for attribution', with a precise date and with X and Y clearly specified.
15 The chapter on Sudan now forms a core part of my study of power-sharing and peace negotiations which also entailed fieldwork in Sri Lanka and Colombia, *Peace as governance: Power-sharing, armed groups, and peace negotiations* (London: Palgrave 2008).
16 Arguably, the same level of caution should also be exercised in comments made in talks and seminars, although this may be more challenging for the researcher to monitor and control since casual conversation may lend itself to over sharing or vernacular language that may be misinterpreted by some.
17 The chapter on Sri Lanka, with the interview removed, is published in my *Peace as Governance*.

Part 2
Access

6 Got trust? The challenge of gaining access in conflict zones

Julie M. Norman

Introduction

Trust is usually a crucial element in gaining access to potential research participants in conflict situations, yet that trust is often difficult to secure. In this chapter, I draw from fieldwork conducted in the Occupied Palestinian Territories to examine different dimensions of research in conflict zones in which issues of trust can influence if and how access is gained. My research focuses on Palestinian popular resistance during the second *intifada*, from 2000 to 2007, in the specific contexts of East Jerusalem and the West Bank. The mixed methods approach I used (including semi-structured interviews with activists, surveys with youth, and participant observation) necessitated that I negotiate different trust relationships to gain access to the field and the research participants. In the following essay, I first discuss how trust from the dominant state or government can determine how the researcher accesses the field site itself. Second, I examine the challenges of gaining the collective trust of an oppressed group or community to gain credibility in carrying out the research. Third, I address how 'special' trust issues can influence access to specific groups within conflict zones, such as militants, activists, prisoners, and children. Finally, I explore practical solutions and specific recommendations for overcoming some of these challenges of trust and access.

Unpacking the terminology

What is trust?

Definitions and expressions of trust can vary between cultures, disciplines, and individuals. Indeed, many 'low-context' cultures typically establish trust through contracts, signatures, and written documentation, while many 'high-context' cultures instead rely on verbal agreements and communal relationships.[1] Similarly, many psychological approaches emphasize the individual, rational elements of trust, while sociological approaches focus on trust's social and emotional aspects. My experience is consistent with Lewis and Weigert's assertion that: 'An adequate conceptual analysis of trust begins by recognizing its multifaceted character', including its 'distinctive cognitive, emotional and behavioral dimensions'.[2] In this sense, it is not accurate to speak of a single, static 'trust' that one either has or doesn't have; rather, there are multiple trusts that may ebb and flow in the context of different individual and collective relationships.

Much of the literature in political science and psychology conceptualizes trust as an individual process based on rational choice, reflecting the *cognitive* dimension of trust. From this perspective, 'trust is based on a cognitive process which discriminates amongst persons and institutions that are trustworthy, distrusted, and unknown'.[3] The cognitive dimension of trust has been analyzed through rational choice methodologies such as game theory, in which trusting relationships are defined by 'an implicit assumption that one person will not deliberately hurt the other to satisfy his own needs'.[4] In the field of international relations, a researcher might try to establish this cognitive trust through standard Institutional Review Board (IRB) requirements such as providing participants with a written statement of research objectives, securing informed consent, and ensuring anonymity and confidentiality.

In my own experience in Palestine for example, I found that these tactics, though necessary at all points in the research, were especially important when I was carrying out the survey portion of my fieldwork. I had structured my research design to include at least 250 surveys[5] gauging youth[6] perceptions and attitudes towards various forms of popular resistance, both violent and nonviolent. Because the surveys asked youth to indicate their opinions on controversial topics such as suicide bombing, and to indicate their past participation in both nonviolent and armed resistance, the youths' willingness to participate depended on their trust of my intentions, and trust that their responses would not be shared with others. Because the nature of survey distribution does not allow for the development of trust over time through the establishment of personal relationships, I had to depend on cognitive methods to quickly establish a rational trust with the survey respondents. Accordingly, I carried a written statement in both English and Arabic, explaining the nature and purpose of my research; secured verbal consent from all participants;[7] and took time to answer questions and explain how responses would remain confidential. I found that steps like these helped establish a rational framework for developing a trust relationship based on clearly stated intentions that appeal to reason and logic.

While cognitive trust measures may be effective in some contexts, and may be appropriate with some methods, research in many conflict zones may require the development of another type of trust relationship. Especially in conflict zones in which agreements, laws, and rules have been violated or abused, the rational, cognitive approach to building trust may not be a strong enough foundation for the development of a trust relationship. Instead, researchers might be better advised to cultivate a more personal, emotional trust with participants. In contrast to cognitive trust, the sociological concept of *emotional* trust refers to an 'affective ... emotional bond among all those who participate in the relationship',[8] such that the betrayal of trust affects not just the issue at stake, but the foundation of the relationship itself. Emotional trust is not based so much on reason or rationale, but rather on personal relations. Researchers may foster this type of trust by spending time in the community, talking with participants in both formal and informal settings, and being cognizant of cultural indications of trust.

In my own fieldwork, I found that emotional trust was especially important in carrying out narrative research. First, many participants required some degree of relational trust of me before even agreeing to an interview, which was often facilitated by a mutual friend or colleague who could vouch for me. One NGO director, for example, initially declined to be interviewed, and was sceptical of my formal paperwork and explanations of my research design. However, when he learned that one of his close colleagues was also a friend of mine, his demeanour changed completely; he immediately invited me to stay for tea, and then for lunch, and we ended up talking for several hours. In accordance with high-context cultural settings, he later explained to me that for him, and many others in Palestine, formal contracts and signatures, which he associated with colonial powers, were less important than someone's word or the referral from a mutual trusted contact in the community.

In addition to setting up interviews, the importance of relational trust was also important during interviews in making participants comfortable enough to share their personal experiences and opinions. Indeed, I found that many activists I interviewed told their stories to me gradually, over multiple meetings, as I spent time in their communities and established personal relationships with them. I was also able to establish relational trust by volunteering my time with communities in capacities not directly related to my research. Specifically, I coordinated a participatory youth media project in several villages and refugee camps in the West Bank, in which I led photography and film/video workshops with local youth groups, and helped youth use media as a tool for expression, empowerment, and advocacy. This project enabled me to develop strong personal relationships with community leaders, youth, and parents that facilitated the emotional trust necessary to conduct my more formal research.

Of course, cognitive and emotional trusts are rarely mutually exclusive; on the contrary, cognitive and emotional trusts complement and reinforce each other. Indeed, both cognitive and emotional trusts contribute to a common platform from which trusting relationships are formed and maintained, enhanced by *behavioural* trust, or social actions that reflect cognitive and emotional trust. As Lewis and Weigert explain: 'When we see others acting in ways that imply that they trust us, we become more inclined to reciprocate by trusting in them more',[9] and the converse is also true. In terms of the researcher, regardless of one's reliance on the cognitive or emotional, trust relationships grow over time based on observed actions. Similarly, Swinth notes that trust is not established automatically, but rather develops sequentially over a 'trust period' in which the participants can observe each others' behaviours.[10] To be sure, in my own research, trust developed over time through multiple trips to Palestine, and return visits to the same specific communities.

Though distinct, these cognitive, emotional, and behavioural dimensions overlap as 'interpenetrating and mutually supportive aspects of the one, unitary experience and social imperative that we simply call "trust"'.[11] It is this multi-faceted conceptualization of trust that will guide the discussion in this chapter.

What are conflict zones?

Just as there are many dimensions of trust, there are many forms of conflict and conflict zones. In this chapter I use the term 'conflict' broadly to apply to: a) 'hot' conflicts characterized by open, direct violence; b) intractable conflicts with varying degrees of active and latent violence; c) situations of state oppression of citizens; d) post-conflict situations; and e) humanitarian situations resulting from conflict, such as flows of refugees and Internally Displaced Persons (IDPs). I situate my own experiences in Israel–Palestine within the category of intractable conflicts, with periods of escalating and de-escalating direct violence; however the Israeli–Palestinian conflict also involves elements of oppression and humanitarian issues, thus the chapter speaks to those types of conflicts as well. While this essay draws from my research experiences in Jerusalem and the West Bank as a basis for providing a practical context, I hope that the questions raised and recommendations provided are useful to researchers in other zones of conflict as well. At the same time, I hope researchers recognize that because research contexts vary both between and within different conflicts, I offer the following observations and suggestions to provide a guiding framework, rather than definitive conclusions, on the role of trust in gaining access in difficult situations.

Gaining access to the field site

One of the initial trust challenges that researchers often face when beginning fieldwork in conflict zones is gaining the trust of the dominant government or regime to secure their entry into the country, without violating the trust of communities in which the research is to be conducted. This primary issue typically revolves around two distinct trust relationships: the researcher's 'relationship' with the dominant polity on the one hand, and his/her relationship with the participants in his/her research on the other.

While access of course varies by conflict zone, many scholars face difficulties in gaining entry to the countries under study. Such cases are common when the government or regime perceives the research to be critical of the state or directly empowering to rebel forces or oppressed communities, and/or indirectly beneficial to such groups by bringing attention to under-reported situations of abuse or injustice. Typical governmental tactics used to hinder research include denying the researcher visas or visa renewals; requiring the researcher to be accompanied by government personnel, often in the name of 'security', covertly following or spying on the researcher; and threatening or acting to arrest or deport the researcher if he/she goes to prohibited areas or meets with certain groups or individuals.

In my own experience, in attempting to conduct fieldwork on nonviolent resistance in the West Bank, the contentious nature of my subject matter raised a red flag with Israeli authorities. Although my research concentrates on nonviolence, I was denied entry to Israel by Israeli security on two separate occasions, following hours of interrogations, strip searches, and a brief internment in an immigration detention centre. During later visits, in which I did manage to secure a visa, thanks to the intervention of Israeli and international colleagues, I still came to expect ten to twelve hours of interrogations with various levels and branches of Israeli security at border control. My experience was not unique; I knew other researchers whose entry was likewise denied, and I met several researchers who found they could not extend or renew their visas after a brief three months in the field.[12]

Denial of entry, visa restrictions, and other government-imposed barriers often put researchers in difficult situations, and raise logistical, methodological, and ethical considerations. While one option is to attempt to eschew the government regulations by either failing to accurately disclose one's intentions or entering the state illegally, such courses of action can put the researcher, as well as his/her research subjects and participants, at significant risk. Furthermore, depending on the research design, the researcher may need to maintain cordial relations with the government to ensure access to officials, records, or resources. Finally, lying about one's research and/or sneaking over borders may violate the ethical code of the individual researcher or his/her institution.

At the same time, 'cooperating' with the government may raise other ethical questions that outweigh commitments to standard procedures. As some scholars have noted,[13] traditional 'ethical' emphases of institutions and disciplines concentrate on methodological formalities, including securing legal approval from host nations and respective government institutions. However, complying with state regulations, even when methodologically possible to do so, can compromise the researcher by forcing him/her to legitimize the regime. As Bourgois states:

> The problem with contemporary anthropological ethics is not merely that the boundaries of what is defined as ethical are too narrow, but more importantly, that ethics can be subject to rigid, righteous interpretations which place them at loggerheads with overarching human rights concerns. How does one investigate power relations and fulfill the researcher's obligation to obtain informed consent from the powerful?[14]

To be sure, while the methodological and ethical implications of circumventing authorities may not be ideal, cooperating with such individuals and institutions and seeking their 'trust' can compromise the researcher's personal ethical code, and/or complicate the trust relationship between the researcher and respondents. Even when deemed practical and necessary, such cooperation can lead to perceptions of legitimizing the regime or oppressive polity, or granting them a degree of power or influence.[15]

In my experience, I was fortunate to find a compromise solution to securing a visa with the kind assistance of a colleague at Hebrew University's Truman Institute for the Advancement of Peace,[16] who wrote a letter of invitation for me to conduct my research in affiliation with the institute. While a few Palestinian activists I later interviewed favoured boycotting all Israeli academic institutions, many others expressed respect for, or at least tolerance of, the Truman Institute, including some activists who had worked directly with the institute on a peace education initiative. I thus felt that, on the one hand, by working through my mid-level civil society contacts in Israel, I managed to avoid 'legitimizing' the usual authorities in securing the visa; on the other hand, I managed to maintain my legality in entering the country and preserve my transparency as a researcher. Furthermore, I found that few participants condemned my 'cooperation' with authorities because Palestinians similarly negotiate with Israel on a regular basis to obtain permits and other travel documents. However, in talking with participants who knew I had been denied entry in the past, I found that the fact that I had experienced even a touch of Israel's treatment towards presumed Palestinian sympathizers helped enhance research participants' emotional trust of me.

Nevertheless, it soon became clear that getting over the border was just the first step of many in gaining access, and each additional step required additional re-negotiations of trust relationships. While the Truman Institute intervention helped Israeli security 'trust' me enough (by association) to grant me the visa, I continued to face regular questions about my purpose and intentions from soldiers at checkpoints and in various locations throughout the West Bank. The soldiers rarely questioned me at the Qalandiya and Rachel's Tomb checkpoints, which link Jerusalem to Ramallah and Bethlehem, respectively, as those routes are fairly well-travelled by aid workers and other internationals. However, I was questioned about my reasons for being at the Huwwara checkpoint near Nablus, and at various 'flying' checkpoints[17] on village roads throughout the West Bank. I usually managed to get by as a tourist or a religious pilgrim, but I was constantly aware of my tenuous 'trust relationship' with Israeli authorities.

At the same time, while my primary community contacts knew me well, I was consistently questioned by research participants about my interactions and affiliations with Israelis, and my cooperation with United States government agencies like the CIA. Indeed, the simple facts of my identity as a US citizen, and my presence in Israel, posed a barrier to my developing trust relationships with respondents initially, many of whom voiced their suspicion that I was a collaborator with the occupying power or its main political and economic ally. My next challenge was then to determine how to develop enough trust to gain access to the communities constituting my research, which I discuss in the following section.

Gaining access to the community and the who, the how, and the what

Once a bargain has been formulated with official gatekeepers, researchers often face challenges of earning research participants' individual and collective trust to gain access to the community or communities being studied. As noted above, the presence of the researcher not only typically raises the suspicions of authorities, but of local communities as well. As Goodhand explains:

> Research [in conflict zones] occurs within an intensely political environment and is unlikely to be viewed by local actors as neutral or altruistic. Researchers ... need to be aware of how their interventions may affect the incentive systems and structures driving violent conflict or impact upon the coping strategies and safety of communities.[18]

According to Goodhand, conflict creates an 'information economy' in which the political situation privileges some voices while suppressing others, thus enabling powerful actors to manipulate the content of information and control its dissemination. This frequent phenomenon typically necessitates the deliberate establishment of a trust relationship between the researcher and respondents, to assure participants that information will be used appropriately. From my own experience, however, I found that achieving seemingly straightforward goals of ensuring security, confidentiality, and transparency involved giving special attention to underlying complexities that manifest themselves in conflict zones which, if overlooked, might erode, rather than enhance community trust.

Security

Ensuring the security of participants is a cardinal task to begin to build trust (cognitive in this case) between the researcher and the researched. However, sometimes steps taken to protect participant security can affect conflict dynamics in such a way that new security threats arise. Jacobsen and Landau bring this possibility to the forefront: 'In conflict zones ... few authorities are willing to protect refugees from those who may do them harm, including researchers whose actions may have less than ideal outcomes'.[19] Although Jacobsen and Landau refer specifically to refugees, nearly all participants in conflict zones research face similar risks relating to the influence of the researcher's presence on the community being studied.[20] Specific security issues that can promote or diminish trust include modes of initial access, methods of research, and sensitivity to delicate topics such as traumatic events or cultural taboos.

Modes of access. Negotiating access through local leaders represents a strategy often used by researchers to approach a community while seemingly protecting the security of both the researcher and the respondents. However, in conflict situations, leadership positions are generally tenuous, and local leaders may be part of a wider, complex balance of power that could easily be upset by the perception of a researcher favouring one leader or group over another. Thus, as Goodhand states: 'An understanding of who wields power and the local dynamics of conflict is an essential starting point for informed security decisions' to avoid upsetting the 'political equilibrium'.[21]

During my own fieldwork, once inside Palestine, I aimed to develop relationships based on cognitive, emotional, and behavioural trust. I spent approximately six months conducting preliminary research and volunteering with different NGOs and community-based organizations, thus introducing me to numerous community leaders and contacts in civil society. The fact that my access to participants was thus based on relationships with multiple leaders enabled me to avoid alienating certain subgroups, which might have occurred if I based my affiliation with one person or organization. Indeed, many activists told me that they would not have met with me if I just worked for 'X', but the fact that I worked through a network of leaders enabled me to establish multiple trust relationships while maintaining my independence as a researcher.

In addition to organizational independence, my range of contacts allowed me to meet with Christians as well as Muslims, Hamas as well as Fateh supporters, peace activists as well as violent resisters, and refugees and villagers as well as urbanites. Differences between these subgroups of Palestinian society range from being clearly evident to simmering beneath the surface. My preliminary research allowed me to identify some of these tensions, and enabled me to structure my fieldwork to avoid privileging one subgroup over another.

Furthermore, identifying or working through a certain leader or leaders without fully understanding other community allegiances could alienate segments of the population, and thus hinder rather than promote the development of a trust relationship. For example, on my initial visits to one village, I was mainly relying on my relationship with one member of the popular committee, and my understanding of the village's resistance efforts was framed through his lens. However, when I later met with another member of the popular committee, I learned that there were tensions between my initial contact and the rest of the group that often manifested itself in a sort of competition in planning actions, attracting participants, and directing publicity. If I had relied solely on my initial contact and his friends and followers in the community, I would have at best overlooked, and at worst alienated, the other community members who were more aligned with the rest of the popular committee.

In other situations where power-sharing agreements do not exist, 'negotiating with the gatekeepers to a community is a highly sensitive process as identifying certain individuals as leaders may endanger them'.[22] Indeed, recognizing local leaders can put those individuals in direct risk as repressive authorities or hostile groups may seek to remove local leaders whom they see as threatening their power base. In these ways, the choices that researchers make in determining their channels of accessing a community can affect the security of both the researcher and the participants, and also affect the quality of the research itself.

Methods of research. Different methodologies can also affect community security, and in turn, trust of the researcher. Participatory methods involving focus groups or large gatherings may reflect researchers' aim of establishing trust through inclusive meetings that allow for multiple voices to be heard. However, such gatherings may present a high-risk situation in active conflict zones in which such assemblies are directly targeted, or in latent conflict zones in which such congregations may be infiltrated by plants or spies. Finally, combatants may use such meetings for their own propaganda, preventing the researcher and community members from engaging in honest conversation.

Recognizing these risks in my own fieldwork, I did not attempt to convene focus groups of activists, but I did rely on participant observation, which put both me and community members in danger of arrest or injury. Israeli security overlooked most activist meetings I attended, though most of these were unannounced and held at undisclosed locations to prevent infiltration. In contrast, the public actions, such as demonstrations and protests, were publicized through activist networks and brought scores of both Israeli soldiers and police, resulting in frequent beatings and arrests of activists. Activists and observers (including international monitors, media personnel, and researchers like myself) were also regularly subject to tear gas, water cannons, and rubber bullets at these events.

Noting the contentious atmosphere at the demonstrations, I complemented my participant observation with narrative research in the form of semi-structured interviews. However, individual interviews can also present security risks. Due to the challenge of access, many researchers identify interview subjects through what Jacobsen and Landau refer to as 'snowball sampling',[23] in which the researcher starts with an initial core group of individuals willing to be interviewed (often identified by a local contact or organization), and then asks subjects to identify others who might be willing to participate. While this method often helps the researcher establish trust relationships by association, snowballing often 'increases the risk of revealing crucial and potentially damaging information to members of a network or subgroup'.[24] To be sure, the snowballing method can create problems within the network if sensitive links between individuals are acknowledged (or, in some cases, not acknowledged enough), or if the researcher, usually in attempts to enhance validity, shares information or opinions from one respondent with another.

Furthermore, the method can be problematic if hostile groups or authorities use researchers' findings or follow researchers' actions to identify networks or subgroups that they perceive as threats.

Researchers can take steps to be aware of these risks, and make methodological choices that best ensure the security of participants in their specific conflict context. In my own research, by working through a network of initial contacts as mentioned above, when my research 'snowballed', it expanded into a number of networks, rather than a single set of contacts. This plurality of sources prevented me from endangering, or becoming dependent on, a single subgroup. I was also careful to ensure confidentiality both within and between subgroups to avoid creating tensions or revealing sensitive information to other community members or to authorities.

Sensitivity. Another security concern emerges when engaging in actual conversations with participants: researchers should be aware of raising issues that might be dangerous or forbidden for community members to discuss. As Goodhand notes: 'Some topics may be taboo because they are too risky while others, while sensitive, may be approached indirectly'.[25] The researcher can thus help foster the trust relationship by having an informed understanding of the conflict as well as cultural dynamics when approaching contentious subjects to avoid alienating or endangering participants. In addition, the researcher should be aware that the discussions he/she provokes may continue or reverberate even after he/she has left the community.

In my experience, my networks of colleagues and contacts assisted me in screening my research devices, such as interview and survey questions, for sensitive subjects. For example, the youth surveys that I conducted asked young people to indicate their degree of support for various forms of resistance, both violent and nonviolent.[26] Specifically, I was curious to gauge youth support for acts of militant resistance against Israeli civilians, including suicide bombs and rocket attacks. Because I knew this would be a sensitive subject, I sought the assistance of colleagues at Palestinian universities before administering the surveys on their campuses to best understand how to present the questions in a way that would engage, rather than alienate, the youth participants. I found that taking the time to get this extra input from local scholars greatly enhanced my capacity to approach these topics with respondents. However, I also found that I had to be in tune to sensitive topics that came up unexpectedly in discussions of the survey or that arose organically in the interviews. Accordingly, I learned to respect participants' reluctance or unwillingness to pursue certain topics, which maintained their own sense of security while also fostering our mutual trust relationship.

As the above discussion indicates, the who, the how, and the what of conducting research in conflict zones all have security implications for the community. Researchers should generally aim to be cognizant of the security risks in their specific contexts to make choices regarding access, methods, and topics that ensure the safety of the participants, individually and collectively. These considerations are necessary methodologically as well as ethically, as such choices tend to shape the researcher's trust relationship with participants, and thus inform the extent of the researcher's access to communities.

Confidentiality

Related to security, the issue of confidentiality can make or break researchers' trust relationship with community participants. Indeed, one of the most significant yet unacknowledged problems relating to participant safety is 'the issue of security breaches arising from researchers' confidentiality lapses'.[27] In addition to contributing to safety concerns, confidentiality is important to encourage both cognitive and emotional trust between researchers and participants, and should be maintained both during and after the research.

How might this be done? One obvious solution is that confidentiality can be preserved by ensuring both privacy and anonymity of respondents.[28] Anonymity is particularly important for preventing hostile authorities or groups from tracing sensitive information to individual sources. However, privacy is also important for protecting participants' responses from others within the community who may disagree with certain controversial opinions. Even if knowledge of such opinions does not put respondents at direct risk, divisive viewpoints can create discord within the community.

Researchers can also be cognizant of how the use of local researchers and translators may threaten participants' sense of privacy and anonymity during the research process. As Jacobsen and Landau explain: 'Using research assistants from the same country or area as the respondent risks transgressing political, social, or economic fault-lines of which the researcher may not be aware'.[29] Indeed, participants' trust of the researcher and the research project often will decline if they worry that their responses may be shared with others in the community, or used against them outside the community. Even when local research assistants are in fact 'neutral', participants' perception of assistants' bias, or association of assistants with a feared or despised group, can often hinder the development of cognitive and emotional trust, thus limiting further access to the individual and community.

During my fieldwork, it was difficult to develop a trust relationship with all participants of course, especially due to my American identity, which unfortunately continues to be a liability in much of the Middle East. However, I developed cognitive trust with most individuals through my assurance of confidentiality, my attention to privacy, and my guarantee of anonymity. I was also sure to be transparent about my research, and to make sure that I had informed consent from all participants. I kept this consent verbal however to ensure participants' security, as the sensitive nature of the research could have endangered respondents if certain opinions on resistance, or reports of previous behaviour, were linked to their names. I further aimed to ensure confidentiality and privacy by conducting most of the fieldwork independently, without local assistants, which helped limit concerns of leakage or secondary bias.

After the research, it is equally important to maintain confidentiality when sharing findings with practitioners, policymakers, and scholars. In some cases, as Goodhand notes, 'There may be a tension between the need for confidentiality and maintaining a strategy of silence in the face of pervasive human rights abuses',[30] creating a dilemma for researchers trying to raise awareness of violations while still protecting their sources. However, it is important for researchers to strive to find means of passing on information while still respecting their trust relationship with research participants.

Participant observation

Participant observation, commonly utilized in conflict zones as either a primary or secondary method, often raises questions about researchers' trust relationships with communities. From one perspective, participant observation can enhance emotional trust, and thus enhance access. However, the establishment of close relationships between researchers and communities can also complicate researchers' transparency and can undercut the cognitive trust developed between researchers and subjects through informed consent. Bourgois raises the essential question: 'We obviously have an obligation to let the people we are researching know that they are being studied ... At the same time, we are taught ... that the gifted researcher must break the boundaries between outsider and insider ... How can we reconcile effective participant/observation with truly "informed consent"?'[31]

Indeed, participant observation encourages researchers to seek a sense of acceptance and trust with local communities so that we have as little effect on social interaction as possible. At other times, relations and trust levels extend beyond the level of observation to participant action, in which the researcher eschews all semblances of objectivity and becomes actively involved in the community dynamics. In conflict zones in particular, some researchers may feel compelled by a moral imperative to take such actions. However, researchers should also be aware that such deep trust relations raise other ethical questions beyond the issue of objectivity. Indeed, relationships can become problematic if the researcher uses his/her privileged 'insider' position to extract information that, when later shared or published, violates the emotional trust established between the researcher and community members. Likewise, research participants may feel a betrayal of trust if shared findings fail to go far enough to bring about anticipated changes. As Goodhand asserts, it is 'crucial that the purpose of the research [be] explained clearly and consistently to community members at all stages of the research process'.[32] Thus, researchers need to find a balance between developing relational, emotional trust, which contributes to access, with cognitive and behavioural trust, to avoid creating unrealistic expectations.

In my research, my presence as a participant observer at various protests and demonstrations helped me to establish behavioural and emotional trust with many activists who came to recognize me at these events. My continued presence at these episodes of resistance gave me access to activists who were hesitant to talk to me at first, but noted that my consistent presence, combined with referrals from colleagues, convinced them to trust me. In addition, my role as a coordinator of media projects with youth groups in several refugee camps and villages in the West Bank further enhanced my relations with community members and helped me establish emotional trust with participants. At the same time, the fact that I lived in Jerusalem and travelled all over the West Bank, rather than residing in one village or camp, facilitated a comfortable space between me and the research participants. While I saw many of the activists and community members regularly, they understood my role as a researcher, so I did not feel that my objectivity or transparency was compromised. I was also honest with participants about the structure and timeline of my research to avoid creating unrealistic expectations.

The ways in which researchers approach security, confidentiality, and level of participation all affect community perceptions and trust, both cognitive and emotional, of the researcher. In addition to these dimensions, researchers should also be aware of how elements of their personal identity affect community perceptions and trust levels. Depending on the specific conflict context, attributes such as nationality, gender, age, religion, race, or ethnic background may present additional challenges to developing trust and gaining access to communities. For me, being a woman had both advantages and disadvantages in terms of trust and access. On the one hand, I was sometimes limited in my participant observation by not having access to traditionally male settings, such as *qahwas* (coffeehouses) or football pitches. On the other hand, the fact that I was a *foreign* woman sometimes gave me access to predominantly male environments if I was with a male friend or colleague, including meetings, parties, and other gatherings. In addition, I was able to meet and talk with women to whom male researchers might not have had access. Being aware of one's personal identity can be helpful for researchers' negotiation of trust relationships with a given community. In the next section, I discuss how researchers can likewise be aware of respondents' personal identities and experiences when developing trust relationships to gain access to individuals.

Gaining access to individuals

In addition to developing trust to access general groups and communities, research in conflict zones requires the nurturing of unique trust relationships with individuals who have been distinctly affected by the conflict, including present or former militants, activists, prisoners, victims of torture or abuse, and child soldiers. Researchers need to give the same attention to security, confidentiality and transparency mentioned above to relationships with these subgroups, yet they must also be sensitive to opening old (or not so old) wounds.

Individuals who have been directly involved in conflict as either participants or victims of violence may still be suffering from the trauma of conflict at the time of research. For example, nearly all of the activists I spoke with had spent time in prison, suffered physical injuries, and experienced the loss of a family member or close friend to the conflict. Researchers thus face unique challenges in gaining access to such individuals and in developing trust relationships with them. As Goodhand observes: 'For traumatized individuals and groups, silence may be a coping, not just a survival, strategy. [Thus] dialogue must always be based on mutual consent'.[33] Indeed, whereas other community members may adopt a strategy of silence to avoid risk, the refusal or hesitancy to speak to a researcher often has another dimension for these special subgroups. Researchers thus need to allow for an extended period of trust development, and respect the decision of individuals who do not give their consent to participate in the research. If or when consent is given, researchers should also be especially sensitive to maintaining the trust relationship during conversations with these individuals by showing restraint and knowing when to stop.[34]

In addition, researchers should avoid implementing Western models of trauma therapy that might undermine local healing practices and potentially erode the trust between the researcher, the individual, and the community.[35] Indeed, whereas most Western models focus on individualized coping strategies, many non-Western approaches emphasize healing within the social context through community-building and/or rituals.[36] As emphasized throughout this chapter, researchers should pay particular attention to the coping strategies employed in the specific context in which they are conducting their research.

Finally, in the period following the fieldwork, researchers should sustain their trust relationship with these individuals by treating them with respect in reports of findings. While this may seem like a rather obvious guideline for the treatment of all research participants, it is important to avoid portraying individuals directly affected by conflicts as solely victims (or perpetrators) of violence. The reason is that, while research centering on victims in particular may be well-intentioned, such framing risks disempowering or exploiting participants.

In my research, developing emotional trust proved to be important in talking with activists who were former militants, prisoners, and/or victims of torture. While many of these respondents were eager to share their stories, others revealed their experiences gradually over time through multiple conversations and visits. For example, I had a series of interactions with one activist who was a popular committee member in a nearby village. First, we spoke on the phone, and he mostly focused on objective accounts of recent resistance activities organized by the village. At our next meeting, I accompanied him to a conference on nonviolent activism where he was more forthcoming about his opinions on different strategies being discussed. Finally, the next time at which I visited him at his family's home, he told me about the ten years he had spent in prison, starting at age 15; the torture and abuses he had been subject to during that time; and the death of his father, also an activist, during the first *intifada*.

Similarly, another activist began our first meeting by telling me the details of a recent demonstration he had organized in his village, making only vague allusions to his past resistance work. After spending time with him and his family in the village however, he later told me about participating in armed resistance as a young man, spending years in prison, surviving attempts on his life, and witnessing the death of a friend during a demonstration. At the end of that conversation he commented that he appreciated having the opportunity to talk about the past and share difficult memories.

In these situations, and in others, I felt that I gradually gained access to individuals' sensitive stories by allowing time for the trust relationship to develop. Though cognitive trust, in the form of assurances of confidentiality and anonymity, were still important in these cases, it was more the emotional trust of evolving relationships, complemented by behavioural trust as these activists witnessed my presence at various events and actions, that enabled them to share difficult experiences with me. Having the patience to wait for these stories, giving respondents the space to bring up sensitive issues at their own pace, and being an active listener during the sharing of hard memories proved to be useful strategies for addressing sensitive topics while respecting the needs of respondents.

Recommendations

Although Palestine represents a unique type of conflict zone in terms of its status as an occupied territory, my experiences as a researcher in the West Bank have reflected many of the concerns related to trust and access discussed in this chapter. I first had to develop a sort of trust relationship with the state of Israel to access the field site. Second, I had to be cognizant of security, confidentiality and participation/transparency issues to gain the cognitive trust necessary to access to Palestinian activist and youth communities. Finally, I had to develop more in-depth relationships with former combatants, prisoners, and victims of violence to establish a sense of emotional trust that would allow them to share their experiences with me.

Based on my experiences, I suggest the following practical recommendations for establishing trust and gaining access in conflict zones:

Before the fieldwork:

- Develop a sound understanding of the conflict dynamics and context of the research.
- Acquire at least a minimum proficiency in language and research skills to conduct the research effectively, and/or convene a team of researchers and assistants with appropriate skills and background.

- Anticipate possible ethical issues and barriers to trust development.

During the fieldwork:

- Constantly monitor the conflict dynamics and the security situation.
- Clearly explain the objectives of the research and obtain informed consent from all participants. Regarding the former, this typically requires having a written statement of one's research objective(s) readily on hand in the appropriate language(s).
- Adapt methods to allow for maximum confidentiality and security for participants by keeping interview data private, maintaining the anonymity of survey respondents, working through multiple networks and using care when selecting research assistants and translators.
- Be willing to show constraint, flexibility and a willingness to stop an interview or observation when necessary and/or appropriate.
- Reflexively consider the effect of the researcher(s) and the research on the community, and honestly examine power relations between researchers and participants.

After the fieldwork:

- Provide feedback to participants when security conditions allow.
- Preserve confidentiality in written reports and public dissemination of findings.

Perhaps the most important recommendation for establishing trust relationships in conflict zones is to allow time for trust to develop. As noted in the theoretical discussion at the beginning of the chapter, trust is not a zero-sum commodity that either does or does not exist; rather, trust develops sequentially over a sustained trust period. Furthermore, rather than being singular or static, trusts grow gradually through cognitive, emotional and behavioural dimensions. Developing trust between researchers and research participants is important in any discipline, but it is especially necessary when conducting research in conflict zones, in which access to the field site, the research community and individual subgroups all depend on the trust relationship.

APPENDIX: YOUTH SURVEY[37]

This survey is for research purposes only. All responses will remain confidential. You may skip any questions you do not want to answer, and you may choose to stop at any time. Thank you for your participation.

Please circle or indicate the most accurate response:

- V0. Age:
- V1. Location
- V2. Gender
- V3. Religion:
  - Muslim
  - Christian
- V4. Level of Devoutness to Faith:
  - High
  - Medium
  - Low
- V5. Political Party:

- Q1. Have you ever received training in popular resistance or nonviolence?
  - Yes
  - No

  If yes, when and where?

- Q2. Have you ever participated in a nonviolent action against the occupation?
  - Yes
  - No

- Q2–2. Have you ever participated in demonstrations or protests?
  - Yes
  - No

- Q2–3. Have you ever participated in a boycott?
  - Yes
  - No

- Q2–4. Have you ever participated in a petition?
  - Yes
  - No

- Q2–5. Have you ever participated in replanting trees on bulldozed land?
  - Yes
  - No

- Q3. Have you ever participated in violent resistance against the occupation?
  - Yes
  - No

- Q3–2. Have you ever participated in throwing stones?
  - Yes
  - No

- Q3–3. Have you ever participated in armed resistance?
  - Yes
  - No

Please respond to the following statements on a scale of 1–5 (1 = Strongly DISAGREE, 5 = Strongly AGREE).

Q4–1. Nonviolent popular resistance is the most effective way to resist the occupation.
1   2   3   4   5
Q4–2. Armed resistance is the most effective way to resist the occupation.
1   2   3   4   5
Q4–3. Both nonviolent and violent resistance are effective ways of resisting the occupation.
1   2   3   4   5
Q4–4. Nonviolent resistance is more *strategic* than armed resistance.
1   2   3   4   5
Q4–5. Nonviolent resistance is more ethical than armed resistance.
1   2   3   4   5
Q4–6. There is a history of nonviolent resistance in Palestine.
1   2   3   4   5
Q4–7. Palestinians have a right to all means of resistance.
1   2   3   4   5
Q4–8. Youth play an important role in resisting the occupation.
1   2   3   4   5
Q5–1. Would you support a nonviolent movement against the occupation?
1   2   3   4   5
Q5–2. Would you support nonviolent demonstrations and protests?
1   2   3   4   5
Q5–3. Would you support a boycott against Israeli products?
1   2   3   4   5
Q5–4. Would you support a violent uprising against the occupation?
1   2   3   4   5
Q5–5. Would you participate in violent actions?
1   2   3   4   5
Q5–6. Do you support throwing stones at soldiers?
1   2   3   4   5
Q5–7. Do you support armed resistance against soldiers?
1   2   3   4   5
Q5–8. Do you support using rockets against civilians?
1   2   3   4   5
Q5–9. Do you support using suicide bombs against civilians?
1   2   3   4   5

Notes

1 The terms 'high-context' and 'low-context' refer to the extent to which people in a given community rely on communication devices beyond their literal speech to convey meaning. The terms were first coined by Edward Hall in *Beyond Culture*

Got trust? The challenge of gaining access in conflict zones   89

(New York: Double Day, 1976) and used later by Raymond Cohen in his *Negotiating Across Cultures* (Washington DC: United States Institute of Peace, 1997) to emphasize how communication styles in different cultures vary due to their field dependence, that is, the degree to which factors outside explicit spoken words affect the conveyance of information. According to Hall, high-context communication tends to be prevalent in communitarian cultures, often characterized by relationship-building, face-saving, nonverbal messages and gestures, and indirect problem-solving and communication strategies. In contrast, low-context communication correlates with individualist cultures, typically characterized by emphasis on efficiency, focus on effectiveness, and reliance on direct questions and observations.

2 David J. Lewis and Andrew Weigert, 'Trust as a Social Reality', *Social Forces*, vol. 63:4 (1985), p. 970.
3 Lewis and Weigert, 'Trust as a Social Reality', p. 970.
4 W. E. Bennis, D. Berlew Schein, and F. Steele, *Interpersonal Dynamics: Essays and Readings on Human Interaction* (Homewood, IL: Dorsey, 1964) p. 223. See also Robert L. Swinth, 'The Establishment of the Trust Relationship', *The Journal of Conflict Resolution,* vol. 11:3 (1967), p. 335.
5 See the appendix for an English translation of the survey.
6 In accordance with Palestinian definitions of 'youth', this population included young people between the ages of 16 and 35 years.
7 The IRB at my home institution, American University, approved the use of verbal consent over written consent to ensure the security of participants, who may have been targeted for their role in resistance activities if the forms were confiscated and/or their identities made known to Israeli authorities. Many survey respondents noted that they would not have participated if they had to record their names, so anonymity was determined by joint agreement.
8 Lewis and Weigert, 'Trust as Social Reality', p. 971.
9 ibid.
10 Swinth, 'The Establishment of the Trust Relationship'.
11 Lewis and Weigert, 'Trust as a Social Reality'.
12 In response to widespread denials of entry, the Campaign for the Right of Entry/Re-Entry to the Occupied Palestinian Territory (OPT) formed in 2006 as a grassroots, volunteer initiative to assist foreign passport holders residing in or visiting the OPT. According to the Campaign, the majority of individuals denied entry are family members of Palestinian ID holders, however, other 'effected groups include professionals and academics who are in the OPT for teaching, research, the arts, business, visiting or volunteering their services. Most of these individuals have never overstayed their visitor's visas or breached any visiting regulations'. See Right to Enter, available at http://www.righttoenter.ps/main.php?mid=7, para 2, accessed 1 March 2008.
13 See Philippe Bourgois, 'Confronting Anthropological Ethics: Ethnographic Lessons from Central America', *Journal of Peace Research,* vol. 27:1 (1990), pp. 43–54; Karen Jacobsen and Loren B. Landau, 'The Dual Imperative of Refugee Research: Some Methodological and Ethical Considerations in Social Science Research and Forced Migration', *Disasters,* vol. 27:3 (2003), pp. 185–206.
14 Although Bourgois in 'Confronting Anthropological Ethics', p. 45 refers specifically to the field of anthropology, the ethical dilemma that he describes pertains equally to researchers in disciplines such as political science and international relations who use anthropological methods.
15 Jacobsen and Landau, 'The Dual Imperative of Refugee Research', p. 194.
16 The Truman Institute conducts significant research on the advancement of peace and justice throughout the world, with a strong focus on the Middle East. It also coordinates a number of bi-lateral projects with Palestinian institutions and NGOs, as well as working closely with Arab-Israeli communities. I continue to be grateful

to the institute for its support of my personal research and for its ongoing progressive, if contentious, initiatives.
17 'Flying checkpoints' are temporary travel barriers erected at various points for lengths of time ranging from a few hours to several months.
18 Jonathan Goodhand, 'Research in Conflict Zones: Ethics and Accountability', *Forced Migration Review*, vol. 8 (2000), p. 1.
19 Jacobsen and Landau, 'The Dual Imperative of Refugee Research', p. 187.
20 ibid.
21 Goodhand, 'Research in Conflict Zones', p. 2.
22 ibid.
23 Jacobsen and Landau, 'The Dual Imperative of Refugee Research', p. 195.
24 ibid.
25 Goodhand, 'Research in Conflict Zones', p. 2.
26 See the appendix for an English translation of the survey.
27 Jacobsen and Landau, 'The Dual Imperative of Refugee Research', p. 187.
28 Goodhand, 'Research in Conflict Zones', p. 3.
29 Jacobsen and Landau, 'The Dual Imperative of Refugee Research', p. 193.
30 Goodhand, 'Research in Conflict Zones', p. 3.
31 Bourgois, 'Confronting Anthropological Ethics', p. 52.
32 Goodhand, 'Research in Conflict Zones', p. 3.
33 ibid.
34 ibid.
35 ibid.
36 See S. Gibbs, 'Post-War Social Reconstruction in Mozambique: Re-Framing Children's Experience of Trauma and Healing', *Disasters,* vol. 18:3 (1994), pp. 268–276; M. Wessells and C. Monteiro, 'Healing Wounds of War in Angola: A Community-Based Approach', in D. Donald, A. Dawes and J. Louw (eds), *Addressing Childhood Adversity* (Cape Town: David Philip Publishers).
37 Although central to my research objective, the youth survey was just one component of my research, which utilized a mixed-methodology approach. I also conducted 88 open-ended interviews with other activists that had a less formal structure and allowed for more flexibility for probing into nuance, and I also engaged in months of participant-observation at various nonviolent actions, meetings, and conferences. The survey thus represents just one dimension of my data collection methods.

7 From cell phones to coffee: Issues of access in Egypt and Lebanon

Courtney Radsch

Introduction

The first question I am usually asked when I sit down for an interview is what I would like to drink. From the vaulted offices of the Arab League to the newsroom of the state-run newspaper to the sparsest house in rural Egypt, taking coffee or tea together is a pleasant ritual throughout the Arab world. In my many trips to the region I find this pleasantry, born of legendary Arab hospitality, is an enjoyable alternative to the hasty business meetings and interviews so common to my home country of America. Doing research in this part of the world poses challenges and opportunities to the investigator, a central one of which is gaining access. Access to informants is tied up with issues of identity and language, cultural awareness and concerns about safety of the subjects as well as the researcher. This article discusses how these issues play out in the field and is primarily based on dissertation research I conducted in Egypt in 2006 and 2008.[1]

The question of access is not only one of access to individuals but to entire countries. The ability to right of entry to a particular site can often depend on the researcher's country of origin and funding sources just as much as interpersonal relations. My research focuses on new media and cyberactivism in the Arab world. I had initially intended to study Lebanon in addition to Egypt but had to drop the former because of practical considerations about funding and safety. Many donor agencies will not give funding for research in countries with a high level travel warning from the State Department, which made it difficult to obtain and maintain funding for Lebanon. Civil violence and the outbreak of war also posed challenges to conducting research there since the airport often becomes a casualty of fighting and travel become difficult and dangerous. Furthermore, people, especially the journalists and activists I interview, tend to be unavailable during such times. And until one gains access to a country one cannot gain access to one's subjects. I found that despite my personal connections in Lebanon I had far greater access in Egypt because of donor funding decisions. Although Egypt is a police state under emergency law, it has been ruled by the same president for more than two decades and is thus relatively stable.

Conducting research in such a political environment poses a challenge to the social scientist and requires negotiating volatile and at times dangerous situations. Trust, access, and confidentiality come into focus in different ways than they might in less difficult situations. The challenges of conducting social investigation in environments where risk accrues to research subjects *and* investigator, as well as some of the cultural and political issues surrounding the feasibility and practicality of doing research in Egypt are the focus of this chapter. In my research on new media and political activism I primarily focus on two vulnerable populations – journalists and bloggers – that have been the targets of state violence, harassment and intimidation. This figures into issues of feasibility and practicality for the social scientist, from the need for personal introductions to subjects' willingness to talk openly and 'on-the-record'. In both cases, however, *wasta*, loosely translated as connections, and *isnad*, the tracing of a chain of witnesses as a criterion of veracity,[2] are especially important for a researcher making initial contact and to build the trust and credibility required to pursue an interview or participant observation. Gaining access almost always begins with mobile phones and ends with coffee.

Reality and virtuality: Ethnographic access and participant observation

My fieldwork involved ethnographic methodology – interviewing, observation, participant observation, focus groups and content analysis of texts (including profiles) produced online – to create the thick description necessary to identify and interpret meaningful structures and discourses.[3] Adopting Wolcott's 'embrace of multiple techniques', my fieldwork techniques include experiencing, enquiring and examining[4] in order to develop and apply theory.[5] Each technique, with the exception of textual analysis, required different levels of access to people in the field. Most of my interviews and focus groups were conducted as participant observation. In participant observation the researcher subjects oneself 'to the set of contingencies that play upon a set of individuals, so that you can physically and ecologically penetrate their circle of response to their social situation' by becoming close to one's subjects and their situations.[6] Or as others call it 'advanced hanging out'.[7] Experiencing through participant observation is the most scientific of methods according to Gans because by allowing people to get close to those being observed 'it allows researchers to observe what people do, while all the other empirical methods are limited to reporting what people say about what they do'.[8] My research emphasized participation or observation depending on the situational context of the moment and the type of access I negotiated.[9] Whereas media content can be studied via content analysis, statistical analysis, or other nomothetic quantitative approaches, the practices and processes that result in the final product are hidden and thus require an ethnographic framework both to collect data and to conduct analysis.[10] Through participating observation I produced detailed fieldnotes of my observations[11] on the contextual specifics of their interactions, the way identity is constructed through interaction, and the positioning that occurs in response, as well as the cultural resources deployed to legitimate or de-legitimate interactional practices.

In order to gain access I sought to immerse myself in the field – both real and virtual. Gaining access to a particular field first requires defining the field of inquiry, an exercise that presents new methodological challenges in the Internet era. In some respect I had to continually seek to define and negotiate the field in which I was conducting fieldwork.[12] In fact, my fieldwork took place in two locations simultaneously, one real and one virtual. I had to be physically located in Egypt to be able to observe journalists and bloggers at work and to fully understand the conditions under which they perform those identities, the hierarchies that structure their fields of practice, and the practices they undertake. But since I was studying bloggers I also had to conduct a virtual ethnography of a virtual world where their identities as bloggers were enacted in cyberspace. In June 2006 I started my blog as a way to keep track of some of my experiences and insights from my first fieldwork trip to Egypt. On this trip I was focused on the mainstream media and journalists rather than bloggers, but blogs were gaining in popularity and I saw it as a way to make my identity and project more transparent to potential informants and provide a way of giving back to the community I was studying. On my second fieldwork visit to Egypt the blog became even more important since clearly having a blog is an essential component of being a blogger and thus enabled me to gain access to the community I was studying as a participant observer.

My research took place in both a physical space defined by geographic and political borders as well as in the deterritorialized space of the Egyptian blogosphere. The Egyptian blogosphere refers to the Internet community of weblogs, known as blogs, that discuss, analyze and opine about the physical entity of Egypt and/or the author's identity as an Egyptian.[13] Thus while I sought access to populations and spaces both real and virtual, on- and off-line and there was some significant overlap, there were also informants who were only accessible in one or the other. Such multi-sited ethnography helped me understand the connections between macro-level forces like globalization, privatization, transnational activism, and American foreign policy with micro-level identities, practices and networks.[14] By de-reifying the Egyptian blogosphere it was possible to find it in Cairo, in Sharqiya, in the Egyptian mainstream media, and in cyberspace.

I employed different strategies to gain access to the real and the virtual, though as technology progressed over the two years I conducted research I found myself using access strategies in different and overlapping ways, as detailed in the case study below. Having identified a few key organizations and individuals I wanted to interview based on my reading and research, I went into the field to begin seeking access to them. The communities of journalists and bloggers I wanted to study are loosely formed and relatively unorganized, so there was no particular gatekeeper or point of access.[15] When

I first went 'into the field' in 2006 I was focused on getting to know professional journalists and their professional worlds in Egypt at a time when blogging had only just begun to make its presence felt there. By 2007 blogs were well-known and had become part of the media systems in both Egypt and Lebanon and the 'field' was quite different than before.

Access and the political environment

Despite the relative opening of the media environment in the Arab world over the past decade, journalists and bloggers continue to face personal and professional intimidation, from repressive press laws and penal codes to detention and arrest.[16] During the period of my research the imprisonment of journalists and bloggers was an all-too-common occurrence in a country where the government uses brute force, from torture to harassment to fines, to enforce its authority over communication space and the media. National security looms large in the communication environment in Egypt, where the Mubarak government is focused on protecting the regime and the political *status quo*. Over the past four years bloggers have been targeted by the Egyptian state for their activism and more recently for their writing.[17] Being aware of the environment in which my research subjects live and work was critical not only to gaining access as a researcher and protecting their safety, but also to ensuring my own safety as I sought to immerse myself in a world so sensitive to state authorities and thus potentially dangerous to myself and my subjects. Making sure that my informants were aware of my efforts to maintain the security of my data through password protection and encryption was an important part of preserving access, credibility and safety. Yet more often than not the knowledge that their opinions and insights would be part of the discourse on media effects in the region gave them a sense of empowerment, and many refused to remain anonymous because this would only be another way for the state to silence them.

The mechanics of doing research

Doing research in the Arab world was usually easier than doing similar research in the United States. In America there often seems to be scepticism and inherent distrust toward the qualitative social scientist, especially those whose methods appear similar to those of journalists, a profession that has lost much respect over the past few years.[18] In the United States it seems one must go through a secretary to arrange an interview or call the press secretary for an official version of events. Business phone numbers and e-mails are used while mobile phone numbers and personal e-mails are guarded much more closely. Although research guides often advise sending letters to make initial contact (which are increasingly sent via e-mail anyway) the researcher must assess the best way to make initial contact based on the cultural practices and norms of the community they hope to study.[19] In the Arab world, however, people do not seem to be as possessive and obsessive about their personal information and will much more readily give you a mobile phone number and a personal e-mail. Most journalists, though they have e-mail accounts, did not seem to respond to e-mail messages consistently and were far more accessible via phone. While few Americans would dream of giving out a friend's cell phone number, once I established rapport with a research subject I found they were often more than willing to provide me with personal contact information for people to which they had access. Mobile phone numbers for even the most senior level officials and executives were easily obtainable from interviewees, perhaps because of the traditions of Arab hospitality, and initial contact made via phone implies a level of *wasta* sufficient enough to at least get in the door. Phones also have the benefit of not leaving a paper trail.

Wasta

Wasta can be loosely translated as connections. In a society where informal networks are institutionalized throughout all class levels[20] *wasta* can be crucial for gaining access to these networks. Coming from the root meaning 'to mediate' *wasta* is a term commonly used to indicate personal connections used to gain access for others. In the literature on *wasta* the term is usually used to refer to the use of personal connections to obtain a job, the intercession of someone on behalf of another to a higher authority, or the connections needed to conduct business.[21] But *wasta* can also refer to the basic need to use personal connections to accomplish regular business and gain access to people not currently in one's network. As Rabo and Utas note, '[w]asta is based on trust, in relations of friendship or patronage' in which anyone who has resources needed by another can become a mediator, or *wasiit*, and can seek or give *wasta* depending on the circumstances.[22] They consider *wasta* as a resource relative to the perceived or real need for mediation.[23] In my research *wasta* meant using my connections to gain access to informants.

Trust is essential for gaining access[24] so I drew on my academic, journalistic and familial networks to get assistance in obtaining contact information for the people I wanted to interview. Occasionally a professor or journalist would send an e-mail introduction or a blogger would use the 'suggest a friend' feature on Facebook[25] to put me in touch with a potential informant. I also made lists of people who had been quoted or interviewed in similar research or on matters related to my research because I felt this indicated a willingness to talk and thus that I would have an easier time gaining access. Yet I found access was difficult to set up in advance and thus did almost all my networking once I arrived in the field, armed with a few e-mail addresses and some names. These networks were broadly construed at the beginning of my research e.g. satellite journalists, state journalists these networks became more focused as I deepened my understanding so that eventually I was seeking access to narrowly defined networks such as Muslim Brotherhood bloggers or liberal activist bloggers.

Isnad

Accessing these groups often required finding a key influential or point-person who would open the doors to others in their social network, and it was not always apparent who this would be. I attempted to establish credibility as a trusted researcher through what I call a modified version of *isnad*. *Isnad* refers to the methodology of Islamic science in which the sayings of the prophet (*Hadith*) are traced through authoritative sources in an unbroken chain of witness in order to verify its authenticity and credibility.[26] Adapting this idea of religious *isnad* to trust and communication, Fandy argues that this practice 'shapes the cosmology of the larger society with regards to trust' and verification.[27] Similarly, I found that *isnad* can be applied in the research setting to establish trust and credibility in a society where personal relations are so important. I also found it diminished concerns that I was a spy given the scepticism towards Americans – especially those who speak Arabic – as potential CIA agents.[28] Americans might call it 'dropping names' though this often has a pejorative connotation. In oral, high-context societies intuition and anecdote are more acceptable as evidentiary claims than in low-context, literate societies.[29] Thus in my initial contact with a potential informant I would explain how I got his or her mobile number and how I knew that person and through whom I had met them etc. This was especially important when I cold-called potential informants with whom I had not connections or *wasta*. Since my informants were part of a relatively contained social category this meant that they often knew each other and thus my dropping of names helped establish my veracity as a researcher and one who could be trusted. By using my modified form of *isnad* and anecdote I found that I was welcomed as a legitimate researcher who should be trusted and helped.

Virtual Wasta *and social networking*

More often than not people were interested in learning more about my research and setting up a meeting in person. Once I made initial contact I sought to create a stronger relationship in which I could gain access to that person's *wasta*. By my second research trip to Egypt I had joined Facebook, a social networking site that had become wildly popular in Egypt by the end of 2007.[30] Facebook is a significant social space where friends communicate, play games, arrange social activities and share social documentation like photos and video. It is a place of social interaction where things/events/movements are produced, perceived, and interpreted and thus formed a key field of investigation.[31] Being in the field required extension into this virtual domain since processes and mechanisms of identity formation, mobilization, and activism took place or passed through these electronic space. Thus I gained access to in-person interviews and activities by becoming a part of their virtual social world as a peripheral member.[32] I occasionally made initial contact through Facebook, briefly introducing myself and my research and asking if they would be willing to chat online or off. Usually, however, I found a friend request waiting for me after an interview or agreed to add an informant during the interview. Towards the end I found myself initiating the process, veering more towards participation in the participation/observation continuum.[33]

I learned that Egyptians use Facebook to make friends and found that adding informants as 'friends' and accepting their 'friend' requests was a good way to enter their social worlds and was almost expected after an interview or meeting. To decline a request would be an insult. Some even questioned why my privacy settings were so high, preventing them from seeing any personal information about me prior to adding them to my 'friends' list, since the vast majority of Egyptians on Facebook appear to have the lowest privacy settings possible. This means that anyone with an account can see their contact and background information, friend list, activities update, pictures and all other personal information on their site. This question often led to interesting conversations about privacy and cultural difference.

Although I was physically 'out' of the field between research trips I was still 'virtually' present in the field because of the nature of my research online using what Hine terms virtual ethnography.[34] As Bernard notes, all participant observation is fieldwork.[35] Furthermore, only via a virtual ethnography of the Egyptian blogosphere could I come face-to-face with the virtual selves created in and inhabiting this virtual space and the networks they create. The continuity of maintaining contact between and around visits with certain bloggers as well as being a virtual present in the Egyptian blogosphere enabled me to gain and maintain access across space and time.

Identity

Access is often dependent on the identity of the researcher, who is stuck with some identifiers like gender, age and race, but able to enact or invoke others depending on context, such as marital status and profession.[36] Some of my 'social attributes'[37] such as being a white American were different than those of my informants, while others, such as being in my late twenties, were not (at least among bloggers). Insider–outsider roles are not a given, rather they are embedded within multiple social identities and their narration.[38] Part of my approach to building trust, establishing my credentials, and putting my informant at ease was to draw on particular parts of my identity that seemed relevant and similar to the person I was talking to or hoped to interview. At times this meant highlighting my identity as a journalist or as a student or as a blogger. Often this meant highlighting the ways in which I was 'like them' in hopes of gaining insider status rather than simply being seen as a Western woman analyzing the Arab Other. By invoking particular personal characteristics at various times I attempted to shift from outsider to insider, enabling me to build trust with my informants and gain different perspectives. Of course I was aware that despite my attempts to negotiate my identity by emphasizing and de-emphasizing particular aspects of my identity, an identity is not entirely 'up for grabs'.[39]

Nationality

On first glance based upon my appearance most of my research subjects assumed that I was an American and thus a Christian. From the outset it was usually assumed that I did not speak Arabic and who had little knowledge of the Middle East, the Arab world or Islam. This was not because of any inherent animosity but rather an image created through media consumption and the effects of US foreign policy in the region. My informants, as people involved in the media industry to some extent, were acutely aware of the way that media frame and narrate Arab identity within Arab–Western relations, especially in the Post-September 11 context. I often felt this initially limited my access both in terms of who would talk to me but also the topics we would cover. I wanted to get beyond the surface and in-depth into the subject matter but often felt hindered by the assumption that I was an American who needed to be educated in the basics; many informants were surprised by the depth of my knowledge of Egyptian and Arab politics, the teachings of Islam and the Arab media system. Perhaps because of my identity as a 'student' or as a relatively young American I saw informants recalculate who I was and how I should be engaged with as our conversation revealed that I was not the 'typical American' they seemed to have assumed me to be.

Being American can be a difficult identity to negotiate in the Arab world because of the negative connotations of American foreign policy and imperialism, especially when attempting to access groups like the Muslim Brotherhood or *salafis* because of American policies and discourse about these groups. Despite my identity as researcher, doctoral candidate and former journalist in the region, I often felt that I needed to invoke my identity as an insider, as someone who was personally familiar with the culture and politics of the region. By stating my status as wife of a Muslim Arab I felt I was signaling that I am familiar with Arab culture, that I know not all Arabs or Muslims are terrorists, and that I am not plagued by the stereotypes they believe characterize most Americans' perceptions of Arabs/Muslims.

As other ethnographers and social scientists have noted,[40] Westerners, and especially Americans, in the field, and especially the Arab Middle East, are often believed to be spies. This concern helped me decide to use my real e-mail address instead of an anonymized one so that the (potential) informant could ascertain that I was who I said I was by my e-mail address and the signature line, which gave my contact information, website and blog URL. I have a description of my research and biography on my website and blog, which I felt made it less likely that I would be seen as a spy or government agent. Hearing me speak Arabic immediately challenged their preconceptions of who I was and what I represented, and almost always drew respect and surprise. Most Arabic speakers acknowledge the difficulty of the language, especially formal *fuhsa*, and freely admit that they themselves do not 'speak Arabic well'.

Language

Language was a key resource in gaining access not only to informants who were monolingual but also to bilingual informants. I also found that Arabic facilitated greater access to Muslim Brotherhood, *salafi* and Islamist bloggers. In my second field visit to Egypt half of my interviews were in Arabic and I was able to participate more fully than my first visit as my language skills had improved. I conducted interviews in Arabic, English and French depending on the preference of the informant, and often switched and mixed them up as we talked about different themes and topics that were better expressed in one language over the other. Over the two years that I conducted fieldwork my language abilities in Arabic improved significantly, and I was able to expand my access to Arabic-only speakers by my second research trip to Egypt. Although I conducted interviews in 2006 with Arabic-only speakers I was forced to rely on a translator, which of course adds an additional element into the researcher–informant relationship and interrupts the natural cadence of conversation. By the second research trip I was able to conduct interviews entirely in Arabic. I was also able to call people and introduce myself, my research and explicate the *isnad* in Arabic, which meant that my pool of informants was much bigger and people were generally impressed and interested by an American who could actually speak Arabic. My ability to speak Arabic and French enabled me to communicate with informants in the language, or languages, of their choice and to understand particular words or expressions that were best expressed in one language or the other. In addition to denoting my familiarity with their culture it enabled them to more fully express themselves in our interview because they could switch in and out of the language as it suited them and depending on the topic. For example, one informant told me that he preferred speaking and writing about democratization in English because this is the language from which the concepts emerge. Arabic proverbs and jokes, on the other hand, were best expressed in the native tongue.

Gender

Gender structures social access to some groups in the Middle East and Arab world, namely religious females. As a woman I was able to access both male and female populations I was studying whereas a male would not have been able to access the conservatively religious unmarried female bloggers. Such 'cross-gender access', as Warren notes, is often more available to foreign women than native women.[41] As a young, married female I was able to spend time alone and in the homes of female Muslim Brotherhood bloggers, for example. By mentioning that I was married, to an Arab and a Muslim nonetheless, I felt that I was eliminating sources of potential tension by implicitly indicating that I was not a wild Western girl tromping through the Middle East on her own, that I was not a threat to the unmarried girls and women or the single men, and that I was at least tangentially 'Arab'.[42]

Being sensitive to how invocations of certain identities are perceived in a given national or professional culture can ease barriers to access. Even within a single interview or relationship with an informant I would draw on different aspects of my identity, highlighting my student status when I sought to gain information and diminish feelings of cultural imperialism or focusing on my identity as a blogger when interviewing other bloggers. At times I wanted to emphasize my experience as a journalist so that we could talk in the journalistic parlance that characterizes the journalistic field and discuss more deeply some of the conceptual issues about the role of journalists in society and norms of journalistic professionalism. Deploying my journalistic identity, however, risked putting the informant on the defensive, especially if I mentioned having worked for the *New York Times*, since this is seen as a respectable and enviable place to work reserved for the best journalists. Thus if I mentioned my previous work I emphasized that I had worked for both the *New York Times* and the *Daily Star* in Lebanon, demonstrating that I respected and was experienced with both Arab and American journalism but without making a distinction or value judgment about either.

One sugar or two?

Much has been written about the 'high-context' culture of the Arab world, where most communication is carried out face-to-face and functions on the basis of who you know, depending more on power and networks of friends than rules or formalities.[43] It is important as a researcher to be sensitive to the role of nonverbal communication in Egyptian culture, and I found that my sensitivity to cross-cultural communication helped me gain and maintain access. While cultural blunders can of course be forgiven, cultural awareness helped me strengthen bonds with informants and likely helped me gain acceptance as someone they would like to help along.

Taking coffee or tea with an informant is a requirement and to refuse is unacceptable – much like refusing seconds at Thanksgiving – and potentially insulting. Great store is put on the notion of 'Egyptian' or 'Arab' hospitality and thus accepting the offer of a drink is a gesture of acceptance and acknowledgment of this. Once I entered a professor's office with a can of soda I had been offered in the previous interview and he was quite upset that he could not offer me something to drink since I clearly already had one. The ritual of drinking together springs from the tradition of Arab hospitality and reflects the different nature of time in the Arab world. Appointments rarely start on time and always begin with small talk. In my experience jumping right into the interview or business at hand is off-putting whereas spending a few minutes chatting often sets a more agreeable tone. Inquiring into the wellbeing of one's family, if the person is a friend or acquaintance, is a sign of respect and cultural awareness.

I also found that business cards are an important and strategic asset. People enjoyed getting a card from me; but one cannot simply give one to a group, each individual should be given a card. On subsequent follow-up interviews or meetings I was sometimes asked for my card again because it had been lost (even if the information was already stored in some sort of electronic device). Furthermore, the cards help establish the credibility of one's identity, especially when embossed with a university or other official logo. This helps reduce suspicions about the researcher being a spy though it does not, of course, eliminate them.

Case study: *Gaining access to Egyptian bloggers*

As described above I conducted semi-structured interviews and focus groups and had lots of informal chats and coffees with informants, and when possible conducted participant observation of events and practices. Watching how journalists and bloggers are involved in an event, such as the April 6 General Strike, gave me a much more nuanced understanding of what happened than interviews alone.[44] Of course some events were unobservable because they happened in the past or while I was not in the field, in which case I had to rely on the accounts obtained through interviews. Furthermore, because bloggers engage in blogging at random, unspecific times and often in the privacy of their homes or in between day-to-day activities, I rarely observed blogging *per se* but rather their interactions and activism as people who are bloggers rather than the actual task of sitting down to write.

On a few occasions, however, I did have the opportunity to observe the act of blogging, though the significance was more in the context in which the need to blog at a particular moment arose than it was about watching someone type away at their computer. In one case I had cultivated a relationship with a particular Muslim Brotherhood-affiliated blogger: visiting his university, meeting for coffee, exchanging e-mails and information about events one or the other might be interested in attending. This blogger was going to bring his friend, who is a blogger of consequence, to meet me at a café. As I was on my way he called me and told me to bring my computer. When I arrived he got online but we had to change the language settings to Arabic so that he could navigate his blog. His friend and fellow blogger had been arrested the day before and he had written a post about it. But his friend and the lawyers said he should take the post offline because the blogger had been transferred to state security and they were afraid that the blog post could put him in greater danger because it talked about a previous arrest and work as a blogger, putting lots of potentially incriminating evidence (from the government's perspective) in a cohesive article that would make it much easier for security to discover than if they had to dig it out for themselves. Shortly thereafter he received a call that the blogger had been tortured and that the security officials had asked about his own blog. This scene demonstrated to me that all interactions with bloggers whether in a formal interview setting or not are always opportunities for participant observation since a blogger can enact this identity at any time since any experience or observation is potential fodder for the blog. Furthermore, my willingness to help was a commitment act that helped build rapport and trust with these informants.[45]

Getting beyond the interview stage and into the community I wanted to study was a mixture of luck and strategy. Often I found that just by being in the right place and being willing to ask for access was sufficient to gain entrée after making initial contact. Perhaps because of the public nature of their jobs and often *personas* or their comfort working with people and taking information from them, my informants were often more than happy to bring me into their worlds, allowing me to see them enacting their roles as journalists or bloggers. For example, on the day of the Qana massacre in Lebanon I was in Al Jazeera's Cairo bureau for what was supposed to be an interview with the bureau chief.[46] But because of breaking news he was out. Instead of squandering my trip there I found a journalist willing to sit and talk. As we wrapped up he told me he had to run and he and his camera crew got into the elevator as I did. Where are you going? I asked. He told me he was going to cover the march by opposition members of the Egyptian parliament to the Arab League. I asked him if I could go and for the next few hours I was able to observe journalists in action, *doing* journalism in a way that no interview will ever convey. The willingness to take a leap and ask for access was critical to my success.

But strategy also played an equally important role. If I wanted to be considered a part of their world I needed to be invited into it. Thus I sought to be seen over and over in places where journalists and bloggers were. I attended press conferences, workshops, finagled invitations to events and basically tagged along whenever possible. I sought to be as involved with this very loosely defined community, a community often only enacted at particular moments, by being in places where they were likely to enact their identities as journalists or bloggers. Bloggers, in particular, are hyperconnected via mobile phones and Internet applications, tools used in the real and virtual spaces they occupy. New technologies were the gateway to participation so I joined listservs, social networking sites like Facebook and Twitter,[47] and kept track of the announcements made on the websites of human rights centres. My presence at an intimate workshop with 12 of the most famous bloggers I was invited to by an academic colleague prompted one blogger to tell me 'You're everywhere!' Because many such events were public they offered an opportunity to observe without participating and without having to expend any resources to gain access.

I gained access and conveyed trust by participating in the blogging life of activists, attending their meetings, conferences and events. At a conference on blogging and human rights early on in my fieldwork I met the famous and influential Egyptian bloggers in a 'safe' environment where I established my credentials as a devoted researcher. Accessing key influential individuals also helped me gain access to others in the community. And unlike some other researchers who passed through and attended a session here or there, I attended the entire nine hours both days. Not only did this give me an opportunity to chat with them and establish connections that I could follow up and conduct interviews, but I could also observe them, their interactions and the points of agreement and contention among them in a way that is not necessarily manifested in their virtual life on their blogs. By the end of the conference I had been accepted as one of the participants and was included in the final group photograph. And just as I wanted to talk to them, many of them wanted to talk to me so that we became subjects of each other. In some ways I was able to enact a form of informational *wasta* in terms of navigating some of the complexities of American academia or providing an interview on my area of expertise. Several of my informants hoped to apply for graduate school in the United States and asked me for advice and information, which I was happy to give.

A turning point came the day before the April 6 general strike in Egypt that included workers and cyberactivists in a common goal. On this day I went from observer to participant-observer and gained a place among the real and virtual community I was studying. It began with a text message from a blogger I had interviewed months before who was also one of the first Egyptian bloggers and an activist: 'Arrests started already. Bloger Malek of malek-x.net and 3 activists from Islamist Labour Party taken to Masr Al Qadima police station for distributing fliers'. This text message made me feel that I had reached a threshold where I was ready to be accepted into the group. At this point I chose to more fully immerse myself as a participant in order to observe how political activism actually took place, how bloggers activated their networks, publicized their efforts and enacted their roles as citizen journalists. I sent messages about what I saw on the streets out to the network via Twitter and wrote blog posts about the strike and my observations, linking to other bloggers and receiving comments from them on my posts. Because of the trust I had built over the months I was granted access to the activist network, receiving the text messages, Twitter updates and e-mails that detailed the mechanisms and processes by which bloggers activate their networks and enabling me to see the structures of these networks. I also sought to go to Mahalla, the site of the worker's strike, where several journalists and bloggers were planning on going in order to document the expected violence. Although an informant had agreed to help me get there, several also warned that it was dangerous and that they themselves were not going to go. I think that my interest and willingness to go proved my commitment to the group and helped further entrench my acceptance and inclusion among this particular group of bloggers. Yet it also underscored the need to draw lines and at times resist seeking access when it puts personal safety at risk. Sometimes just because a door opens the researcher must assess whether she should enter.

Conclusion

Doing research in countries with tumultuous or repressive political systems poses challenges to the investigator and informants alike, but often gaining access comes down to the simple basics building relationships. Online and mobile technologies can be particularly helpful in establishing the initial links needed to gain access because they offer a communicative space outside of the view of the authorities in countries like Egypt and Lebanon and provides an easy way to make initial contact and begin establishing ones *bone fides*. Once the researcher is familiar with the political and cultural context of the fieldwork sites, access becomes a matter of accessing personal networks by deploying relevant and strategic aspects of one's identity.

Issues of access cannot be separated from nationality, which affects the ability of the researcher to obtain funding for particular types of research in particular countries as well as whether that person will be granted a visa to enter the country. Personal and social attributes are often irrelevant in gaining access to the country of fieldwork since funding, visas and other such bureaucratic decisions are bound up in impersonal processes and decision making bodies to which the researcher probably does not have access. This has profound implications for one's research project as it defines the realm of potentiality and feasibility. Without funding most projects are not possible, so the investigator is held hostage to the funding guidelines of the source, regardless of their merit. Changes in security situation can have real and profound impacts on the research project; in my case I had to delay my fieldwork by a semester, revise my prospectus and ultimately discard a country entirely. Egypt is relatively open to Americans on a tourist visa, but it is much more difficult to obtain a research or residency visa. The research must negotiate the need for access with their personal ethics and willingness not to be completely honest with state authorities. Some Arab countries, however, like Syria and Saudi Arabia, can be very difficult for Americans to conduct research in even with a tourist visa since visas can be difficult to obtain and do not guarantee access at the border. Choosing not to enter the country as a researcher but in some other way poses moral dilemmas as well as security ones since the researcher will not have the proper credentials should the authorities inquire. Nonetheless, I chose to enter Egypt on a tourist visa since I was also studying Arabic and found that not being on the state's radar posed fewer problems for my research subjects and myself.

Once you are on the ground in-country, using modern technology and information tools to discover potential access or initial contact opportunities makes access easier to obtain since the only resource needed in many cases is the basic information about time and place. Furthermore, using publicly available information sources also protects those being observed since they do not have to establish any relationship with the researcher.

In many ways access was not only something my informants gave me but gave themselves, refusing to be silenced by an oppressive state. Bloggers resoundingly told me that they started blogging because they wanted to express themselves. They have something to say but nowhere to say it in a state where the media system remains under the heavy hand of the state and is inaccessible to most average citizens. Marginalized populations like the Muslim Brotherhood, homosexuals, and Bahai lack traditional media outlets and political representation; they say that with no newspapers and the inability to even express themselves at times in their own homes, online media and interest by researchers is empowering and demonstrates the effects of these media. The profound need to express oneself publicly coupled with the desire to effect change in their societies is reflected in the willingness to talk openly and 'on-the-record' about their experiences. Their refusal to remain silent and muzzled made access something they seemed to want to give because it would enable them to gain something for themselves and for the cause of freedom of expression.

Notes

1 I would like to thank the NSEP Boren Fellowship program for awarding me a fellowship to conduct fieldwork in Egypt in 2008 and the Social Science Research Council for the Pre-Dissertation Fellowship for International Collaboration to conduct research in Egypt in 2006.
2 *Isnad* is an Arabic term used in Islamic sciences and is explained later.
3 Clifford Geertz, *The Interpretation of Cultures: Selected Essays* (New York: Basic Books, 2000), p. 7.
4 Harry F. Wolcott, *The Art of Fieldwork* (Walnut Creek, CA: Rowman AltaMira, 2005), pp.44–46.
5 Michael Robert Evans,. "The Promises and Pitfalls of Ethnographic Research in International Communication Studies," In Mehdi Semati (ed.), *New Frontiers in International Communication Theory* (Lanham, MD: Rowman & Littlefield, 2004).
6 Erving Goffman, *On Fieldwork* (Prospect Heights, IL: Waveland Press, 2001), p. 154.
7 Gottlieb, *Ethnography: Theory and Methods* (Thousand Oaks, Calif.: Sage Publications, 2006), p. 49.
8 Herbert J. Gans, 'Participant observation in the era of ethnography', *Journal of Contemporary Ethnography*, vol. 28, no. 5 (1999), pp. 540–548.
9 R. M.Emerson and M.Pollner, 'Constructing Participant/Observation Relations', in Emerson, R. M.(ed.), *Contemporary Field Research: Perspectives and Formulations* (Prospect Heights, IL: Waveland Press, 2001), p. 241.
10 As Wolcott (1999) notes, ethnography can describe process or an outcome (41). This research adopts what he terms 'ethnographic techniques' but does not aim to produce an ethnography. Rather the goal is to produce 'a kind of account of human social activity out of which cultural patterning can be discerned' Harry F. Wolcott, *Ethnography: A Way of Seeing* (Walnut Creek, CA: Altamira Press, 1999), p. 68.
11 Robert M. Emerson, Rachel I. Fretz, and Linda L. Shaw, *Writing Ethnographic Fieldnotes* (Chicago: University of Chicago Press, 1995).
12 Emerson and Pollner, 'Constructing Participant/Observation Relations', in R. M. Emerson (ed.), *Contemporary Field Research: Perspectives and Formulations* (Prospect Heights, IL: Waveland Press, 2001).

13 The methodological and analytical rationale involved in designating and defining the Egyptian blogosphere are outside of the scope of this chapter. For discussions on defining the field of inquiry and community of study in cyberspace see Christina Hine, *Virtual Ethnography* (Thousand Oaks, CA : Sage, 2000); Marc A. Smith and Peter Kollock. *Communities in Cyberspace* (New York: Routledge, 1999).
14 Mitchell Duneier, 'On the Evolution of Sidewalk' in R. M. Emerson (ed.), *Contemporary Field Research: Perspectives and Formulations* (Prospect Heights, IL: Waveland Press, 2001), p. 177.
15 Patricia Adler and Peter Adler, 'Observational Techniques' in Patricia A. Adler, Peter Adler, N. K. Denzin and Y. S. Lincoln (eds),*Handbook of Qualitative Research*,(Thousand Oaks, CA: Sage Publications, 1994), pp. 377–382.
16 Courtney C. Radsch, 'Satellite Television in the Arab World', *Oxford Analytica* (22 April 2008). Courtney C. Radsch, 'How Al Jazeera is Challenging and Improving Egyptian Journalism', *Reset: Dialogue on Civilizations* 22 June 2007, available at http://www.reset.org, accessed 1 March 2008.
17 Courtney C. Radsch, 'Blogging in Egypt', *Reset: Dialogue on Civilization* vol. 103 (Rome, 2007), available at http://www.resetdoc.org, accessed 1 March 2008.
18 George Kennedy and Daryl Moen, *What good is journalism? How reporters and editors are saving America's way of life* (Columbia: University of Missouri Press, 2007), p. 2–3. *The State of the News Media 2007* (Washington, DC: Project for Excellence in Journalism, 2007), available at http://www.stateofthenewsmedia.org/2007/, accessed 30 May 2008.
19 Martha S. Feldman, Jeannine Bell and Michele Tracy Berger, *Gaining access: a practical and theoretical guide for qualitative researchers* (Walnut Creek, CA.: AltaMira Press, 2003).
20 Diane Singerman, *Avenues of Participation* (Princeton: Princeton University Press, 1995), pp. 11–18.
21 Robert Cunningham and Yasin Sarayrah, *Wasta: The Hidden Force in Middle Eastern Society* (Westport, CT: Praeger, 1993); Robert Cunningham and Yasin Sarayrah, 'Taming Wasta to Achieve Development,' *Arab Studies Quarterly* vol. 16 no. 3 (1994); Kate Hutchings and David Weir, 'Understanding networking in China and the Arab World: Lessons for international managers,' *Journal of European Industrial Training* vol. 30 no. 4 (2006), pp. 272–290. Ahmed A. Mohamed and Hadia Hamdy, 'The Stigma of Wasta: The Effect of Wasta on Perceived Competence and Morality', The German University in Cairo, Faculty of Management Technology *Working Paper 5* (2008).
22 Annika Rabo and Bo Utas, *The Role of the State in West Asia* (Istanbul: Swedish Research Institute in Istanbul, 2005), p. 118.
23 Rabo and Utas, *The Role of the State*, p.119.
24 Feldman, Bell and Berger, *Gaining Access*.
25 www.facebook.com is a social networking site where people can post a wealth of personal information and connect with people through networks and friend requests.
26 Kimberly Y. Schooley, 'Cultural Sovereignty, Islam, and Human Rights–Toward a Communitarian Revision,' *Cumberland Law Review* vol. 25 (1994), p. 651; Mamoun Fandy, 'Information technology, trust, and social change in the Arab world,' *The Middle East Journal* vol. 54, no. 3 (2000).
27 Fandy, *Information Technology*, p. 383.
28 Richard G. Mitchell, Secrecy and fieldwork (Newbury Park: Sage, 1993), ch. 6.
29 R. S. Zaharna, 'Understanding cultural preferences of Arab communication patterns,' *Public Relations Review* vol. 21 no. 3 (1995), pp. 241–255.
30 The List: The World's Top Social Networking Sites, *Foreign Policy* (2008), available at < http://www.foreignpolicy.com/ > , accessed 12 April 2008.
31 Geertz, *The Interpretation of Cultures*, p. 7.

32 Adler and Adler, 'Observational Techniques', p. 380.
33 Emerson and Pollner, 'Constructing Participant/Observation Relation'.
34 Hine, *Virtual Ethnography*.
35 Quoted in Wolcott, *The Art of Fieldwork*, p. 81.
36 Emerson and Pollner, *Constructing Participant/Observation Relations*; Carol Warren, 'Gender and Fieldwork Relations', In Robert Emerson (ed.), *Contemporary field research: perspectives and formulations* (Prospect Heights, IL: Waveland Press, 2001). pp. 208–223.
37 Emerson, *Contemporary field research: perspectives and formulations*, p. 116.
38 Paul Atkinson, Amanda Coffey and Sara Delamont, *Key Themes in Qualitative Research* (Walnut Creek, CA: AltaMira Press, 2003), p. 41.
39 Shehata, *Ethnography*, p. 258.
40 Warren, 'Gender and Fieldwork Relations'; Shehata, *Ethnography*.
41 Warren, '*Gender and Fieldwork Relations*', p. 215.
42 I was referred to several times as half-Arab by my informants, which signalled acceptance and inclusion.
43 Gary Weaver, *Culture, Communication and Conflict: Readings in Intercultural Relations* (Boston: Pearson, 2000); Edward Hall, *Beyond culture* (New York: Anchor Books, 1989). Fandy, 'Information technology, trust, and social change in the Arab world'.
44 Atkinson, Coffey and Delamont, *Key Themes in Qualitative Research*, p. 100.
45 Clifford Geertz, *Deep Play: Notes on a Balinese Cockfight* (Berkeley: University of California Press, 1979), p. 85.
46 The Qana massacre refers to the July 30, 2006 attack by Israel on a village in Lebanon that killed 28 people, more than half of whom were children.
47 www.twitter.com is a microblog that allows users to send short, instant messages online and/or through mobile phones. These messages are then relayed to anyone who has signed up to follow that user via SMS.

8 'That is not what we authorised you to do ... ': Access and government interference in highly politicised research environments

Susan M. Thomson

The purpose of this chapter is to provide an overview of the strategies used to gain access to potential respondents and to deal with government interference in my research project in Rwanda from April to October 2006. I had planned to spend one year in the field (April 2006 to April 2007) but the government of Rwanda revoked my letter of permission in September 2006. I spent a month with government officials, learning the 'true version' of how 'things really are in Rwanda' rather than 'wasting' my time talking to 'peasants' and 'unimportant people' who 'are all liars anyway'.[1] The Rwandan government took my passport, with a promise to return it once I had been 're-educated' about its initiatives to promote national unity and reconciliation in the wake of the 1994 genocide. Long before this official government interference, I had already traversed the uneven terrain of entering Rwanda, identifying two local partner agencies to sponsor the research, and had successfully gained access to the 'terribly closed' rural world of ordinary, peasant Rwandans.[2]

My research was based in Southern Rwanda as it is home to the largest pre-genocide Tutsi population, and remains demographically similar since the genocide.[3] It is also home to a cross-section of individuals from each of Rwanda's three ethnic groups – Hutu, Tutsi and Twa. Few in Southern Rwanda had any direct experience of the mass killings of Tutsi prior to the 1994 genocide, making it an ideal site to consider government claims of historical unity as friends, family and neighbours had lived relatively peaceful until late April 1994 when the genocide started.[4] Hutu and Tutsi living in the South also worked together to resist the genocide in its early days, but were eventually overcome by the well-oiled genocidal machine of the previous government.[5] I also had prior knowledge of the region, when I lived in Butare town (now Huye) while employed with the United Nations (1997–98) and the United States Agency for International Development (1998–2001). Having lived in Rwanda for almost five years, I felt compelled to embark on research which could contribute to an understanding of how ordinary Rwandans made sense of the political and social processes of the post-genocide Rwandan state. The purpose was to allow ordinary Rwandans to express themselves as individuals, in their own words, as they seek to re-establish livelihoods, re-constitute social and economic networks, and reconcile with neighbours, friends and, in some cases, family since the 1994 genocide.[6]

The first goal of this chapter is to provide an overview of the demands, difficulties and tactics used to gain access to highly politicized research sites such as post-genocide Rwanda. Thinking about issues of access at the design stage is essential as *how* you carry out your research, *whom* you talk to, and *what* you talk about can help you navigate intensely political environments where research is unlikely to be viewed by local actors as neutral, or altruistic. With knowledge of and continued sensitivity to local realities, researchers can mitigate the difficulties of identifying a representative sample and better assess the often biased or self-interested evidence compiled during fieldwork. I instantiate the importance of continued awareness of local realities in two concrete examples, one with a respondent and one with government, in the last part of the chapter.

My research took place within a context of discreet government surveillance as well as chronic violence and extreme human duress,[7] which further limited my ability to gain access to the social spaces and enter the private locations where ordinary Rwandans live. It also involved extensive interviewing with a respondent pool that was difficult to access as few are willing to talk openly about their experiences during the 1994 genocide. Exacerbating access to potential respondents is the prevalence of emotional trauma among Rwandans – Hutu, Tutsi and Twa – who survived the genocide.[8] My research also involved obtaining permission from the Rwandan government, and the need to identify and work with government-approved local partners.

The second purpose of the chapter is to explore government interference in the research process. Interference can take a variety of forms from the obvious milling about of a government official during an interview, to questioning and/or intimidating the respondent after the researcher has left about the content of the interview, to more direct obstacles, like failing to produce promised permissions documents, or openly misleading the researcher. In my case, the interference was subtle as a number of actors worked on behalf of the government to make sure I would 'write about only what I saw'. That the post-genocide government of Rwanda sought to obstruct my research did not surprise me, since it skilfully practices information management in eliminating virtually every form of dissent.[9] I first discuss the tactics of interference that I identified towards the end of my fieldwork. I then explain the techniques employed to safeguard the identity of respondents, while assuring my safety as well as that of my research assistants in ways that protected the integrity of the research. I also consider the possible impact of government interference on my research findings, and suggest ways to deal with the possibility of interference when designing and implementing your research project.

Research procedures

Permission to enter 'the field'

Thinking about entering 'the field' requires some preliminary preparations before the researcher makes her descent. In addition to booking one's travel, procuring the necessary visas and vaccinations, and ensuring a secure place to stay upon arrival, there are a number of preliminary steps to think through, notably delimiting the field-site, establishing organizational ties and identifying potential respondents. Even projects grounded in participant observation as the primary method are buoyed by interviews and genealogical research that requires forethought and planning. How research is to be carried out, who will participate and how the material gained will be safeguarded and used are thought through for academics during the ethics process, and fine-tuned during fieldwork. Practitioners or development workers who undertake research as part of their job description may have a different set of constraints; for example, purpose-driven research for donors to assure continued funding of existing projects rather than the problem-driven research that academics tend to undertake. They are more likely to already have local partners in place, as their employment with an international organization or development agency explains their their presence in the country. Regardless of the purpose of one's research, the support of the host government is often required, which makes knowledge, of what kind of research the government is willing to support, important and is best taken into account at the design stage.

In post-genocide Rwanda, as in many other countries in Africa, academics require permission from the highest level of government for three reasons. One, to allow governments to ensure that the research is appropriate to their development or peacebuilding agenda; two, as a way for the government to register and keep track of foreign researchers; and three, to provide a letter of introduction to government officials and local partner organizations who work with the researcher on a more regular basis during the period of fieldwork. My project required permission from the Ministry of Local Government (MINALOC), who authorized interview topics and informed local government officials that I had its permission to be in rural areas to talk to ordinary Rwandans. The research also included interviews and participant observation in several of Rwanda's prisons; speaking to prisoners required an additional letter of permission, addressed to the director of each prison I visited, from the Ministry of Internal Security (MININTER).

Before the government would even consider my request for a research permit, I first needed to identify a local partner who would 'sponsor' my research. I knew that my choice of partner would impact who I could I talk to and how. For this reason, I decided to pursue partnerships with two local partners,[10] one who I knew had close ties to government (partner A) while my other partner (partner B) had more autonomy and was even critical of government policy on occasion. I nurtured the relationships with both local partner organizations about 18 months prior to entering the field. We worked largely by e-mail. One of my partner organizations only had three computers for a staff of 27, meaning that most of our correspondence was by post with the occasional telephone call. Rwanda has reliable postal and telecommunications networks and this was never a hindrance. Both partner organizations have websites and before contacting them by e-mail to request that they sponsor my research, I researched their respective mandates, programmes and activities, target audience and beneficiaries. I also met with representatives of each organization in the diaspora and tried to learn as much as I could before approaching them. This knowledge was valuable as we negotiated the nature and scope of our partnership. In my initial letter to each organization requesting that I be taken on as a partner, I was able to show where my research dovetailed with their activities. My requests to partner with each organization were approved in late 2005.

My research about the life stories of ordinary Rwandans before, during and after the genocide was broadly in line with the type of research that the Rwandan government wanted to support. It took about a week to get the letter of permission from MINALOC, and the process required several face-to-face meetings with the personal assistant of the minister. The process was quick, with four to six weeks being the average length of time for the government to grant its permission. I attribute this to pre-fieldwork preparations, notably the choice to partner with a local organization that worked with foreign researchers on a regular basis. What I did not realize at the time was that my primary local partner, partner A, was charged with reporting back to the assistant to the minister at MINALOC about whom I spoke to in the field, and what we spoke about.

Surveillance appeared early in my relationship with partner A. Meetings with eight senior members of government, including two ministers and three senators, were 'necessary' before I could get to apply for a research permit from MINALOC. During these meetings, I presented each official with a list of interview topics, my *curriculum vitae* to show my ability to carry out the project, and a one-page overview of the research and its expected outcomes. The one-page overview included a paragraph on my chosen research partners and the nature of our relationship to show how we would work together and how each party would benefit from the partnership. Each meeting ended with the official waxing poetic on the success of the government in restoring peace and security since the genocide. I was reminded by everyone to keep regular contact with partner A, and not to believe everything people told me. Most interesting was the consistency of the message; there was virtually no variation in what each official told me. Even more interesting was the very different versions of the truth that arose as ordinary Rwandans were most willing (given the right introduction and conditions) to talk to me about their lives before, during and after the genocide. In highly politicized research environment, it is important to recognize the government's version of events, as well as the narratives of other actors, and to understand how each version of the truth may impact fieldwork, notably accessing possible respondents and then interpreting the information they share with you. Knowledge of the government's consensus version about life in post-genocide Rwanda proved helpful during interviews as I began to recognize it when I heard it and was able to modify my interview technique accordingly, and in some cases abandon the interview altogether if it was yielding biased or partisan information.

During the first month of fieldwork it became apparent that my partner A contact was 'checking in' on me as he repeatedly suggested I not believe everything I heard from ordinary Rwandans, and asked numerous questions about how things were going with my conversations with 'unimportant people'. At first, I perceived this as small talk but eventually came to appreciate the role of his organization, as well as my own role, in Rwanda's information economy. Research involves making choices about which voices are heard and whose knowledge counts. The government was not necessarily interested in the life stories of all Rwandans; it was only keen on those voices that supported its vision. My contact at partner A understood this and I soon did as well, engaging in a cat-and-mouse game of trying to gauge what he wanted to hear during my reporting sessions, with what I was willing to tell them about what I was learning from my interviews with so many 'unimportant' Rwandans. My strategy was to tell him as little as possible, and to ask my respondents about the best ways to avoid having others – be it neighbours, government officials or civil society representatives like my contact with partner A – observe our conversations together. I did not try to hide the fact that my contact at partner A was asking about who was saying what. Instead, I shared with some of my respondents what partner A wanted from me, and asked them for suggestions on how to avoid telling him what was really being said. This usually resulted in a deepening of the interview relationship, as my respondents were delighted that I seemed to understand the constraints they were under in the daily lives and was willing to discuss how to avoid the glare of 'people who make decisions in Kigali that affect us out here [in rural Rwanda]. Those people in Kigali tell us what to do when they come here. You ask me what I think and I tell you. Then you tell me next time how you took my news to [partner A contact] in Kigali. It is very good'.[11]

Respondent recruitment

None of the 37 individuals who agreed to participate in the research were identified through organizational contacts, although both the government and my local partners recommended that I do so. Instead, I accessed respondents principally through personal networks, ordinary people that I would meet at the market, walking in the hills or on the taxi-bus. I have a basic knowledge of Kinyarwanda, the sole language of more than 90 per cent of Rwandans, and was able to speak about everyday things, such as shopping in the market,

Access and government interference 113

asking about one's family or work, and ordering a drink at a local kiosk. I also kept Kinyarwanda language books with me at all times, both as a learning tool and to show that I was trying my best to speak to ordinary Rwandans in their mother tongue.[12] I tracked potential respondents through their social networks as everyday life in Rwanda, like rural areas in other countries, is not confined to a geographical entity. Much like the footpaths and back roads that link individual homesteads to one another, I choose to follow the linkages between individuals.

In the early days of respondent recruitment and before agreeing to any formal interviews, I spoke informally with many ordinary Rwandans about their lives before, during and after the genocide. As the individual spoke, I made, with permission, notes about the individuals she referred to. Individuals spoke of family, friends, neighbours as well as their interactions with government officials before and after the genocide. Some of the relationships were positive, others negative. Regardless of the nature or quality of the relationship, I tried to follow up with each of the named individuals. This approach provided 167 names. I was able to contact 95 individuals of whom 37 agreed to participate. Many of my respondents said that they agreed to participate in my research because I did not access them through organizational contacts and made an effort to meet them in the places 'where they live' or 'in the fields where they work' (interviews, 2006).

My contact at partner A provided a list of names of people I was supposed to interview. I still did not know at the time that my contact within my partner organization was reporting back to MINALOC about the progression of my research. As time passed, he became more interventionist in bringing members of his organization to my residence to interview, usually in his presence, demanding to see my research notes, and offering to 'verify' the narratives of people he did not send to me as 'all Rwandans are liars'. After some wrangling, in which I repeatedly refused to share even the names of my respondents, let alone the content of our discussions, we agreed that I would inform him of my interview schedule. My strategy was to share with him the date of select interviews, but never the time. I then organized to meet respondents very early in the morning, from 4am in some cases, in the rural areas where they lived. Respondents were willing to speak with me early in the morning. City-folk, such as my partner A contact or local government officials, did not keep 'country-hours' and I never saw any officials during the dawn hours, a point that was not lost on any of my respondents as they spoke freely with me, pleased with the opportunity to speak to an outsider. The words of one respondent are emblematic: 'It is good for me to talk to an outsider like you because I can't share my stories with people around here'.[13]

Another sign of interference was the repeated requests from partner A for a summary of what was being said by whom; as he became more forceful in requesting the information, I was glad that several safeguards to maintain the confidentiality of interview material were in place. Pre-fieldwork preparation proved invaluable once again as I had already instituted a system of not recording the names of respondents anywhere in my fieldnotes and of using a fresh notebook for each meeting, lest I lose the notes, or a local official ask to see them. Where a name might appear in an audio recording, I blanked out that section of the tape before transcription by a member of the research assistance team.[14] I also blanked out any information that could be used to identify a particular respondent, such as the names of relatives or friends, or associational memberships. These safeguards were taken to protect the anonymity of respondents in case the government wanted to see the interview notes, and also to ensure their confidence as part the trust-based relationship I shared with respondents. Meticulously following these safeguards meant that any backlash during the research process, or as a result of any publications that ensued from the research, would ensure that Rwandan government officials would be unable to locate individual respondents.

I eventually learned that partner A was concerned that respondents were making negative comments about the government, and could bring sanction against his organization. He was, after all, accountable to government for my actions. Once this concern became apparent, I interviewed the individuals he brought to my doorstep, treating them as a collective voice about the power dynamics between the government and civil society, but also between civil society organizations and their membership.[15] The circumscribed autonomy of partner A, and the way in which it impacted the research, provide important insights on the surveillance of foreign research projects and local power dynamics within civil society organizations in particular and the community level more generally. It also provided increased rapport with some respondents in the shared experience of dealing with local elites became a bonding one. For example, the rapport I shared with ordinary Rwandans, as well as the density of social networks in Rwanda, was confirmed when I met one of my respondents during a trip to the market. His sister's cousin was one of the individuals brought to my home by my partner A contact. She said that members of the organization in a community where some of my respondents live were told by my contact what they could and could not say during the interview. If the individual spoke on themes other than those 'authorized', the privileges of membership would be revoked, including loss of access to health care and support for school fees.

Gaining access

Access to respondents

I knew from my previous period of residence that it would not be easy to gain access to the personal lives of people who had their lives torn asunder by genocide. To facilitate access and to demonstrate my seriousness, I lived, as much as a white foreigner could, as ordinary Rwandans lived. I walked everywhere, and only took public transportation when I had to go any extended distance (I managed distances of less than 10 kilometres on foot; my translator for the day would often meet me at the agreed site rather than walk). This gave me a certain cachet as it became evident to many people that I was ready and willing to travel considerable distances to see them. Some of the most revealing conversations were in the hills surrounding the valley where I lived, where I walked every evening and met a broad cross-section of ordinary Rwandans, some of whom were participating in the life history aspect of the research. When I bumped into participants outside the formal interview setting, I did not say hello unless they greeted me first. This was out of respect for their privacy as questions about how and why we knew each other could have arisen.

I anticipated that Rwandans would speak their minds when they felt secure and comfortable. And speak they did; the life history approach resulted in 348 hours of raw interview material, with an average of 9.4 hours per respondent. I was sensitive that some topics would have to go untouched. The approach was to listen empathetically to what individuals deemed important, and not to pry. I never pressed individuals to speak about things they did not want to discuss; I proved my reliability with my awareness of and sensitivity to the fact that there were people, things, and places I did not seek to know. The close relationships that developed were a reaction to my interest in people's understanding of and feelings about events and changes, in their lives, particularly since the genocide. That I was only interested in what individuals were willing to share and the fact that I had a permission letter from the government minimized personal risk for respondents as my presence in communities was officially sanctioned; respondents who agreed to participate in the research understood its risks and some weighed this against the therapeutic benefits of having a sympathetic outsider to talk to.

In fact, many individuals thought that if I a was researcher, and so interested in their lives as few before had been, then I must by definition be a therapist. Most individuals were aware of the role of therapists since the genocide as the post-genocide government had organized post-traumatic stress counselling units for survivors of the genocide and for individuals who needed emotional support following participation in the *gacaca* grassroots justice courts. 'Therapist' was a role I could not escape, and many individuals asked me during the long walks to and from interview sites if their behaviour was 'normal', or confided to me their troubles and heartaches. This was an added layer of stress for me as I spent most of my days listening to the narratives of individuals who survived the genocide, had been raped, or tortured, or had witnessed killings, or who had killed. While personally difficult as I sometimes took on the pain and suffering that individuals shared with me, the therapist image also meant that the combination of my empathy and respect made me privy to significant and intimate details of people's lives that could have been otherwise unobtainable.

Layers of surveillance, modes of interference: Two examples

Two principal examples from fieldwork illustrate the demands of research in highly politicized environments and highlight the importance of continued sensitivity to local realities. The first example shows how an empathetic act can potentially threaten relationships with respondents and undo hard-earned trust and respect. In the second example, I discuss the experience of having my research permit withdrawn and share the strategies I used to assure my safety as well as that of my respondents.

'What made you think you could touch her?'

A condition of my research permit was the need to pay a visit to the local government official in each administrative centre the first time I visited the community in question. This was the norm, and I gladly paid these courtesy calls to present my letter of permission from the central government. Meeting local officials gave an air of respectability to the research, and respondents understood that I was serious about hearing their life experiences, which was further evidenced by my repeated visits at the agreed upon times at the agreed locations. As fieldwork progressed, and I met and spent time with more people, the importance of understanding alliances in Rwandan social life became more apparent, as the following example shows.

During a courtesy call at the administrative offices of a rural community about 40 kilometres southwest of Butare town, a woman whom I did not know was wailing uncontrollably and was screeching at the end of a long hallway of closed doors. Who or what was upsetting her was unclear. About ten minutes later, I was called in to meet the official I had come to see, and he asked me what was going on with this crying woman. I said I did not know as he ushered me out the door, having approved my request to conduct interviews with some of the residents in his bailiwick. I had expected my courtesy call to take much longer, and so I sat outside on a low wall to wait for one of my translators so we could walk the short distance to the agreed interview meeting place. Shortly after, the wailing woman was unceremonious dumped outside, onto the concrete slab that served as the front entrance of the office block. She eventually stopped crying, laying prostrate and seemingly exhausted from whatever bad news she had just received. She eventually pulled herself together, and I gave her a meek smile as she walked past where I was sitting. There were about 15 Rwandans in attendance. I did not think about this event again, as incidences of heartbreak and sorrow such as the one I had witnessed were relatively commonplace.

The next week, I was back and was leaning on the same wall outside the offices of the local authorities as I waited for my translator to arrive. I was about 15 minutes early and the same woman who had been wailing the week before appeared. The government had organized a wake to symbolically rebury the bodies of those individuals from the area who had died during the

Access and government interference 117

1994 genocide. The government had instituted a new policy in early 2006 that local offices were to become the official repositories of the remains of genocide dead, officially as a genocide memorial, but also to control access to the memorials as some tombs were being broken into as people sought to bury even unidentified remains on their own land. The woman was upset because she believed her husband and two of her children were among the bodies to be reburied, and she had spent significant time and energy asking for their bones to be given to her so she could bury them 'properly' on their land. The wake was scheduled to start, and I slipped into the crowd to bear witness. The wailing woman of the previous week was standing two or three people in front of me, and I could see her hunched shoulders and hear her efforts to choke back tears. The ceremony lasted about 20 minutes, and as the crowd dispersed, the woman stood motionless over the new, official burial site. Soon, we were the only two standing before the gravestone. She sighed deeply and I put my arm around her shoulder and gave her a gentle squeeze to say 'sorry for your trouble'. She winced, and I pulled away. We stood silently over the gravesite for another 15 minutes or so. She left and I continued milling about, waiting for my now-late translator to arrive.

When I eventually arrived at the agreed upon interview location, the woman I was scheduled to interview was incensed: How could I have offered my support to her enemy? Didn't I know that her husband had been killed by the husband of that Hutu woman I touched? Didn't I know that the woman was making trouble at the offices of the local authorities? She thought I knew Rwandans better than that! I did not know much about this woman's life history as we had yet to have our first formal interview. Taken aback by the vehemence of her questioning, I offered to leave. Which raised her ire even more: 'So now my stories are not good enough for your project? I thought you cared about me. Ha, you are just like the authorities. You take what you need and then leave us [not clear who 'us' refers to]. I thought you were different ... '. I further explained that I had offered to leave as a sign of respect for her feelings. I explained that I did not know the woman in question but that I was truly sorry for her loss, just like I was sad and sorry for all that my respondent had suffered during and since the genocide.[16] We sat quietly together, and I held her hands in mine for about 20 minutes. She soon sat up straight, and we looked at each other in silence for a few minutes, and she went on to explain that I had to be more careful about who I spent my time with and to remember that I was an 'important person' (someone with social standing). We talked for a long time, well into the late afternoon, about her perceptions on government policy and how it keeps people apart rather than bringing them together. I was never sure of the nature of our 'alliance' (to use her word) after this, but I certainly understood that something important had happened as it became clear that this respondent expected me to defend her interests; she saw me as her ally, and in treating other Rwandans in what I perceived to be a similar situation in the same way, was revealing to me. In entering the private spaces of my respondents, I was not only revealing the obvious inequalities between researcher and researched, but also began to open the door on the arbitrariness that constrained the lives of both women, my respondent and the stranger. Even a compassionate touch of the 'wrong' individual could bring unexpected negative consequences although in this case the incident resulted in a stronger relationship with this particular respondent. I never saw the woman that I met at the local office again although I did think of her whenever I saw a grave site, a regular occurrence in post-genocide Rwanda.

'We don't need that kind of research'

Part of my research design was to interview prisoners accused of genocide. I received the appropriate permissions from MININTER and began interviewing prisoners in early August 2006. My prior work with the UN also played a role here; I knew that the Director of Prisons for the local prison I was visiting would ask the head of prisoners (male and female) to identify individuals for me to interview. There was no question of informed consent in the prisons because of the power relationship between the prison administration and the prisoners themselves. I was supposed to submit a list of names of individuals that I wanted to interview. Instead, I asked for six individuals, three women and three men, who had confessed to their crimes and had already gone through the *gacaca* traditional justice process, as well and six individuals who had not confessed their crimes and were awaiting trial. As expected, the head of prisoners were brought to me and they identified several individuals who were willing to speak to me.[17] About three weeks into the process of meeting unnamed prisoners, the Director called me into his office to ask for a list of the names of the individuals who had 'agreed' to speak to me. I did not record anything except the necessary demographic details for each participant as a safety precaution; the focus was on recording the narrative. I suspect that the Director knew the names of each prisoner, but his insistence and my inability to share the names resulted in a summons from the Ministry of Local Government asking me to come to Kigali (the capital city) 'to discuss my research project'.

I sat outside the office of the individual who requested to see me for three days before I was called in to explain what I was doing interviewing 'Hutus about their experiences of genocide. We know what they did, and we don't need that kind of research'. I showed my research permit to the assistant of the minister, as well as the research summary and list of interview topics that supported my application for a research permit to show that I was well within the boundaries of what I was 'allowed' to do. The official suggested at this point that perhaps my research project 'be shut down' as it was clearly against government policy. It eventually emerged that the research looked too favourably among the experiences of prisoners, and that 'what I needed was to stop talking to ordinary people who were filling my head with negative ideas'. The official then told me to stop interviewing and I told them that I would have to undergo 're-education'. My interviews with survivors continued, but all other interviews were stopped. My passport was taken away, with a promise to return it when my 're-education' was complete. The official also gave me a list of government officials in Kigali to see, and assigned a junior government official to escort me to five *ingando* (citizenship re-education) sessions and take me to seven *gacaca* court sessions so that I could observe 'the good work of the government in restoring peace and security' to Rwanda.[18] I was required to check in with this person every night; in turn he informed his superiors of what I was doing and who I was with.

When the government stopped my research, the safety of everyone associated with the research was a grave concern. I never felt that my physical safety was at stake as relations with the government remained cordial, if sterile throughout. I was deeply concerned for the safety of my respondents and my research assistants. I understood that the government considered my research findings to be potentially threatening. For that reason, I submitted to their plan of 're-education', and did exactly as my government handler asked me to do when asked. The process included a requirement of meeting senior members of the government, the Rwandan Patriotic Front (RPF). My handler gave me a list of names and phone numbers of the most senior of party officials from government, civil society and the private sector. I visited each one dutifully, expecting admonishment on every occasion. Usually, and somewhat surprising to me, very few of them knew why I was visiting and we often just chatted for a few minutes about my research. Some had heard of my 'situation' and were uninterested in receiving me. Others spoke for more than an hour about the accomplishments and achievements of the RPF in stopping the genocide and restoring peace and security 'to all of Rwanda'.

During these visits in Kigali, I was also able to visit the Canadian Embassy and request a new passport. That process took about four weeks, and I snuck out of Rwanda early one Sunday morning in October 2006. I took the bus from Butare to Kigali late Saturday afternoon, bought my ticket to Nairobi with cash, checked in at a five-star hotel under an assumed name, hopped in a taxi at 4.30am and checked in at the airport. I timed my departure to correspond with Rwanda's Patriotism Day celebrations, which I knew would be heavily attended by members of the security forces. I also thought I could leave once I got my passport, as the government knew I was stranded until they returned the document to me. There were no police checks from town to the airport, and the airport was on a skeleton staff, which did little to calm me until the aircraft successfully left Rwandan airspace.

Surveillance and interference: Some reflections

My research, as evidenced by the two examples presented above, experienced both surveillance and interference from ordinary people and government officials alike. While embarrassed by my female respondent for not understanding the politically sensitive nature of alliances and status in a rural community, I learned an important lesson about empathetic listening. Had I left the home of my respondent when I first felt the need to go, that could have negatively impacted on the outcome of my research. My hasty departure may have closed off access to the private lives of some of my respondents in a particular community. The main concern was not that I touched the wailing/mourning woman, but that I was insensitive to what it meant for my respondent. If I am offering support to her perceived enemy, then I had better offer at least that and more to her. Her reaction was more than traumatic, it was also evidence of the weak political and social position of Tutsi widows of the genocide. Fortunately, I was able to learn from this experience, and while the respondents' emotional safety (and perhaps mine) was at risk, there was never a concern of lasting enmity. This is an important consideration in polarized research settings and affirms the need to think about who you will interview and how at the research design stage while allowing for enough flexibility to adapt the research to suit local constraints. Another lesson is to engage tense situations with respondents and to prepare yourself to deal with such situations. Individuals who have lived through violence can exhibit strong reactions to seemingly compassionate acts in unexpected ways. Intense interviews on sensitive topics are gruelling for respondent and researcher alike and while it is necessary to accommodate the preferences of respondents, it is also important to protect yourself. I did this by trying to interview only in the mornings so that I could spend the afternoon recuperating if necessary.

The experience of having my research cut short impacted the research in a number of positive ways. First, in offering to 're-educate' me, the government actually availed a frontline look at the tactics and techniques it uses to control Rwanda's political and social landscape. Initial feelings of fear, both for my physical safety and that of my respondents, soon subsided to a sense of privilege of being able to spend so much time in the company of Rwandan élites. Since my research was grounded in the voices of ordinary Rwandans, I quickly recognized the sweeping generalizations and over simplifications of Rwandan history that the government relied upon to legitimize its rule, which allowed me to further contextualize and situate the narratives of my respondents. The government's attempt to influence my thinking on its reconstruction and reconciliation successes since the 1994 genocide was equally revealing as I was able to see first hand how the government organizes the flow of information, and determines what counts as the 'truth' in post-genocide Rwanda. Talking to Rwandan élites was not part of my research design, but listening to them speak positively influenced my research in the end. Government interference and surveillance is likely in intensely political research sites such as post-genocide Rwanda and it is important to listen to as many possible view points from a broad cross-section of actors. Indeed, awareness of multiple view points is helpful in understanding and interpreting the individual 'truths' that people share with you, as is the ability to compare and contrast these alternate versions with the dominant version of the truth.

The insights and knowledge gained during my 're-education' also provided a source of solidarity between some of my respondents and me. The embedded nature of the life history interview method meant that I had spent considerable time over several months getting to know people, listening to life stories and sharing everyday experiences with them, and word spread quickly that I was no longer allowed to work. None of my respondents were surprised with the news, most of whom would pass by my residence to pay a visit, as is the custom in Rwanda. This surprised me as I had expected respondents to keep their distance, given my precarious situation. More than half of my respondents visited me at home, and several sent their hellos. I was heartened by the continued interest of many respondents in the research despite the obvious interference of the government.

The many steps I had taken during the design phase of my research and the modifications I made early on in my fieldwork to assure that each of my respondents understood the purpose of the research, and its attendant risks, before agreeing to participate paid off when my work was halted. Several respondents shared with me that they were proud to be part of a project that the government recognized as critical of its policies. This spoke to individual convictions for the research, and verified that the consent they had accorded at the outset of the research was still valid. This was an important lesson as it raised questions about the validity of informed consent over an extended period of time in politically volatile environments. Had my respondents reacted differently to the news that the government was stopping my research, I could have confronted a situation where the majority, if not all, of my respondents withdrew their consent in the final days of the project.

Conclusion

This chapter has shown that research in highly politicized research environments is both necessary and possible with forethought and planning that takes into consideration local realities from a variety of perspectives. A sense of humility is a useful starting point as is maintaining a sense of flexibility in adapting to field conditions. Equally important is the need to identify how the local information economy operates as this directly impacts access to both the field site and to possible respondents. Maintaining good working relationships with actors on all sides of the political divide is also important. The strategies I employed during fieldwork, notably my efforts to gain the trust and protect the safety of my respondents were thought out prior to entering the field and tweaked to local conditions during fieldwork. The primary lesson of the chapter is that research in highly politicized environments must be grounded in a nuanced understanding of local conditions, and in awareness of whom to talk to, how to speak with them and on what topics.

Notes

1. Fieldnotes, Rwanda 2006.
2. Danielle de Lame, *A Hill Among a Thousand: Transformations and Ruptures in Rural Rwanda* (Helen Arnold, trans. Madison: University of Wisconsin Press, 2005), p. 14.
3. Alison DesForges, *Leave None to Tell the Story: Genocide in Rwanda* (New York: Human Rights Watch, 1999), pp. 432, 489, 592.
4. The genocide started in Kigali, the capital city, on the night of 6 April 1994. The killing started in Southern Rwanda almost two weeks later, around 21 April 1994. See DesForges, *Leave None to Tell the Story*, pp. 438–439. For analysis of how the genocide unfolded across the country and its local dynamics, see Scott Straus, *The Order of Genocide: Race, Power, and War in Rwanda* (Ithaca: Cornell University Press, 2006), pp. 65–94.
5. DesForges, *Leave None to Tell the Story*, pp. 494–499.
6. Research on the politics of ordinary, peasant people is the exception rather than the rule in Rwanda. See David Newbury and Catharine Newbury, 'Review Essay: Bringing the Peasants Back In: Agrarian Themes in the Construction and Corrosion of Statist Historiography in Rwanda', *American Historical Review*, vol. 105 (2000), pp. 832–878.
7. On government surveillance and the broader political context and related human suffering, see, for example, Jennie E. Burnet, *Genocide Lives in Us: Amplified Silence and the Politics of Memory in Rwanda* (University of North Carolina at Chapel Hill, Department of Anthropology, unpublished doctoral dissertation, 2005), particularly pp. 205–260; de Lame, *A Hill Among a Thousand*, particularly chapter 1; Human Rights Watch, *Uprooting the Rural Poor in Rwanda* (London: Human Rights Watch, 2001); International Crisis Group, *Rwanda at the End of the Transition: A Necessary Political Liberalisation?* (Nairobi: ICG, 2002). The reports of Human Rights Watch (www.hrw.org) and the UN's Integrated Regional Information Network (www.irinnews.org) are also useful.
8. Ndayambajwe found that 95 per cent of his sample exhibited symptoms of trauma or post-traumatic stress. See Jean Damascène Ndayambajwe, *Le Génocide au Rwanda: Un analyse psychologique* (Butare: Université Nationale du Rwanda/ Centre Universitaire de Santé Mentale, 2001), pp. 17–24. The psychosocial unit of AVEGA, the main organization working with women survivors of the genocide, estimates that 78 per cent of their beneficiaries show symptoms of trauma (Author's interviews, Rwanda 2006).
9. Johan Pottier, *Re-Imagining Rwanda: Conflict, Survival and Disinformation in the late 20th Century* (Cambridge: Cambridge University Press, 2002), particularly pp. 9–52 and 109–129; and Filip Reyntjens, 'Rwanda, Ten Years On: From Genocide to Dictatorship,' *African Affairs* vol. 103 (2004), pp. 177–210.
10. I do not identify my local partner organizations by name for fear of creating problems for my research respondents, my research assistants or representatives of the organizations.
11. Author's interview, Rwanda 2006.
12. Christian M. Overdulve, *Apprendre la langue rwandaise* (The Hague and Paris: Mouton, 1975); Eugène Shimamungu, *Le Kinyarwanda: Initiation à une langue bantu* (Paris: L'Harmattan, 1998).
13. Author's interview, Rwanda 2006.
14. I relied on the assistance of four translators/transcribers, all of whom were unknown to each other. As an additional safeguard, each member of the assistance team signed a written contract attesting that they would do their utmost to safeguard the narratives of each individual whose voice they were translating.

15 Civil society in Rwanda has been co-opted by government, and its mandate is broadly to implement the government's development agenda. See, for example, Chris Maina and Edith Kibalama (eds), *Civil Society and the Struggle for a Better Rwanda. A Report of the Fact-finding Mission to Rwanda organised under the auspices of Kituo Cha Katiba* (Kampala: Fountain Publishers, 2006).
16 At this point, I dispatched my translator to bring a phone card so that the respondent could call a trauma counselor if the respondent wanted to do so. She was exhibiting the tension and anxiety of a person in the midst of a traumatic episode. I had organized with partner B to give a list of names and phone numbers to persons who had their trauma triggered as a result of our conversations.
17 The life history interview allowed prisoners to speak in their own voice about the conditions of their detention. The information gathered was qualitatively different than that gathered outside as the interview setting was more sterile, and was certainly surveilled as we sat in a dark corner in the room outside the Director's office.
18 Fieldnotes, Rwanda 2006.

Part 3
Veracity

9 Researching repellent groups: Some methodological considerations on how to represent militants, radicals, and other belligerents

Carolyn Gallaher

Introduction

In the summer of 1996 I settled on a dissertation topic – the militia movement in the US. I did so with equal parts excitement and fear. I was excited because I felt I could make a mark with my study. At the time, most studies of social movements were focused on left-oriented, progressive movements. My study could contribute to the then small, but burgeoning scholarship on right wing movements.[1] I also came to my project with some trepidation. In 1995 the movement's most infamous adherent, Timothy McVeigh, had parked a rental truck packed with a ton of explosives in front of the Murrah Federal Building in Oklahoma City, Oklahoma. The bomb blast ripped the face off the building, killing 169 persons inside. Like others in the movement, McVeigh believed a 'new world order', spearheaded by the United Nations (UN), and assisted by Jewish 'sympathizers' in the US government, was emerging. It was, they argued, poised to install a one-world, communist government. Militias saw themselves as the last line of defence against the new world order, and many believed a war against the federal government was imminent. As I was in the process of discovering, the movement's ideas were a repellent mix of anti-Semitic conspiracy theories[2] and apocalyptic thinking.[3]

As a case study for my dissertation I chose the Kentucky State Militia (KSM). At the time, the group was growing in strength and influence. Indeed, by 2001, the Anti-Defamation League (ADL) had labelled KSM 'the strongest active militia in the US' (Anti Defamation League 2001). KSM was also accessible because it operated 'above ground'. The group hosted monthly public forums – 'Citizens for a Constitutional Kentucky' (CCK) – where leaders recruited new members and educated local people on the militia's world view. Group leaders also worked with sympathetic lawmakers in the Kentucky General Assembly to forward pro-gun legislation and block bills it found problematic.[4]

The goal of my research was to understand the role of race and class in the movement's politics. To do so I adopted a methodology based on participant observation at CCK meetings and selected interviews with militia leaders and those of affiliate groups. Like most graduate students doing fieldwork, I encountered my fair share of problems. I made clumsy attempts to secure interviews. Sometimes I asked questions in a convoluted manner. In one interview the batteries in my tape recorder died with no backups on hand. I also had trouble organizing field notes of the CCK meetings I attended. I arranged some entries thematically and others temporally. These were problems to be sure, but I felt somewhat prepared to deal with them because they had been addressed in my methodology courses or in conversations with fellow graduate students returning from the field.

As I conducted my research, however, I also encountered problems for which my training did not prepare me. These problems were specifically related to the repellent nature of my informants. Perhaps my biggest problem was dealing with the emotions my research unleashed in me. Before starting my project, I had assumed I could keep an emotional distance from the hateful, conspiratorial things I would hear. I was surprised, however, by the intensity of my reactions. Sometimes I felt angry and wanted to tell my informants just how wrong I thought they were. Other times I felt queasy and anxious. I wanted to leave a meeting even though I knew I was getting 'good' data.

I also felt guilty about how I dealt with my emotions. To get the data I needed I learned to hold my tongue and to keep my emotions in check during interviews. When someone said something particularly galling, for example, I usually scribbled something in my notebook to avoid making eye contact. The how-to manuals I consulted suggested that arguing with informants or reacting judgmentally to their views would put them on the defensive. An informant on the defence is more likely to stop an interview, or to dig his heels in and defend a position on ideological grounds rather than present the nuances of his views. While my strategy ensured successful data collection, I also worried it signalled a tacit approval on my part. I felt like I was being dishonest to my informants, and as a result, to myself.

I was also unprepared to deal with the fact that my informants might want to use my university connections for their own purposes. During the middle of my research project a militia member asked me to appear on a public access TV show produced by a militia member. I believe I was asked to participate in order to provide a veneer of legitimacy to the show; my connection to the university brought with it a sense of respectability. The request also suggested my worries about sending signals of approval might not be unfounded.

In retrospect, I came to see the situation in which I found myself as an ethical grey area. My methodological training prepared me for the standard problems of fieldwork, but I felt unprepared for the ethical and emotional nuances of doing fieldwork with groups like these. In this chapter I propose some ethical guidelines for dealing with groups I label here as repellent.[5] In doing so it is not my intention to reject or even replace existing guidelines on research ethics but to augment them for people doing research on difficult groups. I begin the chapter with a short definition of what I mean by the term repellent. I then review two common models for research ethics – the 'institutional' and the 'critical' – and point to gaps in these guidelines as they pertain to research of repellent groups. In the second half of the chapter I outline an ethical strategy for the study of repellent populations and discuss the strategy with reference to my dissertation research on the militia movement in the US and to a lesser extent on my recent work on Loyalist paramilitaries in Northern Ireland.[6]

Defining repellent populations

The term repellant is sufficiently broad to include behaviours that run the gamut from the merely annoying to the truly despicable. It is also a relative term. I may intensely dislike someone a colleague holds in high regard. Here, however, I use the term repellent – causing distaste or aversion – not to refer to perks of personality and preferences thereof but to an ideology that promotes dominating other groups in society. These sorts of ideologies may be found across the political spectrum. Under this rubric, warlords, guerrillas, paramilitaries, and even some states could be classified as repellant. These groups must, of course, be sufficiently large and organized to present a coherent discourse and back it up with action. While my definition here suggests that violence is part and parcel of the domination process, it need not be. That is, the repellent category also includes groups who provide the vocal and written justification for their quest of domination over other groups in society, even though they leave the actual violence to others.

Although this definition is neither scientific, nor particularly rigid, my purpose here is not to delineate the boundaries of the category so much as it is to assist researchers who find themselves in situations like the one I describe above. Indeed, some flexibility for perspective is necessary. When I embarked on a 2002 study of the Ulster Volunteer Force (UVF), a Loyalist paramilitary in Northern Ireland, for example, most people regarded it as being on the repellent side of the conflict. The Irish Republican Army (IRA), the UVF's main counterpart, had a substantial international backing, and IRA men were routinely labelled with romantic terms such as 'freedom fighter'. Loyalists, by contrast, were more typically described as 'criminals' and 'thugs'.[7] However, I also realized that if a Protestant student from Northern Ireland wanted to do a study of the Republican side of the conflict, they would likely view the IRA as repellant. And, they would probably face many of the same conflicted emotions I did. My goal, then, is not to concretize a definition of repellent but to describe a relational moment in which any researcher could find her or himself.

The evolution of research ethics

The idea that research should be guided by ethical principles took shape in the post World War II period. In this section I discuss two models for ethical behaviour in the research of human subjects. The first is a formal, institutional model established by government mandates and monitored by

Institutional Review Boards (IRBs). IRBs generally govern research conducted at universities, medical centres, and think tanks where research is funded by government agencies. The second is a set of informal guidelines developed out of what Denzin and Lincoln[8] call 'interpretive and critical paradigms'. These paradigms include, but are not limited to Marxism, feminism, queer theory, constructivism, and postcolonial studies.[9] While the particulars of these paradigms vary by discipline, all of them call into question the assumptions underpinning traditional social science research.

The IRB model

For much of the twentieth century, researchers had few guidelines beyond the scientific method to guide their research on human subjects. Most researchers assumed that their studies would be judged by the degree to which their methodology followed the norms of scientific research – i.e. testable hypotheses, 'clean' data, and replicable experiments. Ethics was not a priority for scholars doing research on human subjects. Indeed, a number of egregious cases suggest it played no role at all.

The most infamous example is the medical experimentation conducted in Nazi concentration camps during World War II.[10] Joseph Mengele, the head doctor at Auschwitz, was notorious for doing arbitrary experiments that had little if any scientific value. In one experiment Mengele tried to physically connect a pair of twins, effectively turning them into Siamese twins by interconnecting veins in their hands.[11] In another case, Mengele used an X-Ray machine to see if it could be used to sterilize women. Most of Mengele's victims died. Survivors report being tortured or seeing someone else being tortured.

The notorious Tuskegee Syphilis experiment in the US provides another egregious example of unethical behaviour in human experimentation. In the 1930s the US Public Health Service in Tuskegee, Alabama launched a study of the progression of syphilis in human subjects. At the time, there was no known cure for the disease. The subjects of the study – 400 African-American men – were infected with syphilis without their knowledge or consent and tracked against a control group of 200 healthy African-American men. Most men thought they were receiving free medical services when they agreed to participate in the study. By the 1940s penicillin was discovered as an effective treatment against syphilis but the Tuskegee men were never treated with the medicine.[12]

Even as late as the 1960s ethical violations continued in state-run medical institutions. The Willowbrook State School, an institution on Staten Island, New York for 'mentally defective' children, permitted doctors to conduct an experiment on the effectiveness of gamma globulin in treating hepatitis.[13] The school already had a high incidence rate of hepatitis, but doctors in the study infected healthy children with the disease. The parents of the children in the study consented to their children's participation, but many were not fully informed of the risks involved, including liver damage later in life. Evidence also suggests that some parents thought their children were receiving preventative care against potential hepatitis infection rather than the actual infection.[14]

Ethical lapses were also common in the social sciences. A classic example is Laud Humphreys' study on the 'tearoom trade', a euphemism for men who use public restrooms to have anonymous sex with other men. Humphrey's research design included participant observation at several park restrooms and a survey instrument. He gained access to the tearooms by acting as a 'watchqueen' – alerting men in the bathroom if police were nearby. From his vantage point Humphreys was able to collect data about the social behaviours surrounding the practice, including the use of non-verbal cues to signal a desire for sex and a willingness to participate. Humphreys also collected licence plate information from men using the 'tearooms'. After his participant observation was completed, Humphreys used his licence plate data to obtain addresses of the men using the tearooms. Along with a graduate student Humphreys then conducted a survey of each household along with a control group. When collecting the data Humphreys and his assistant misrepresented themselves as doing a social health survey. Humphrey's dissertation was eventually published as a book[15] and promptly created an ethical firestorm. Critics accused Humphreys of participating in an illegal act by not calling police and suggested he had invaded the privacy of the men in the tearooms by not informing them that he was collecting data on them.[16] He was also accused of causing 'psychological distress' among the men whose homes he visited. Many were married and not living as openly gay men.[17]

Media attention and subsequent public outcry to abuses such as these contributed to attempts to formalize an ethical code of conduct for human subjects research. During the Nuremberg Trials, for example, judges hearing cases against Nazi doctors added a statement to their verdict outlining 'permissible medical experiments'. The ten axioms in the verdict are now known as the Nuremberg Code.[18] Likewise in the US, reaction to abuses at Tuskegee and Willowbrook, among others, sparked a formal response, the 1979 Belmont Report,[19] which remains the definitive guideline for US government-funded research on human subjects.

While the Nuremberg Code dealt specifically with medical ethics, the Belmont Report was written with 'behavioural' research in mind. It has, therefore, become the basis for IRBs overseeing social science research. Belmont highlights three ethical principles that should guide human research – respect for persons, beneficence, and justice. Out of these broad categories several directives are formulated for the implementation phase of research.

The first is *informed consent*. Many of the abuses outlined above were seen as egregious because the subjects of study had limited information about the nature of the studies/experiments in which they were participating. Indeed, some participants were not even aware they were being studied. Informed consent requires that researchers explain the nature of their research to potential subjects and that potential subjects be given the opportunity to provide (or withhold) their consent to participate.

A second principle is *disclosure of risk*. A risk assessment is designed to ensure that participants have complete knowledge of the risks involved before assenting to participate in a study. Willowbrook parents, for example, signed poorly worded consent forms that contained only partial information about the risks their children faced.[20] Likewise, the Tuskegee men had no idea they could eventually die due to their participation in the study. Today, when researchers seek informed consent they must present subjects with a statement outlining all known risks involved in the study. Moreover, before embarking on a project, a researcher must demonstrate that a study's benefits (individual and/or societal) outweigh the risks involved for participants.

A third directive concerns the *protection of vulnerable populations*. Throughout the twentieth century, vulnerable populations were often subjected to experimentation that other groups in society were rarely exposed to. The vulnerable tended to be chosen for experiments not because a given problem affected them more frequently or severely than other groups in society, but because they were easier to access and provided little resistance. Institutionalized persons, for example, were easy to reach because of their confinement. Likewise, for much of the twentieth century, the institutionalized were unable to refuse participation since they were not allowed to make their own decisions (or were incapable of doing so). As a result, the Belmont Report suggests that research samples should only contain vulnerable people if the problem or issue being studied is specific to them.

Critical ethics

Most scholars situate the rise of critical ethics in the early 1980s with the rise of the 'crisis of representation'. The crisis began in Anthropology when Clifford Geertz laid out an interpretive paradigm for his discipline.[21] He called on his peers to build interpretations on *thick descriptions* of the people, rituals, customs, and events that make up a culture. Geertz rejected the idea, however, that an anthropologist could provide a definitive account by doing so. Indeed, the 'natives' anthropologists studied, and perhaps lived among, were actively representing their culture to the anthropologists studying them. As such, the anthropologist could only represent a representation. Geertz argument called into question an important assumption undergirding social science research at the time – that the researcher could uncover *the* truth.[22]

The crisis of representation also led scholars to question the assumption of objectivity in social science research. The role of environmental determinism in early twentieth century geography provides a telling example. Proponents of environmental determinism posited that climate and topography explained variations in human development. Tropical climates and mountainous regions were believed to produce morally inferior, lazy people while temperate climates produced industrious, risk-taking cultures.[23] Disciplinary critics today see the theory as an attempt to justify and legitimize exploitation in the colonies. The theory allowed the discipline to be relevant to imperialist forces in American and European governments.[24]

Feminists, critical race scholars, and queer theorists also called into question the ways in which 'othered' groups were represented in social science research. Feminists noted, for example, that statements about social organization were often based on data collected only on men.[25] Likewise, critical race scholars argued that behaviours common among minority groups were classified as deviant not because of some inherent quality but because they varied from a white norm.[26]

Implicit in all of these findings is a recognition that the research process is woven through with unequal power dynamics. Researchers, as experts, are able to shape how research subjects are presented and as a result policies that address their needs and concerns. Indeed, even if a study follows the strictest IRB protocols, it can still cause damage to research informants by presenting them in stereotypical, uncomplicated ways. Not only can marginalized people internalize negative imagery about themselves, they can also be the victims of poorly thought out policies based on them.

The crisis of representation is much broader and deeper than this brief synopsis suggests. However, some ethical guidelines that follow from these views have gained wide purchase in critical corners of the social sciences. Three are especially widespread. The first concerns truth claims. When researchers reject the idea that there is one truth, then what they can say about an issue is necessarily constrained. The critical approach suggests that results are *partial* and *situated*. Knowledge production occurs in place and time. How one sees the world depends directly on where they see it from, and how they see it given that vantage point. Moreover, how a viewpoint is portrayed is further complicated by the 'noise' a researcher brings to the data. Researchers must account for how their biases affect the collection and analysis of data. In sum, critical ethics rejects the notion of 'value-free inquiry based on a God's-eye view of reality'.[27]

A second ethical guideline to stem from the crisis of representation concerns the practice of *decentering*. Despite claims to objective measurement, traditional social science has often used subjective yardsticks to measure the social world. For much of the twentieth century, for example, academics were white, heterosexual, males. Perhaps not surprisingly, the norms by which they measured deviance were those with which they were most familiar. The critical response to this situation calls for scholars to uncover and ultimately deconstruct the biases at the centre of mainstream discourse. Scholars have tended to do so by illustrating how 'othered' populations live and see the world. In doing so, they represent difference as it is rather than how the dominant groups in society sees it.

A third guideline deals with how to mitigate the affects of the often unequal power relationships that exist in the field between researcher and researched. The starting assumption is that researchers have power over their informants and must therefore seek to neutralize that power differential. At a macro level, researchers should try to break down the wall between researcher and researched so that the research process is collaborative. Some scholars argue for shared ownership of research.[28] Others argue that researchers should share rough drafts or other tentative conclusions with their informants before publication. And, informants should have veto power over representations with which they disagree. Still others argue that instead of approaching a community with an extant research project in mind, researchers should let the community determine what needs to be studied.[29] Some scholars have also pushed to break down the wall between research and advocacy. This approach is called participatory action research.[30]

Ethical gaps

While IRB and critical ethics provide important safeguards, they contain important gaps for those researching repellent populations. I detail specific problems below, but I begin with a broad discussion of the assumption underpinning both models. The specific problems I discuss later in this section are related to these assumptions.

In the IRB model, ethics is defined and operationalized with reference to the rights of those being researched. The goal is to protect the research subject from the researcher. This is a laudable goal, and a necessary one given the history of human experimentation. However, research is not a unidirectional process. It is relational and transactional. Emotions (anger, laughter, ambivalence), expectations (honesty, fairness, a *quid pro quo* arrangement), and things (information, gifts, contacts) can flow both ways, whether properly or not. At present, the IRB model only considers the flow in one direction, from researcher to researched. At one level this makes sense. The IRB cannot govern persons outside of the institutions in which they are housed. However, it can govern how a researcher should act when the flow from research subject to researcher presents an ethical dilemma. In short, ethical guidelines should cover both sides of the research transaction, ensuring that both parties are protected, albeit in different ways.

In the critical model, by contrast, the guiding principle is to unyolk research from the exploitative practices of colonialism, racism, sexism, etc. In this context, research has tended to focus on the exploited. When abusive practices are discussed, it is usually in relation to how the 'other' sees, copes, and resists them. As Denzin and Lincoln[31] explain the rise of critical paradigms in the academy:

> a new generation of graduate students across the human disciplines ... were drawn to qualitative research practices that would let them give a voice to society's underclass (p. 16).

Indeed, over time, critical methods, and the ethics attached to them, have come to be associated almost exclusively with research on (and often in collaboration with) exploited, vulnerable, and otherwise sympathetic groups.

This equation is not, of course, written in stone. It is quite possible for scholars who study repellent groups to take a critical perspective. However, many of the guidelines are inapplicable for the study of repellent groups. In her study of women in the hate movement, for example, Blee notes that feminist methods had little to offer her project:

> The feminist scholarly principle of basing interviews on rapport and empathy is helpful for groups that are 'conducive, whimsical, or at least unthreatening',[32] but it hardly seems appropriate when the groups are hostile or frightening (p. 12).

In the remainder of this section I discuss specific problems that arise from these lacunas. I begin with a discussion of protections for researchers. I then discuss questions of power in the field. I conclude by examining how to handle *quid pro quo* relationships.

Researcher vulnerability

One of the most important contributions of the IRB model of ethics is the inclusion of protections for vulnerable populations. Researchers who want to study vulnerable people today must follow rigorous protocols, often involving layers of bureaucracy. Likewise, scholars who write about traditionally 'othered' groups today are far less likely to assert group uniformity, present aberrant behaviours as those of the whole, or make glib observations.

While these represent important strides in the field of ethics, vulnerability is not exclusive to research subjects. Indeed, there are occasions when the researcher may find herself in a vulnerable position vis-à-vis. a research subject. In her book *Inside Organized Racism: Women in the Hate Movement*, for example, sociologist Kathleen Blee describes trying to arrange a site for an interview with a Neo-Nazi woman.[33] She 'wanted me to be blindfolded and transported to an unknown destination in the back of a truck'. Blee recounts that another potential interviewee 'proposed a meeting in a very remote racist compound to which I would have to be driven by a racist group member' (p. 17). In my own research I was asked by one potential militia informant to prove that I was not an FBI agent. The potential informant was angry and seemed agitated, and I found myself in the unenviable position of trying to prove a negative. In another instance, while I was doing research in Northern Ireland an ex-prisoner stipulated that he would only grant me an interview if I agreed to come to his home. While I had met other informants in their homes, this informant's request made me nervous. Not only did he commit particularly heinous crimes, published accounts suggested he was still active with a Loyalist paramilitary unit in his hometown.

None of these anecdotes are meant to suggest that the tables are turned and that repellent groups have the upper hand in research settings. Rather, as Blee puts it, both parties are 'equally unsafe'.[34] The researcher may feel put into a situation that is neither comfortable, nor entirely safe, while an informant may feel anxiety about meeting outsiders and worry about infiltration by government agents. While IRB and critical ethical models rightly lay out protections for vulnerable peoples, there are no similar guidelines for how researchers should protect themselves.

Levelling power in the field

A related problem with the ethical paradigms discussed above concerns *how* to level the researcher's presumed power over the research subject. The tactics that have evolved to deal with this differential – sharing rough drafts, seeking input on research topics, providing veto power to informants, and so forth – have become commonplace in many social science disciplines. However, if a researcher of a repellent population were to employ these same strategies, he would likely find himself in a political, if not ethical, bind. Most people, for example, would balk at giving a neo-Nazi group the right to veto a researcher's conclusions. Similarly, most would recoil at the idea that a local warlord be allowed to set a researcher's agenda. In my research on the militia movement, for example, I never considered letting my informants set my research agenda for me; I had no interest in examining *prima facie* the conspiracy theories they promoted as key problems. Doing so would have given them credence they did not deserve.

Context helps explain a good deal of the incompatibility here. Critical approaches to ethics emerged out of a sustained period of academic self reflection. Academic complicity in colonialism and imperialism abroad and oppression of minorities at home were a stain on the social sciences. The methodological guidelines critical scholars established were designed to rectify these sins by rejecting not only the assumptions of traditional social science research (i.e. objectivity, neutrality) but many of the methods attached to it as well (i.e. distanced data collection). Indeed, critical work has often been tinged with missionary zeal. Noddings argues, for example, that caring for other humans should form the moral core of research. Collins asserts that a 'visionary pragmatism' should frame feminist research and encourage scholarship that is politically useful for the oppressed. Bell talks about developing a radical black female subjectivity through her work. Christians declares that 'neutrality [in research] is not pluralistic but imperialist'.[35]

This dialogue presents two problems. First, by so closely associating the critical with support of and advocacy for sympathetic populations, research on repellent populations has until recently been all but ignored.[36] Second, by linking the critical with the moral, those who study repellent groups may reasonably ask what a morality of the study of repellent groups would look like. Should a moral approach to the repellent involve trying to change them?

Likewise, what, if anything, should a researcher do to mitigate or minimize a repellent group's vulnerability in an interview? And, what, if anything, does the researcher owe a repellent group as she/he crafts a representation of them?

When research subjects have ulterior motives

Both the IRB and critical models assume that research can be an exploitative process. A researcher takes advantage of knowledge about research subjects (i.e. their race, gender, or disease history) for their own purposes. The annals of human subjects research make such protections welcome additions to the research process.

However, neither model fully addresses how to avoid the opposite scenario – potential exploitation of researchers by research subjects. Though rarely discussed, such interactions occur frequently. Researchers who study poor communities, for example, often find that community leaders expect something in return for granting access to their communities. They may want help setting up a meeting with an NGO or assistance getting development funds. Likewise, people who study refugees often find that refugees are more willing to share their stories if the researcher can provide something in return – help finding a lost relative, assistance getting a better housing assignment, etc. To varying degrees, potential research subjects regard the research process as a *quid pro quo* relationship.

Neither the IRB nor the critical model adequately addresses how researchers should deal with such expectations. Most IRBs require researchers to include a statement in the research consent form indicating whether participation is compensated, and if so how (e.g. with a payment or free medication for the duration of a clinical study). While an important safeguard, monetary or in kind compensation does not capture the full spectrum of things a research subject might want for his or her participation. In many cases potential subjects do not want money; they want intangible things like access to a scholarly community, for example.

For its part, the critical model assumes that such *quid pro quo* relationships are not only acceptable but should be built into the research process. Indeed, the critical response to exploitative research practices of the past is to ensure that contemporary researchers give back. Research should be useful for the groups or communities studied; leaders should be able to marshal a researcher's data to receive grant funding, affect a change in policy, or encourage a new political approach.

For scholars studying repellent groups, neither model offers adequate protection. The IRB model does not, for example, cover the variety of 'free' things a participant might want from a researcher. When I was doing my study on the militia movement, for example, I called the IRB board to ask if it was appropriate for me to participate as an 'interviewer' on a public access television show produced by a militia member. I was worried about my reputation and wanted some guidelines on how to protect it while still maintaining my access to the group. As I discovered when I phoned my university IRB, however, the office only had protocols for protecting my informants. The IRB officer's only concern was whether I would be filming the interviews. He told me I would have to rewrite my consent form and submit it for re-approval if I wanted to film my interviews. When I told the officer I would not be in charge of filming, he responded bureaucratically, telling me that I would not be 'out of compliance' with the IRB if I did the show. While I certainly wanted my study to remain in compliance, I wanted even more for someone to help me sort out the KSM request, and whether it would be a good or bad idea for me to be seen on militia TV.

The critical model of ethics had even less to offer me. Indeed, the assumption that research subjects are sympathetic leads to the belief that such help is warranted. Unfortunately, the sorts of help my informants wanted from me (the respectability attached to my university connection) was not something I wanted to give.

Some starting points for an ethics of researching repellent populations

Approaching dangerous subjects safely

When studying dangerous groups, researchers have to take precautions that peers studying more sympathetic groups do not. The first and most important thing a researcher can do to ensure their safety is to be honest about who they are and what they are doing. As such, researchers of repellent groups should never go 'undercover'.

A number of fascinating studies have been conducted by people going undercover. Fielding, for example, posed as someone interested in joining the National Front, a neo-Nazi group in Britain. Carolyn Ellis studied the Guinea, fisher-folk on the Chesapeake Bay with a distinct dialect, culture, and kinship structure.[37] Although the Guinea were not dangerous, they were suspicious of outsiders, so Ellis told community leaders she was writing a paper on fishing, and taped conversations she had with Guinea people without their knowledge. In between full disclosure and undercover methodologies there are a variety of deceptive or less than honest tactics researchers have used to collect data. Some scholars, for example, don personas in the field. When he conducted a study of police room interrogations, for example, Richard Leo 'played' a conservative tough guy so that the conservative men on the force he was studying would open up to him.[38]

While undercover research is more frowned upon than not, there is no clear consensus that it should be off-limits.[39] Those who oppose undercover research argue that it is against the ethical principle of informed consent. Many also note that going undercover is unnecessary. Even people in hard to infiltrate groups will agree to talk if the researcher can allay his or her fears. And, sometimes such fears are easy enough to allay. Hate groups, for example, worry less about a researcher's political perspective than his or her potential affiliation with a local police force or federal law enforcement agency. Scholars also argue that adopting a persona can distort research results. Informants often react to the personalities in front of them. By adopting a distinct persona rather than neutral persona, a researcher is likely to get a version of what his subject thinks a person with that persona wants to hear.

Those who support undercover research argue that it is the only way to get access to difficult communities. Separatist groups, for example, are virtually impossible to research because members view outsiders as contaminated. Only true believers can be brought into the circle. Others argue that deception is appropriate so long as the benefits of the research outweigh any potential harm to the informants. Some scholars go as far as to suggest that researchers should have evidentiary privilege similar to the privileges held by doctors and lawyers.[40]

In this chapter I side with the view that undercover research is unethical.[41] And, I would add to the arguments discussed above the following justification. In a situation where a researcher is studying a repellent group, a blown cover could lead to violence against the researcher. Not only has trust been broken, but repellent groups often view violence as an acceptable mechanism for dealing with perceived problems. In no situation should a researcher risk his life or health to get the data. Risk to life and limb may be appropriate for law enforcement, but not academia. Indeed, a number of pitfalls may confront an academic in such a situation. By putting oneself undercover, for example, a researcher increases the likelihood that he will witness something illegal. Such information may be off-limits to an ordinary, above ground researcher, and may in fact allow for a more thorough portrait of a group, but having such information also puts a researcher in legal jeopardy.

If I had gone undercover in the KSM, for example, and a member divulged to me that KSM's commander was planning an attack, I would have become a witness to a conspiracy to commit murder. Moreover, having such information does not necessarily mean that I would have been able to use it properly or effectively. Going to the police would be the obvious thing to do in such a situation, but the police would need to investigate my claims before making an arrest, and the process could not only blow my cover, it could proceed too slowly to stop an attack. Going to the police could also present its own dilemmas. Under the same scenario, if KSM was already under police or federal surveillance, it is possible I could have been pressured to assist in the investigation. Saying no to such a request could lead police to view me with suspicion. Saying yes would force me to spy on my informants and put me in breach of IRB ethical codes that prohibit lying to research informants about the uses of data collected.[42]

When a researcher fills out IRB forms they should be required to consider how they will mitigate potential risks to their person in the course of a research project.[43] Many scholars who research dangerous populations do these sorts of inventories on their own. However, requiring a researcher to consider the issue is a useful exercise because it forces a more specific accounting of the measures that will be taken to ensure safety.

Leveling the field

Although power dynamics between researcher and researched are often balanced in research involving repellent populations, researchers still maintain the upper hand in one important area – the power of representation. As 'experts' in university settings, researchers have access to media outlets and public policy circles their informants do not. They can, therefore, shape a group's coverage in these circles more than the group itself can. As such, researchers must consider, albeit in modified ways, how to level this dynamic. Worrying about this may seem unnecessary, even wrong, to some readers. Why, for example, be fair to groups that are patently unfair to other groups in society? However, such an approach is consistent with the role of a social scientist – to explain social dynamics. Policy makers, governments, and law enforcement agencies can only deal with repellent groups effectively if they understand how such groups are organized, see the world, and react to it. Indeed, stereotypes will not help policy makers limit the threat and spread of such groups.

The primary responsibility a researcher in this situation is to ensure that his or her research subjects recognize the portrait painted of them. This does not mean that the researcher cannot analyze, and ultimately proffer judgments on these views. However, it does require a researcher to be fair to a group's self-presentation. Indeed, researchers should mitigate the potential to dismiss their subjects' self-presentation by searching not only for contradictory evidence, but complementary data as well. A researcher will not always find 'exculpatory' evidence, but in searching for it will ensure that such evidence was not overlooked.

When I first began studying the militia movement, for example, I was struck by how frequently my interview subjects would tell me they were not racist.[44] Their self-presentation did not square with the watchdog accounts I had read of the movement.[45] These accounts routinely presented the movement as racist and anti-Semitic. And, I was tempted to write off my informants' comments as mere spin. As I spent more time in the field, however, I found a contradictory set of facts regarding the movement's claims to be non-racist. I discovered, for example, that one of KSM's members was a former Ku Klux Klan (KKK) member. Despite the member's connections to the KKK, the leadership had allowed the man to remain in the organization, and had in fact defended him against critics.[46] I also discovered that the movement's ire at the UN was based on an antipathy for the 'third world' – a term I came to see as code for non-white people. However, I also discovered that the movement's two signature issues while I was in the field had little to do with race. The movement wanted to legalize industrial hemp in the state and also prevent a biosphere designation in a state park in the southern portion of the state. As I grappled with how to approach this information, I came to see that my presentation of the group should highlight the contradictions. The militia's self-presentation glossed over internal contradictions within the movement, but neither was race the central factor of the movement's politic. Rather, the most interesting finding for me was how race and class intersected in the movement's rhetoric. And, it also led me to believe that progressive activists could develop campaigns to draw people out of militia movements by targeting their class-based concerns.

A second example can be seen in my research on Loyalist paramilitaries.[47] In the wake of the 1994 ceasefire and the 1998 peace agreement in Northern Ireland both Republican and Loyalist paramilitaries became involved in the drug trade. The Loyalist side has, however, taken more heat for its participation than Republicans have. The gangster trope is commonly deployed by politicians and commentators to describe Loyalist paramilitaries. Leading Loyalists are typically dubbed 'godfathers' while street level members are called 'thugs'.[48] Moreover, Loyalists political leaders are routinely scolded to 'clean up their own house'.[49]

When I interviewed ex-prisoners with the UVF I asked them about the group's participation in the drug trade. Most admitted off the record that UVF men were engaged in selling drugs, but they were also adamant that the UVF leadership had a zero tolerance approach to drugs. One informant explained to me that once a member was caught selling drugs he was stood down from the organization. Such statements were difficult to square with the ample evidence of UVF involvement in the drug trade on the street.[50] However, I also wanted to be fair to the leadership's self-representation, to give it a hearing. What I discovered after many interviews and much background research was that the UVF leadership *was* opposed to drugs. However, it was also fighting a rear guard action against younger members heavily involved in the trade.[51] While the leadership wanted to get rid of the drug sellers in its ranks, the peace accord it signed onto prevented it from taking care of the drug problem in its midst by standing down the dealers and backing up the stand down orders with a threat of execution. Murder, even an internecine one, is sufficient grounds for revoking the privileges associated with the peace accord. In short, I could not dismiss the UVF's claim to have a no-drugs policy. Rather, I came to the conclusion that the police force should take a more aggressive role in policing Loyalist drug crimes instead of expecting Loyalist paramilitary leaders to do the job. The paramilitaries are certainly capable of policing their own drug dealers but their means for doing so (executions, kneecappings, expulsions from the province, etc.) are not consistent with human rights.

Dealing with quid pro quo

Some quid pro quo is natural in any research project. Over the years I have purchased soft drinks, coffee, and sandwiches for people I was interviewing. On occasion, my informants have picked up the tab. One informant, for example, took the check from the waiter's hand and when I protested told me he could not let a person driving a car like mine (a beat up Datsun) pick up the tab. When I interviewed UVF men in Northern Ireland, I often shared cigarettes with them (and they with me). I found that sharing a vice was usually a good way to start an interview because it put me and my interview subject on equal footing. Sharing is a natural social lubricant. It provides a baseline of civility and trust, and it humanizes the interviewer and interviewee for each other.

There are, however, a variety of problems with more substantial quid pro quo transfers, especially in research on repellent populations.[52] For starters, scholars who study these groups are not always in a position to reject requests for help on political and/or moral grounds. Indeed, most researchers strike a delicate balance between divulging who they are functionally (academics doing a research project) and who they are politically (e.g. a feminist or a socialist). When I did research on the militia movement, for example, I presented myself truthfully as a Ph.D. student doing my dissertation on the militia movement. I told potential informants, again truthfully, that I wanted to get beyond the stereotypes of the movement in the press to gain a better understanding of the movement. But, I never divulged upfront that I was liberal, although I never lied if someone asked me outright. Only one person ever inquired about my specific views.

In retrospect, I think some of my informants probably knew I disagreed with them while others thought I was curious or even sympathetic. The silence on the issue seemed, however, to suit us both. It allowed me to figure the movement out without undue suspicion of my motives by the group. And, it allowed the movement to suspend its suspicion of me and explain itself to an outsider who agreed to take it seriously.

These sorts of uneasy truces are part and parcel of most research encounters with repellent groups. However, a research subject may also choose to disrupt that delicate balance in order to secure something greater. That moment came for me when I was asked to participate on a public access TV programme produced by a militia member. The informant who asked me to participate indicated that he was asking me because I would look 'proper' on TV. I eventually agreed to participate on the programme after consulting my dissertation advisor and the IRB at my university. But, I regret doing so today. My style of interviewing – to tease out how a person sees the world – worked well as a data collection method. It kept informants from going on the defensive and allowed me to see the nuances in their view. However, my style was too soft for TV. It made me look like a supporter because I did not ask oppositional or 'in your face' questions.

In retrospect, I believe I should have told my informant that I could not participate on the programme because it would have called my objectivity into question to be on a show run for and by members of the movement. I did not use the excuse at the time because I took seriously the critique of objectivity and felt it would be dishonest to claim an objectivity I did not believe was possible. If I had a similar request today, I would have no qualms saying no. I still believe that true objectivity is impossible, but I see academic and strategic value in claiming it and striving for it. Objectivity may not be possible, but permitting the appearance of subjectivity or partisanship is not the same as recognizing that objectivity is impossible. I would define this view as a form of strategic objectivity.[53] It allows a researcher to maintain a critical distance from research subjects, to find balance as they walk the tight rope that research on repellent populations often entails.

Conclusion

This chapter is an attempt to lay out some ethical guidelines for researchers working on repellent populations. Such guidelines are necessary to address the lacunas in both the IRB and critical models of research on repellent populations. For its part the IRB model provides no protections for researchers. These protections are not frequently necessary in social science research on sympathetic populations, but they are vital for people doing research on repellent groups. The critical model, by contrast, assumes empathy between a researcher and their informants. Such empathy rarely exists for those doing research on repellent groups, and as such the methods entailed in the model are inapplicable, at best, and inappropriate at worst.

This chapter provides three starting points for consideration. The first suggestion is that IRBs incorporate protocols to protect researchers. Such measures will help researchers keep their safety in mind. Second, the chapter suggests that researchers develop mechanisms for representing repellent groups fairly. Academics can best contribute not by trying to draw people out of repellent movements but by explaining them to groups who have to deal with them (NGOs, government agents, police, etc.). These groups often have only stereotypical representations of such groups to go from. Finally, the chapter suggests that a 'strategic objectivity' can help researchers avoid *qui pro quo* expectations by their research subjects. This chapter is, however, neither exhaustive nor comprehensive. It is my hope that it can spur further conversations and guidelines for researchers doing work on repellent groups.

Notes

1 See especially Sara Diamond, *Roads to Dominion: Right-Wing Movements and Political Power in the United States* (New York: Guilford Press, 1995). In the intervening decade a number of important studies of right-wing movements have been published. Kathleen Blee, *Inside Organized Racism: Women in the Hate*

144 Researching repellent groups

   Movement (Berkeley: University of California Press, 2003); Abby Ferber, *White Man Falling: Race, Gender, and White Supremacy* (Lanham, MD: Rowman and Littlefield, 2000) among others.
2. Joel Dyer, *Of Rage: Why Oklahoma is Only the Beginning* (Boulder: Westview, 1997); Daniel Levitas, *The Terrorist Next Door: The Militia Movement and the Radical Right* (New York: St. Martin's Press, 2002)
3. James Aho, *The Politics of Righteousness: Idaho Christian Patriotism* (Seattle: University of Washington Press, 1990).
4. Carolyn Gallaher, *On the Fault Line: Race, Class, and the American Patriot Movement* (Lanham, MD: Rowman and Littlefield, 2003).
5. In this chapter I build on Nigel Fielding's seminal essay on researching 'unloved' populations in his 'Mediating the Message: Affinity and Hostility in Research on Sensitive Topics', in Claire Renzetti and Raymond Lee (eds), *Researching Sensitive Topics* (California: Sage, 1993). While I extend and specify the category, Fielding is arguably one of the first scholars to call into question the difficulties facing researchers of unsympathetic groups.
6. See Carolyn Gallaher, *On the Fault Line* and Gallaher, *After the Peace: Loyalist Paramilitaries in Post-Accord Northern Ireland* (Ithaca: Cornell University Press, 2007) respectively for full accounts of these projects.
7. Peter Taylor, *Loyalists: War and Peace in Northern Ireland* (London: TV Books, 1999).
8. Norman Denzin and Yvonna Lincoln, 'Preface', in N. Denzin and Y. Lincoln (eds), *The Sage Handbook of Qualitative Research* (Sage: Thousand Oaks), pp. 1–32.
9. Norman Denzin and Yvonna Lincoln, 'Introduction: The Discipline and Practice of Qualitative Research', in N. Denzin and Y. Lincoln (eds.), *The Sage Handbook* (Thousand Oaks, CA: 2005), pp. 1–32.
10. Lucette Lagnado and Dekel, Sheila, *Children of the Flames: Dr. Josef Mengele and the Untold Story of the Twins of Auschwitz* (New York: Penguin, 1992).
11. Louis Snyder, *Encyclopedia of the Third Reich* (New York: Da Capo Press, 1994).
12. Fred D. Gray, *The Tuskegee Syphilis Study* (New York: New South Inc., 2002).
13. Ruth Faden and Tom Beauchamp, *A History and Theory of Informed Consent* (New York: Oxford University Press, 1986).
14. Faden and Beauchamp, 'A History of Theory'.
15. Laud Humphreys, *Tearoom Trade: Impersonal Sex in Public Places* (Chicago: Aldine Publishing Company, 1968).
16. David Warwick, 'Tearoom Trade: Means and Ends in Social Research', *The Hastings Center Studies,* vol. 1 (1973) pp. 27–38.
17. See Warwick, 'Tearoom Trade' and Clifford Christians, 'Ethics and Politics in Qualitative Research', in N. Denzin and Y. Lincoln, (eds), *The Sage Handbook.*
18. The Nuremberg code can be found on the Department of Health and Human Services webpage available at < http://www.hhs.gov/ohrp/references/nurcode.htm>
19. The Belmont Report can be found on the National Institutes of Health webpage available at <http://ohsr.od.nih.gov/guidelines/belmont.html> .
20. Faden and Beauchamp, 'A History of Theory'.
21. Clifford Geertz, *The Interpretation of Cultures* (New York: Basic Books, 1973).
22. Denzin and Lincoln, 'Introduction: The Discipline and Practice of Qualitative Research', in Denzin and Lincoln (eds), *The Sage Handbook.*
23. Friedrich Ratzel, *Anthropogeographie* (Stuttgart: J. Engelhorns Nachf, 1921); Ellen Churchill Semple, *American History and its Geographic Conditions* (Boston: Houghton, Mifflin, 1903).
24. Richard Peet, 'The Social Origins of Environmental Determinism', *Annals of the Association of American Geographers,* vol. 75 (1985) pp. 309–333; N. Smith, *American empire: Roosevelt's geographer and the prelude to globalization* (California: University Press, 2003). At the time, the Anthropologist Franz Boaz also

called the theory into question, albeit on different grounds. He argued that environmental determinism was suspect because it could not account for the varied 'fates' of societies that arose in the same climate zones, see D. Livingstone, *The Geographical Tradition* (London: Blackwell, 1992).
25 Jan Monk and Susan Hanson, 'On not excluding half of the human in human geography', *Professional Geographer*, vol. 34 (1982), pp. 11–23.
26 bell hooks, *Black Looks: Race and Representation* (Boston: South End Press, 1992).
27 Denzin and Lincoln, *The Sage Handbook*, p. x.
28 Stephen Kemmis and Robin McTaggart, 'Participatory Action Research', in Denzin and Lincoln (eds), *The Sage Handbook*, pp. 559–603.
29 Linda Tuhiwai Smith, *Decolonizing Methodologies: Research and Indigenous Peoples* (London: Zed Books, 1999); Ward Churchill, *Struggle for the Land: Indigenous Resistance to Genocide, Ecocide, and Expropriation in Contemporary North America* (Maine: Common Courage Press, 1993).
30 Patricia McGuire, *Doing Participatory Research: A Feminist Approach* (Amherst: University of Massachusetts Press, 1987); Orlando Fals Borda and Muhammad Rahman, *Action and Knowledge: Breaking the Monopoly with Participatory Action Research* (New York: Apex Press 1991).
31 Denzin and Lincoln, 'Introduction: The Discipline and Practice of Qualitative Research', in Denzin and Lincoln, (eds) *The Sage Handbook*, p. 1–32.
32 Here Blee is quoting Nigel Fielding, 'Mediating the Message', in C. Renzetti and R. Lee (eds), *Researching Sensitive Topics* (California: Sage, 2003) p. 148.
33 Kathleen Blee, *Inside Organized Racism: Women in the Hate Movement* (Berkley: University Press, 2003).
34 Nel Blee, *Inside Organized Racism*, p. 118.
35 N. Noddings, *Caring: A Feminine Approach to Ethics and Moral Education* (Berkeley: University Press, 1984); bell hooks, *Feminist Theory from Margin to Center* (Boston: South End Press, 1984); bell hooks, *Black Looks: Race and Representation* (Boston: South End Press, 1992); Christians, 'Ethics and Politics in Qualitative Research', p. 148; Patricia Hill Collins, *Fighting words: Black Women and the Search for Justice* (Minneapolis: University Press, 1998).
36 In the last decade critical scholars have begun to examine dominance rather than how dominance is resisted. There are now vibrant subfields on whiteness. See David Roediger, *Towards the Abolition of Whiteness* (New York: Verso, 1994); Noel Ignative, *How the Irish became White* (New York: Routledge, 1995); Mat Wray and Annalee Newitz, *White Trash: Race and Class in America* (New York: Routledge, 1997) and on masculinity Rachel Adams and David Savran, (eds), *The Masculinity Studies Reader* (Oxford: Blackwell, 2002); Raewyn W. Connell *Masculinities* (Australia: Allen and Unwin, 2005). However, studies of social movements defending dominance remain relatively rare and methodological guidelines for them even rarer.
37 Nigel Fielding, *The National Front* (London: Routledge, 1981); Carolyn Ellis, *Fisher Folk: Two Communities on Chesapeake Bay* (Lexington: University Press of Kentucky, 1986).
38 Richard Leo, 'Trial and Tribulations: Courts, Ethnography, and the Need for an Evidentiary Privilege for Academic Researchers', *The American Sociologist*, vol. 26 (1995), pp. 113–134; Charlotte Allen, 'Spies Like Us: When Sociologists Deceive their Subjects', *Lingua Franca* (November, 1997), pp. 31–39.
39 See Allen, *Spies Like Us* and Christians, *Ethics and Politics in Qualitative Research*.
40 See Fielding, *The National Front*, for example, and Leo, 'Trial and Tribulations'.
41 By undercover I mean here a person who hides the fact that they are doing research.

42 In 2001 as I was putting the finishing touches on my book manuscript about the militia movement, the commander of KSM was arrested for multiple gun violations (see the Epilogue in my book for an extended discussion). It is quite possible that KSM was under surveillance while I was doing my research. And, although I often complained to friends that my informants rarely talked about their guns, I am glad in retrospect they did not. I could have faced a real version of the scenario laid out above.
43 One of the most trenchant critiques of IRBs is that they are primarily designed to protect the institution from lawsuits and other legal challenges. In a small way, this suggestion addresses this critique by forcing the IRB to consider the need of its employees.
44 Gallaher, *On the Fault Line*.
45 Morris Dees, *Gathering Storm: America's Militia Threat* (New York: HarperCollins, 1996); Daniel Junas, 'The Rise of Citizen Militias: Angry White Guys with Guns', in C. Berlet (ed.), *Eyes Right! Challenging the right wing Backlash* (Boston: South End Press, 1995), pp. 226–235.
46 Gallaher, *On the Fault Line*.
47 Gallaher, *After the Peace*.
48 Jim McDowell, *Godfathers: Inside Northern Ireland's Drug Racket* (Dublin: Gill & Macmillan, 2002).
49 Gallaher, *After the Peace*.
50 J. McDowell, *Godfathers: Inside Northern Ireland's Drug Racket*.
51 Gallaher, *After the Peace*.
52 Even some scholars who research sympathetic groups take issue with participant action research. I leave these critiques aside here, instead focusing on why the model is, at the very least, inappropriate for research on repellent populations.
53 Here I am indebted to the notion of 'strategic essentialism' developed by feminists and postcolonial scholars. Strategic essentialism is a political move oppressed people may employ when dealing with an oppressor. The idea is to downplay differences and present a united front over and against an enemy/oppressor. The term strategic is used to indicate that those employing essentialism are aware of internal differences and are presenting the coherent front strategically, to meet short term objectives.

10 Interpreting truth and lies in stories of conflict and violence

Lee Ann Fujii

Angélique[1] told a harrowing tale. 'They said I had Tutsi blood', she explained. Her voice was soft, her demeanor sombre. It was our first meeting after a long day of multiple interviews. I was in Rwanda to talk to rural people who had lived through or participated in genocidal violence. The year was 2004 – ten years after a civil war that had installed a new regime and a genocide that had cost the lives of half-a-million people.

We sat side by side on a damp log, the ground still wet from rain. I was eager to hear her story, for here was a woman, I had thought, who was Hutu but had nonetheless been targeted because her mother was Tutsi. Angélique continued. Some neighbours had dug a hole where she hid for the night with her youngest strapped to her back. Her rescuers covered the hole with leaves. The next day, Angélique and her baby fled to safety with Tutsi from the area.

Angélique's experience would have been another piece of data I was collecting on mass violence that took place in Rwanda between 1991 and 1994. Her story was consistent with those from other genocide survivors I had interviewed as well as published testimonies.[2] Survival, as Angélique's story illustrated, was often a matter of luck and the life-saving gestures of neighbours, friends, and strangers.

Each time I travelled to the research site where Angélique lived, I looked forward to learning more. As the interviews continued, however, Angélique became less precise. The more I probed, the sketchier her story became.

Angélique seemed to have other things on her mind. Her present life was filled with hardship and struggle. After the war, she had returned with the other refugees who had fled across the border, but the government denied her 'survivor' status. Worse, the other Tutsi survivors also denied she was a survivor. Angélique was consequently ineligible for benefits the government had promised to genocide survivors, which included new housing and assistance with school fees for her children.

By our fourth interview, it started to occur to me that Angélique had made up the entire story of her escape. Her statements were not adding up. When I asked why her former Tutsi friends would have denied she was a survivor like them, she said it was because her husband was Hutu. This seemed odd since other survivors I met had been married to Hutu. When I asked her what had become of her husband, she said she did not know. This, too, struck me as odd – that no news of her husband had ever reached her through other refugees, as was common with other refugees to whom I had spoken. When I asked about her parents' background, she gave similarly vague answers. At one point, she went beyond all credibility and claimed that her father had had 39 wives. Polygamy was common in this part of the country but I had never heard of any man having more than two or three wives. I was beginning to doubt everything she was saying.

How should researchers deal with questions of veracity in post-violence settings when the stakes run particularly high? To what extent should researchers trust personal narratives and local histories that are generated in politically sensitive contexts?

This chapter argues that the value of oral testimonies that researchers collect in places that have recently suffered violent conflict does not lie solely in the truthfulness of their content. It also lies in the meta-data that accompany these testimonies. By meta-data, I mean the information people communicate about their interior thoughts and feelings. Meta-data are important indicators of the current social and political landscape and how that landscape shapes what people are willing to say to a researcher. These meta-data are indicators of how reliable the data are and what answers they provide. By failing to attend to these meta-data, analysts risk mis-interpreting ambiguities, overlooking important details, drawing incorrect conclusions, and leaving informants vulnerable to reprisals or harassment for having talked to the researcher. Attending to meta-data is therefore vital to protecting informants and for arriving at robust explanations and theories about violence and its aftermath.

Types of meta-data

When I conducted my fieldwork in 2004, it had been ten years since the genocide and civil war in Rwanda. In that period of time, memories change. People forget some details and mis-remember others. They re-arrange chronologies, confuse sequences, and give greater weight to some moments over others. In addition, institutions of all kinds, from prisons to schools, socialize people to construct the past in certain ways.[3] Most of the prisoners my interpreter and I spoke with, for example, had been in prison for at least eight years, some close to ten. In that amount of time, it is likely that prison culture helped to produce one particular way of talking and thinking about the genocide.

Violent episodes may also have much greater salience for some communities than others, regardless of how much time has passed. In the United States, for example, whites and blacks from the same community recall a past lynching that occurred in their town very differently, with members of the black community retaining the details while many whites had forgotten them.[4]

Interpreting truth and lies in stories of conflict and violence 149

The forum in which people recall past violent events can also shape the testimonies that people provide. Truth commissions privilege certain types of narrative over others. The Peruvian truth commission, for example, was eager to hear women's stories of victimization but not their stories of heroism.[5]

All these factors enhance the importance of meta-data in our fieldwork and analysis. In the following sections, I discuss five types of meta-data: rumours, inventions, denials, evasions, and silences. The importance of these and all forms of meta-data lies in what they tell us about the informant, the power relations in the informant's community, and the relationship between researcher and informant. Meta-data, in short, bear directly on the quality of data researchers can expect to collect in post-conflict or post-violence settings.

Rumours

Ethnographers of war and violence have noted the prominent role that rumours play in periods of extreme uncertainty and insecurity. Cut off from other sources of information, rumours help people make sense of the situation. They may even stand in for knowledge, as Anna Simons argues in the case of Somalia.[6]

Rumours can arise about researchers for similar reasons. In places that have recently suffered violence, mistrust of outsiders is particularly acute. Linda Green, for example, talks about the rumours that arose about her and her research assistant when she began going to Mayan women's homes to interview them (after conducting initial interviews in public places). As Green explains: 'Above all else they had not wanted the *gringa* to be seen coming to their house.[7] Under the scrutiny of surveillance the women were afraid of what others in the village might say about them and me'. Like Green, I, too, encountered many rumours about my interpreter and me during the course of my fieldwork. Not only did these rumours circulate within the community, they also passed between the research sites to the prisons (through visitors) and back again from the prisons to the communities.

The most troubling of these rumours were those that painted my activities as threatening and thus worthy of suspicion. At one interview in the prisons, for example, a prisoner asked if a rumour he had heard was true. The rumour was that I and my team had gone by his house and my driver[8] had tried to question his young child about the war, over the protests of the mother who insisted the child was too young to have known anything about the war.

I denied this rumour in the strongest terms possible. I then used this exchange as an opportunity to investigate how prisoners vetted information they heard through visitors to the prison. I asked this prisoner how he and the other prisoners could tell whether news they heard from the outside was true or not. He said it was possible to tell in some instances, when, for example, the rumour contained precise details, such as, in this case, an accurate description of my car. In other instances, the prisoner admitted it was not possible to tell. Since vetting was difficult, rumours stood in for truth and hence, easily enhanced people's suspicions of us.

We heard similar rumours in the research sites. One woman we interviewed several times, whom I call Thérèse, was visibly nervous talking about the genocide. She articulated her fears more than once. At our third interview, she told us that every time we came, she worried that we would ask her about 'the politics of the genocide'. The rumour she had heard was that my interpreter and I were working for the Rwandan government and that we were talking to people about the impending *gacaca*, a government initiative that established community-based courts to try the 120,000 people who had been imprisoned for allegedly having participated in the genocide.[9] At the time of my fieldwork, *gacaca* was scheduled to begin nationwide in the coming months. I tried to use this opportunity to understand why Rwandans traded in rumours. Thérèse explained that rumours were part of everyday life. 'Even if you stay at home, you always hear rumours about yourself', she stated matter-of-factly. Given the ubiquity of rumours, what Thérèse feared was not who my interpreter and I really were, but who her neighbours said we were. It was the identities her neighbours had assigned to us, and not our real identities, that cast suspicion on Thérèse for having talked with us.

Over time, Thérèse's fears subsided; so, too, did her neighbours' suspicions of us. At a later interview, Thérèse even confirmed that her neighbours no longer regarded us suspiciously, but had come to think of us as 'friends' dropping by for a visit. She herself likened our visits to that of a priest – we come for short visits, then we leave, but we always come back again. The shift from threatening government agents to welcome visitor reassured me that our continuing presence was not getting Thérèse into trouble with her neighbours or local authorities. It also indicated that she had begun to trust us.

Rumours such as these also illustrate the extent to which field research is a two-way street. As many scholars have pointed out, not only are researchers studying their informants, their informants, in turn, are studying them back – to figure out who the researcher really is and whether the researcher is a source of potential threat.[10] Thérèse's neighbours, in other words, were simply trying to figure out whose interests my interpreter and I really represented. Making such determinations is critical in settings rent by violence, when social relations are fragile or fractured.

Rumours thus point to the source of people's fears about what is at stake if they agree to talk to the researcher. If people believe that the researcher is acting in ways that appear threatening or overly aggressive (like approaching a prisoner's child without his knowledge), there is clear reason for informants to be less than forthright in interviews. If however, people come to believe that the researcher is who she says she is, then people should have less reason to be mistrustful and fewer reasons to lie or prevaricate.

Inventions

Perhaps more threatening to a researcher than rumours are false, embellished, or made up stories. Indeed, most researchers will use well-known techniques, such as triangulating different sources, to ferret out lies in order to get closer to the 'truth'.

Not every story, however, lends itself to determinations of truth. People's beliefs about how the world works, for example, cannot be subject to a truth test. Similarly, the value of people's narrations about their experiences of violence – what they saw, did, felt, or heard – does not necessarily lie in their factual accuracy or objective truths, but in the meaning that the narrator endows particular events, moments, and timelines. Stories situate the narrator in a larger context; thus all the details of the story, including inaccuracies, fabrications, embellishments, and inventions, are revealing. As noted oral historian Alessandro Portelli explains:

> Oral sources are credible but with a *different* credibility. The importance of oral testimony may lie not in its adherence to fact, but rather in its departure from it, as imagination, symbolism, and desire emerge. Therefore, there are no 'false' oral sources … 'wrong' statements are still psychologically 'true,' and … this truth may be equally as important as factually reliable accounts (emphasis in original).[11]

As Portelli teaches us, the stories people tell – inventions and all – are valuable because they reflect the speaker's state of mind, interests, aspirations, and desires. All these elements tie the speaker to her larger community and reveal different kinds of truths, such as the psychological truths Portelli points to and the emotional truths that Leigh Payne describes. For Payne, emotional truths may be based on fictional accounts of violence but nevertheless say quite a bit about the kinds of atrocities that perpetrators or regimes commit.[12]

In my own work, I pondered the value of my interviews with Angélique after I began to suspect she may have made up her story of escape. The point at which I doubted everything she had been saying was when she claimed her father had had 39 wives. Thirty-nine seemed implausible, and as John Dean and William Whyte[13] note, when a story appears implausible, there is reason to question it.

It was at that point that I knew that Angélique had been spinning tales but was her purpose deception? While at first I felt annoyed that she would lie to me, I soon came to believe that her purpose for making up a story was not deception, but rather to make sense of her current situation. Angélique's present was difficult to bear, both in material and psychological terms. The war had left her a widow with many children to feed; her house was small and shabby, even by local standards. She felt marginalized and rejected by the other Tutsi who had denied she was a survivor. Given her situation, it may have been better not to know what happened to her husband, particularly if he had participated in the killings of Tutsi.

At the same time, Angélique's story of being hunted down for having 'Tutsi blood' may have contained elements of truth. To borrow Payne's term, Angélique's story might have been emotionally true even if parts were factually false. Angélique's mother may have been Tutsi, giving her good reason to have feared being targeted. Her father may have been a man of some means and had multiple wives (though perhaps not 39). This would have given Angélique first-hand knowledge of being associated with someone of social standing or prestige, making her present circumstances all the more difficult to bear.

Angélique was not the only person to exaggerate or embellish. Sophie was around 80 years old when we first met her in 2004. During the genocide, she had managed to rescue 20 people by hiding them in her small house. Despite her advanced age, Sophie was vivacious and seemed to relish the attention our visits brought. And while she loved to tell stories, dates were usually a blur to her. 'It's been ten years', she explained when she could not remember the specific year in which a certain event had taken place. Sophie did not claim to remember everything, but like most good storytellers, she was committed to whatever story she did tell. Did Sophie embellish at times? Undoubtedly. Did these embellishments turn her stories into lies? I would argue not. Sophie's stories were not litanies of facts but narratives with characters and plots. It was not dates that were important to Sophie, but who did or said what to whom and why.

Like Angélique, Sophie, too, felt marginalized by the rest of her community. Unlike Angélique, however, being marginalized for Sophie meant having greater freedom to say and do what she wanted. It made her more forthcoming, not less. Being more forthcoming did not necessarily make Sophie's stories more reliable in terms of factual or chronological accuracy, but it did make them more available to cross-checking with other sources. By contrast, when the details of Angélique's story became less precise and more fantastical, it became harder to confirm any part of the story, even with her. Indeed, it was my inability to gain greater clarity from Angélique that made me suspect the veracity of her story as a whole. And when I began doubting everything that Angélique had told us, I began to ask different questions of the data she provided. Why would someone make up a story like that? What is the story behind the story? Angélique's testimonies hinted at the value she placed on being recognized as a 'survivor' and a 'victim'. The value she placed on these categories did not seem to reflect purely material motives – what she could obtain from the government or a foreign researcher by being classified as a 'survivor'. It had to do with a type of social hierarchy that was in place at the time, a hierarchy that placed survivors near or at the top. This hierarchy had left Angélique at the bottom with no obvious way to advance. Claiming that others had denied her survivor status and perhaps, a prestigious pedigree via her father, were ways to mitigate the disappointment she felt about her current situation. Angélique's invented life story, thus, seemed to be an example of a 'uchronic' story. It was not a story of what was, but rather, what should have been.[14] In this alternative version, Angélique's dignity and social importance are restored.

I interpreted Sophie's embellishments, by contrast, as coming from a place of critique. Sophie had strong opinions and enjoyed expressing them. Indeed, Sophie seemed to relish the opportunity to show that she was not like her neighbours by openly criticizing other people. For Sophie, the goal of relating stories was not to invent a new life history that made it easier to cope with present realities, as seemed to be the case with Angélique. It was to demonstrate her willingness to speak openly and frankly about anything.

As the contrasting examples of Angélique and Sophie show, narratives of violence, even those filled with inventions, inaccuracies, fictions, and lies, can embody all sorts of truths – emotional, psychological and moral. Angélique's stories embodied her aspirations for a better life and her disappointment with her current reality. Sophie's stories shed light on her moral code and the value she placed on speaking out rather than hiding her true thoughts. Researchers should mine their data for all forms of truth and not prejudge the data based on a hasty judgments.

Denials

Another discursive strategy that shaped people's testimonies was denial. I encountered denial when talking to people who were not genocide survivors but survivors of violence that occurred after the end of the civil war and genocide.

The most memorable encounter occurred in the northern research site of Kimanzi. I had asked the local authority if there were any women *rescapées* who might be willing to talk with me. By using the word *rescapé(e)*, I had assumed that my meaning was clear – that I had wanted to talk with survivors of the violence targeted at Tutsi civilians, which had taken place in the region in January–March 1991. When the female *rescapée* the local authority had sent, arrived for her interview, I had certain expectations about how the initial interview would go. Genocide survivors were usually quite willing to talk about their experiences during the violence. Thus, when I began with questions about the period of 1990–94, I was taken aback when she answered by focusing on the period after 1994.

Q. Where did you live during the period of 1990 to 1994?
   I lived here in the *secteur* Kimanzi, *cellule* R–
Q. What happened to you during this period?
   I encountered some problems from the war. Especially the war of 1997 when they struck me with knives and machetes.
Q. Who struck you during the war of 1997?

It was the *Inkotanyi* [sobriquet of the Rwandan Patriotic Front or RPF, the rebel army that had invaded Rwanda in 1990 and eventually took power in 1994].

Q. Why did the *Inkotanyi* strike you in 1997?

I don't know why. They were killing people. They wouldn't even let the children go because the day they struck me, they left with my two small children, the youngest was still nursing and the other [who] was born just before the youngest.

Q. What did the *Inkotanyi* do with your two children?

They killed my two children and threw them into the forest. It was the neighbours who picked up the bodies.

Q. Before 1997, did you ever have problems with violence?

No. Again, when I arrived home, the *Inkotanyi* also killed my husband and I was left all by myself in this awful world.

Q. Were you there when your husband was killed by the *Inkotanyi*?

No. The hospital kept asking my husband to find me some nutritious food to help me get better. My husband disappeared when he went to Ruhengeri [town] to find me some meat.

Q. Was there violence here in [*cellule*] R – before 1997?

No. The problems started after the arrival of the *Inkotanyi* in Rwanda.

Q. When did the *Inkotanyi* arrive here at [*cellule*] R –?

I remember that they arrived here in 1997 after having made all the Rwandans return, from Zaire, and they started to kill the people.

In this short passage, I made three attempts to get this woman to talk about the period of 1990–94 and each time, she refocused the question on the period she wanted to talk about – the 'war of 1997'. To highlight her victimization, she denies that any violence took place in her *cellule* before 1997. Instead, she links all the violence in her community to the arrival of the RPF, when she and her family became targets for killing. She also dates the RPF's arrival to 1997, overlooking a particularly bold RPF attack that had occurred in her region in January 1991, which her neighbours (who were also Hutu) had no problem recalling.

This informant was not unique in her denial of violence that occurred prior to her own victimization. Other women who lost husbands after the war and genocide also maintained that there had been no violence before they and their families became targets. While I did not find their denials credible (in light of other testimonies), I did not think of their denials as simply lies or deceptions. Instead, I realized that what was paramount for these women was their own victimization. Only by allowing these informants to speak about their experiences of violence could I get them to acknowledge, however grudgingly, that others were targeted for violence at an earlier point in time. It was as if acknowledging the violence perpetrated against other victims took away from their status as victims. In a way, they were right. In its *gacaca* initiative, the RPF-led government had reserved the term 'survivor' (and by extension, the category of 'victim') for people who had escaped the genocide.

By doing so, the government was effectively denying the experiences of victims of other forms of violence, most notably, violence that the RPF had committed against Rwandan civilians.[15] Furthermore, by restricting my questions to the period of the 1990–94 civil war and genocide, I, too, was designating these women's experiences as irrelevant since the data they were providing fell outside the temporal boundaries I had established for my research.

What these women's denials taught me was that informants do not experience violence in the same neat, analytic packages that we researchers use in our fieldwork. Rather, people experience, remember and recount violence through the lens of their own victimization. This meant that I could not pre-specify a designated time period and expect that informants would go along with my categories, especially when my demarcations did not match their experience, or worse, denied them. Had I denied these women the opportunity to tell their stories, I would have unwittingly contributed to large gaps in my data.

Evasions

In addition to denials and inventions, I also encountered strategies of evasion and avoidance on the part of some informants. Some people avoided answering particular questions; some answered by omitting important information; others avoided being interviewed altogether. Avoiding interviews did not always mean that the person had something to hide. Similarly, agreeing to be interviewed did not indicate any level of openness on the part of the informant.

People who avoid being interviewed may do so for quite mundane reasons. During the course of my fieldwork, for example, I came across people who were bored by the interview process and preferred doing something else with their time. In other cases, avoidance did seem to signal that the person had something to hide.

The most blatant example of evasion I encountered in the field was with a man I call Robert. The local authority suggested we talk to Robert because he had become *conseiller* or local head of 'Ngali' after the war. Robert was also a genocide survivor. Since we were having trouble finding people that day (because it was market day and most people were not at home), I jumped at the opportunity to interview him.

Entering his house, I noticed that Robert seemed to be fairly well off by local standards. He had a young wife and a daughter who greeted us in French. There was a scale on a table near the front door, indicating that he was a merchant of some kind. As we sat down, he made a big show of welcoming us into his home. Throughout the interview, he played the part of cordial host, all the while clutching a wad of 100 Rwandan francs bills in his hand.

I began the interview as I had with other genocide survivors – with the expectation that this man would talk openly about his experience during the genocide. As the interview progressed, however, I noticed that rather than getting more detailed (as was usually the case with survivors), his answers became more general. He began the interview saying that he had seen everything. He explained that in 1994, Hutu were being trained to kill Tutsi. He also volunteered the name of the local person who was in power at the time of the genocide. As I continued my questions, however, he began to claim he did not know the answers.

Q. How did the attackers know who the Tutsi were?
I don't know how they knew that, but they had made lists well in advance and used those at the time of the killing.
Q. They made the lists before the shooting down of the president's plane?
I don't know when they did it.
Q. Did the war that started in 1990 change anything here in Ngali?
We heard that there was a war at the border, that the *Inyenzi-Inkotanyi* [common reference to the RPF] were attacking Rwanda. The friendships between the people began to erode and what do you know, there was a conflict between the ethnic groups, saying that the *Inyenzi* were Tutsi.
Q. After having arrived at R – [the *secteur* where he fled], what did you do next?
We stayed at my father-in-law's until the arrival of the *Inkotanyi*.
Q. When did the *Inkotanyi* arrive at Ngali?
I don't know because I wasn't here at Ngali.
Q. At R –?
I don't remember. I was in the house [of my father-in-law]. I didn't go out at that time.
Q. Were you threatened during the time you were staying at your father-in-law's house?
I was threatened.
Q. Who threatened you?
It was the people who destroyed my house who were threatening me – the Hutu people who were hunting the Tutsi people.

This entire exchange struck me as odd for a survivor. Many prisoners, including confessed killers, claimed to have seen everything and then became vague when I asked them to give details of what precisely they saw or did. This man was showing the same tendency. With prisoners, even those who had confessed their participation in the genocide, I understood this vagueness to be a strategy to deflect guilt or minimize responsibility for their deeds. This man was a genocide survivor so his evasions perplexed me. He states that there were lists circulating, but claims not to know who had drawn up the lists or when. Yet, if such lists had existed (and other testimony corroborated this point), local people must have helped draw them up since only locals would have known which households were Tutsi.

He then says that he fled to his father-in-law's house and stayed there until the arrival of the RPF. He also says, however, that he did not know when the RPF arrived in Ngali (his own *secteur*). This was not believable since his father-in-law's *secteur* adjoins Ngali. It was also odd that when I brought the question back to his own experience being targeted, he avoids specifying which Hutu were targeting him. Were they outsiders? Neighbours? Militia? Instead, he resorts to the unassailably general statement that 'the Hutu were hunting the Tutsi'.

All of these evasions puzzled me. Then, as we were leaving the man's house, my interpreter pointed out that Robert must be the brother of a prisoner we had recently interviewed. This prisoner was also a Tutsi genocide survivor and had told us a complicated story of how he came to be imprisoned after the genocide. While the details of his story were a blur to me at the time, what I did recall was his emphasis that it was family problems that had landed him in prison and nothing else. My interpreter had figured out the link when she recognized the names Robert had given for his parents (in response to a standard set of questions I asked at initial interviews).

Another clue that Robert was being deliberately evasive was when he told us that he had only one brother, who had died in the genocide. What he neglected to mention was that he had another brother who was languishing in prison. That omission was clearly telling but telling of what? After our initial interview, which did not last long, we asked Robert if we could come back another day. He readily agreed. We made an appointment to talk with him again in two weeks time. When we returned on the appointed day, he was nowhere to be found. We left a message with his wife that we would return on another specified day. On the next appointed day, he was absent again. We then asked the *responsable* (local authority) if he had seen Robert. The *responsable* made his own inquiries but said he could not locate him either. It was obvious that Robert was trying to avoid us. His behaviour piqued my curiosity, for why would a survivor have reason to hide from a researcher conducting research on the genocide? He had been among the victims of the genocide, after all, not one of its perpetrators.

Because he had avoided meeting with us, I decided to inquire about Robert to others. From multiple testimonies, I arrived at a picture of a man who was not well liked even before the genocide. After the genocide, dislike turned to fear. The new authorities made Robert the new *conseiller* of Ngali. Robert used this position of authority to have numerous residents imprisoned and killed. I asked people if they thought Robert was trying to exact revenge. All said no, that it was not revenge that motivated Robert, but greed. He was after his victims' property.

Robert's story illustrates how closely tied power and violence could be at the local level. As *conseiller*, Robert wielded almost absolute power over the lives of local residents. This level of power sounded similar to the stories I had heard about the local leader of the genocide and the power he was able to wield. With the backing of higher authorities, both he and Robert used violence to consolidate their power and pursue their private interests. Robert's story thus lent greater credibility to the stories I heard about the leader of the genocide (who was already dead by the time of my fieldwork).

More generally, the case of Robert cautions researchers against viewing victims as innocent and perpetrators as the only actors capable of violence. It speaks to the need to strip these categories of their normative assumptions. It also suggests that analysts should not treat the stories of victims as necessarily more accurate than other actors' testimonies, since victims, too, have their own interests to withhold information. In the case of Robert, I heard that he had worked with former *génocidaires* to imprison and kill people after the genocide. It is no wonder he remained vague about the identities of genocide perpetrators when I asked him these questions.

Silences

Like evasions, silences, too, can be polyvalent. Their meanings can be multiple and contradictory. They can both hide and reveal.

I had expected people to be silent on one subject: sexual violence. I had read about how widespread mass rape was during the genocide[16] and did not expect anyone to talk about it. I also chose not to ask about this aspect of the genocide directly as I felt unprepared to broach such a sensitive and potentially traumatizing subject. Instead, I waited for informants to bring up the topic themselves. Only three people did so. One was a local resident in my northern research site, who said he had heard that former Rwandan army soldiers had committed sexual violence against Tutsi women and girls in a neighbouring *secteur*. Another was a female genocide survivor who, while fleeing, ran into two local killers, one of whom threatened her with rape. She managed to escape. The third was a prisoner who maintained his innocence. He related a story of how his cousin and an accomplice had killed multiple members of his (the prisoner's) family and raped a girl hiding at his mother's house.

These cases were the exceptions. People were, for the most part, silent on this subject. That silence reflected not only the sensitivity of the topic, but also a general disbelief that sexual violence could occur in one's own community. One (male) Tutsi survivor insisted, for example, that there had been no rape in his community during the genocide because he had never heard anyone talk about it. When I asked him if a woman who had been raped would feel free to talk about it, he conceded she would not.

People's silence about sexual violence also seemed to reflect a universal shame about this form of violation. As an anthropologist of Croatia points out, victims who talk about their rape generally bring more, not less, shame to themselves and their families. For this reason, they often choose to remain silent as a way to protect their families.[17]

In addition to silence on sexual violence, people were also largely silent on the more general topic of atrocities. When people talked of killing, they did so with an economy of words: 'We cut him' or 'they killed him'. I often inquired as to the instruments of death. The answers were consistent but perfunctory:

hoes, clubs, axes, and machetes. People occasionally volunteered details about atrocities but it was rare.

Unlike talk of rape or sexual violence, silence on atrocities is not universal or common across societies. The Mayan widows that Green interviewed, for example, readily described the atrocities committed against them and their families during *la violencia*. As Green (1999, 75) explains:

> The women, without prompting, took turns recounting their stories of horror. Using vivid detail, they would tell of the events surrounding the deaths or disappearances of their husbands, fathers, sons, brothers, as if they had happened the previous week or month, rather than six or eight years before.[18]

French journalist Jean Hatzfeld[19] elicited similarly detailed accounts of the atrocities that a group of genocide survivors from a southeast region in Rwanda lived through and witnessed. Why was I unable to elicit similar details? Perhaps I did not ask the right questions or establish the requisite level of rapport with informants. I chose not to ask direct questions about the most intimate details of the violence because such questions felt too invasive. I had no obvious entry point. Perhaps it was my own norms that kept me from broaching this subject, despite being keenly interested in expressive forms of violence. Or perhaps it was the realization that 'interviewing is also interrogation, and many subjects will not allow it to penetrate beyond a certain level of generality'.[20] In other words, perhaps I knew instinctively not to ask.

Silences require careful handling since one explanation does not fit all. In the case of sexual violence, I interpreted the silence to mean this was a topic not to be broached – by me or anyone else. In the case of atrocities, I was uncertain as to the reason for the silence but did not think to discuss it with my interpreter or other colleagues and friends in Rwanda.

Silences are not always shared, however. Individuals can also be silent on specific subjects. Their silence does not necessarily mean they are less truthful or forthright than those who are more talkative. Thérèse, the informant who likened our visits to that of a priest, said very little about the genocide during our many interviews, but was quite open about all other topics. Robert, by contrast, claimed to have seen everything but told us very little.

Silences can also be a collaborative effort between the researcher and informant. As Kay Warren points out, 'strategic ambiguities' always arise in narratives about war and violence. Often, such ambiguities are not invitations to probe more deeply, but rather subtle admonishments to the researcher to respect certain topics as 'off limits'.[21] As Liisa Malkki remarks about her own fieldwork experience in the 1980s interviewing Burundi refugees living in Tanzania:

... the success of the fieldwork hinged not so much on a determination to ferret out 'the facts' as on a willingness to leave some stones unturned, to listen to what my informants deemed important, and to demonstrate my trustworthiness by not prying where I was not wanted.[22]

Like Warren, Malkki, and others who have studied war and violence up close, I, too, never pressed anyone to talk about anything he or she did not want to discuss. When I encountered hesitation or resistance, I used the opportunity to ask questions about entirely different topics to demonstrate my willingness to respect the informant's boundaries. 'Not asking' was one way I could demonstrate my trustworthiness, and thus help to maintain certain silences.

Conclusion

This chapter has argued that meta-data are important elements of fieldwork. They are not ancillary to fieldwork practices or strategies; they are at the core of the many decisions we make in the field when choosing informants, interlocutors, enumerators, research assistants, and translators. Meta-data add to the rigour of our studies by acting as a gauge for the quality of the narratives we are collecting, particularly in post-violence settings. They alert us to possible silences and gaps in testimonies. They point us to actors whose experiences may have been silenced by current political or social conditions, or to actors who wish to avoid saying too much. They teach us how to evaluate and analyze our data, which are particularly important tasks when determinations of truth with a capital T are not possible or appropriate. Finally, meta-data are crucial for minimizing harm in the field. They point to the importance of dispelling rumours and allaying suspicions so that those who agree to talk to us do not bring unwanted attention on themselves.

Meta-data arise in every encounter in the field, no matter what methods the researcher is using. Surveys or other forms of one-shot interviews are no less vulnerable to systematic denials or silences than multiple interviews. People are no less apt to embellish their stories to a native-born enumerator than a foreign researcher. Thus, all researchers should pay attention to the meta-data that may be shaping their research.

Failing to attend to meta-data can have clear consequences for a study's findings. Systematic silences, evasions, and denials, for example, can obscure the identities of perpetrators, lead to under- and overestimations of participation in violence, and foreground the experiences of certain actors, such as victims, while downplaying those of other actors, such as victims-turned-perpetrators. Rumours about who the researcher is can create barriers before the research has begun, making the very people in whom the researcher is interested less likely to talk honestly, openly, or at all.

There are multiple ways to read and adjust for meta-data. One strategy is to interview people multiple times over an extended period. Multiple interviews enable the researcher to respond to the fears and suspicions that are likely to exist in post-conflict settings. Knowing that informants can face reprisals from many quarters – neighbours, colleagues, family members, state agents – should force the researcher to find ways to ensure people's safety, not only during the period of research but just as importantly, long after the researcher has left the field.

A second strategy that researchers might incorporate is to invite informants to conduct their own interview of the researcher – to flip the tables so to speak. The questions informants raise may speak directly to their reasons for and concerns about agreeing to interviews, their aspirations for establishing a relationship with an outsider, and their assumptions about what they might get in return for their time. By allowing informants to ask questions (and not just answer them), the researcher might learn of people's concerns directly without having to guess or assume. The standard one-way interview will not always bring these issues out in the open.

A third practice that scholars might incorporate is more systematic self-reflection while in the field. This process might involve regular dialogue with research assistants and colleagues in the country about rumours and gossip that commonly arise about outsiders and those that arise specifically about the researcher. In my experience, my interpreter did not always relay this information to me so I had to ask. Researchers might also take note of puzzles that arise from everyday conversations and interactions, and revisit those puzzles to see if time in the field has helped to resolve them. Researchers should also reflect on the source of that clarity – why previous puzzles suddenly make sense when they did not before.

Researchers usually acquire a certain amount of local knowledge while in the field; it is the immersion into local cultures and perspectives that slowly shifts and transforms the researcher's own sense of what is normal and credible. With sustained fieldwork also comes the opportunity to build trust and rapport, not only with informants but also acquaintances, friends, and colleagues. This trust becomes the main avenue for identifying, interpreting, and responding to meta-data. Some scholars deny that trust and rapport automatically come with time. As Konstantin Belousov *et al.* argue, in 'crisis-ridden research settings', rapport between researcher and researched may actually diminish over time.[23] As Staffan Löfving, too, observes: 'Lying, misinformation and direct silence adhere to the communicative tool kit of people in politically unstable circumstances'.[24] While strategies of dissimulation may indeed constitute strategies of survival in conflict and post-conflict settings, meta-data can help researchers make sense of the ambiguities and complexities that such strategies generate. Through meta-data, researchers can indeed find the truth in lies and answers to questions we did not know we had.

Notes

1 All names of people who participated in my research and place names below the level of province are fictitious to protect identities.

2 'African Rights, Death, despair, and defiance' (London: African Rights, 1995), Alison Des Forges, *Leave None to Tell the Story* (New York: Human Rights Watch and Fédération internationale des ligues des droits de l'homme, 1999).
3 Leigh Payne, *Unsettling accounts* (Durham: Duke University Press, 2008), p. 20.
4 Charlotte Wolf, 'Constructions of a lynching', *Sociological Inquiry*, vol. 62, no. 1 (1992), pp. 83–97.
5 Kimberley Theidon, 'Gender in transition: Common sense, women, and war', *Journal of Human Rights* vol. 6, no. 4 (2007), pp. 453–478.
6 Anna Simons, *Networks of dissolution* (Boulder: Westview Press, 1995).
7 Linda Green, *Fear as a Way of Life* (New York: Columbia University Press, 1999), p. 75.
8 In addition to a full-time interpreter, I worked with a driver who was skilled at navigating the rough, dirt roads that led to each research site and looking after my very old car.
9 This number has since gone down through government release programmes. On *gacaca*, see Lars Waldorf, 'Mass justice for mass atrocity: Rethinking local justice as transitional justice', *Temple Law Review* vol. 71, no. 1 (2006), pp. 1–87.
10 Patrick N. Peritore, 'Reflections on dangerous fieldwork', *The American Sociologist*, (Winter 1990), pp. 359–372; Alessandro Portelli, *The Death of Luigi Trastulli and Other Stories* (Albany: State University of New York Press, 1991), pp. 30, 64.
11 Portelli, *The Death of Luigi Trastulli*, p. 51.
12 Payne, *Unsettling Accounts*, Chapter 7.
13 John P. Dean and William Foote Whyte 'How do you know if the informant is telling the truth?' in Lewis Anthony Dexter (ed.), *Elite and Specialized Interviewing* (Evanston: Northwestern University Press, 1970), p. 126.
14 Portelli, *The Death of Luigi Trastulli*, Chapter 6.
15 On RPF war crimes, see Des Forges, *Leave None to Tell the Story*, Roméo Dallaire, *Shake Hands with the Devil* (New York: Carroll and Graf Publishers, 2004), and Maria Beatrice Umutesi, *Fuir ou mourir au Zaïre: Le vécu d'une réfugiée rwandaise* (Paris: L'Harmattan, 2000).
16 See, for example, Peter Landesman, 'A Woman's Work', *The New Your Times Magazine* (15 September 2002), pp. 82–134.
17 Maria B. Olujic, 'The Croatian war experience', in Carolyn Nordstrom and Antonius C.G.M. Robben (eds), *Fieldwork Under Fire* (Berkeley: University of California Press, 1995).
18 Green, *Fear as a Way of Life*, p. 75.
19 Jean Hatzfeld, *Dans le nu de la vie: Récits des marais rwandais* (Paris: Éditions du Seuil, 2000).
20 Peritore, 'Reflections on dangerous fieldwork', p. 360.
21 Kay B. Warren, *Indigenous Movements and Their Critics: Pan-Maya Activism in Guatemala* (Princeton: Princeton University Press, 1998).
22 Liisa Malkki, *Purity and Exile* (Chicago: University of Chicago Press, 1995), p. 51.
23 Konstantin Belousov, Tom Horlick-Jones, Michael Bloor, Yakov Gilinkskiy, Valentin Golbert, Yakov Kostikovsky, Michael Levi, and Dmitri Pentsov, 'Any port in the storm: Fieldwork difficulties in dangerous and crisis-ridden settings', *Qualitative Research* vol. 7, no. 2 (2007), p. 156.
24 Staffan Löfving, 'Silence and the politics of representing rebellion: On the emergence of the neutral Maya in Guatemala', in Paul Richards (ed.) *No Peace No War: An Anthropology of Contemporary Armed Conflicts* (Athens: Ohio University Press, 2005), p. 89.

Part 4
Security

11 Maintenance of personal security: ethical and operational issues

Julie A. Mertus

Introduction

In recent years, expectations have changed within academia and among policy analysts regarding the appropriateness and feasibility of conducting research in dangerous situations. While in the past, researchers were implicitly or explicitly forbidden from entering zones of 'hot conflict', today most researchers expect to be free to go nearly anywhere and investigate nearly anything. Entering insecure areas, however, is particularly risky today, given the post-Cold War shift to intra-state conflicts, and the rise in terrorist activity and other non-state or trans-state violence. While humanitarian practitioners have increasingly adopted safety-conscious measures in their fieldwork, academic researchers lag far behind. Academic researchers could learn from humanitarian actors how to assess security risks and take appropriate measures. The goal of this chapter is to enhance the ability of academic researchers to conduct their own risk assessment and to explore other practical measures to enhance their personal security. Having read this chapter, researchers should be able to make more informed decisions as to whether to initiate research in a dangerous area and when to call it quits and return home.

This chapter is divided into three main parts. First, it begins with a statement of the causes of insecurity and the ethical imperative of 'personal security' (also referred to as 'care of self'). Second, it surveys the explosion of interest in safety amongst practitioners, and in particular the proliferation of training literature. Finally, drawing from this literature, the chapter explains the importance of conducting risk and vulnerability analyses, and concludes with suggestions for other practical safety measures for academic researchers working in dangerous situations.

The problem

Researchers working in difficult situations are often a self-sacrificing and even reckless lot. They work long hours, travel across insecure borders, shrug off sexual harassment and other forms of mistreatment that they would never tolerate back home, expose themselves to incurable diseases and stay up all night at the internet café blogging their exploits to an often tiny, but admiring, audience. In some circles, being the target for machine-gun fire is a sign of greatness. In others, it is a sure sign of stupidity. In any event, it is a clear indication that basic ethical standards have not been observed.

The ethical imperative of researchers to do no harm to the population that they study has long been established. In the field of human rights, this has led to extended recognition of the responsibility of anyone conducting fieldwork to anticipate any risks of harm to others that may arise in connection with their work and the need to take steps to minimize the possibility of such harm.[1] Less acknowledged, but equally important, is the responsibility of researchers to anticipate and counteract the potential harm to oneself. The types of harm that may await researchers includes not only the kind of harm to physical security that gun fire, bombings, landmines and natural disasters invoke,[2] but also the physical and psychological damage inflicted by detention and imprisonment, sexual harassment and other mistreatment designed to derail the possibility of working in the area. Additional critical concerns result from the severe stress of working with traumatized populations, living under the watch of an authoritarian state, travelling in highly militarized zones, and exposing oneself to continual danger.[3]

Care of the self is integrally related to care for others. At the heart of both types of care is a belief in human dignity and the equal moral worth of humankind. Whenever people act in ways contrary to their own human dignity, they threaten these fundamental tenets at their root. The impact could be direct and immediate. For example, a researcher who overlooks the potential risks of their work and who disregards their own vulnerability may endanger not only their own security but also the security of their interview subjects. At the same time, the impact of disregarding personal security may also be more indirect and long-term, as when a researcher takes enormous personal risks in tracking down a story and in so doing fosters the creation of a downgraded security standard for others to follow.[4]

Security concerns have never been greater for in-country researchers. Developments in communication and transportation technologies have made it easier for a wide range of researchers to travel to the heart of conflicts. During the American/Vietnam War, to take one illustration, only a handful of journalists went to the battlefields; academics, for the most part, provided commentary and analysis from afar. Beginning with the Balkan wars of the 1990s, however, the scenario changed significantly. Dubbed the 'first war that Europeans could hitch-hike to', the Bosnian war was home to floods of journalists and academics, many of whom had no training whatsoever in personal security. To compound matters, these neophytes find themselves entering into conflict zones that posed considerably more hazards for civilians than in earlier times.

In a speech that would be heralded for its poignancy following the bombing of the US Embassy in Baghdad which took his life, Sergio Vieira de Mello (former UN High Commissioner for Human Rights) summarized the new and dangerous scenario as follows:

> Contemporary armed conflict is seldom conducted on a clearly defined battlefield, by conventional armies confronting each other. Today's warfare often takes place in cities and villages, with civilians as the preferred targets, the propagation of terror as the premeditated tactic, and the physical elimination or mass displacement of certain categories of populations as the overarching strategy ... Meeting [humanitarian] needs has become more difficult, as the dividing line between soldiers and civilians has grown blurred.[5]

The risks described by de Mello are particularly high during complex emergencies,[6] or profound and prolonged social crisis, 'where there is total or considerable breakdown of authority resulting from internal or external conflict and which requires an international response that goes beyond the mandate or capacity of any single agency and/or the ongoing United Nations country programme'.[7]

Academic researchers can find their ability to obtain permission to reside legally in such a country to be frustrated due to the lack of a central authority and the resulting anarchy. In the absence of a central government, or when one is too weakened to be effective, researchers are tempted to turn to local militia and warlords for *de facto* permission to do such basic things as enter and exit the country (or, in particular parts of the country), to gain access to refugee camps and/or to use warlord controlled roads. This situation undermines researcher neutrality and opens the door for manipulation by local armed groups.[8] Furthermore, by interacting directly with and advocating on behalf of high risk or marginalized populations, workers also put themselves at greater risk of being targeted by armed factions.[9]

The risks of relying on the state in situations where the state is a serious perpetrator of violence and abuses cannot be overstated. Academic researchers studying conflicts in which peacekeepers have been deployed face an entirely new set of challenges connected to misconceptions about the nature of peacekeeping.[10] Peacekeeping does not guarantee the end to violence against civilians. In fact, in some cases, an internally-declared peace may signal the onset of different forms of violence targeting civilians, such as kidnapping and corruption.[11] The presence of peacekeepers can lead to a false sense of security, encouraging researchers to take risks that they should only take in peacetime. So too can the presence of armed guards, armoured vehicles and bullet proof vests. Researchers who avail themselves of these accoutrements of twenty-first century war games are most likely to place themselves unnecessarily in danger. Instead of searching for new gimmicks to protect themselves, researchers should be trying to equip themselves with better information to guide their decision making. Fortunately, they have a place to turn for information, as humanitarian practitioners have produced a plethora of training manuals and guides with general application to academic researchers.

The security scramble

The intensity at which international institutions have pushed back against any possible downgrading in standards for security has been incredible. Leading the surge of interest in security, the United Nations (UN) has moved away from an *ad hoc* agency-by-agency response to crisis and has instead shifted towards a more organized and coordinated stance.[12] In 1998, the UN began building an institutional infrastructure for security with the creation of the Office of the UN Security Coordinator (UNSECOORD), a unit which later became part of the UN Department of Safety and Security (UNDSS). During his tenure, former Secretary General, Kofi Anan, persistently advocated for increased and consistent funding for UNSECOORD and solicited donations from Member States to the Trust Fund for the Security of UN Personnel.[13]

Alongside its institutional approach to safety, the UN has also focused on developing training programmes for field staff, as well as hiring security officers for regional headquarters and field offices.[14] In January 1998, the UN released *Security in the Field: Information for Staff Members of the United Nations System*, a handbook that provided information related to the UN security management system and also addressed hostage taking, security for children, gender-specific issues (with a strong focus on sexual harassment and violence), as well as stress management.[15] Several months later, in May 1998, the Commission of the European Communities published a working document on the *Security of Relief Workers and Humanitarian Space*, which, among other issues, explores how the provision of aid in itself affects certain conflicts and occasionally propagates insecurity and how donor agencies and other financial sponsors can also create unnecessary additional risk for staff.[16]

These issues have been further explored by Koenraad Van Brabant, one of the most influential scholars on security management. After authoring numerous articles and reports on the topic from 1994 to 1999, Van Brabant produced a landmark document that is still considered one of the most comprehensive analysis on staff safety, *Operational Security Management in Violent Environments: A Field Manual for Aid Agencies* (published by the UK Overseas Development Institute (ODI)).[17] The text, commonly referred to as the bible of staff security, is intended to be a practical reference guide that offers a systematic approach for the management of security concerns, including risk assessment, threat analysis and prevention, safety planning and communication coordination. A year later, in March 2001, Van Brabant complemented his 'how to' field manual with a text addressing the role of management in security decision-making. *Mainstreaming the Organizational Management of Safety and Security: A review of aid agency practices and a guide for management* offers in-depth analysis of initial attempts by 20 organizations to strengthen staff safety that suggests recommendations to further improve organizational security.

While Van Brabant is widely admired as a leading scholar whose work has shaped the direction of the security discipline, the International Committee of the Red Cross (ICRC) draws kudos as a leading organization in this area. The ICRC has offered some of the most definitive work on security, with the *Code of Conduct for the International Red Cross and Red Crescent Movement and Non-Governmental Organizations (NGOs) in Disaster Relief*, published in 1994, long serving as the standard in the field.[18] This seminal text has served as a starting point for more recent ICRC training manuals, such as the March 2008 ICRC comprehensive guide *Stay Safe – International Federation's Guide to a Safer Mission.*[19]

Nongovernmental organizations have followed suit with their own trainings and manuals on in-country security. The seminal work specifically addressing NGO concerns is *The People In Aid Code Of Best Practice in the Management and Support of Aid Personnel.* This widely-accepted NGO best practice guide emphasizes a strategic, participatory and transparent approach to the management of human resources, with security concerns integrated across management based on best practices in the field.[20] Sara Davidson, on behalf of the Relief and Rehabilitation Network, drew up the first published version of the code between 1995 and 1997 after extensive consultations with humanitarian organizations worldwide. Driven by humanitarian agencies in the UK and Ireland, with funding from the UK government's then Overseas Development Administration, input on best practices also came from UN agencies as well as from humanitarian organizations from elsewhere in Europe and the United States. Most recently revised in 2003, the guiding principles espoused in the *People In Aid Code* are still considered the industry benchmark.

In sum, many excellent guides on the safety of humanitarian staff exist – far too many to mention all by name here. Surprisingly, the lessons from these guides rarely find their way into trainings for academic researchers. The problem is not a lack of interest in security. On the contrary, the number of universities and independent research institutions interested in training their researchers in security protocol has escalated. The problem seems to be a lack of connection between the academic and practitioner worlds. Academic researchers have a lot to learn from humanitarian practitioners on enhancing personal security.

Enhancing personal security of academic researchers

Risk assessment

Mike O'Neill, the Director of Security for Save the Children, recommends that 'before deployment to the field every aid worker should be conversant with her/his respective organizational mission and how that mission/

organization is likely to be perceived by stakeholders in the area of operation'.[21] In similar fashion, academic researchers should remain cognizant of their mission – as defined by their own research plan – and become knowledgeable of how their research intervention is likely to be perceived. In addition, regardless of the scope of their mission, they should have a foundation of knowledge of the conflict (actors, history, patrons, etc.) and endeavour to understand the most likely threats to be encountered on the ground.[22] The process of gaining and weighting this kind of information is known as a 'situational analysis' and 'risk assessment'.[23]

Standard practice in any Red Cross or United Nations training for pre-deployment of field staff to troubled areas begins with a situational analysis and risk assessment with the explicit goal of obtaining the most information possible to make an informed decision on whether and how to operate in-country.[24] Academic intervenors, in contrast, take great pains to assess risks to the subject of the research while overlooking risks to the researcher. A risk assessment surveying the entire security environment, however, would also be of great utility to them and indeed their research plan. A risk assessment not only helps to inform the decision as to whether or not to go into a country, but also helps to reduce the risk once researchers find themselves in a dangerous environment. Some academic researchers may resist conducting such an extensive analysis, asserting that it is not within their mandate. Risk analysis is essential to perform an evaluation of likelihood of harm to self and others and, thus, it is clearly of relevance to research design, implementation and results.

A risk assessment involves scrutiny of both the external factors and internal threats that may affect the security environment. External factors include an analysis of the:[25]

- →**History of communal conflict and state-sanctioned violence** – *According to all sides in the conflict, what are the historical and the current reasons for conflict? Is there a history of struggle over resources, long-standing discrimination and exclusion, chauvinism, racism and patterns of mobilization based on identity groups?*
- →**Identification of political elites** – *Who controls the state, and how is that authority exercised in terms of the allocation of resources, privileges and opportunities?*

What sections of society do they come from and what privileges do they enjoy?
- →**Identification of external players** – *What has been and is currently the role, overt and covert, of regional and international players? What is their interest in the state?*
- →**Existence and functioning of legal institutions and observance of the rule of law** – *Do all people view legal institutions as functioning fairly? Do all people have equal access to the legal system and are political disputes likely to be resolved peacefully through legal institutions?*

Maintenance of personal security: ethical and operational issues 171

- →**Trends in protection of human rights** – *Has the state agreed to the domestic enforcement of international human rights standards and to what extent do all people enjoy full protection in line with these standards?*
- → **Military developments** – *How much power does the military hold over local political decision making? How likely is a threat to the established political order arise from either the state-sanctioned military or from other armed groups?*
- → **The economy/resource base and infrastructure** – *To what extent are resources distributed fairly and to what extent do structured inequalities exist between groups? What kind of challenges does the infrastructure pose to safe travel (i.e., how safe are the roads?); provision of medical care (i.e., if a foreigner is hit in a car accident or contracts a terrible illness, what kind of medical care is available?*
- → **The crime profile** – *Is crime opportunistic on the part of one or a few individuals, or is it likely to be organized crime? Are there criminal groups linked to an armed group, for example, is it exporting drugs or diamonds and importing weapons in return? Is it linked to political interests, such as the 'thugs' that get used by political power-brokers to intimidate and attack their opponents or instigate 'mob violence'? Or is it a criminal group working on its own account, enriching itself through illegal activities?*
- →**The nature of the current conflict** – *How do all international and external parties to the conflict identify the nature of the conflict? Can it be said to be a struggle over scarce resources, a rebellion by an oppressed group, an illegal/legal attempt of a state to retain control over its own territory, etc.? Are terrorism tactics being used in the environment, and if so what are their nature? Are the attacks against political and military targets or against an 'illegal foreign presence'?*
- →**The probability of natural disaster** – *How likely is an earthquake, hurricane, flood or other natural disaster? Should a natural disaster hit, what kinds of preparations have been made for emergency evacuation?*

The identification and analysis of possible external factors helps to identify and prioritize potential threats to the researcher, such as: artillery fire, mines, car-jacking at gunpoint, sexual harassment and abuse, and exposure to disease. The likelihood of impact must be continually monitored because it changes over time and is often determined by the current attitudes within the country to international interveners generally and, in particular, to those states likely to be associated with the researcher. In addition, the likelihood that a particular researcher would have her security threatened may be lessened should the researcher understand the social norms and codes of the society and act respectfully in light of them.

Vulnerability assessment

Another consideration for researchers in assessing risk is their own vulnerability. There is not necessarily a single risk assessment template for all academic researchers entering into a conflict area. Different researchers may face different threats because of their origin, affiliation, age or gender. Vulnerability may increase or decrease according to one's own particular exposure to threats. Van Brabant helpfully suggests a list of questions for humanitarian aid workers that could be applicable to academic researchers as well:

- Are you at risk of military or terrorist activities – e.g. because of the location of your [interview or participant observation] sites and travel routes, [and] the timing of your movements?
- Are you at risk of targeted political action – e.g., because of the politics of your home government; the simple fact of your being foreigners/ Westerners; the identity of your[translator, driver or other local assistants]; the nature and balance of your relationships with different interest groups in a conflictual situation; the position you have taken in any of your previous publications or any other public statements you have made?
- Are you at risk of criminal acts – e.g., because of the (perceived) value of your assets; the location of your office or residence ...; the nature of your travel movements; the proximity or hindrance of your presence ... to criminal gang activity?
- Are you at risk of angry and aggressive actions by disgruntled populations – e.g., ... because of the controversial nature of your research?[26]

Ultimately the degree of a particular researcher's vulnerability will depend on the appropriateness and effectiveness of the security measures that they have taken to reduce the risk.[27] Each researcher should decide for themselves how far they are willing to go in protecting themselves and the threshold of unacceptable risk. To take one illustration: for some academic researchers, it is time to go home when it becomes clear that a research plan cannot be accomplished without the aid of an armed guard and the enlistment of an armoured vehicle. For others, these measures would be completely acceptable and even anticipated.

The ABCs of threat and vulnerability analysis[28]

A threat and vulnerability assessment can be conducted in different ways, but they all should answer the following questions:

Why could an attack happen (crime, political reasons, ransom, revenge)?

Who poses the threat (criminals, army, armed factions, fanatics, dissatisfied workers beneficiaries)?

What are the likely targets (expatriate staff, visitors, family members or local staff)?

How could an attack happen (weapons, ambush, bombs, robbery, hostage taking)?

Where are we most vulnerable and where are the likely locations for any attacks?

When could an attack happen and when does the possibility of an attack increase?

Other security measures

For academic researchers conducting a situation analysis and risk and vulnerability assessment is just the beginning of the creation of a personal security plan. Prior to departure researchers entering dangerous situations should take the precaution of registering with their country's embassy or consulate,[29] ensure that they have a reliable and safe means of communication and transport, and obtain all necessary immunizations and medications. Researchers should also consider making copies of their travel documents and passport and leaving at least one with a reliable contact back home.

Any piece of information discovered in the possession of the researcher is subject to being confiscated, read and misused against the researcher and the research subjects. For this reason, researchers should plan on leaving behind phone books, research notes and other work product that could lead to harassment and abuse should it fall into the wrong hands. For the same reasons, researchers should be careful to not keep much information on their laptop computers. Provided that secure e-mail is available, researchers can use it to safeguard their research notes. As soon as data is entered into the computer, it can be e-mailed to a safer location. Even with assurances that communication channels are safe, researchers should still use a code when identifying local sources in research notes.

The designation of a supportive person residing outside the conflict area can be incredibly important. Not only can this person be the recipient of e-mailed data and the holder of copies of important documents, but they can also act as a researcher's conscience. Sometimes, in the heat of the moment, field researchers will be tempted to move outside their comfort zone. Prior to their arrival in-country, researchers should think about acceptable levels of risk and communicate their decision to a colleague who will remain at home, who will be able to remind the researcher of their personal security planning and, if necessary, be able to call an over-zealous researcher home.

Once in-country, the researcher should review local media sites and local colleagues to check on their sense of the situation on the ground, gaining information about specific safety developments, such as landmine placement and removal, and the recovery and removal of small arms stockpiles. If humanitarian work is being conducted in the area, the researcher should ascertain how they employ security precautions; asking, for example, the extent to which security precautions are employed and, if possible, establish/ join a security coordination network. Whenever possible, the researcher should also check in on their embassy or consulate to record their arrival. Throughout the entire length of time spent in-country, the researcher should continually take the pulse of the security environment and prepare for sudden changes.

Conclusion

Humanitarian practitioners have long realized that an effective mission does not require a tradeoff with personal security. On the contrary, humanitarian work in dangerous places is more likely to be effective if security measures are enhanced across the board – that is, for both those on the delivering and on the receiving sides of the humanitarian equation. Academic researchers would do well to learn from practitioner experiences with risk assessment and security analysis. The ethical imperative to take care of oneself in the field is strong, and the pragmatic justifications for security-awareness are evident. The best academic work comes not from unconsidered risk-taking but from careful application of security measures.

Notes

1 See, e.g., 'Statement of Ethical Commitments of Human Rights Professionals', in *Consolidating The Profession: The Human Rights Field Officer,* Humanrights professionals.org, *available at* <http://www.humanrightsprofessionals.org/images/statement%20of%20ethical%20commitments_nov%2028%202007_website.pdf>, accessed 17 March 2009.
2 See Cate Buchanan and Robert Muggah, *No Relief: Surveying the Effects of Gun Violence on Humanitarian and Development Personnel* (Geneva: Centre for Humanitarian Dialogue, 2005); Leanne Olsen, *A Cruel Paradise: Journals of an International Relief Worker* (Toronto: Insomniac Press, 2002).
3 See, e.g., John Burnett, *Where Soldiers Fear to Tread: A Relief Worker's Tale of Survival* (New York: Random House, 2005).
4 In Bosnia, for example, it was the author's experience that the tendency of certain journalists and humanitarian aid workers to accept great personal insecurity lowered the bar on security for all other researchers in the region.
5 Sergio Vieira de Mello, 'Meeting of Special Rapporteurs/Representatives, Experts and Working Groups of the Special Procedures of the Commission on Human Rights' (Geneva: United Nations, May 31, 1999).
6 Frederick M. Burkle, 'Complex Emergencies: An Introduction', *Prehospital and Disaster Medicine,* vol. 16 no. 4 (October–December, 2001).
7 Consolidated Appeal Process Guidelines, Inter-Agency Standing Committee (13 April, 1994), available at <http://www.reliefweb.int/cap/CAPSWG/CAP_Policy_Document/Guidelines/CAPguid94.doc> accessed 17 March 2009.
8 Mark Turner, "We are helpers, not martyrs': UN aid workers are increasingly becoming targets in the war zones they try to assist*', Financial Times* (7 October, 2000).
9 See e.g., Catherine A. Bertini, 'Protecting the Protectors', in Yael Danieli (ed.), *Sharing the Front Lines and the Back Hills: International Protectors and Providers:*

Peacekeepers, Humanitarian Aid Workers and the Media in the Midst of Crisis (New York: United Nations, 2002), pp. 64–67.
10 Arne Nils Kastberg, 'Risk and Protection for UNICEF Field Staff', in Yael Danieli (ed.), Sharing the Front Lines and the Back Hills: International Protectors and Providers: Peacekeepers, Humanitarian Aid Workers and the Media in the Midst of Crisis (New York: United Nations, 2002), pp. 72–77.
11 '2007 "One of the Deadliest Years" for United Nations Personnel, Staff Union Says: At least 9 Peacekeepers, 33 Civilian Staff Members Killed During Year', UNDPI Press Release ORG/1489 (New York: UNDPI, 2 January 2008), available <http://domino.un.org/UNISPAL.NSF/9a798adbf322aff38525617b006d88d7/b657b e76c84ac934852573c5004f2cda!OpenDocument> accessed 17 March 2009.
12 'UN Security Structure', UNDAC (2006), available at <http://ochaonline.un.org/OchaLinkClick.aspx?link=ocha&DocId=1005295> accessed 17 March 2009.
See also 'United Nations Joint Logistics Centre Brief Description', UNJLC (12 June 2006), available at <http://www.unjlc.org/about/unjlc_brief_discription> accessed 17 March 2009.
13 UNIS, 'Secretary-General Kofi Annan Promises Major Reform of UN Peacekeeping Calls on Member States to Provide Funds, Improve Decision-making', UN Press Release UNIS/PK/39 (23 August 2000).
14 UNIS, 'Secretary-General, at Staff Security Summit, Urges States to Ratify Treaty on Safety of United Nations and Associated Personnel', UN Press Release SG/SM/7869 (29 June 2001).
15 Security in the Field: Information for Staff Members of the United Nations System, United Nations, Office of the United Nations Security Coordinator (New York, 1998), available at <http://www.reliefweb.int/library/documents/security.pdf> accessed 17 March 2009.
16 'Security of Relief Workers and Humanitarian Space', EU Commission (1998), available at <http://aei.pitt.edu/6712/> accessed 17 March 2009.
17 Koenraad Van Brabant, 'Operational Security Management in Violent Environments: A Field Manual for Aid Agencies', Humanitarian Practice Network at the Overseas Development Institute (London, June 2000), available at <http://ngosecurity.googlepages.com/GPR8.pdf> accessed 17 March 2009.
18 ICRC, 'Code of Conduct for the International Red Cross and Red Crescent Movement and Non-Governmental Organizations (NGOs) in Disaster Relief' (Geneva: ICRC, 1994)(with subsequent revisions).
19 Lars Tangen; John Dyer; Karl Julisson, 'Stay Safe: Stay Safe – International Federation's Guide to a Safer Mission', International Federation of the Red Cross, IFRC security Unit (Mar 2008), available at <http://www.reliefweb.int/rw/lib.nsf/db900sid/OCHA-7DBHYA/$file/113700-stay_safe_management-EN.pdf?openelement> accessed 17 March 2009, pp. 23–24.
20 Sara Davidson, 'People in Aid Code of Best Practice in the Management and Support of Aid Personnel', People In Aid, Relief and Rehabilitation Network Paper 20 (1997), available at <http://www.peopleinaid.org/code/>, accessed 17 March 2009.
21 Mike O'Neill, 'Ask the Experts', InterAction (2000), available at <http://www.interaction.org/library/detail.php?id=5476> accessed 17 March 2009.
22 Tangen, Dyer, and Julisson, 'Stay Safe', pp. 25–27.
23 Ibid.
24 See, e.g., ICRC, 'Seminar on the Security of Humanitarian Personnel in the Field for Non Governmental Organisations (NGOs)' (Geneva: ICRC, 5 December 1997).
25 These are drawn from many sources, with the most reliance on Tangen, Dyer, and Julisson, 'Stay Safe', pp. 23–24.
26 Ibid., p. 50–51.

27 David Lloyd Roberts, 'Staying Alive: Safety and Security Guidelines For Humanitarian Volunteers In Conflict Areas', The International Committee of the Red Cross (revised, 2005), available at <http://www.reliefweb.int/rw/lib.nsf/db900sid/RURI-6LJUCY/$file/icrc-safety 30jan.pdf.pdf?openelement> accessed 17 March 2009.
28 Tangen, Dyer, and Julisson, 'Stay Safe', p. 26.
29 O'Neill, 'Ask the Experts'.

12 Impact on research of security-seeking behaviour

Amy Ross

Introduction

This chapter explores the nexus of *research* and *security* in conflict zones, or what have been called 'warscapes'.[1] Peoples and places experiencing violence and mass atrocity are notoriously difficult to study. In addition to the dangers to researchers attempting to collect data, interviews obtained in conflict zones are precarious and problematic. Perpetrators are often recalcitrant to discuss events that might be self-incriminating, and the victims of violence may be placed in further danger if they attempt to denounce the crime. In particular, for the victims of violence, reporting local events to outsiders might be so dangerous that many choose to remain silent, or give false information, rather than risk further trauma.

Although clearly a complicated project, it is imperative to conduct research on violence. Social science research would be of rather poor quality without quantitative and qualitative data directly related to the human beings who produce, resist, and survive in (and despite) conflict zones. Often this research must be conducted in the sites where the violence has occurred and where there is the danger of further damage, especially to those who remain in the conflict zone after the researcher has returned to his/her home country and institution.[2]

This chapter probes the intersections, contradictions and potentially dangerous collisions between 'research' and 'security'. The discussion focuses on how violence and danger influence the data we collect/create, our conclusions, and the relevance of our work. The discussion is organized around several broad questions. First, in the section entitled **Security and silence**, I discuss the difficulties of attempting to do research on violence, within conditions of violence, while looking after the safety of oneself and others. How do efforts to be safe in the midst of danger influence the research collection process? Second, discussing **Trauma, testimony and data**, I address the complexity of obtaining and understanding information from informants who have suffered trauma. When are the data important enough (if ever) to justify the potentially disruptive presence of a researcher, and how does one make these kind of assessments? Finally, in **Human security and the relevance of research** I discuss the difficulties of transforming the lived experiences of informants in conflict zones into something called 'data' that can be used to communicate meaning to scholarly and other audiences. As researchers in conflict zones, what rights (if any) do we have to work within 'life-rafts' of relative safety, amidst a sea of suffering, and what responsibilities exist concerning the relevancy of the research?[3] How does the broader absence of the basic needs of human security (such as adequate food, shelter, health care) intersect with and influence research on the conditions of violence?

I address these questions based on my experiences, illustrating the discussion through specific examples.[4] The goal is to generate further questions rather than provide answers; this essay is a polemic rather than a 'how to' primer. The central dilemma involves attempting to be safe in a dangerous world.

Security and silence

One night in Guatemala I found myself on the side of a dark road, surrounded by a group of agitated young soldiers with machine guns. While the conditions were chaotic and confused, I remember thinking very clearly that this was the wrong place to be. Whatever else you do with your life and work, I told myself, avoid situations in which a pack of nervous teenage boys might have the means and motivation to shoot you.

I was with Rigoberta Menchú Tum, the Guatemalan Mayan author and activist and the recipient of the 1992 Nobel Peace Prize. We were returning from the highlands, Santa Cruz de Quiché, to the capital late at night in May 1993. Our party was stopped at a military check point on the outskirts of Guatemala City. Guatemala was in a state of emergency as the country was experiencing a coup following then-President Jorge Serrano's dissolving of Congress. A curfew was in effect. It could be that we were pulled over as a matter of routine, within the context of the state of exception. Or it is possible that the military was displeased with Rigoberta's decision to make a surprise trip to El Quiché, her first time home since her exile a decade before. If we were specifically targeted, this compounded the possible dangers.

The soldiers had told the men in our group to step to the side while they talked to Rigoberta.[5] I moved over to stand next to Rigoberta, who immediately told me to go stand with the males in our group, and I realized my mistake – of course it was the men being led away, to an even darker area off the road, who were in more danger than Rigoberta herself. Rigoberta got us out of the situation through the sheer force of her personality. At one point in the drama she stood before the soldier-boys with their twitchy fingers on the trigger and said: 'I am *La Premio Nobel* (the Nobel Laureate) and I will be going back to the capital now'. The soldiers, young Mayans themselves, became suddenly respectful and stepped aside: We were eventually allowed back into our vehicles and on our way. Once back in Guatemala City, we spent the night at the offices of CONAVIGUA (the association of widows of the violence). Everyone slept together on mats in the room at the back of the building, in case the house was attacked from the street.

That particular dangerous situation occurred while 'accompanying' a human rights activist rather than conducting social science research. The practice of 'accompaniment' was adopted by solidarity groups (mostly from the United States and Europe) to provide support for human rights activists in Central America living with the threat of violence. In theory, the presence of an 'international', and a potential witness, with a vulnerable person could deter violence against these potential targets. But I wanted to be more than a body – I wanted to study the dynamics of violence and power in Guatemala, and (attempt to) make a contribution in the realm of ideas. I also knew that such work would take me into difficult situations, like the frightening episode on the side of the road with Rigoberta and too many guns. In the context of conflict and danger, I would have to figure out – if I could – how to be safe. The difficulties would go beyond a concrete moment of having machine guns pointed in my face. I would have to consider the security of others – before, during and after my intervention. And I would have to develop appropriate methodologies in order to understand and interpret the data I was collecting.

Is it possible to be safe in an unsafe world? How can one seek safety, when trying specifically to study the absence of security? It is, I believe, necessary to look after one's own safety, but also incredibly presumptuous. Why should the researcher be safe while everyone else suffers fear and the consequences of violence? At its worst, security-seeking behaviour on the part of a researcher can put others at risk.

In the context of Guatemala, where I worked between 1989 and 2002, the issue of security, for oneself as a researcher and for others, loomed large. During the decades of violence in Guatemala, an estimated 45,000 persons 'disappeared', 200,000 persons were killed, more than 600 villages were wiped off the map, some 200,000 Guatemalans were forced into refuge in neighbouring Mexico, and more than a million Guatemalans were internally displaced.[6] In addition to the brutality of political murders, massacres and other acts of overt violence, much of the populace suffered from poverty and discrimination in their daily lives. In the context of such conditions, an armed insurgency formed in the 1960s. While the rebels failed to actually take power as in neighbouring Nicaragua in 1979, or to even develop a plausible capacity to do so as rebels did in El Salvador in the 1980s, the existence of the armed rebellion in Guatemala provided the rationale for a violent counter-insurgency campaign which involved widespread attacks on the civilian population.

In addition to its intensity and extent, a significant aspect of the violence in Guatemala was the fact that it was denied. The massacres of entire villages in the highlands were conducted secretly – the army claimed that it was fighting a war against terrorists or communists – and largely failed to receive international attention as mass atrocity.[7] 'Disappearances' were essential to 'deniability'.[8] In the absence of a corpse, the state could deny that a crime had even occurred. Ignacio Martín-Baró, a prominent social psychologist, observed that the power of this particular form of terror was the state's ability to deny responsibility for these crimes while simultaneously making the entire society aware that it could kill with impunity.[9]

These diabolical features of 'disappearance' shaped my initiation into Guatemala. When I had first arrived in the country I lived with a family in Guatemala City while studying Spanish. Their oldest child, Gustavo, had been 'disappeared'. One afternoon as he was leaving the university, armed men driving a car without plates had grabbed him. Gustavo's family went to the police and became intimidated by the questions: 'Was your son a rebel? Maybe he went to join the guerrillas? Who was he with, who were his friends, who were the witnesses? Give us their names and addresses!' Gustavo's family met others at the morgue while looking for Gustavo's body and joined the Mutual Support Group for Families of the Disappeared (GAM).[10] The phone threats then began: 'Stop looking or you will lose another'. A family crisis deepened as some family members insisted they must keep 'looking' (which meant political activism) and others worried about further violence. The mother became ill. The father laid down the law – everyone must do everything to spare further pain. In the two months I lived in the house I rarely saw anyone go out except when necessary – to work and to the market for food. Gustavo was rarely mentioned. Very little conversation took place at all.

I became obsessed, in that house, with Gustavo's story. I wanted to know more, but raising the subject of the absent son provoked further pain, and causing additional injury to my hosts felt like a violation in itself. In such an intense climate of fear and insecurity, where the stakes were so high, it was extremely difficult to pursue research, especially research directly associated with the violence.[11] The lack of security was especially intense for Guatemalans (academics and activists) attempting to acknowledge and address the violence and associated structures of power. One of the first challenges I was confronted with was the fact that the most obvious way to avoid risk was to stay silent. To even broach the subject of the violence and its meanings, much less to raise the question of responsibility, was venturing into dangerous terrain. Often, the very fact that a researcher would be foolish enough to ask such a question would convince the respondent that answering truthfully would be a mistake. Who could possibly trust someone indiscreet enough to ask such a question? To talk about such topics was to raise one's voice to a shout in a culture where people were afraid to even whisper.

To research violence required talking to those most affected by the violence. However, the violence itself created the conditions under which seeking information about the violence could provoke further repression. Rather than initiating conversations and/or interviews, I listened a lot. I spent years and years with my mouth shut. In a strange way, it helped that my first few years in Guatemala were spent learning Spanish and Central American politics and history. Because my knowledge of the language and society was so minimal, I had to listen rather than speak.

By the time I began dissertation research in 1994, I had experience and a degree of familiarity with Guatemala that worked in my favour. Years of involvement with the country meant that I knew, to an extent, when and where to observe. Some of the most important interviews and participatory observation in Guatemala occurred with my notebook closed. Most importantly, over the previous decade I had established a community of friends and colleagues in Guatemala, who trusted me enough to share their opinions. Much of my research in Guatemala was informed by the access that these associates provided to sensitive sites and information.

When I reflect on my experiences in Guatemala, I realize that my sense of security, and that of others, was predicated on my knowing how to observe silences and absences more than engaging in speech. In most instances, interviews and participatory observation could only be conducted if I had a long-term association with the appropriate person to facilitate my access. Once granted access, I had to be constantly vigilant of when and how I asked questions, and the impact of my presence on activities I observed.

Trauma, testimony and 'data'

Obtaining and analyzing the data that results from research conducted in difficult situations is complex, whether one is seeking information from victims or perpetrators. It is challenging both to obtain 'data' from persons who have suffered trauma, and to transform their lived experiences into an analysis that can be used to communicate meaning to scholarly and other audiences. Similarly, it is difficult to include the 'perpetrators' voice in the research data and analysis. While the categories of 'victim' and 'perpetrator' are far from separate and static, the relevant issue is how to get at the essential sources of information.[12] The risks and potential adverse impact of collecting data has to be weighed against the possibility that the data will be sufficiently useful to justify the potentially disruptive presence and activities of a researcher.

In Guatemala, fear of repercussions was a major obstacle to discussing the violence. In the countryside, many of the perpetrators of the violence still lived in the communities, often maintaining positions of influence and power. While I was conducting fieldwork observing the Guatemalan truth commission and its activities collecting testimonies in the countryside, the fear was apparent. Many of those providing testimony were fearful of signing their names to their statements, although this was a requirement in order for the information to be analyzed by the staff and included in the final report. Villagers refrained from discussing the violence, preferring to 'guardar el silencio,' (watch one's tongue) due to ongoing fears, rather than solely the trauma of the past.[13] Perpetrators rarely called themselves that – to this day I have yet to meet a war criminal that doesn't consider him/herself a war hero.

In theory, sharing one's personal, painful experience serves to make the experience 'real' and hence assist in the recovery of a victim.[14] A South

African Truth and Reconciliation Commission poster proclaimed 'Revealing is Healing', and the authors of the Guatemalan Commission for Historical Clarification's final report, 'Memory of Silence', asserted that truth-telling would 'dignify' and therefore contribute to the recovery of the victims.[15] Yet relating traumatic experience is always a subjective activity, making its interpretation very complex. Elaine Scarry argues that the pain suffered by the body in extreme duress, such as under torture or through physical assault, constitutes the 'unmaking of the world', in that the experience is impossible to express in language. The pain associated with a traumatic experience, whether experienced in the flesh or emotionally, may jeopardize the ability of a victim to communicate that experience in coherent testimony. In South Africa, for example, during hearings focusing on human rights violations, victims relating their experiences would often leave the stage without finishing their testimony. Although these people had been prepared (to a certain extent) by Truth and Reconciliation Commission 'briefers', when the moment arrived to speak, victims would become overwhelmed by the pain of the experiences they were trying to relate. In other cases, although the victim's presentation would appear coherent, later the victim would complain that he/she had failed, in the short time available, to truly relate experiences.

Speaking about traumatic experience must be preceded by the establishment of a 'safe' place in which to talk.[16] In South Africa, the political transformation of 1994 had contributed to the lessening of political violence (except in KwaZulu Natal) and therefore an increased sense of safety in discussing political issues.[17] By the time victims stepped forward to tell their stories to the South African Truth and Reconciliation Commission, security conditions had significantly improved. In contrast, in Guatemala, the lack of a profound political transition (despite the signing of the 1996 peace agreement) meant that conditions of fear persisted through the period of my research, particularly in the countryside. Hence in addition to the emotional pain of reference to the violence of the past, individuals sharing their traumatic experience in Guatemala further faced fears regarding the impact of that testimony on future security. Many of the people responsible for the violence remained in a position to cause additional trauma, and those providing testimony were conscious of this danger.

Efforts to remain secure impact the abilities of victims, perpetrators and observers to relate the circumstances of violence. These conditions complicate the project of data collection and analysis. Testimony based on trauma is influenced by the fear of further danger and the fallibility of memory, and the way in which the so-called 'fog of war' can colour the recollection of the events. As Tim O'Brien observes: 'In any war story, but especially a true one, it's difficult to separate what happened from what seemed to happen. What seems to happen becomes its own happening and has to be told that way'.[18] While observing the collection of testimony in the South African Truth and Reconciliation Commission and the Guatemalan Commission for Historical Clarification, I learned that my research must be grounded on the premise that the manner in which 'the truth' is constructed must be understood within the context of the specific conditions shaping the security, or lack thereof, associated with the establishment and functions of the sites in which the testimony was narrated.

Human security and the relevance of research

Conducting research on violence, pain and trauma is challenging for the researcher, the informants and the readership. With the effort and expense involved, there is, arguably, a duty to make the data worthwhile. On the one hand there is the very real need to attempt to do social science research in societies experiencing intense violence and conflict, and on the other a complicated set of concerns about how that research (knowledge) is produced, and for whom. In particular, it would be grotesque to use the life experiences of informants as mere 'data' for our social science research, or, worse, for advancing our careers. The duty becomes particularly clear in the context of conducting research where one's interlocutors not only face direct security threats, as engaging with the researcher may lead to reprisals or violence, but where one's interlocutors lack many of the basic preconditions for human security, facing poverty, threats to health, and precarious living conditions.[19]

Can research in conflict zones benefit the people most affected by the violence, especially when substantial elements of the affected population lack the basics of human security, such as food and shelter? How to make one's work worthwhile, such that the costs and risks of the research (for researchers and those we encounter) might yield greater human security? I was most recently tested by this dilemma during fieldwork in Northern Uganda, where I found my own position of relative privilege complicated the fieldwork. Specifically, the data I was seeking – local reactions to the International Criminal Court (ICC) – seemed quite remote from the reality of my interviewees, given conditions in the Internally Displaced People's (IDP) camps, where more than 90 per cent of the population struggled to survive.

The powers and positionality of the researcher (in this case, a 'white' North American) and the subjects (in this case, Ugandan victims of violence) complicated the collection and interpretation of data. In my experience (and in my opinion), it is extremely difficult to visit an IDP's camp without being interpreted as a non-governmental organization (NGO) representative. Often I was identified (wrongly) as someone there to provide 'aid' – that is to offer something – when in fact I was there to *take* something – interviews that I could translate into data and knowledge.

Moreover, the data I sought to extract was designed for a research project that seemed very far from the actual needs of the population. Perhaps the readers of the scholarly journal where my research would (hopefully) appear might gain some insights concerning social theory, geographies of justice, and the dialectics of violence, power and the production of space from my work. Collecting data on the opinions of the IDPs concerning the ICC was relevant to my work, but in what way was it relevant to the welfare of the 1.7 million persons displaced and facing extreme mortality rates? How did my research fail to address the needs of the population most affected by the violence? How, and in what ways, was my research and its publication venues (dictated by the terms of my tenure-track position) at odds with the promotion of human security? Respondents seemed confused or insulted when asked to participate in a research study on the place and space of justice. 'Why are you here, if not to help? What can you give us? Oh, so you want to TAKE something from us ... our time, our life stories, a taste of our trauma? For what? For your book? Why tell you what we want? Isn't it obvious? Are our needs so mysterious? What would YOU need if you were forced from your home and made to live in a camp without possibilities for employment or subsistence agriculture, where it takes eight hours to get water?'

In one instance, after taking an interview, I asked the respondent if he had anything to ask me. He said: 'May I have your pen?' I was mortified. I had been asked that question all morning and at that moment, I was down to my last pen. I had to decide whether to help this particular person, which would mean relinquishing my last pen, and ending my interviews for that day. I had travelled thousands of miles, spent thousands of dollars and hundreds of hours working to get to this site in order to get interviews; I felt that I needed to carry on working. Yet as I tried to explain that I needed my pen, I could see the look of doubt and distrust in the young man's eyes. I looked like someone who could spare a pen. At another time, I was asked by a camp leader what I would do with the information I was collecting. I told him that I would write an article for an academic journal. I asked the camp leader if I could reciprocate for the time he had spent with me by sending a copy of my article when it was published. He laughed and said: 'Sure send your paper. When we get it (here he made a gesture of rolling a set of papers into a log) we can put it into the fire and maybe have a hot dinner, if there is any food. Send a book! Ha ha'. This response highlighted the ways in which those I sought to interview faced more than security threats in the possibility of the infliction of physical harm, but also the absence of conditions of basic human security.

In certain cases, permission to conduct interviews was given on the condition that I refrained from making any reference whatsoever to the International Criminal Court. (Camp leaders said that the ICC inspired fear.) In those circumstances, I was therefore confronted with the challenge of researching locals' opinions of the ICC, without mentioning the institution itself. In Northern Uganda, parents of abducted children and other concerned community members were encouraging combatants who were abducted as children to leave the Lord's Resistance Army (LRA) in exchange for an amnesty deal (a 'package'). Some were alarmed that reference to an international court and prosecutions would discourage the amnesty process and therefore deter the 'returnees' (this was the preferred term, rather than 'rebel' or 'ex-combatant'). I thus had to re-word my interview questions and cautiously analyze the data. I concluded that I had failed to understand the essence of what my interviews could ascertain, but this 'failure' became a productive element, as I became better at interpreting the claims made by those speaking in the name of the 'victims' of the violence.

Often, members of the military were present (or near-by) during the interviews. Fear of LRA retaliation also seemed to influence the tenor and context of the interviews. Having belligerents close by severely constricts the ability to ask questions and trust answers. There is also a serious challenge in crossing between and among the communities. How does going to an IDP's camp impact the security of its inhabitants? How does interviewing perpetrators present risk situations for the researcher as well as others in the community? In the grounded daily practices of the researcher, how does one visit both a refugee camp and a military base? How does one collect and interpret interviews from the rape victims, and those accused of rape? What if the rape victim was also a murderer, as in the case of a 'child mother' I interviewed in a camp for returnees? She had been abducted at the age of twelve, along with a sister and two female cousins in front of her grandmother's home. The LRA killed her grandmother on the spot and dragged the girls away. The youngest kept crying at which point the LRA demanded that the three older girls kill the youngest, or be killed themselves. During the course of this interview, the young woman (holding a baby in her lap) seemed confused whenever I asked what she wanted to happen to the men that abducted her (and turned her into a sex-slave and domestic servant). She continually referred to her rapist as her 'husband'.

In addition to visiting the camps, I also sought out the highest level LRA defectors, as they would be likely to know of the ICC and have opinions related to its interventions in Uganda. After a great deal of effort and negotiations with the Ugandan military commander in Gulu, I was granted an interview with two high-level LRA commanders who had defected, received amnesty, and joined the Ugandan army (the UPDF). I was instructed to wait in the restaurant of the largest hotel in Gulu: the 'military hotel' as the army frequented the bar, and met with government and other officials on the expansive grounds. The interview was very productive, from my point of view, as the respondents described their decision to leave the LRA and accept amnesty. We talked extensively. Several hours later the UPDF officer who was observing the interview (the precondition) told me that it would be polite to buy the gentlemen lunch, so we ordered food for them, and then I paid the bill and left the men. Later, a Scandinavian NGO worker told me that one of the men was a notorious LRA commander, who 'specializes in 12-year-old virgins'. I was reimbursed for the lunch through my grant from the University of Georgia. In the course of gaining important information for my research, I had unintentionally also assisted the army in its handling of these defectors.

Conclusion

Conducting research on violence and human rights abuses among populations in conflict zones which lack food, water and shelter – the basic needs that underpin human existence and therefore security – requires sophisticated methodologies and training in ethics-based research design. In certain cases, the research interests of the social scientist might fail to address the critical security interests of the population most affected. In my case, asking questions in Uganda about the meaning of a courtroom in The Hague has seemed, at times, to be remote from the human needs and security of those I was interviewing.

It is difficult to be safe anywhere on earth, and perhaps most of all in a conflict zone. The activity of attempting to collect data (such as interviews and observations) *on violence within conditions of violence* can provoke further danger for researchers and informants. The illusion (or presumption) that the researcher should be 'safe' can be misleading, especially if the researcher's security seeking behaviour is a higher priority than consideration for the security of informants. Often the decision to remain silent (to keep one's mouth shut rather than ask a question in order to generate 'data') is the most productive for both knowledge-production and attempting to remain safe. Even in the event that the interviews are obtained, understanding the data in a context where the material (violence, insecurity) is both the product and the producer of violence and insecurity requires critical thinking and creative methodologies.

Returning to my earlier example of standing on the side of a dark road with machine guns pointed at Rigoberta's entourage, in retrospect I believe that as I embarked on a decade of research in Guatemala during some of the most intense periods of repression, I deliberately ignored the thought that my own security was at risk. My relative privilege seemed obvious in light of what Guatemalans were experiencing. I told myself that it would be nonsensical to worry about myself when everyone around me was in greater danger. Of course this was ridiculous – foreigners were victims of violence in Guatemala as well. But the converse of that illusion was an important realization: I had to be hyper-vigilant concerning the impact of my actions on others. Moreover, this attention to security needed to take into account more than what photojournalist Ron Havelhas referred to as 'the bang-bang of war'.[20] Beyond the physicality of violence, security and the lack thereof influence every aspect of our work – the projects we design, the people we interview, the data we collect and the meaning of the product.

Notes

1 Caroline Nordstrom, *Shadows of War; Violence, Power and International Profiteering in the Twenty-First Century* (Berkeley: University of California Press, 2004).
2 I write from the perspective of travelling 'to' a difficult site. In many cases, researchers are studying their own social realities and might actually lack the

Impact on research of security-seeking behaviour 187

ability to leave, as in returning home to some safe campus, country, or institutional setting. Alternatively, 'home' may lack security for those returning, and universities and other sites of research production can also be very 'difficult' places.

3 I believe that every research site can be considered a 'difficult situation' whether in the form of a sterile laboratory, dusty archives, or a bloody battlefield. Knowledge production is intimately and inextricably linked to the production of power, and every site of knowledge/power production can be considered a 'difficult' site, especially for critical thinking and creating relevant scholarship. For the purposes of this volume, I understand 'difficult situations' to be directly related to scenes of intense violence. But, of course, there are other equally violent and difficult situations that happen in 'normal' landscapes such as the bedroom or the boardroom.

4 Carolyn Ellis and Arthur Bochner, 'Chapter 28: Autoethnography, Personal Narrative, Reflexity: Researcher as subject' in Norman K. Denzin and Yvonna S. Lincoln (eds) *Handbook of qualitative research* 2nd edition (Thousand Oaks, CA: Sage, 2000), pp. 733–768.

5 For all future researchers of/in conflict zones, please note: When the situation gets to the point that the men are separated from the women, violence is on the horizon.

6 Comisión para el Esclarecimiento Histórico, *Guatemala: Memoria del silencio* (Guatemala: UNOPS, 1999).

7 Beatriz Manz, *Refugees of a Hidden War: The aftermath of counterinsurgency in Guatemala* (Albany: State University of New York Press, 1988).

8 Aryeh Neier, 'Human Rights and Accountability' lecture, Townsend Center for the Humanities, University of California, Berkeley, April 1994. See also Naomi Roht-Arriaza, (ed.) *Impunity and Human Rights in International Law and Practice* (Oxford: Oxford University Press, 1995).

9 Martín-Baró was one of the six Jesuit priest/professors killed by the military in San Salvador in November 1989 (along with the housekeeper and her daughter).

10 As early as 1984, and despite considerable risk, the Mutual Support Group for Family Members of the Disappeared (GAM) was formed and began visible protests in front of the National Palace, with pictures of missing relatives. GAM was particularly effective in bringing together *ladino* activists and Mayan survivors, and organized extensive marches and demonstrations in the capital. GAM's activities met with fierce repression: two of the founding members were killed in March and April 1985.

11 See Manz, *Refugees of a Hidden War*, 1988, and Beatriz Manz, *Paradise in Ashes: a Guatemalan journey of courage, terror and hope* (Berkeley: University of California Press, 2004).

12 The construction of the binary of 'victim/perpetrator' is itself an area of research production that demands further study, but is beyond the scope of this chapter. See R. Charli Carpenter, *'Innocent Women and Children: Gender, Norms and the Protection of Civilians* (England: Ashgate, 2006) and Erica Bouris, *Complex Political Victims* (Bloomfield, CT: Kumarian Press, 2007).

13 Matilde Gonzáles, *Se Cambiá el Tiempo; Conflicto y Poder en Territorio K'iche' 1880–1996* (Guatemala: Asociación para el Avance de las Ciencias Sociales en Guatemala, 2002).

14 See, for example Judith Lewis Hernan, *Trauma and Recovery: The Aftermath of Violence-from Domestic Abuse to Political Terror* (New York: Basic Books, 1992); and Rebecca Coffey, *Unspeakable Truths and Happy Endings: Human Cruelty and the New Trauma Therapy* (Maryland: The Sidran Press, 1998).

15 CEH, *Memory of Silence*, prologue.

16 Hernan, *Trauma and Recovery*, p. 155.

17 Despite the transformation in 1994, a great sense of insecurity due to common crime and violence persisted in South Africa.

18 Tim O'Brien, *The Things They Carried* (New York: Penguin Press, 1990), p. 78.
19 The broad view of human security, articulated in the Commission on Human Security's 2003 report, *Human Security Now*, suggests that the definition of security should be broadened to include hunger, disease and natural disasters, in addition to war, genocide and terrorism, because these in fact kill more people. See http://www.humansecurity-chs.org/.
20 See Havel's interview in the documentary, *Crimes of War*, by the Crimes of War Project (2002).

Part 5
Identity, Objectivity, Behaviour

13 Fieldwork, objectivity and the academic enterprise

Marie-Joëlle Zahar

> Our narratives have become our prison ... Evidence to the contrary is just disregarded or rejected as incredible
>
> Kofi Annan[1]

This contribution reflects on a particular set of hurdles linked to the use and misuse of the notion of objectivity as it relates to fieldwork in internal conflict situations. My awareness of the pitfalls of research in civil war situations goes back to my time as a Master's candidate attempting to research the Lebanese civil war. At the time, a number of professors expressed concern about potential 'sources of bias' in the study:[2] not only was I Lebanese but I had been 'involved' in the conflict as a political analyst and journalist before returning to academe. There were concerns that I would thus be more sympathetic to the actors of the civil war that I wanted to study. One person, in particular, could not understand my intuition that militias needed to be understood in organizational, indeed in institutional terms. 'How can you use the notion of institutions to understand such rag-tag as militias?' was the approximate way in which this member of the jury addressed me. It was 1993, a year when the Bosnia war exploded on our television screens, with Serb forces regularly described as roaming gangs of killers.[3] It thus seemed genuinely puzzling that I would choose a term associated with order, predictability, and rules, to understand such a disorderly, unpredictable, and unruly phenomenon. To which I replied: 'I see no problem in so doing. The mafia was particularly violent. No one ever doubted it was organized and violence was an integral part of the organizational process'.

I extrapolate from this experience because I have come to realize that fieldwork in conflict zones is particularly conducive to 'biases' though not necessarily of the sort social scientists commonly worry about. The rest of the chapter proceeds as follows. First, I discuss the notion of objectivity in the social sciences. I argue that not only is objectivity an ideal, it might actually be a false god. Then, I draw a connection between objectivity and the academic enterprise, highlighting the manner in which our search for objectivity is particularly blind to a specific kind of biases derived from the reification of sovereignty as the organizing principle of the state system. I describe the structuring role that the concept of the state plays in political science. I then argue that it impacts our research agendas in a number of inter-related ways: 1) by restricting the scope of inquiry; 2) by framing the manner in which we theorize about specific phenomena; and 3) by restricting the scope of solutions proposed by our analyses. In other terms, if theories are about description, explanation and prediction, each and every step of the way stands to be tainted by our conceptual blinkers. In sketching out these problems, I pay specific attention to and draw examples from the study of non-state armed actors.[4] The last part of this contribution reflects on the implications of the argument for fieldwork in conflict zones and attempts to develop a set of common-sense rules to raise our awareness and minimize the impact of the conceptual blinkers that we carry with us to the field.

I. Knowledge and objectivity: The social sciences between holy grails and false gods

Knowledge is one of the few goods that have been sought, though not consistently or exclusively, for themselves. Its discovery and transmission are the fundamental purpose of academic life. This is the extent of agreement in the academic community. Beyond this statement of professional purpose, social scientists disagree fundamentally on the 'best' way of achieving this good.

Two broad approaches to knowledge drive most social science research. Ideographic approaches to knowledge start with particular cases chosen because of some affinity between the researcher and their subject. This is said to result in detailed, context-sensitive research that captures specificity and provides rich and thick description. Nomothetic approaches seek to conceptualize particular sequences in terms of larger but similar sets in order to predict. The urgency behind prediction, which in the field of international relations is associated with the study of war, has been identified as an attempt to learn from the past and avoid the repetition of harmful events.[5] Our concerns with the ideographic and nomothetic aspects of research capture the essence of the debate over the best way to enhance knowledge.[6]

But social scientists do not only disagree about the best starting point, they also fundamentally disagree about method. Techniques to achieve objective knowledge have been defined by two conceptions of science: positivism and critical rationalism.[7] Positivism is usually (but not exclusively) associated with inductive research; critical rationalism is closely linked to deductive research.

Empiricists see the scientific enterprise as the 'carefully controlled, neutral observation of empirical events', which ultimately allows the discovery of regularities or patterns of relationships between observable events. This positivist conception is premised on the assumption that facts speak for themselves and that grasping the facts allows for discovery of the world. But there are those who disagree with this premise. They argue that theory is not the result of observation but that observation is made possible by theories which allow the identification of regularities.

Critical rationalism is associated with the work of Karl Popper and with his description of observation as 'theory-laden'.[8] Such presuppositionist theories offer an alternative conception of science 'that emphasizes the conventional nature of scientific practices and the fallible character of scientific explanations and predictions'. Social scientists operating within this framework employ a panoply of instruments, ranging from creative insights and practical reason to formal logic to approximate the truth about the world.

I do not intend to delve into the particulars of the controversy over objectivity in the social sciences. Others have done so far more eloquently.[9] Rather, I want to elaborate the premises of my own position on the subject. As a student of comparative politics and international relations interested in a phenomenon – militarized ethnic strife – located at the interface of two subfields of political science, I identify with what is known as the 'centre' – i.e. political scientists who pursue 'theoretically informed political analysis focusing on one or more countries, through diverse conceptual lenses and utilizing a variety of data, contemporary or historical, qualitative or quantitative'.[10] This pragmatist approach seeks to 'negotiate not only the difference between complexity and parsimony, but also the wide epistemological chasm between realist and relativist perspectives'.[11] It simultaneously acknowledges the importance of objectivity and the difficulty, indeed the impossibility of achieving it.

Disinterested positivistic objectivity is a grail that we might strive for but never achieve. This is not because of our failure, as analysts, to separate ourselves from our object of inquiry. Even when totally foreign to a situation, we interpret events through our own categories of understanding and these induce biases into our analyses as I will endeavour to demonstrate further below.[12] But if value-free empirical enquiry is either an ideal or a delusion, it does not follow that prescriptive research should not be guided by criteria. If disinterested objectivity is beyond reach, it does not follow, at least not to my mind, that relativism is all we are left with. Not all goes when it comes to research. In that respect, the basic ideal of objectivity remains useful as a methodological warning against sloppiness.

This of course brings up the issue of the intrinsic link between knowledge and power, the discussion of which has a long and rich intellectual history. Weber was the first to recognize the uneasy coupling between science and politics.[13] In his study of sexuality, Foucault cogently demonstrated that categorization was not just a way of generating knowledge but of generating power of a specific kind, productive power.[14] In my own practice, in my effort to link problem-specific analytic constructs with case-specific interpretations, I remain prey to the trap of productive power. Impartiality is my, admittedly imperfect, way out of this quandary. I understand impartiality as an ethic of research that strives toward a balanced and reflexive approach to analytic constructs and thick interpretation, navigating the muddy waters between the two in such a way as to ensure that thickness does not prevent engagement with analytic constructs while at the same time making certain that the singularities, the voices of the particular are not silenced by the weight of the many.[15]

All I want to suggest, at this point, is that our observation of 'facts' is clearly informed by the way in which we view the world but that as we go about collecting these 'facts' we need to exert a conscious effort to avoid gross distortion to make them fit predetermined categories. This, I would describe as an attempt to uphold the integrity of fieldwork research. I elaborate on both statements below.

II. Hidden distortions: Studying non-state actors in a world of states

In civil conflict situations as in all ethnographic or case-study research, investigators 'enter an already established social setting to discern its patterns and meaning'.[16] Such situations test the researcher's impartiality in a number of ways.

The intensity of conflict may trigger a number of emotional responses that interfere with one's judgment and perceptions of the environment. The militarized nature of these conflicts places most researchers in a new situation. The fear, apprehension, and anticipation, as well as the practical obstacles triggered by military operations can interfere with the thoroughness of the research and consequently with its completeness and the extent of its partiality. The brutality of the violence – sometimes directly – witnessed by researchers stands in the way of a disinterested approach to the field. This is not specific to fieldwork in situations of conflict. Indeed, 'the personal emotional experience and state of mind during fieldwork have an impact on the way fieldworkers, in being their own instruments, practice their research'.[17] In an extremely incisive article on the topic, anthropologist Baz Lecocq makes the point that it does not only colour our views on matters studied, 'it is decisive on whether or not one does see anything in the first place, or even on whether or not one wants to see anything at all'.[18]

Researchers are also likely to seek shortcuts to secure information. In the context of civil wars, 'urban bias' has been identified as a common shortcut.[19] Ease of access and a greater sense of familiarity lead researchers to privilege information coming from capital cities at the expense of information coming from rural areas. But capital cities are also more tightly controlled by governments which may, among other problems, privilege a governmental narrative. Another danger lies in reinterpreting local events in light of a 'grand narrative' which gives an overarching national logic to civil wars. 'National' conflicts may be and have often been used by citizens to settle local scores with little connection to the political fault lines.[20] For example, Tanner's work shows that the ethnic cleansing campaign in Bosnia and Herzegovina (1992–95) was as much the result of an intentional master plan as it was the expression of local dynamics of conflict that turned common folk into their neighbours' executioners.[21]

These are serious enough problems. However, I submit that the most important pitfalls are not located in practical issues as much as they lie in more conceptual questions rendered especially relevant in situations of internal conflict.

We live in a world of states. The vagaries of history have given the national state primacy over contending principles of political organization.[22] Following the end of World War II international institutional arrangements have reified the state as the universal political entity. This has dire consequences for subnational secessionist movements and other non-state actors challenging the legitimacy of a given state. The results are nowhere better spelled out than in the words of Mohammed Selim:

> When they ... operate in the international system, nonstate actors confront certain problems that state actors do not usually experience. Lacking a political base and the conventional means of conferring legitimacy, these actors find the legitimacy of their representation to be always in question. They must be concerned with the issue of being heard, perceived, and recognized by nation-states and international organizations ... As the nonstate actors become more visible and draw more international support, they run the risk of being portrayed by their adversaries as mavericks threatening international legitimacy.[23]

Drawing from my own research, the same set of conclusions can easily be reached with respect to most if not all non-state armed actors operating in the international system. Analysts have made much of a fundamental fact of insurgency, its relative weakness vis-à-vis governments.[24] Another fundamental fact of insurgency is as important though less recognized. This is the legitimacy gap that separates a government (no matter how illegitimate de facto) and insurgent groups (no matter how factually legitimate in the eyes of a large swathe of the population). Commenting on the manner in which we define militias, Alice Hills makes this point cogently.

> Militia are usually described as taking part in some form of inter (or intra) group fighting within a geographical area, and as belonging to a specific group or leader. However, they cannot be defined solely in terms of their role as agents of warlord power ... because commentators (...) refer to 'opportunistic freelance armed militias', as well as to clan militias operating check points along trade routes. The groups labelled militia in the 1990s may enforce recognition within their own societies (by virtue of their possession of arms), but the fact that they operate in fragmenting states means they lack the formal recognition.[25]

This fundamental fact has structuring effects on the manner in which practitioners and analysts approach non-state armed actors.

In practice, the international community tends to privilege state actors. Governments are natural interlocutors, including in situations of internal conflict. There are concerns, one might add legitimate ones, that any decision by states and international organizations to open talks with non-state armed actors might be used to legitimate the otherwise reprehensible actions of the latter. In the late 1990s, this conundrum resulted in a 'crisis' at the United Nations; UN conflict-resolution practitioners simultaneously recognized the need to talk to relevant actors in conflict zones, including non-state armed groups, to alleviate the suffering of civilians and faced accusations that such talks were being used as a cover by some such actors who were responsible for gross violations of human rights.[26]

One consequence has been the tendency to privilege state actors when setting up peace talks. A brief look at the composition of the negotiating teams involved in the Ta'if (Lebanon conflict) and Dayton (Bosnia and Herzegovina conflict) Accords reveals a majority of state officials rather than militia representatives. Lebanese parliamentarians, last elected in 1972, who met in Ta'if in 1989 to put an end to the Lebanese civil war that none of them had incidentally fought. Likewise, President Slobodan Milosevic of Serbia and President Franjo Tudjman of Croatia negotiated the Dayton Accords of 1995, not the leaders of the Bosnian Serbs and Bosnian Croats. Peace negotiations between Arabs and Israelis in Madrid initially excluded the Palestine Liberation Organization with the United States and Israel preferring that Palestinian negotiators be included on the Jordanian negotiating team. Even in places like Angola and Mozambique where insurgents have won a seat at the negotiating table, this legitimacy deficit translated into government resistance to acknowledge their adversaries as equals. For the most part of 1991–92, Mozambican negotiations stumbled over the difficulty of finding a formula that acknowledged the government's sovereignty while guaranteeing RENAMO's (Resistencia Nacional Moçambicana) acceptance as a political party on a par with the ruling FRELIMO (Frente de Libertação de Moçambique) party.[27] In Angola, its fears heightened by the experience of the stillborn Gbadolite agreement,[28] UNITA (União Nacional para a Independência Total de Angola) sought guarantees of parity in the security realm by insisting on demobilization and equal reinsertion of MPLA (Movimento Popular de Libertação de Angola, ruling party) and UNITA troops in the army.

The reality of a world of states has affected the opportunity structure of insurgents, rebels, militias and other non-state armed actors;[29] it has, equally significantly but less obviously, affected the research agenda of political science and the lenses through which we approach the study of ethnic conflict. In the next part of the chapter, I argue that this impact can be observed in three realms: 1) the scope of inquiry; 2) the theoretical referents that frame our research; and 3) the scope of our prescriptive solutions.

II.I Restricting the scope of enquiry

Conceptual blinkers have had two detrimental effects on the definition of the phenomena that we ought to study in relation to civil wars: they initially led to an effort to distinguish non-state armed actors from states, then to an effort to distinguish them from civilians. Each carried with it a host of definitional problems that restricted the scope of enquiry into the causes and mechanisms of internal conflict.

Inter-state conflicts have extensively come under the microscope of analysts of international relations; this has not equally applied to civil wars and/or ethnic conflicts. Not until the dismemberment of the former Soviet Union and Eastern Bloc did the internationalization of ethnic conflict impose itself as an inescapable reality of contemporary politics.[30] Consequently, the study of militias involved in such conflicts was both sparse and largely descriptive[31] if not journalistic. The term warlord, for example, is 'applied to prominent clan and faction leaders using armed civilian followers to impose their policies and ambitions. It is normally used in a derogatory sense because it is assumed that their power is neither traditional nor legitimate but has been gained through intrigue and intimidation'.[32] To the extent that analytical approaches to militias, warlordism and rebels can be discerned, these often centre on the assumption that such groups are overwhelmingly driven by extremist ideologies and/or profit.[33]

A cursory look at the literature on the Lebanese conflict is instructive. Lebanon's civil war lasted over 17 years (April 1975–October 1991). Of the plethora of books and articles covering different aspects of the war, less than 10 per cent address the functioning of the various militias which, for all intents and purposes, were the major actors of this conflict. Of these, a majority dealt with the ideology of the groups. In my own dissertation research on the most institutionalized of all Lebanese militias, the Lebanese Forces, by 1998 I could only find three articles discussing topics other than their belief-set. Two of the three described the organizational structure of the militia and they were written by the same author.[34]

This is by no means a characteristic peculiar to this conflict. In spite of the length of the Angolan (1975–2006) and Mozambican (1975–92) conflicts, there are few accounts of either UNITA or RENAMO that focus on the groups' organizational structure. Nor are there comparatively many organizational or institutional studies of the Fuerzas Armadas Revolucionarias de Columbia in spite of their long history which dates back to 1964. Instead, a plethora of articles have been published that look at the violence meted out on society by these groups[35] as well as at their involvement in black market activities such as diamond-mining in the case of UNITA and the drug trade for the FARC.[36]

Not only are there few studies of non-state armed actors but these also draw a sharp distinction between the logics underpinning the actions of state and non-state actors. They also draw a clear line between non-state combatants and civilians.

Neither states ...

In their efforts to distinguish non-state armed actors from states, analysts have played up the notions of rationality and interest. It is common parlance in some circles to refer to non-state armed actors as irrational or greedy thus incapable of the compromises necessary in the name of the putative national interest. Nowhere is this distinction more evident than in the distinction between old and new wars proposed by Mary Kaldor.[37]

Several approaches to the study of non-state armed actors surmise that decisions regarding political action derive from a group's beliefs.[38] Where states are described as rational decision-makers, non-state armed actors are deemed irrational. The excessive violence used by such actors is often used as proof of their irrationality. How could someone rational engage in mass slaughter as was the case for the Bosnian Serbs or in the sort of mutilations that accompanied the breakdown of civil peace in locales such as Liberia or Sierra Leone? Authors conclude that the objectives of such groups are incommensurable with the search for peace. Such actors are likely to hold total goals of the sort that preclude compromise and lead to a zero-sum approach to conflict-resolution. They are also less vulnerable to costs and willing to go to great lengths to achieve their objectives. Such premises underpin the development of categories of insurgent identifications such as terrorist and total spoiler.

Alternative approaches highlight the profit motive. There are two variations on this economic theme. One depicts non-state armed actors as mercenaries; the other paints them as brigands. Some analysts do not even consider rebels and insurgents as actors in their own right. Instead, focusing on their usually highly asymmetric alliances with outsiders, analysts contend that such groups do not and cannot exercise political autonomy. Patrons are seen as the real political actor and the non-state armed actors are downgraded to the rank of puppets. Such arguments have been used widely in reference to insurgents, revolutionary movements, and guerrillas, as well as in inter-state conflicts. Several analysts of the situation in Mozambique, for example, have insisted on approaching RENAMO as 'a domestic instrument of Rhodesian aggression (1976–80) and apartheid destabilization (1981–89)'.[39] Similarly, successive US administrations have tended to view Central American revolutionaries as either Cuban or Soviet proxies. Thus, the intractability of the conflicts is a function of the strategic designs of external actors with a stake in the outcome of a particular internal conflict.

Another line of argument emphasizes the use of military capabilities to extract economic resources in an environment of political and economic collapse. To quote David Keen, 'the apparent "chaos" of civil war can be used to further local and short-term interests. These are frequently economic: to paraphrase Carl von Clausewitz, war has increasingly become the continuation of economics by other means'.[40] Authors stress what they see as a fundamental difference: in the case of warlords, rebels and militias, this profit is personal and private. In the words of John McKinlay: 'There is no ... mitigating Robin Hood tendency which might show [warlords] to be redresser[s] of global inequality'.[41]

This kind of interpretation finds echoes in resource competition theory which suggests that ethnic conflict would remain insignificant if not connected to processes and opportunities for economic survival.[42] From this perspective, sole emphasis on the search for economic gain suggests that the looming prospect of decreasing benefits is an essential pre-condition for compromise. This is the implication of Keen's argument in *The Economic Functions of Violence in Civil Wars*, when he maintains that economic interests have actually led to the persistence of violence. Although this logic has been used as a justification for policies such as arms embargoes and other economic sanctions, the connection between economic losses and willingness to compromise is not always substantiated by evidence.[43]

Nor civilians ...

It has become common sense among practitioners and analysts alike to assert that the 'new wars' of the post-cold war period differ from earlier internal conflicts in at least one aspect: the use of civilians as targets and objectives of warfare. It is indeed 'accepted wisdom' to flag the high number of civilian victims in the (un)-civil wars of the last decade with numbers hovering in the vicinity of 80 per cent of the total casualty count. Particularly illustrative is the title of a contribution by Cynthia Enloe to *The Women and War Reader:* 'All the Men are in the Militias, All the Women are Victims'.[44] This image, imprinted in our consciousness by media coverage of the conflicts in the former Yugoslavia, in Sierra Leone, or of the genocide in Rwanda, is only partially correct. Often, analysts and practitioners draw too stark and artificial a separation between combatants and civilians in such contexts.

Civil wars are not fought by regular armies; armed civilians, conscripted willingly or forcibly, provide the bulk of fighting forces on one, if not both sides of these conflicts. The Rwandan genocide, for example, was carried out in large part by the Interahamwe; however, it also involved the participation of a number of Hutu Rwandans. The line between civilian and combatant is blurred by a number of practical considerations with methodological consequences: How do we think about part-time soldiers? How do we conceive of the immediate families of combatants? What to do with civilians who do not bear arms but provide the logistical backbone of the guerrilla or insurgency? How do we reconcile childhood's innocence with the growing number of child soldiers?

Defining non-state armed actors out of politics

Our definitions of non-state armed actors are by and large unsatisfactory. Analysts have tended to draw stark lines between these actors and the governments that they fight as well as between them and the civilians that they abuse or alternatively claim to represent and protect. Research has highlighted the end of ideologies; it has asserted the end of conflicts fuelled by grievances and the dawn of a new era of greed-driven wars; we have then relaxed this to speak about motives v opportunities. In the process, we have reduced the relationship between non-state armed actors and local populations to a dichotomy between the power of guns and the powerlessness of society. Gun-toting, drug-trafficking thugs such as the Colombian FARC were said to rule over communities by fear; they could not have a more organic relationship to those civilians in the midst of whom they operated. The labels used to describe armed groups reflect the sharpness of the division. Gone were the revolutionaries, the rebels and the insurgents of olden days; in their place, a plethora of brigands, warlords, war criminals and terrorists took centre stage in civil wars. Civilians, for their part, are increasingly labelled 'vulnerable groups', a distinction that echoes research related to the debate over greed and grievance which highlights the fact that combatants are angry, jobless, young men (and their victims, by extension, women, children and the elderly).

Though cursory, this review suggests that our understanding of non-state armed actors has contributed to defining them out of politics. Nowhere is this more clearly spelled out than in the debate on greed and grievance. However, the interplay between politics and economics cannot be disregarded. Indeed, '[w]hile criminal organizations function in a parapolitical way, attempting to control and regulate in order to increase income, insurgent groups work in a reversed sequence, using their income to promote their activities as underground governments'.[45]

II.2 Limiting our theoretical referents

Consciously or not, the primacy of the state has translated into a dominant discourse that influences research agendas. In the following section, I suggest a few consequences of the manner in which this state-centric focus has impacted our definitions and understanding of non-state armed actors.

Defining civil wars out of the study of war

Until recently political scientists knew relatively little about the phenomenon of militarized internal strife. International relations theorists trained to focus on inter-state conflict initially failed to recognize civil wars as a legitimate object of study. Most civil wars fell under the label proxy wars as their protagonists were seen primarily through a Cold War prism. This accounts, in part, for the surprise of analysts when, following the collapse of the Soviet Union, internal conflicts did not decline in numbers and intensity.

Even when civil conflict came under the purview of International Relations, the discipline's frames affected the manner in which these wars were studied. For example, definitions of war excluded many subnational conflicts from early comparative quantitative research on the grounds of their not meeting standard casualty thresholds.[46] To date, most quantitative studies require the state to be involved as a protagonist to code an internal conflict as a civil war though analysts have considered a number of ways to account for the threshold of severity in civil wars.[47]

Defining civil wars as the realm of anarchy and chaos

Early research on civil war attempted to transpose the notion of anarchy from the international to the domestic realm. Analysts emphasized state failure as an equivalent to the descent into anarchy. This resulted in overemphasis of the dividing lines between protagonists to the expense of the myriad instances of cooperation and orderly interactions that do take place in the midst of chaos.[48]

Another manifestation of this overemphasis on chaos is the insistence by many to focus on looting and terror in studying the mobilization techniques of non-state armed actors.[49] This comes to the expense of the study of the myriad links that might develop between combatants and civilians, which may account for this mobilization and even translate into popular support for the rebellion. As discussed above, of the myriad military groups involved in ethnic conflicts, few were systematically studied from organizational or institutional perspectives.[50]

In ongoing research, I investigate the impact of identity, economic factors, strategic considerations and organizational structure on the nature of ties between civilians and combatants with a focus on the Lebanese Hizballah. Preliminary results indicate that identity is a poor predictor of congruent interests between combatants and society, that economic agendas can not only prolong wars but also improve the lot of civilians, that the nature of a group's grievances matters and can provide an entry point into engagement on issues of human security, and that the degree of organizational complexity and coherence, not only of the armed factions but also of the local populations, affects the nature of interactions.[51]

Defining rationality out of internal conflicts

Another consequence of the way in which we define and understand non-state armed actors impacts our appreciation of the violence in civil wars. Whereas early studies have tended to describe it solely in terms of brutality, irrationality and thirst for blood, recent research is forcing us to rethink these analyses. This is one of the most positive developments in the study of non-state actors whereby political scientists, sociologists and anthropologists are investigating the micro foundations of violence.[52] They have established that political violence may have local functions not only for the combatants but also for communities.[53] One of the most interesting aspects of this new stream of literature focuses on the reframing of local feuds in light of the larger conflicts.[54] Its warning to us is stark and refreshing: there is no *a priori* reason to think that state violence and non-state violence are not comparable; nor is there any solid ground to thinking that violence is irrational and therefore not amenable to analysis.[55]

II.3 Limiting our prescriptive horizons

Many analysts concerned with the study of non-state armed actors hail from the discipline of political science and more specifically from the subfield of international relations. But political science, like all disciplines, has its own conceptual and methodological 'blinkers'. Analyses of how best to stabilize the peace and ensure 'human security'[56] have erred precisely because of these blinkers. In other terms, there has been devolution of the concepts of peace and human security into state-centric forms.

Peace as stability

In political science, debates have singled out spoilers as the single most important threat to peace processes. Spoilers are of course those actors or groups who use violence and derail peace.[57] Stabilizing the peace has thus become partly synonymous with containing spoilers. This has resulted in two streams of literatures. The first focuses on overcoming the political commitment problem by devising power sharing schemes that provide the leaders (and not the followers, a distinction to which I will return momentarily) of armed groups with incentives to give up violence. This approach seeks to achieve regime security, the security of those in power, in the hope that they will exercise restraint and give up violent action. The second focuses on the containment of followers, addressing issues of demobilization and disarmament of combatants as part of the larger task of security sector reform (more on this later under the discussion of human security).

Research on spoilers often conceives of barriers to exit in purely military terms. The commitment of outsiders is necessary to deploy all available instruments, including military force, in defence of the peace process.[58] As traditional peacekeeping proves increasingly inadequate, peacekeepers are often called upon to use force and tame volatile environments.[59]

Yet, barriers to exit need not be understood uniquely in military terms. Indeed, several styles of foreign intervention provide more or less efficient barriers to exit.[60] Some custodians of peace privilege compellence; others manipulate incentives.[61] While coercion and incentives are not necessarily mutually exclusive, intervention styles have implications for the sustainability of peace. Custodians can understand peace implementation in one of three ways: compliance, process or peacebuilding. In practice, however, only the first two meanings of peace implementation find echoes in the politics of intervening third-parties. The short time span of these strategies is detrimental to stability. The custodians' obsession with exit strategies compounds the problem as it translates into a tendency to use 'force' to deal with bottlenecks. Such methods are unlikely to forge meaningful long-term relationships between former adversaries or to create a strong belief amongst them in the goals and values of conflict-resolution. Whether outsiders can generate the kind of conflict-transformation envisaged by the proponents of peacebuilding seems unlikely.[62]

Human security as peace

The need to recognize differences between state and human security and the corollary importance of protecting and promoting the latter have not only become well-established in academic discourse; they have gained credence and popularity in the media and, through them, the general public. It is all the more interesting and problematic then, to realize that analyses that purport to investigate ways of restoring human security remain caught in a state-centric paradigm. In spite of the realization that security is a three-tiered edifice, current prescriptions remain located at the two most political echelons. There are few systematic analyses that focus on the need for an integrative vision and seriously consider the development of grassroots efforts to promote the human security agenda.

Narrowing the horizons of the possible

The two problems identified in this commentary are consequential at the level of policy design and practice. In spite of the hopes of many policy-oriented academics, there is no one-to-one correspondence between our analyses and policies. Our analyses have become prisoners of our statist conceptual lenses, preventing academics from providing a counterpoint that prods policy ahead. Worse, they might even contribute to the promotion of insufficient and problematic policies. Three examples serve to illustrate this argument:

• *The inability to account for violence's ability to morph*: This results in policies that ultimately threaten human security at the grassroots. For example, the inability to seriously tackle combatant reintegration is directly linked to the increase in criminality in many post-conflict situations. This criminality, in the absence of effective and functioning state security institutions, creates a security gap. Analysts have acknowledged the existence of this gap but few have articulated the logic linking criminal violence and war-related violence in comprehensive ways.[63]

• *The perpetuation of a reactive rather than a proactive agenda*: This is the tendency to deal with symptoms rather than causes. In post-conflict situations, reactive agendas prioritize disarmament and mobilization, thus curbing the expression of violence, rather than dealing with integration which would have addressed some of the root causes that lead to violence in the first place (such as economic need, social marginalization and the like). Such reactive agendas create disillusions in the ranks of former combatants. They make it all the more difficult to get the kind of grassroots support that is needed for sustainable peace.[64]

- *The under-specification of phenomena essential to the sustainable promotion of peace and human security*: DDR is a whole and the success of demobilization and disarmament depends in large part on the success of reintegration. Yet our efforts to understand successes and failures have focused on the technical aspects of D/D to the exclusion of serious research on reintegration (often left to 'softer social sciences' such as anthropology). State-centric tools of power-sharing and security sector reform to dominate debates on restoring peace and human security to the expense of longer-term conflict prevention and combatant reintegration.

III. State-centrism as a threat to the integrity of fieldwork

The hegemony of the state in both theory and practice poses an acute dilemma to researchers interested in civil conflict. On the one hand, the advancement of knowledge and the search for sustainable solutions require a complete and (as) accurate (as possible) picture of the situations at hand. On the other hand, the overwhelming presence of the state as a universal organizing principle and an inescapable theoretical construct often mediates and influences scholarship on ethnic groups.

Because of their lack of legitimate status, non-state armed actors are often left out of negotiated political settlements. But their military capabilities and their legitimacy in the eyes of even small proportions of the populations should alert us to the need to gain a better understanding of these groups, be they warlords, militias, rebels or insurgents. Not only do they possess the means of mounting challenges to international stability, they are also societal actors in their own right and deserve as much analytical attention as other, state-sanctioned, actors such as parties, interest-groups, and the like.

Having said so, one must also address the possibility that, in giving a voice to the voiceless, researchers could also fall prey to impartiality and biases of a different kind. These can fall under one of two headings: either accepting the counter-hegemonic discourse of the non-state actors at face-value or imposing upon them our own interpretation of the situation and romanticizing their reality.[65]

Each of these can be detrimental to our understanding of the dynamics of internal conflict. State-centric biases inform our research questions, our definitions, and our conceptual lenses in ways that hinder a thorough understanding of the non-state actors involved in these conflicts. Oversight of the possibility that these groups are indeed independent and representative actors has been identified as one of the reasons disputes fail to be settled in an orderly and civilized fashion.[66]

I would argue that it has also stood in the way of the elaboration of lasting peace agreements. Analytically, poor understanding of the organizational aspects of non-state armed groups can be blamed for part of our failure to grasp the dynamics of civil wars. Our reticence to accept non-state armed actors as a fully legitimate topic of inquiry in the social sciences is a reflection of the reality that, although a major contender in most militarized internal conflicts, they are – by the mere fact of their illegitimate status – usually sidelined during negotiation processes.

Counter-hegemonic approaches, on the other hand, tend to accept the non-state armed actors' viewpoints too uncritically. This causes worry among traditionalists who believe that 'if ethnopolitical groups are given special legal status in international and domestic law, it could provide the impetus for innumerable claims and counterclaims, which would lead to protracted conflicts and leave few existing states intact'.[67] This kind of bias also fails to estimate the extent to which ethnic mobilization is based on real grievances and the extent to which it is the work of political entrepreneurs.[68]

My argument in this account has been a plea not to allow statist theoretical lenses to prevent us from studying non-state armed actors. In closing, I want to suggest that the risks and biases integral to fieldwork in conflict situations can be minimized by following a number of basic rules having to do with research design as well as with what I call our methodological ethic in the field.

First, and foremost, is a careful research design including attention to alternative explanations. Indeed, the most effective bulwark against our conceptual blinkers remains careful attention to the multiple explanations that can, theoretically, account for a given phenomenon. This is the safest way to avoid distorting the facts collected during fieldwork and twisting them to fit our pre-determined categories. While it is clear that fieldworkers are situated and that they cannot pretend to disinterested objectivity, it is also clear that a careful assessment of our data, as against the multiple explanations that might account for a given outcome, can minimize the extent to which our theoretical and conceptual blinkers distort our perception of the reality.

Once in the field, three rules of thumb constitute, to my mind, a sound methodological ethic that partakes in minimizing the distortions that I highlighted in this contribution. First, we ought to privilege participant-observer techniques allowing direct and (as) unmediated (as possible) observation. There are, in anthropology, those who argue that fieldworkers cannot and indeed, should not, seek to remain benign visitors and neutral observers. They claim instead that a fully integrated position in society is necessary to understand the way in which a social position influences what and how one perceives.[69] I would not go as far as to suggest that understanding the world of non-state armed actors requires the observer to become a participant. However, it is important to gain as close access to these groups as possible in order to understand their internal logics. Given the manner in which they are usually framed, especially by the governments against which they fight, it is highly likely that the greater our dependence on third parties to understand non-state armed actors, the greater the risk that we will see them not for what they are but for how the third party in question, be it a facilitator, an interpreter or a research assistant, perceives them to be. This danger is magnified in instances where the limitations in our language skills prevent direct conversations with our interlocutors. A second rule of thumb is meant to prevent us from being instrumentalized and unconsciously becoming the voice of either governments or non-state armed actors. Simply put, the fieldworker must consciously attempt to seek out as many opinions by talking not only to non-state actors but to their domestic opponents, external observers and civilians from all walks of life. Only then can he or she be relatively confident that they are gathering a diversity of opinions and covering an array of perspectives from which they will seek to reconstruct the extremely complex reality of the situations they are trying to understand. The third rule of thumb builds upon the second and extends it into the realm of the written sources that constitute our bibliographical material. Much like our conversations, these should reflect a conscious attempt to get different assessments of the situation from secondary and primary sources with differing perspectives and ideological positions on the subject matter.

None of these suggestions is particularly new to fieldwork researchers. We must just realize that given the theoretical and practical pitfalls associated with ethnic conflict situations, abiding by these guidelines is essential for the validity of our contributions to knowledge.

Notes

1 Kofi Annan, 'The Golden Rule for Ending Conflict', *The Globe and Mail* (Toronto), 16 February 2007, p. A17.
2 This later became the basis for my Ph.D. dissertation. Marie-Joëlle Zahar, *Fanatics Mercenaries Brigands ... and Politicians: Militia Decision-making and Civil Conflict Resolution* (Montreal: Department of Political Science, McGill University, 2000).
3 To cite but two examples, see Michael Ignatieff, *Blood and Belonging: Journeys into the New Nationalism* (Toronto: Penguin, 1993) and John Mueller, 'The Banality of "Ethnic War"', *International Security*, vol. 25, no. 1 (Summer 2000), pp. 42–70.
4 Marie-Joëlle Zahar, 'Protégés, Clients, Cannon Fodder: Civilians in the Calculus of Militias', *Managing Armed Conflicts in the Twenty-first Century*, a special issue of *International Peacekeeping*, vol. 7, no. 4 (Winter 2001), pp. 107–128.
5 Peter Evans 'The Role of Theory in Comparative Politics: A Symposium', *World Politics*, vol. 48 (October 1995), p. 3.
6 This is the induction v deduction debate so familiar to students of international relations. See 'Symposium: Methodological Foundations of the Study of International Conflict', *International Studies Quarterly*, vol. 29 (1985), pp. 121–136.
7 Mary Hawkesworth, 'Contending Conception of Science and Politics: Methodology and the Constitution of the Political', in Dvora Yanow and Peregrine Schwartz-Shea (eds), *Interpretation and Method: Empirical Research Methods and the Interpretative Turn* (Armonk and London: M.E. Sharpe, 2006), pp. 29–41.

Hawkesworth's crisp description of positivism and critical rationalism provides the basis for the summary of both approaches.

8 Karl Popper, *The Logic of Scientific Discovery* (New York: Basic Books, 1959); see also Karl Popper, *Conjectures and Refutations: the Growth of Scientific Knowledge*, 4th ed. (London: Routledge and Kegan Paul, 1972) and *Objective Knowledge: an Evolutionary Approach* (Oxford: Clarendon Press, 1972).

9 See, for example, Dvora Yanow and Peregrine Schwartz-Shea (eds), *Interpretation and Method: Empirical Research Methods and the Interpretative Turn* (Armonk and London: M.E. Sharpe, 2006); Ian Shapiro, Rogers M. Smith, and Tarek E. Masoud, *Problems and Methods in the Study of Politics* (Cambridge: Cambridge University Press, 2004); Brent Flyvbjerg, *Making Social Science Matter: Why Social Enquiry Fails and How it Can Succeed Again* (Cambridge: Cambridge University Press, 2001); Sanford Schram and Brian Caterino (eds), *Making Political Science Matter: Debating Knowledge, Research, and Method* (New York: New York University Press, 2006).

10 Atul Kohli, Introduction, 'The Role of Theory in Comparative Politics', p. 1.

11 Rudra Sil, 'Problems chasing methods or methods chasing problems? Research communities, constrained pluralism, and the role of eclecticism', in Ian Shapiro, Rogers M. Smith, and Tarek E. Masoud, *Problems and Methods in the Study of Politics* (Cambridge: Cambridge University Press, 2004), p. 321 fn. Sil further argues that small-N comparisons which aim to link problem-specific analytic constructs to case-specific interpretations remains the best strategy to this end.

12 More on this later in the chapter, with specific respect to the manner in which our 'objective concepts' can influence our approach to empirical situations in the field.

13 Max Weber, 'The Meaning of Ethical Neutrality', in Edward Shils and Henry Finch (trans.), *Methodology of the Social Sciences* (New York: The Free Press, 1949).

14 Michel Foucault, *Archaeology of Knowledge*, A.M. Sheridan Smith (trans.) (New York: Pantheon, 1982).

15 In this regard, see Anne Norton's discussion of what she terms the totalitarian tendencies of problem-driven research. Anne Norton, 'Political Science as a Vocation', in Ian Shapiro, Rogers M. Smith, and Tarek E. Masoud, *Problems and Methods in the Study of Politics* (Cambridge: Cambridge University Press, 2004), pp. 67–81.

16 William May, 'Doing Ethics', *Social Problems*, vol. 27, no. 3 (February 1980), p. 362.

17 Baz Lecocq, 'Fieldwork Ain't Always Fun: Public and Hidden Discourses on Fieldwork', *History in Africa*, vol. 29 (2002), p. 273.

18 Lecocq, 'Fieldwork Ain't Always Fun', p. 280.

19 For example, see Stathis Kalyvas, 'The Urban Bias in Research on Civil Wars', *Security Studies*, vol. 13, no. 3 (2004), pp. 160–190.

20 Stathis Kalyvas, 'The Ontology of "Political Violence": Action and Identity in Civil War', *Perspectives*, vol. 1, no. 3 (September 2003), pp. 475–494.

21 Samuel Tanner, 'Saisir la violence de masse: Le nettoyage ethnique en Bosnie et l'apport d'une perspective locale et d'une approche de réseau', *Déviance et société*, vol. 31, no. 3 (2007), pp. 235–256.

22 For more on the vagaries of history and the alternative presents that were not to be, see Charles Tilly (ed.), *The Formation of National States in Western Europe* (Princeton, NJ: Princeton University Press).

23 Mohamed Selim, 'The Survival of a Nonstate Actor: The Foreign Policy of the Palestine Liberation Organization', in Bahgat Korany and Ali Hillal Dessouki, eds, *The Foreign Policies of Arab States* (Boulder: Westview Press, 1984), pp. 260–261.

24 See, for example, James D. Fearon and David D. Laitin 'Ethnicity, Insurgency, and Civil War', *American Political Science Review*, vol. 97, no. 1 (2003), pp. 75–90.

25 Alice Hills, 'Warlords, militia and conflict in contemporary Africa: A re-examination of terms', *Small Wars and Insurgencies*, vol. 8, no. 1 (1997) pp. 39–40.
26 See, for example, Paul B. Rich, 'Warlords, state fragmentation and the dilemma of humanitarian intervention', *Small Wars and Insurgencies*, vol. 10, no. 1 (1999) pp. 78–96.
27 Author interview, Alfiado Zunguza, Executive Director, JustaPaz – Centro de Estudo e de Tranformação de Conflictos, Maputo, 16/03/2006. According to Zunguza, FRELIMO accommodated RENAMO during the negotiations for two interrelated reasons. First was the loss of outside support at the end of the Cold War. Second was the realization that they could not win the war. The negotiations were not a situation that either party really wanted but neither had much choice. FRELIMO understood that the regular army could not defeat the guerrilla. As a precondition, FRELIMO had to recognize RENAMO as a (proto) political party, not just armed bandits. See also Martin Rupiya, 'Historical Context: War and Peace in Mozambique', in Jeremy Armon, Dylan Hendrickson and Alex Vines (eds), *The Mozambican Peace Process in Perspective*, special issue of *Accord – An International Review of Peace Initiatives.*, no. 3 (1998), p. 15.
28 At Gbadolite, the government's agenda was limited to ensuring a single-party system, the exile of Savimbi, and the end of American support for UNITA (Solomon 2002, 54).
29 Esman defines the political opportunity structure as 'the constitutionally sanctioned rules of access to political and economic resources'. Milton Esman, *Ethnic Politics* (Ithaca and London: Cornell University Press, 1994), p. 45.
30 According to Ryan Stephen, specialists in international relations have generally tended in their writings to underestimate the significance of ethnic conflict if not to ignore it altogether. Ryan Stephen, *Ethnic Conflict and International Relations* (Aldershot: Dartmouth, 1990), pp. 1–50. However, 'the frequency with which ethnic conflicts have erupted in recent years and the speed with which they have been internationalized has led to a change in this situation', K.M. de Silva and S.W.R. Samarasinghe, *Peace Accords and Ethnic Conflict* (London and New York: Pinter Publishers, 1993), p. 2.
31 Laqueur's extensive study of guerrillas is a case in point. Walter Laqueur, *Guerrilla: A Historical and Critical Study* (London: Weidenfeld and Nicolson, 1977).
32 Alice Hills, 'Warlords, militia and conflict in contemporary Africa', p. 36.
33 R.T. Naylor, 'The Insurgent Economy: Black Market Operations of Guerrilla Organizations', *Crime, Law and Social Change*, vol. 20 (1993).
34 Kamal Beyoghlow, 'Lebanon's New Leaders: Militias in Politics', *Journal of South Asian and Middle Eastern Studies*, vol. 12, no. 3 (1989), pp. 28–36; Lewis Snider, 'The Lebanese Forces: Their Origins and Role in Lebanon's Politics', *Middle East Journal*, vol. 38, no. 1 (1984), pp. 1–33; and Lewis Snider, 'The Lebanese Forces: Wartime Origins and Political Significance', in Edward Azar et al., *The Emergence of a New Lebanon: Fantasy or Reality?* (New York: Praeger, 1984).
35 See, for example, Glenda Morgan, 'Violence in Mozambique: Towards an Understanding of Renamo', *The Journal of Modern African Studies*, vol. 28, no. 4 (December 1990), pp. 603–619; Wolfgang S. Heinz, 'Review: Guerrillas, Political Violence, and the Peace Process in Colombia', *Latin American Research Review*, vol. 24, no. 3 (1989), pp. 249–258; Jutta Bakonyi and Kirsti Stuvøy, 'Violence & social order beyond the state: Somalia & Angola', *Review of African Political Economy*, vol. 32, no. 104 (2005), pp. 359–382. For a nuanced understanding of RENAMO's violence see Jessica Shafer, 'Guerrillas and Violence in the War in Mozambique: De-Socialization or Re-Socialization?' *African Affairs*, vol. 100, no. 399 (2001), pp. 215–237.
36 See, for example, Benjamin Ryder Howe, 'Revolutionaries or Crooks?' *Foreign Policy*, vol. 122 (January–February 2001), pp. 98–100; Assis Malaquias, 'Diamonds

are a Guerrilla's Best Friend: The Impact of Illicit Wealth on Insurgency Strategy', *Third World Quarterly*, vol. 22, no. 3 (June 2001), pp. 311–325; Philippe Le Billon, 'Angola's political economy of war: The role of oil and diamonds, 1975–2000', *African Affairs*, vol. 100 (2001), pp. 55–80.

37 Mary Kaldor, *New and Old Wars: Organized Violence in a Global Era* (Stanford: Stanford University Press, 1999) and 'Old Wars, Cold Wars, New Wars and the War on Terror', *International Politics*, vol. 42 (2005), pp. 491–498. See also comments on the New Wars thesis in Stathis Kalyvas, "New" and "Old" Civil Wars: A Valid Distinction?' *World Politics*, vol. 54 (October 2001), pp. 99–118.

38 Exclusivist and narrow, these beliefs are contrasted with the transformative ideologies that insurgents held in the Cold War era. See, for example, Michael Ignatieff, *Blood and Belonging: Journeys into the New Nationalism* (New York: Viking Press, 1993).

39 João Honwana, 'Implementing Peace Agreements in Civil Wars: The Case of Mozambique', paper presented to the Workshop on Peace Implementation, Center for International Security and Cooperation, Stanford University, (15–16 September 1998), p. 2.

40 David Keen, *The Economic Functions of Violence in Civil Wars*, Adelphi Paper 320 (London: Oxford University Press and The International Institute for Strategic Studies, 1998), p. 11.

41 John MacKinley, *Globalisation and Insurgency* (Oxford: Oxford University Press/International Institute for Security Studies, 2002), pp.38–40.

42 This builds on the relative deprivation hypothesis, which links conflict to relative economic deprivation. See James C. Davies, 'Toward a Theory of Revolution', *American Sociological Review*, vol. 27, no. 1 (February 1962), pp. 5–19; and Ted Robert Gurr, *Why Men Rebel* (Princeton: Princeton University Press, 1970). Critiques of relative deprivation theory highlight that: 1) the poor lack resources and opportunities to rebel; and 2) that there is a collective action problem involved in organizing a rebellion of economically deprived sectors of society. For the first set of critiques, see Harry Eckstein, 'On the Etiology of Internal Wars', in *Struggles in the State: Sources and Patterns of World Revolution,* George A. Kelly and Clifford W. Brown Jr., eds (New York: Wiley, 1969) pp. 168–195. For the second set see Mark Lichbach, 'What Makes Rational Peasants Revolutionary? Dilemma, Paradox, and Irony in Peasant Collective Action', *World Politics*, vol. 46, no. 3 (April 1994) pp. 383–418. This critique is based on the theory of collective action. See Mancur Olson, *The Logic of Collective Action* (Cambridge: Harvard University Press, 1965).

43 In spite of common wisdom to this effect, it is not clear that economic wealth is associated with a hardening of positions and a refusal to negotiate or, conversely, that economic hard-times necessarily bring about a softening in political stances. For example, a stark reversal in financial fortunes is one of the conditions that made the 1993 Oslo Accord between Israel and the PLO possible. The PLO had suffered economically from the downfalls of the second Gulf War during which the organization lost its rents from Arab Gulf states. However, one should qualify the argument in two ways. At the same time as Fatah initiated negotiations with Israel, smaller less prosperous members of the PLO refused to follow suit although they were similarly affected by the downturn in PLO economic fortunes. More significantly though, the shift in PLO positions away from ideological intractability can be traced back to 1974 when the organization was at the pinnacle of financial wealth.

44 Cynthia Enloe, 'All the Men are in the Militas, All the Women are Victims: The politics of masculinity and femininity in nationalist wars', in Lois Ann Lorentzen and Jennifer Turpin (eds), *The Women and War Reader* (New York: New York University Press, 1998), pp. 50–62.

45 Naylor, 'The Insurgent Economy: Black Market Operations of Guerrilla Organizations', p. 14
46 These definitions limit the phenomenon to violent conflict between the organized militaries of two or more independent political entities with a threshold of 1000 casualties. See Jack Levy, 'The Causes of War: A Review of Theories and Evidence', in P.E. Tetlock, ed., *Behavior, Society and Nuclear War*.
47 For discussions of and variations on these issues see Nils Petter Gleditsch, Peter Wallensteen, Mikael Eriksson, Margareta Sollenberg and Håvard Strand, 'Armed Conflict 1946–2001: A New Dataset', *Journal of Peace Research*, vol. 39, no. 5 (2002), pp. 615–637; Nicholas Sambanis, 'What is Civil War: Conceptual and Empirical Complexities of an Operational Definition', *Journal of Conflict Resolution*, vol. 48, no. 6 (December 2004), pp. 814–858; Errol A. Henderson and J. David Singer, 'Civil War in the Post-Colonial World, 1946–92', *Journal of Peace Research*, vol. 37, no. 3 (2000), pp. 275–299; Bethany Lacina, 'Explaining the Severity of Civil Wars', *Journal of Conflict Resolution*, vol. 50, no. 2 (2006), pp. 276–289.
48 See, for example, Barry R. Posen, 'The Security Dilemma and Ethnic Conflict', in Michael Brown (ed.), *Ethnic Conflict and International Security* (Princeton: Princeton University Press, 1993), pp. 103–124 and William Rose, 'The Security Dilemma and Ethnic Conflict: Some New Hypotheses', Security Studies, vol. 9, no. 4 (2000), pp, 1–51.
49 See, for example, Mats Berdal and David Keen, 'Violence and Economic Agendas in Civil Wars: Some Policy Implications', *Millenium: Journal of International Studies*, vol. 26, no. 3 (1997), pp. 795–818; John Mueller, 'The Banality of "Ethnic War"', *International Security*, vol. 25, no. 1 (Summer 2000), pp. 42–70; Paul Collier, 'Rebellion as a Quasi-Criminal Activity', *The Journal of Conflict Resolution*, vol. 44, no. 6 (December 2000), pp. 839–853. For an alternative account of the manner in which security ought to be conceptualized in intra-state conflicts see Stephen Saideman and Marie-Joëlle Zahar (eds), *Intra-State Conflict, Governments and Security: Dilemmas of Deterrence and Assurance* (London: Routledge, 2008).
50 See, for example, Timothy Wickham-Crowley, *Exploring Revolutions: Essays on Latin American Insurgency and Revolutionary Theory* (New York: Sharpe, 1991); Rex Brynen, *Sanctuary and Survival: The PLO in Lebanon* (Boulder: Westview Press, 1990); Charles King, 'The Benefits of Ethnic War: Understanding Eurasia's Unrecognized States', *World Politics*, vol. 53 (July 2001), pp. 524–552.
51 See, for example, Marie-Joëlle Zahar, 'Violence against Civilians: Irrational Impulse or Calibrated Strategy? Lessons from Hizballah (1984–2002)', paper presented at the annual meeting of the International Studies Association, Montreal, Quebec (Canada), March 2004.
52 Stathis Kalyvas, 'Wanton and Senseless? The Logic of Massacres in Algeria', *Rationality and Society*, vol. 11, no. 3 (1999), pp. 243–285; Benjamin Valentino, 'Final Solutions: The Causes of Mass Killing and Genocide', *Security Studies*, vol. 9, no. 3 (Spring 2000), pp. 1–59; Roger MacGinty, 'Ethno-National Conflict and Hate Crime', *American Behavioral Scientist*, vol. 45, no. 4 (December 2001), pp. 639–653; Stuart J. Kaufman, 'Symbolic Politics or Rational Choice? Testing Theories of Extreme Ethnic Violence', *International Security*, vol. 30, no. 4 (2006); Peter Langford, 'The Rwandan Path to Genocide: The Genesis of the Capacity of the Rwandan Post-colonial State to Organise and Unleash a Project of Extermination', *Civil Wars*, vol. 7, no. 1 (2005), pp. 1–27.
53 Stephen C. Lubkemann, 'Migratory Coping in Wartime Mozambique: An Anthropology of Violence and Displacement in "Fragmented Wars"', *Journal of Peace Research*, vol. 42, no. 4 (2005), pp. 493–508.
54 Stathis Kalyvas, 'The Ontology of "Political Violence": Action and Identity in Civil Wars', *Perspectives on Politics*, vol. 1, no. 3 (2003), pp. 475–494.

Fieldwork, objectivity and the academic enterprise 211

55 For a dissenting opinion see Chaim Kaufmann, 'Rational Choice and Progress in the Study of Ethnic Conflict: A Review Essay', *Security Studies*, vol. 14, no. 1 (January–March 2005), pp. 178–207.
56 The concept of human security grew out of a realization that international relations were studied from a Eurocentric perspective, underlining the need to interrogate generalizations borne of the experience of great powers and European states. At core, it holds that security cannot be reduced to state or national security because this presupposes a specific kind of state-society relations. Indeed, the security of individuals is not only endangered by threats emanating from outside but that it can be endangered by states that abdicate a central element of sovereignty, the contract to protect citizens against harm. As the recent report of the International Commission on Intervention and State Sovereignty highlights, such abdication can be intentional or it can be a consequence of state weakness and inability to fulfill obligations in this regard.
57 Stephen John Stedman, 'Spoiler Problems in Peace Processes', *International Security*, vol. 22, no. 2 (Fall 1997), pp. 5–53.
58 See Stedman, 'Spoiler Problems in Peace Processes', and Barbara F. Walter, 'The Critical Barrier to Civil War Settlement', *International Organization*, vol. 51, no. 3 (1997). This is one of the main lessons of a study that analyzed sixteen cases of peace implementation. Stephen John Stedman, *Implementing Peace Agreements in Civil Wars: Lessons and Recommendations for Policymakers*, IPA Policy Paper on Peace Implementation (New York: International Peace Academy, 2001).
59 The commitment of international actors is seldom sufficient. In part, outsiders seldom consider pacifying conflict zones as a strategic objective that could justify expending human and military resources to keep the peace. In those rare occasions where pacification is defined as a strategic objective by outside interveners, as was the case with Syria's involvement in implementing Lebanon's Ta'if Agreement or with NATO's presence in Bosnia and Herzegovina, the commitment of outsiders does indeed go a long way to controlling the volatile environment.
60 Stephen John Stedman, 'Peace Processes and the Challenges of Violence', in John Darby and Roger MacGinty (eds), *Contemporary Peacemaking: Conflict, Violence and Peace Processes* (Houndmills, Basingstoke: Palgrave Macmillan, 2003).
61 Incentives can be of two kinds: material (economic carrots) and political (power sharing formulas securing access to the State). Material incentives create an instrumental loyalty towards the peace process; this loyalty is likely to endure only as long as the 'carrot' that generated it. Power sharing formulas are often thought to be a more efficient barrier against the resurgence of violence because they provide security to the protagonists.
62 Marie-Joëlle Zahar, 'Understanding the Violence of Insiders: Loyalty, Custodians of Peace, and the Sustainability of Conflict Settlement', in Edward Newman and Oliver Richmond (eds), *Spoilers and Peace Processes: Conflict Settlement and Devious Objectives* (Tokyo: United Nations University Press, 2006). See also Stuart J. Kaufman, 'Escaping the Symbolic Politics Trap: Reconciliation Initiatives and Conflict Resolution in Ethnic Wars', *Journal of Peace Research*, vol. 43, no. 2 (2006), pp. 201–218.
63 One glaring exception is the Center for the Study of Violence and Reconciliation in South Africa which has produced a series of important studies that establish the link between failures of reintegration and the level of every day insecurity in the townships by speaking of criminal violence as an expression of the continued marginalization of most poor black South Africans and the disappearance of 'legitimate outlets' for the expression of violence provided by the struggle against apartheid.
64 When leaders receive lucrative packages and positions in power while foot soldiers get next to nothing, revolts are likely to occur. Such was the case in the DDR

process involving RENAMO in Mozambique. When political interests at home dictate risk-averse policies to donor countries, resulting strategies are often incoherent. For example, Western donors seek to reform security in the West Bank and Gaza but they quibble over the payment of police salaries out of aid packages for fear of being perceived to fund 'terrorists'. Analysts and policy-makers then wonder why disgruntled policemen turn to violence and terror. When the international community tries to address the problem, it fails to probe its role in either creating or worsening it. In an interesting article, Walter argues that the recurrence of conflict is often linked to the disenchantment of foot soldiers which facilitates mobilization for the next round. Barbara F. Walter, 'Does Conflict Beget Conflict? Explaining Recurring Civil War', *Journal of Peace Research*, vol. 41, no. 3 (2004), pp. 371–388.

65 A good example of this kind of 'romanticizing bias' is provided by the early literature on civil society in Latin America.
66 This argument has been presented by Ted Gurr and Barbara Harff in *Ethnic Conflict in World Politics* (Boulder: Westview Press, 1994).
67 Gurr and Harff, *Ethnic Conflict in World Politics*, p. 153.
68 This is the case of Serbian nationalism as discussed in Mihailo Crnobrnja, *The Yugoslav Drama* (Montreal and Kingston: McGill-Queen's University Press, 1994).
69 See the discussion of these perspectives in Lynn Hirschkind, 'Redefining the "Field" in Fieldwork', *Ethnology*, vol. 30, no. 3 (July 1991), pp. 237–249.

14 Dilemmas of self-representation and conduct in the field

Stephen Brown

Introduction

Researchers often forget that while we conduct fieldwork, we are ourselves the object of other people's research. A variety of actors are constantly gathering different types of information on us. Most directly, the people we interact with in the course of our research activities, such as interviewees and archivists, form an opinion of us that can influence our access to information. As researchers we are highly dependent on people's goodwill and voluntary cooperation; how we present ourselves to them can thus have a significant impact on our research opportunities. At the same time, other people also collect information on us, out of professional interest or simply curiosity, ranging from fellow passengers in a mini-bus or a waiter at a restaurant to secret police. This information can circulate informally and sometimes formally, through gossip networks and possibly paid informants, in ways that we cannot control – or even track. Not all of this has a direct impact on our research, but the way we interact with people – and the way we represent ourselves – often has a significant indirect influence on our work, including on our emotional well-being.

When the tables are turned on researchers and we become the object of interest, we might prefer to remain vague about our own opinions or hide our own beliefs, not to mention aspects of our personal lives. Likewise, when conducting extended fieldwork in one place, the behaviour and information we reveal outside the research context, including in our spare time, can have an impact on our ability to conduct research. In environments where information spreads quickly, being seen, for instance, socializing with one particular group of actors or having a more intimate relationship with an individual can compromise our 'reputation' as a serious and unbiased (or sympathetic) researcher. Not socializing at all might not be sustainable and moreover projects another image that can be interpreted negatively as well. Furthermore, what we reveal in a seemingly innocent or private context can circulate, at times inaccurately, and do harm to our research relationships and even our sense of security. Examples include cohabitation or having children out of wedlock; being gay, lesbian or bisexual; or belonging to a specific religious group or being an atheist. Dissimulation or lying about these issues may avoid some problems, but raise other ones, such as internal conflict and ethical concerns.

To what extent does our personal conduct matter when in the field, especially when 'off duty'? When asked about personal issues that may reveal a controversial answer, how should we respond? Using examples drawn in part from my own experiences, this chapter explores the issues of self-representation and conduct in research situations and sites. It addresses a series of dilemmas upon which other researchers may wish to reflect before being placed in similar situations. I try to avoid being normative and recommending a specific course of action, preferring to promote awareness and invite reflexivity on the part of the researcher. Thinking through these issues ahead of time can help prevent awkward situations and other problems that can handicap and sometimes even abort effective fieldwork. It will also help researchers choose a course of action that is based on the particularities of their research method and site, as well as their own personal situation, most likely to lead to productive research.

The false separation of the selves

It is tempting, but misleading, to think that while in the field we can just separate our 'on-duty' researcher selves from our 'off-duty' selves. We all play certain roles, assume certain *personas*, in our everyday lives. While in the classroom, I present myself very differently from when I am having a drink at a colleague's house. I don't reveal the same level of personal information to students as I do to friends. In my home country, I have no concern that being seen in public with certain people or in a certain place, being heard to hold a certain opinion or belonging to a certain group will hamper my everyday professional activities or otherwise cause me any problems. I live in a country where, gossip aside, most people make a clear separation between personal and professional lives. Strong legal provisions at various levels offer protection. Moreover, I work in an institution that by its very nature promotes freedom of thought. My position as a tenured professor provides me with a particularly privileged level of professional security and how people perceive me does not have a significant impact on my day-to-day life or well-being.

When conducting research in the field, I lose that luxury. A researcher's self-presentation and reputation are important for obtaining and maintaining access to information, which is in fact a *sine qua non* of fieldwork, and poses additional challenges in 'difficult situations'.[1] This is especially the case for those conducting interviews that are longer and more in-depth than mine, or that require permission to consult an archive.[2] Those collecting life-histories require multiple sessions, while researchers involved in lengthy participant-observation or 'thick' ethnographic studies normally live for an extended period of time in a 'host' community. In such cases, the goodwill of local people and of gatekeepers among power elites is often essential to be able to begin, pursue and complete research. Formal (government) or informal (local 'traditional' authority) research clearance can be withdrawn and individual participants can refuse to collaborate, thereby potentially jeopardizing the project as a whole. Such decisions can be based on opinions and beliefs about us and our work, which may not be accurate but are to a large extent influenced by our behaviour both while 'on duty' and 'off'.

Information about visiting researchers circulates in networks normally beyond our ken. On occasion, I have received an echo of the fact that people were talking about me and my work. For instance, while conducting research in Nairobi in 2001 on international responses (or lack thereof) to so-called 'ethnic clashes' in Kenya, a Kenyan NGO official told me that I was making Western aid and embassy officials 'nervous'. Given what I was finding, I did not interpret this as a bad thing *per se*. It actually confirmed my sense that I was onto something important that many would prefer to leave unexamined.[3] In fact, this person reported this back to me in the context of expressing support for my research, mentioning that it would be extremely difficult for a Kenyan to do it. (Kenyans would be more susceptible to intimidation and any NGO that supported the research could find its donor funding cut or withdrawn.) Perhaps he meant it in part as a caution, though I felt no need to modify my behaviour as a result.

Though I did not quite think it through at the time, this indicated that subsequent people I contacted might already know something about me and my work and prepare their responses in consequence. Beyond the sensitivity of my topic, other information about me could be circulating: Was I seen as astute and well-prepared or naïve, ill-informed and easy to lead astray? Open to new ideas or had I already made up my mind on what I wanted to find? Objective or a trouble-maker? Perhaps shortly after I began this field research, word had already gone out across Nairobi on what kind of a researcher and a person I was. I am unable to gauge how this affected my research, positively or negatively, in terms of the quality and veracity of information. For the work I was doing, access was not difficult to negotiate and probably not affected. Where there is a higher risk that key informants could refuse to participate or that a person of authority could shut down the research project, the implications of such 'nervousness' could be much worse.

The separation of the public and the private is a fiction that is hard to maintain in most research sites. The majority of research in difficult situations takes place in a far more intimate setting than the example I give above, interviewing mainly Western officials and national elites in a very large urban area. Information circulates much faster in smaller cities and faster still in small towns, rural settings or refugee camps, including through an informal communication network sometimes known as the 'bush telegraph'. We researchers are alien oddities and we often inquire about sensitive or unusual issues. It is normal for people to be curious about, discuss and judge us. How best to prepare for this fact?

Professional conduct

Earlier chapters in this volume deal in great depth with ethical and security issues, as well as how to obtain access. Marie-Joëlle Zahar's chapter specifically analyzes the implications of our perceived or actual identity and interests. It is amply clear that professional conduct is important. Our ability to gather useful information and sometimes even our personal security depend on it.

Here I will allow myself to be normative: While 'on duty', researchers should generally be polite, respectful, punctual, patient, humble, appropriately dressed and non-judgmental, among other things. Demonstrating a commitment to protecting the interviewees' identity, if requested, and otherwise respecting the ethical codes of research are also particularly important. At times, however, we might need to push a bit harder to get a proper answer to a question – but we also need to gauge when insisting will actually be helpful. There can be a fine line between good investigative technique and what could be interpreted as inappropriate rudeness. When meeting with interviewees or other people in the context of our research, we need to be attentive to their clues on when to move from pleasantries to discussing 'business' and on when to change topics, move on to the next question or bring the meeting to an end. I try to leave my ego at the door and absorb as much as I can from the interview. On only very few occasions, have I felt hostility from an interviewee, even contempt, mainly for people like me in general: white or Western graduate students or academics who fly in, poke around and fly out, writing a Ph.D. thesis or publishing and perhaps even making a career on other people's life-and-death problems. This is a valid critique and I try not to take it personally. On almost all occasions, however, people I talked to were extremely gracious and generous with their time, setting a tone that I needed only to follow.

My own experience, however, does not cover the range of possible interlocutors. Almost all of the people I have interviewed are either Western officials working in Africa or a relatively Westernized local elite, be they in government, academia or 'civil society', based in the capital city. Every single one of my hundreds of research interviews to date has taken place in a European language. I have never used an interpreter. As such, the cultural divide is not so vast. We speak the same language, both literally and figuratively, and my interviewees are used to talking to people like me. If I unknowingly commit an offence, they will be more likely to contextualize it. The task is far more complicated for researchers interacting with everyday people in cultural contexts where they do not know local codes. Under such circumstances, appropriate behaviour is less intuitive and researchers are far more likely to be the object of interest – and potentially being misunderstood. Greater preparation, for instance on language and societal norms (including dress codes), and increased attention to subtle cues can mitigate this risk.

Most researchers are sensible and sensitive enough to realize the importance of professionalism while conducting research. Beyond the few comments above, I do not wish to draw up a list of do's and don'ts. So much of it is basic common sense. What is less obvious, however, are a few other aspects of self-representation, to which I now turn: 'off-duty' behaviour, more intimate relationships and responding to personal questions.

Off-duty behaviour

As mentioned above, people like me – and presumably most people reading this book – can, during their everyday activities, keep a relatively clear separation between their life at work and their personal lives. It is not complete or unproblematic, but relatively easily managed. In the field, especially under difficult circumstances, this is next to impossible. The public and the private spheres can become almost indistinguishable. In some instances, including when using feminist methodologies, the bonds of empathy and shared experience can actually be prerequisites for research.

It is very hard to keep secrets in the field; news travels fast by bush telegraph. Foreign researchers are easily identified, especially if white in a country with few white people. When I worked for the United Nations in Oman, I remember an Omani co-worker, who greeted me one morning and said: 'So you went to Nizwa last weekend ... '. Apparently, a friend of his – whom I did not even know – had seen me and reported back to him. Another officemate once told me that she had seen my car parked at a specific residential area the previous night. She then (half?) jokingly asked: 'Who is she?' These were innocent enough questions, but it certainly felt like surveillance.[4]

While conducting Ph.D. research in Lilongwe, Malawi, I had no car; I took public transportation where available and did a lot of walking. I soon realized people knew a lot about me. Hawkers remembered what I had bought or even just looked at, sometimes months later. A private security guard at the main post office once greeted me by name, though I had never had a conversation with him before. On occasion, taxi drivers already knew where I was staying before I told them. What else was circulating about me? In particular, was the company I was keeping a problem? The majority of people with whom I socialized during my four months in Malawi were American, most of whom worked for the US government, mainly the US Agency for International Development. A few others worked for the UN or an NGO. Most worked in the health sector, whereas I was conducting research on democratization, so at least I did not interact with them in the course of my work. I considered myself very lucky to have found interesting and kind people who included me in their social activities and helped me find temporary accommodation. They also kept me from feeling bored and isolated.

Did this come at a price? It is hard to tell. I have no doubt that many Malawian officials and donor representatives (my main interlocutors) saw me around town, noted with whom I was socializing and associated me with the

American government crowd – or heard about it through the grapevine. Once a US Embassy security guard let me through to someone's office without checking for identification or phoning ahead – clearly against security protocols – presumably because he thought I was an American official. This identification with American government circles probably compromised people's perception of my objectivity. Few probably even realized that I was Canadian, especially since I was at the time based at an American university. I would like to believe that my explanation of my research and my interview questions would have made clear that I was not taking the US government's line, or any other's. Still, how could what was 'known' about me not colour people's perception of me and interaction with me?

What else did people 'know' or think they knew about me? As a graduate student on a low budget, I actively sought out free accommodation. I stayed at eight or nine different places during my four months in Lilongwe, mostly as a house-sitter, though sometimes as a guest. (Many expatriates were happy to have someone like me stay in their home while they were away on holiday or mission to keep an eye on things. I in turn jumped at the chance of having the run of a real house, access to a kitchen, telephone and a television, once even a car.) Did people impute anything about my relationship with my various hosts, be they male or female? In the course of various conversations, I heard many tales about which foreigner was sleeping with whom. I once heard back about a conversation at USAID about whose boyfriend I was or was not.

Should I have behaved any differently while in Malawi? Should I have cloistered myself in a cheap hostel and avoided being associated with anyone in particular? It would probably have improved my image as an objective researcher, but at what cost? It would have reduced my productivity in some ways, notably by eliminating easy access to a telephone, which was necessary for setting up interviews. (This was in 1997–98 and I did not use a cell phone in the field, as one now can do quite easily.) It certainly would have had a strong negative impact on my emotional well-being. Field research can be intense and isolating. Having drinks or dinner with people, going to a party or partaking in weekend leisure activities do much to restore balance. It also would have created a new security problem, not so much for me personally as for my laptop. As far as I could tell, nobody really seemed to care about my 'off-duty' activities – but not all situations are so innocuous. At times, the company we keep can have a tangible influence on our research and security, especially in difficult situations.

Consider the example of a relatively young European male employed by the United Nations in a Central American country emerging from civil war.[5] By day, he worked in his office, representing an international organization closely involved in the negotiation and implementation of peace accords. In his spare time, he liked to hang out with senior members of the former guerrilla army, then in the midst of reconfiguring itself as a political party. This was clearly a great opportunity for him to learn about revolutionary movements and hear first hand about the struggle. He presumably also sympathized with their politics. His fraternization did not go unnoticed. Complaints found their way back to his UN superiors about his lack of neutrality, followed by death threats. He was urgently reassigned to a UN office in another county.

Should he have behaved differently? Does being a UN official by day mean that he cannot have drinks in the evening with whom he wants? Should his boss have prohibited him from this type of activity? Or at least warned him? Or should he have been more discreet about meeting in public or at least have been prepared for the consequences, however extreme they turned out to be? Is declining to have drinks with actors on one side in a politically polarized situation the wise thing to do or is it a conservative bureaucratic reaction to a potentially fascinating opportunity? After all, he did not take this posting to stay home and watch videos or just hang out with other UN international staff.

There are no clear answers. As researchers, we want to maintain a positive reputation, often linked to impartiality and objectivity. At the same time, we need to work under conditions that protect our mental well-being, which is after all necessary for productive fieldwork. Moreover, declining social invitations could actually be considered rude and also be detrimental to our reputation. The challenge is to find the balance that is right for us, given the particularities of our fieldwork – methodology, duration, types of partners – and our own personal needs.

Don't date the data?

The thorniest question related to off-duty behaviour is probably the issue of romance and – let's not hide behind euphemisms – sex. When in the field, do we have to become asexual? Or is it OK to flirt, go on a date, engage casual sex or enter into a relationship? Though some thesis advisors warn their students not to 'date the data', I want to avoid the should-or-shouldn't approach to this issue. Many people I know have actually formed lasting, loving relationships with someone they met while conducting research, either another expatriate or a person from that country. The longer the research trip, the more likely we are to get involved with someone in the field. And these relationships can affect our research in various ways. Individual researchers can make their own choices; I want to help them understand the issues and think them through.

As mentioned above, doing research can be a very isolating experience. Paradoxically, it can sometimes also be a very intense one, where close personal relationships can form very quickly, especially when in what this volume identifies as 'difficult situations'. Being away from home and from family and friends can lead to an almost instant intimacy with others who are in a similar position. These social circles can sustain our research by helping us decompress, as well as serve as support networks in times of stress, provide helpful guidance and help us resolve certain problems. A close relationship

220 *Dilemmas of self-representation and conduct in the field*

with a specific person can do all of this, as well as provide additional personal support. A relationship with a local person in particular may also provide useful insight into local culture and help improve language skills.

Also, being in a strange environment can make us suspend our usual behavioural self-regulation. In a sense, we feel that 'the normal rules don't apply' and can find ourselves doing things we would never do in our regular lives, in part because we are faced with new situations and opportunities. Moreover, we know that our fieldwork will come to an end and we will go home, sometimes without any plan to return. We tend to think that, as in a trip to Las Vegas, 'What happens in the field stays in the field'. Sometimes, the Jiminy Cricket that is our conscience stays home or, put in Freudian terms, our id supplants our super-ego. Solitude and boredom can make us do a number of things we would not normally do, not all salacious. In my case, these included participating in a weekly 'dart night' at a USAID employee's home or attending a volleyball tournament where the players were almost all expatriates. I found this somewhat embarrassing, since these are not types of activities I partake in at home and furthermore participating so willingly in an 'expat scene' did not correspond to the image I had of myself in the field. Still, such social activities can be useful coping mechanisms that enhance mental well-being and thus actually make a research trip more successful than it otherwise would be.

On the topic of romance and sex, I prefer not to discuss my own personal experiences. Instead, I draw on an example provided by Heidi Postlewait in a book she co-wrote with two former UN colleagues, *Emergency Sex and Other Desperate Measures*. In it, the three friends take turns chronicling a decade of work on various UN peacekeeping missions. Of the three, Postlewait is most detailed about her love life and coins the term that found its way to the book's title, though by no means is it the central theme of the book. She clearly illustrates the rapid and at times urgent intimacy that often develops in difficult situations. In the following passage, she describes how, while working for the UN Mission in Somalia, she and a Somali translator, with whom she is having a relationship, come under sniper fire:

> Yusuf and I get up and run around to the safe side of the building. And then the strangest thing happens. I want to rip my clothes off, rip Yusuf's clothes off, and just fuck him right there. I can feel this pounding inside me and I can't wait. It has to be right now, not in ten minutes, not five. Now. An Emergency. Emergency Sex.[6]

In an interview, Postlewait explained the rapid closeness and physicality as follows:

> Everything is intensified and magnified – friendships, your faith, your desire to stay alive. Andrew [Thomson, a co-author of the book] said something about the sex being an antidote to that feeling of being near

death. 'Emergency sex' is a metaphor for that intensity. People out there don't have their usual family support systems. You don't have a daily routine. You're really needy. You're seeing terrible things. In a month, you're in a kind of relationship that would take three or four years here [in the United States]. They don't generally last [...] which is probably a good thing.[7]

Only rarely are UN mission or research trips that dangerous, but otherwise stressful conditions can provoke a similar response. How might romance and sex affect our research?

Anecdotal evidence suggests that a woman is more likely to be judged more negatively than a man for entering into a sexual relationship in the field. Postlewait's encounters certainly received far more attention in book reviews and newspaper articles than did her male co-authors'. Same-sex relationships are usually more stigmatized than heterosexual ones. In some cases, extra-marital sex or homosexuality may even be illegal in the research site.

It is virtually impossible to keep such secrets in the field – and we need to therefore assume that information will circulate. Our attempts to present ourselves as an 'objective' researcher can suffer greatly if we are known, for instance, to be literally in bed with the US Embassy or a politicized identity group and thus widely assumed to be figuratively in bed with them as well. Moreover, many researchers will find that men and women mingle more freely in their home country than at their research site. In such circumstances, a man and a woman being seen together or being known to have spent time alone together is likely to lead to assumptions about the nature of the relationship. Even if it is a platonic friendship, people may well assume it is a sexual relationship – and reputations may suffer. In many places, no matter how chaste she really might be, a woman who entertains one or more men in her hut, hotel room or other dwelling, or is even seen drinking with a man in public, is liable to be considered promiscuous or even labelled a prostitute.

Once something is 'known' about us, once a negative reputation is made – whether based on truth or not – it is almost impossible to undo. Opportunities and goodwill may evaporate and, in some circumstances, we may find ourselves *persona non grata* in the very place we need to be to carry out our research. As researchers, therefore, we need to make informed decisions on getting romantically involved or even giving a public impression that a relationship may be sexual, weighing the personal benefits against the probability of negative impact on research. The only real mistake would be to assume that no one would know, that it is purely our own business, that what we do in our spare time does not matter.

Answering personal questions

Even if our on- and off-duty conduct in the field is beyond reproach by local standards, we are sometimes faced with personal questions that we may not wish to answer. Though it may be no secret in our regular lives back home, we may prefer to avoid revealing at the research site certain information that may lead to us being stigmatized – such as religious affiliation (or not believing in God); living with a partner or having children without being married; or being in a same-sex relationship. We can avoid some problems by not revealing this information or by lying. However, such strategies can lead to other problems, including unease with ourselves for lacking honesty.

Friendly people all over the world engage in conversation with outsiders and solicit information on what we may consider to be our private lives. Women especially are often asked about their marital status or if they have children. (I suspect that men are more likely to ask the former and women the latter.) Though seemingly innocuous, such questions can actually become loaded. Saying she is single may lead directly to a difficult question on why. It could also expose her to an undesired increase in sexual attention. Saying she is married can lead to problematic comments, such as 'If your husband really loved you, he wouldn't let you be here on your own' or 'What kind of a woman are you to come here and leave your husband behind?' Revealing that we are cohabiting can provoke a negative moral judgment. Being in a same-sex relationship is most often considered far worse, even if legally married (as is possible in a few places). When engaging in research, it is certainly generally desirable to avoid being overtly condemned or denounced as immoral, including being branded a sinner. Researchers might not want to share openly other types of personal information as well, despite being quite open about it at home. For instance, they might prefer not to reveal being Jewish in a country where they think saying so could impede research or put them in an awkward or vulnerable situation. Likewise, being openly lesbian, gay or bisexual might cause problems in some places.

What to do when asked personal questions if an honest answer might be counterproductive? What kind of strategies can we adopt? One possibility is to lie. I have heard of a professor who systematically tells her single female students going to do work abroad to invent a husband and wear a wedding ring. I completely understand why a researcher may chose to do so, especially if she feels it enhances her personal security or prevents her from being seen as a threat by other women. Though useful and perhaps advisable under some circumstances, I find it a bit odd that a professor recommend premeditated falsehoods across the board. Lying in such a way is based on negative assumptions about the behaviour of people in the research site and their inability to deal with the truth and difference.

Though lying may provide an easy answer, it can exact its own price. Researchers may have moral qualms about lying or consider it an inappropriate way to establish a research relationship, which normally requires a bond of trust. Moreover, for people who are proud – or at least not ashamed – of their status, lying can leave researchers feeling displeased with themselves. For instance, sexual minorities from an environment where 'coming out' is the norm, hiding or lying about their sexual orientation may cause inner conflict or feelings of personal cowardice and betrayal of the self or the community. The same could be true in other examples, such as religion. Moreover, 'coming out' as gay, Jewish, or some other potentially stigmatizing identity could actually constitute an opportunity to break down stereotypes and fight prejudice.

Lies might also prove difficult to sustain, especially when spending an extended period of time in one research site. For instance, people may begin to doubt the existence of an alleged spouse or fiancé(e) if there are insufficient signs of communication, such as letters, or content that betrays a platonic relationship, for instance phone calls that people may overhear or actively listen in on. As a result, the researcher could earn the reputation of being a liar, which harms research relationships.

My strategy is to be as evasive as possible about information I would rather not share, without lying. For instance, in English, we can try to use non-gendered words like 'partner' to avoid revealing a same-sex relationship. In many languages, however, nouns have masculine and feminine forms. A way around this is to use an unspecified 'we' or refer to the relationship itself instead of the spouse. For instance, an exchange with a taxi driver in Rwanda in 2007:

Him: Are you married?
Me: Sort of. I am in a common-law relationship, which in Canada is almost the same as being legally married.

I do not know what he made of my response, but we moved on to another topic.

It is harder to dodge the question of children. In many societies, childless people can be objects of pity. A man and especially a woman without a child are often considered incomplete, unfulfilled, not fully adult, sometimes even unwilling to or incapable of meeting societal duties. Reproducing is also tangible proof of a man's virility.

I used to have what I thought was a great explanation for my lack of offspring. I vividly remember –probably because of my discomfort at the time – a discussion I had with a friend of the Nicaraguan family I was living with in a working-class neighbourhood of Managua in 1987. Our conversation went something like this:

Him: Do you have any children?
Me: No, I don't.
Him: Why not?
Me: I'm too young to have kids.
Him: How old are you?
Me: Twenty.
Him: I already had two kids by the time I was 20.
Me: Different cultures, I guess [*laughs uncomfortably*].

I am now too old to offer that explanation of my childlessness. Maybe I could just say because I am not married – though then they would probably ask me why that was … Last time someone expressed sympathy for my childlessness, I admitted to not really wanting to have children of my own. It has the advantage of being true, but that might stigmatize me as a selfish person. My answer left the person who asked, a Kenyan woman who had just expressed her joy at having two children of her own, looking rather horrified. I tried to assuage her pity for me by assuring her that in my culture not having children was not seen as a terrible thing. She did not look convinced, but we were able to shift conversation to another topic. I am not sure how effective cultural relativism-based arguments are.

Religious affiliation is not often raised in my everyday life – nor is it likely to be in the 'off-site' lives of most researchers. The topic of religion, however, has come up much more often in the field. Pentecostals have quizzed me on my beliefs and tried to get me to attend a service at their church. One hotel registration form (at a Holiday Inn, of all places, in Southern Oman) had a line for me to indicate my religion. I am not sure why; probably something to do with liquor licensing and maybe having a mini-bar in my room. I just left it blank and no one objected. I have yet to develop a proper response to what seems to most to be a simple question. Especially in places where having a religion is akin to having an ethnic group, my lack of one risks baffling people – and may be seen as the worst possible answer.

Truth-telling has the advantage of simplicity and sincerity, as well as respect for the interlocutor, but could make research more complicated – either because people will be unfavourably predisposed or seek to disengage. It could also make a researcher uncomfortable if the truth is something he or she would rather not talk about. Lying, however, can also cause the researcher some discomfort and lies may be revealed later on, breaking any bond of trust. Either way, the researcher's discomfort with these questions can cause him or her to respond awkwardly or aggressively, neither of which is propitious for building a research relationship. Even answers that dissimulate the truth, without outright lying, may sit uncomfortably with the researcher, as it feels less than honest.

One way to avoid uncomfortable questions is to not ask them of other people, thus making it a topic of conversation. This might also not be possible, depending on the type of research being conducted. In many cases, asking personal questions may be part of the research process. We also risk being perceived as overly formal and disinterested, even rude and lacking in reciprocity. In some cases, it might be possible simply to respond firmly that we do not wish to discuss such personal matters – at the risk of being found cold and distant – and then change the topic, for instance to local politics, on which most people will happily speak volumes. Better yet, a witty non-response can go a long way, even if rehearsed.

Conclusion

This chapter has addressed some of the most pertinent issues of self-representation and conduct while undertaking field research and their impact on fieldwork. It has presented the particularities of conducting research in difficult situations, notably the impossibility of separating our personal lives from our fieldwork in a context where we, as outsiders, are highly visible and information about us circulates in ways we cannot know. It also explored the challenges and possible strategies for responding to them, namely 'on-duty' conduct, 'off-duty' behaviour, including intimate relationships, and how to deal with personal questions that inevitably arise.

As researchers, we are faced with a number of dilemmas. How we choose, whether consciously or unconsciously, to respond to them can have a significant impact on our research relationships, our access to necessary information and sometimes even the viability of our research. How to find the right balance between professional conduct and personal well-being, even outside the narrowly defined research context? When might lying or dissimulation enhance research productivity more than being explicit with the truth? What are the trade-offs in adopting one strategy, rather than another? And how can we make informed decisions based on unknown (if not fully unpredictable) consequences? What to do when all options can potentially interfere with the quality of our research and our personal well-being while conducting fieldwork?

The right option – if there is one – depends on the idiosyncratic mix of who the researcher is, who the interlocutors are and what the situation on the ground is. This will often require a snap judgment, which could prove in retrospect not have been the wisest choice. To improve the odds of dealing with the situation as well as we can, the best strategy is to think through ahead of time how best to conduct ourselves and how best to react to hypothetical situations and thus be prepared if and when they arise.

Notes

The author wishes to thank Susan Thomson for her helpful comments and suggestions.

1 See in particular Chapters 6 to 8 in this volume.
2 My field research typically involves several weeks or months in a distant country, most often in Africa, working on my own or perhaps with one other Western researcher. Most of my research consists of one-on-one semi-structured interviews that last 60 to 90 minutes. I normally meet with someone only once during a research trip, though I might interview them again on a subsequent research trip.
3 The result of this research was published as Stephen Brown, 'Quiet Diplomacy and Recurring "Ethnic Clashes" in Kenya', in Chandra Lekha Sriram and Karin Wermester (eds), *From Promise to Practice: Strengthening UN Capacities for the Prevention of Violent Conflict* (Boulder: Lynne Rienner, 2003), pp. 69–100.
4 This example and two other ones below pertain to UN employees rather than actual researchers. As foreigners temporarily in the country, some of their experiences are relevant to my discussion here. As staff members of an international organization, however, they benefit from easier access and greater institutional support than researchers, including if the situation becomes truly difficult. Their off-duty behaviour is less likely to have an impact on their work, especially when they enjoy diplomatic immunity. NGO officials are presumably more affected by

these issues than UN staff, but less so than most researchers that lack institutional backing.
5 This is a true story, but I am being deliberately vague about the details to protect the person's identity.
6 Kenneth Cain, Heidi Postlewait and Andrew Thomson, *Emergency Sex and Other Desperate Measures: A True Story from Hell on Earth* (New York: Hyperion, 2004), p. 139.
7 Suzy Hansen, 'Sex and drugs in hell: The authors of *Emergency Sex and Other Desperate Measures* talk about keeping body and soul together in the killing fields of Cambodia, Somalia and Haiti', *Salon.com*, 8 July 2004, available at <http://dir.salon.com/story/mwt/feature/2004/07/08/emergency_sex/index1.html>, accessed 3 May 2008.

15 There and back: surviving field research in violent and difficult situations

Olga Martin-Ortega and Johanna Herman

The objective of this book has been to offer perspectives from authors experienced in dealing with the complex challenges of planning and carrying out research in difficult situations, especially those which are not necessarily apparent to someone who has not been in the field. This conclusion provides a practical way of applying these perspectives. All readers, but especially new researchers, may find this chapter helpful in the planning and preparation stages of their research. We recommend of course that readers also refer to the relevant chapter for more in-depth treatment of particular areas of interest.

Getting started: practicalities

Surprise obstacles will always come up in your research, especially when your travels take you to conflict zones and other difficult settings, but sensible planning will help you to prepare for dealing with any potential problems in a way that will minimize its impact on your work.

The first step in all research is of course the research proposal. When you consider your research questions, spend time identifying any potential obstacles in your specific study. This analysis should enable you to shape the research. For example, if it appears the security situation will be too volatile for you to gain access to a particular area, it may be necessary to change your focus before you go, to avoid a situation where you might arrive in a country and are then unable to access your research participants. A thorough knowledge of the country history and current political situation is needed for you to assess the potential risks and the appropriate response.

The amount of time available to you and possible limitations on access will affect your work, so it is necessary to develop strategies appropriate to your resources and access. Firstly, think about the amount of time that will be necessary to complete your research. This will be based on the nature of your research questions and methodology: interviews with government officials in a capital city will involve different resources and challenges to engaging in participant observation or conducting focus groups at several sites across the country, or conducting repeated interviews in one particular community. In terms of the timing of your trip, try to be flexible and consider the country context. You may have a fixed idea of when is convenient for you but if it falls during monsoon season and you wish to do a lot of travelling, it may not be the best time to go. Similarly be flexible about scheduling so as to accommodate the availability of your key interlocutors. Additionally, you may need to plan your research around local holidays or diplomatic scheduling; government officials or UN staff may be on holiday during the summer. Above all, you will need significant lead time for the preparation and planning of your trip.

Although it is important to conduct as much desk research as possible before going, particularly to assist you in narrowing down people you wish to contact or organizations you wish to work with, greater information and contacts will often be available once you arrive in the country. The selection of communities that you wish to work with or villages of particular interest may be difficult to determine from abroad. As a result, it is important to build in time to follow up with contacts and organizations that you will only be able to access once in the field.

Access to the country will be a vital issue. There are often obstacles to obtaining a visa in countries in conflict or recuperating from it. In their respective chapters, Julie Norman and Susan Thomson explore the challenges of access in a country where authorities may have reason to be worried about researchers or their outputs. If a visa requires sponsorship, you may need to consider how a certain institutional affiliation may affect your research. Again, approaching potential institutions, organizations or individuals to sponsor you can take some time. You may also need to demonstrate financial security for the period that you are in the country, and this will be something you need to plan for, although a letter from your university or funding body may suffice. Seeking illegal entry to a country, or making misleading statements regarding your research is likely to put you at risk and also to violate your university's ethical code.

The logistics you will need to undertake will depend a great deal on the type of research that you intend to carry out and the difficulties of the specific location. You will probably want to organize at least your first week's transport and accommodation before going. If you can determine what can be arranged in advance and what will have to be done in the country, this will enable a more efficient use of time. It is likely that you will need a great deal of currency with you, since in many sites of research credit cards will not be accepted and ATMs are unlikely to be available. It is important to consider how to travel securely with currency, as the amount you may carry may be of considerable value – even the equivalent of an individual's yearly salary.

Julie Mertus offers several good suggestions for ensuring your security before you depart, including agreeing with a trusted individual in your home country that you will check-in with them periodically, that they will hold copies of your passport, as well as acting as your voice of reason to tell you when you have gone beyond your agreed boundaries of safety.

The practicalities of your trip will include not only logistical organization but also approval by your institutional review board (IRB) or other ethics committees. This can be a time-consuming process that you will need to factor into your planning. As Judy Hemming demonstrates, it is not always an easy process and may sometimes requires interviews with the board, or negotiations over particularly contentious points. The approval may also be necessary in order to obtain any letter of support for a visa application from your institution.

Going to the field

Once you have begun your field research, a host of additional issues will arise. In this section we consider some of the lessons drawn from the chapters in relation to ethical considerations, gaining access to your participants, the validity of data, safeguarding personal security, your personal behaviour and perceived identity.

Ethical considerations

Research in social sciences is subject to specific ethical standards, usually set by professional organizations, governments, universities, funding bodies, or some combination of these. Your research is likely to be developed in the context of an institution that has its own research ethics framework and will require you to commit to them prior to funding or approving any proposal.

Broadly these ethical demands comprise the following:[1]

■ The research should be designed, reviewed and undertaken to ensure integrity and quality.

■ Research staff and participants should be informed fully about the purpose, methods and intended possible uses of their research and the risks involved in their participation. In many instances, this information is required to be given in writing so that participants can give informed consent.

■ Respect should be given to the confidentiality of the information supplied by the participants and their anonymity when requested or required.

■ The participation of research participants should be voluntary, free of all coercion. On most occasions you will be required to obtain their permission to be interviewed and for their data to be used in writing and may need to obtain clearance from them prior to the publication of the results or any other outputs. Further, you might be required to make your participants aware of and consent to the arrangements made for the management and security of the data and the preservation of anonymity.

■ The research should avoid harm to research participants. This includes not only the obligation to minimize physical or psychological harm, discomfort or stress to your participants, but also to avoid social risks such as risk to social standing, privacy, personal values and beliefs, links to their families and the wider community, their position within occupational settings as well as avoiding propitiating the consequences that revealing information related to illegal behaviour may have. All these risks are particularly pertinent in the research settings we are treating as 'difficult situations'.

■ There should be explicit statement of any conflict of interest or impartiality that conditions the independence of the research.

However, as John C. King notes, this and other professional guidelines often take a narrow view of ethical considerations. There are complex ethical problems that need to be addressed and King uses a dramaturgical metaphor to demonstrate how many of the authors have managed to adjust to unanticipated ethical dilemmas and ensure the success of fieldwork much as a playwright adjusts to ensure that the 'show must go on'. His analysis of how authors adapted their 'performance' illustrates the importance of flexibility to realize your research vision and develop new knowledge.

As a researcher you will be responsible for following institutional rules, from the initial proposal to the final stages of publication and beyond,[2] and will have to navigate what King calls a 'complex ethical thicket'. Research proposals must indicate how ethical standards will be met, and gaining approval may not always be a quick and easy process, as demonstrated by the experience of Hemming. Her chapter shows that universities may act on concerns that are not strictly to do with ethics, but relate to image and the context of a competitive international environment. It may be helpful to reflect upon how to present your research so as to minimize any negative interpretations as well as highlighting the unique and positive aspects of your work.

As we noted already, obstacles in the ethics approval process can affect both your logistics and your proper research. An IRB may place restrictions upon research that can adversely affect its outcome. For example Hemming was asked to interview her subjects away from their places of work, which she felt would affect their comfort and safety. However, an IRB may sometimes deny consent outright. If it looks as though you will not receive approval, it may be that you need to change the focus of your research, subject to careful consideration regarding its impact on outcomes, and in consultation with a supervisor, if appropriate.

Ethics regulations may not only change your research, but also require additional time and effort to accommodate the rules. This may particularly be the case with respect to informed consent. Norman found that anonymity was key in gaining the trust of participants, and she gained special dispensation from her university to conduct interviews accordingly. Hemming gave every interviewee her business card instead of a consent form. There may be other creative ways to fulfil these and other ethical requirements. University procedures can be long and bureaucratic at the best of times, and ethics committees examining applications involving 'difficult situations' tend to move particularly slowly and cautiously. Even if you respond to all queries and provide additional information, the institution may insist upon certain rules such as a requirement of obtaining written consent.

There and back: surviving field research in violent and difficult situations 231

In addition to the university's or funding body ethics code, you will also need to consider whether you require any research permission from authorities in the country you are travelling to. It took four months of consulting with the relevant national ministry and engaging with the local authorities for Elizabeth Levy Paluck to obtain the relevant permissions for 14 research sites. Such engagement also entails careful but honest presentation of research to suspicious authorities. The most appropriate strategy will depend on the country context, but your approach to authorities may be assisted by letters of support or introduction obtained in advance from your university or other organizations.

As a researcher you have ethical obligations not only to your interlocutors, but also towards your research staff, particularly if you are working with NGOs and/or research teams. Several chapters address the management of relationships with research staff, both to ensure that they are complying with ethical standards, but also to safeguard their security and wellbeing. As Paluck shows, if you have partnered with an NGO and are working with some of their staff or using their vehicles and equipment, it is sensible to follow their security rules even if you feel they are more stringent than those you would apply to yourself. She also recommends including a meal as part of the per diem for members of your research team, to ensure that they are well fed while out in the field, rather than setting aside all funds to take back to their families without addressing their own needs.

Gaining access to your participants

As the varied experiences in this book have shown, although the type of research and situation may change, it is always necessary to gain access to and the trust of individual participants, and often also government officials and others in religious organizations, NGOs, academic institutions, and so on. It is important to understand the cultural, historical and contextual dimensions of trust. As Norman rightly points out, these can vary between cultures, disciplines and individuals, and as Courtney Radsch reminds us, access is often dependent on the identity of the researcher, and both inherent and social identifiers which have different meanings in different contexts. It is thus important to consider how you will be viewed in the country of research. Would your credentials – your university, the organization that funds your research, etc. – mean anything to government officials or to individuals? Would the fact that you come from a specific country have any impact on participation in your research? Does it create suspicion or does it give you a certain reputation? Is the fact that you have a specific ethnic or racial origin, or religious background an impediment or an opportunity? These factors are important to take into account.

On a recent trip to Liberia to research the rebuilding of the rule of law, the authors of this chapter found that the mention of their affiliation with a school of law in both our written and oral introduction to our project was helpful in gaining access to important actors, including a high-ranking member of the judiciary, because the legal profession is highly regarded in that country. In addition, although most participants were not familiar with our funding body, mentioning the institution in the explanation of our research made it possible to interview a top UN official who agreed to see us due to a personal connection to that institution. Clarity about purpose, financial support, and institutional connections is not only important for compliance with IRB requirements; it may offer opportunities for the work itself, although of course it may also create obstacles.

As Norman explains, the formal IRB requirements (providing participants with a written statement of research objectives, securing informed consent and ensuring anonymity and confidentiality) are important but not always helpful in obtaining access. On occasion they might even be counter-productive, as they might intimidate people or even put them at risk, for example the requirement of written consent. Gaining trust can be as crucial as fulfilling all of the formal requirements.

Several authors draw attention to the difficulties of dealing with certain governments when negotiating access. You may be required to comply with their national regulations, and to be aware before entering the field that the government in question may refuse to support certain types of research. As several chapters in this book show, it is crucial to make the right alliances in the country to assure this access. However it is equally important to understand what the affiliations with those organizations that facilitate government favour will mean to your participants. Susan Thomson's choice of an NGO with strong links to the Rwandan government to be her research partner, having guaranteed her initial access, had repercussions in the way she had to conduct her research and protect her participants and data. In contrast, Norman's affiliation with an Israeli academic institution opened the door to the Occupied Territories and did not lead to her rejection by the Palestinian participants, thanks to her very careful choice of a prestigious, non-stigmatized institution.

On occasion the relationships with local organizations who act as sponsors or partners may depend on personal ties, colleagues, or colleagues of colleagues, which can make things easier. However, any choice of partner can also have risks, so it is important to research thoroughly before making an informed decision, and to carefully monitor the impact it has on your research as it develops in the field. You may find that you have to develop creative solutions for dealing with these agents in the field, as both Thomson and Paluck did in Rwanda with their respective NGOs. You need to consider how to present your association to certain institutions or your personal and professional connections to the communities/people to which you seek access. As Paluck shows us, in some situations it may be beneficial to be seen as part of an NGO, particularly in a volatile security situation, or where NGOs may be trusted by communities. However, in other situations if NGOs are seen as aligned with the government or a specific political persuasion, it may be

There and back: surviving field research in violent and difficult situations 233

preferable to highlight your independence as an individual researcher without renouncing agreed affiliations.

Whether you decide to work with a partner organization or not, gaining access to local participants will always present challenges. Each researcher and each group of participants, and situation itself, are different but there are some important general issues to consider. The trust of the participants can be obtained by creating a network of connections and the impact of your own behaviour, which can contribute to the likelihood of acceptance from your participants. Radsch explains how connections are crucial to gaining access to informal networks, and how accessing certain groups often depends upon support from the right, influential, person. Thomson adapted her personal behaviour to facilitate access, putting emphasis on living as a local, using public transport, going to the market regularly and making strong efforts to speak the local language. Norman gained access to different groups through affiliating to a network of local leaders and community organizations, while spending months working as a volunteer as part of her preliminary research. Their experiences illustrate how preserving independence as a researcher is important, although it can be difficult to avoid being seen as supporting a particular point of view. Thomson illustrates this difficulty in her chapter, where showing sorrow for one individual prompted an angry reaction and initial rejection from another potential participant. It is important to remember, as Radsch demonstrates, that sometimes gaining certain access is a mixture of luck and strategy. Luck cannot be predicted, but good strategy can make it easier to seize opportunities when they arise.

The validity and relevance of your data

In situations of conflict, or in countries recovering from violence, a researcher will find that there are many reasons why he/she may feel that he/she is not getting the 'truth' from interviews. If a researcher feels unable to trust interviewees, this may mean that they interpret this as inaccurate data and thus of no use. However, as Lee Ann Fujii demonstrates in her chapter, there is much to be drawn from such data, even if it cannot be corroborated and evaluated as factually accurate. As she reminds us, people's stories embody 'other truths' – emotional, psychological and moral. Understanding personal narratives that may not seem to add up can actually reveal a great deal about the person recounting them. This means that it may be hard to put the experiences of people into categories for research purposes, and when a victim tells you their story, such distinctions may seem artificial. It is important to remember that working in a difficult situation does not mean that you hold your research to a different standard than usual, but using meta-data will enable you to determine the quality of your data and fill gaps in your research that you would otherwise not have been able to.

In the attempt to ensure a good relationship with potential interviewees and to obtain information that you can trust, gaining an awareness of discussion and rumours circulating regarding your purpose and presence in the community is key. Fujii illustrates how a researcher can be viewed as suspect where there are rumours about her identity. It takes time to build this trust, not only with the interviewee but in the wider community in which you are acting. It could help, if your time and research design allow for it, to try to build this trust through conducting multiple interviews over a period of time in order to hear and react to the rumours and ideally refute them. You may also want to assign some time where your interviewee is able to ask questions, both at the beginning when you introduce yourself and the research project, and at the end when they have seen the questions you have posed and may be concerned about the purpose and use of their answers. Carolyn Gallaher puts forward a strong argument that it is unsafe for a researcher to try and work 'undercover' particularly when working with repellent groups. She has found that people in hard-to-reach groups will agree to talk, if the researcher can explain the purpose of research and reassure them as to his or her own lack of affiliation with police or other law enforcement bodies. She also found that it could be counterproductive in terms of the veracity and validity of data to adopt an alternate persona, as the subject may act in the manner that they think someone with that persona will want to hear. Therefore, to obtain relevant data, it may be better to present oneself as neutrally as possible.

Carrying out research on politically sensitive or emotional topics could be particularly challenging. Researchers may encounter a lack of answers or responses, leading to a deficiency in terms of relevant data. In this situation the development of mutual trust can help you establish an enabling environment for your participants to open up on such issues. Thomson showed her participants an understanding of the important need to protect any information collected due to potential government surveillance, which created bonds and deepened their trust relationship. This helped her access data that would otherwise have been concealed to her. Norman asked her Palestinian colleagues the best way to ask questions on youth support for violent resistance, in order to engage the youth participants rather than alienate them. Seeking advice on the cultural context in this manner could provide you with more relevant answers than a question framed by your understanding as an outsider. However, Fujii also demonstrates that silence on certain issues such as sexual violence or atrocities may be important for establishing trust and showing respect for the boundaries of interviewees. It is important to acknowledge that there might be certain issues to which we simply cannot gain access and that participants' reluctance or unwillingness to pursue certain topics must be respected. For this reason, consideration of the necessity of certain types of data for your research, and the impact on your work if you are not able to gain any data on this area, is essential. It will be helpful to reflect on your own capacity to overcome socially and emotionally tense situations, and to bear in mind the delicate balance between pursuing your objectives and respect for the boundaries of those you are working with.

There and back: surviving field research in violent and difficult situations 235

It is also important to try to avoid preconceived ideas about persons and their identities, or to accept uncritically representations that are portrayed to you as reality. The fact that someone has been termed a 'victim' may colour your view of their subsequent behaviour or lead you to assign more weight to their story. Fujii shows that victims may become perpetrators, or, as Amy Ross' account of her encounter with a young mother in Northern Uganda exemplifies, may already have both roles. Conversely, it may not be the case that repellent groups are necessarily lying to you. Gallaher demonstrates that analyzing the claims of repellent groups and not dismissing them out of hand as spin or propaganda, can generate findings that could potentially help NGOs, activists, the police, and other parties in understanding the group's actions and undermining their support base.

Ultimately, it is important to remember that meta-data involves information and experiences beyond the scope of the original inquiry, and/or acquired outside the planned modes of information-gathering. For Fujii, meta-data can be as important as the actual details gathered from an interview. Meta-data can help researchers make sense of many of the ambiguities and complexities found in the field. Ross also points out the importance of silences, and how much she learnt from listening. Thomson's forced 're-education' programme provided her with interesting extra information that she had not foreseen when designing her research. Field research in such instances can be not only an information collection exercise but also a learning experience, both professionally and personally.

Safeguarding personal security

In safeguarding personal security, it is vital to consider not only risks to physical security but also to your psychological health.

Physical security

Most academic institutions include risk assessments as part of the research proposal phase. When deviation from good research practice (in terms of security and health and safety standards) results in unreasonable risk of harm to the researcher and research participants, most institutions consider this to be research misconduct. Depending on the institution these risk assessments may not be completely adequate for your type of research, as your institution might not be so familiar with dealing with fieldwork or have in place the more complex strategies that larger humanitarian organizations do. In some cases it is wise to do a personal risk assessment even if you have completed forms for your institution, as Mertus suggests. To identify general and the latest specific risks, use academic literature and newspapers, travel guides and embassies' websites. On many occasions your vulnerability does not only depend on your behaviour but also on internal and external elements related to you and your background. Internal elements can affect how the local population sees you due to nationality, origin, religious or political affiliation, age, or gender, while examples of external elements are the international policies of your government. These variables are out of your control but you can prepare strategies to alleviate their effects.

From such an assessment you can prepare a security plan. It is very likely that your university or institution has a security protocol or even provides training, which you could combine with the specific tips offered by Mertus in her chapter. To these we would add the necessity of obtaining insurance or being clear about the details of insurance that may be provided by your institution. You will want to confirm that your proposed activities are covered under this policy and that the country is not excluded, particularly in the event that evacuation is necessary, and ensure you have all the necessary documents and phone numbers related to your insurance readily available.

We suggest that your security plan also considers any potential changes to your trip. Once in the field you may be invited to participate in activities you have not foreseen or to go to areas that were not in your initial itinerary. It is worth trying to anticipate such possibilities in advance and deciding which activities are completely out of the question for you. You may only have a partial understanding of the situation and may be persuaded into a situation of unnecessary risk. For example, if you have made a firm decision before entering the field that you would not travel to certain parts of the country, meet certain types of groups or individuals, etc., it may make you reconsider taking a chance once you are there.

Our most recent fieldwork provides an example of making these types of decisions. We had designed our research, and obtained university permission, to be based only in Monrovia, and our security plan was devised accordingly. During our trip we were invited to visit one of the counties outside the capital with an NGO. We would have travelled by NGO convoy to the village and be hosted by them there for three days, however we would have returned on our own in a taxi, a lengthy trip on damaged roads and in an insecure environment. We had not previously considered security arrangements for travel outside Monrovia in our risk assessment, and although this trip could have provided additional information, we decided we were unable to objectively consider the implications of taking the return journey on our own and decided to keep to our security plan of not leaving the capital. In this regard, we would highly recommend Mertus' advice to have a person in your home country or institution with whom to evaluate any proposed deviations from your trip. As already mentioned having someone at home will give the objective view of whether such a change is advisable or not in terms of your security.

As Mertus says, each researcher should decide for themselves how far they are willing to go in protecting themselves, and the threshold of unacceptable risk. Ross makes the important point that in the field we feel less vulnerable and relatively protected because we are external to the conflict, and that the local people are in much greater need or more vulnerable. This may

There and back: surviving field research in violent and difficult situations 237

contribute to a false sense of security. It is not necessarily the case that as outsiders we are less vulnerable, for example our position may even make us a particular target for crime.

When dealing with the security of your participants, it is extremely important to be conscious of the risks they run when agreeing to participate in your research. In sensitive situations they could face not only political repression and social ostracism, but even risk their lives and those of their family members. The use of translators or research assistants also complicates security. They might have obligations and ties of which you are unaware, so what appears to you as a relationship of trust, and even a legal one if you have a contract with them, may not be as valuable to them as the relationship they might have with the government or other groups or individuals. Thomson offers some tips on preserving the anonymity of your participants, including techniques for coding the names and personal information that could identify participants, deleting information on audio recordings before they are heard by others, and security of written and electronic copies of documents. As Mertus warns, any piece of information you physically hold could be confiscated, read and used against you and your participants.

Finally, there may come a time in which it is not wise for you to continue your research, both for your own safety and that of your participants, and in extreme cases it may be necessary that you leave the country. Thomson was forced to develop an escape plan, and in particularly unstable situations this could be something to prepare for a worst case scenario.

Emotional wellbeing

Most of the chapters have shown the need to be aware of the impact your research trip might have on your emotional wellbeing. To address the risk of such impact it is important to be conscious of your own capacities, strengths and weaknesses, not only as a researcher but also as a human being. The level and type of personal involvement and the duration and nature of your research will depend on your own character and personality. You might want to think about how the experience of sharing both happiness and sorrows with local people in difficult or conflict situations may affect you and, how you plan to deal with it before departing.

Several authors have drawn attention to the difficulties of dealing with certain governments when negotiating access. The fact that some governments seek to control access to information and outcomes of research should not prevent us from pursuing our research objectives. Nonetheless, however, it is important to anticipate the possibility of government action, considering some of the experiences that our authors have endured, such as spending hours of interrogation, being strip searched or detained, being placed under house arrest or in 're-educational' programmes or having to flee a country in the middle of the night. Such treatment can affect not only our security but also our wellbeing. During research in difficult situations, there will always be some degree of stress. From our comfortable position at home it may be hard to determine the consequences that incidents of insecurity or even violence may have on us.

Even in the absence of repression or risk, it may be unsettling to learn that your research is considered useless or irrelevant by your interlocutors, who may be in desperate circumstances, and who may be the very people you believe your research will assist. Ross' experience in a Ugandan IDP camp, where participants were more concerned about being given a pen or food rather than learning about the outcomes of her research, illustrates this well.

In addition to your own personal wellbeing, you should consider the wellbeing of your research participants and how involvement in your research may affect them. It is important to think carefully about how to phrase or ask about sensitive subjects or topics that could put the participant in danger or have an impact on their emotional and mental health. This is highly dependent on context and may need to be adapted to respond to realities on the ground. Questions can be phrased so as to enable interviewees to only give you as much information as they are comfortable with sharing, both in terms of their safety and welfare. In addition, it is important to consider the effect of other behaviour that is not directly related to your research, such as eating or drinking in front of participants who may themselves be hungry or observing religious rituals.

Your personal identity

Your research is inevitably conditioned by your identity and how you appear to others. In other sections we have considered how this might affect your access to participants and your physical safety. Here we consider how it may affect your individual interactions. As Radsch points out there are some identifiers, like gender, age or race, which the researcher is stuck with, whilst others depend on the context and how the researcher may make use of them, such as profession and marital status. Several chapters have highlighted the difficulties that being white or Western present when one seeks to develop a trust relationship in a non-white or non-Western setting. These difficulties can be somewhat mitigated with careful self-presentation. Part of Radsch's approach to building trust was to establish her credentials by drawing on particular parts of her identity that she thought were relevant and similar to the person she was interviewing. In so doing, she sought to convey that she was 'like them' in the hope of gaining insider status, as did Thomson. On the other hand, you may feel that, as a researcher, you have an obligation to present yourself as neutrally as possible in order to elicit the best response from your interviewees. It may also be the case, as Marie-Joelle Zahar highlights, that when studying non-state actors, objectivity may be impossible to achieve and it is more useful to acknowledge that you may be influenced by a statist point of view and adjust your work accordingly by being open to alternative conceptual frameworks and explanations.

There and back: surviving field research in violent and difficult situations 239

Complications can arise if your research does not involve sympathetic actors. As Gallaher outlines in her chapter, remaining silent when talking to repellent groups may make you feel complicit. You may therefore want to think about how you will feel listening to opinions you do not agree with, and how you will want to handle a situation where it is assumed that you are sympathetic. Although Gallaher does not advocate using a false persona, or going undercover, it is important to plan how to answer questions about your political beliefs if they are divergent from the groups you are working with. Gallaher's experience of being asked to appear on a television programme funded by the militia group she was studying, also raises the issue of how activities outside of your research but connected to your subjects may impact the continuation of your work. It could be helpful to think about what your research subjects may ask from you: for example they may want to use your academic credibility or contacts, and this could impact your professional objectivity, work and future research. Awareness of this possibility could prepare you to consider how you could deal with any awkward requests.

There are not only potential difficulties with your direct relationships with your research subjects. For researchers who are in the field for long periods of time, there is also the possibility that your social life can impact your research. As Stephen Brown points out in his chapter, there is no right or wrong way to decide how or whether to change your behaviour in the field. It is up to you to decide upon your comfort level but may be helpful to think about it in advance. When you are away from home and working in a country where conditions may be difficult, both in terms of security and facilities, the balance between work and wellbeing is very important. You will probably make friends and socialize, seeking some degree of rest and relaxation. However, this may impact your research and position in unanticipated ways. Rumours can very quickly and widely circulate and it can be difficult to keep a clear separation between your professional and personal lives. While in your home life, it may be the case that who you socialize with has no bearing on your work, however this could be very different in the field where there is a close-knit international community. You may choose to decline some invitations as inappropriate because accepting them would lead to problematic assumptions about your professional affiliation or even personal relationships.

Whether you volunteer information about yourself or not, you will need to consider how you answer personal questions about your sexuality, marital status or religion. How to respond will depend on your judgment about your situation and comfort level with sharing or concealing parts of your identity. If you choose to lie, it may nonetheless be difficult to keep up the pretence for a prolonged period of time. Although you may feel uncomfortable with such questions, in some contexts sharing such personal information may be seen as an essential part of building trust and some people may not understand that you do not wish to disclose such information. Brown suggests being evasive without lying, and it may help to practice some responses so that you are not taken by surprise.

After you leave: writing up and publishing

After you leave you will have to make sense of the vast material you have collected. Often researchers can feel exhausted after an intense experience and even want to block out everything related to the trip, including their research topic. However painful it may be to go back to it, it is advisable to work on it while interviews and details are still fresh in your mind and not so distant that your experiences will be misinterpreted.

If you have not managed to write up field notes or transcribe interviews while still in the field, this should always be the first step. Just as with any notes in the field, these should be kept secure to maintain the anonymity of sources before clearance of referenced comments.

When it comes time to write up your research, you will face the significant challenge of how to deal with clearance. In this sense, you may need to deal with issues that emerged during your time in the field, such as any failure to obtain informed consent from certain sources, the use of information which was acquired confidentially, or how to avoid distortion of research outcomes by being faithful to your data without distorting or omitting data that does not fit your expected results. Chandra Lekha Sriram's chapter demonstrates the challenge of ensuring continued confidentiality of sources while meeting criteria for publication. There may be demands that data and sources are treated not just rigorously but transparently, which can create difficulties where sources have only authorised their citation by generic identification categories, or have not authorised any citation. When considering interviewees' desire for anonymity, it is important to think about how to preserve their identity and at the same time make use of their information. And as Sriram's dilemma demonstrates, it can be difficult to maintain that anonymity where publishers demand files. On occasion, as she shows, you might have to take the painful decision either to exclude some information where sources cannot be reached for clearance, or to share your sources under strict controls.

And a final thought ...

Although the preparation necessary for conducting research in conflict areas and other difficult settings may seem daunting, it could turn out to be one of your most rewarding experiences, filled with opportunities to learn a great deal about specific research topics and also to engage with other cultures and people and even to discover more about yourself. On your research trip, there will definitely be challenges that you will not expect, but also encounters and relationships that could surprise you. It is a privilege to be able to conduct this research and contribute to knowledge and understanding of some of the most pressing issues of the day. You have already made a good start by trying to identify the potential issues and picking up this book. It will be a great experience ... **ENJOY!**

Notes

1 Based on the six principles of ethical research laid out by the ESRC as fundamental for their funding of social science research and as a guide for other institutions, found in the ESRC Research Ethics Framework (REF), 2005, available at http://www.esrcsocietytoday.ac.uk/ESRCInfoCentre/Images/ESRC_Re_Ethics_-Frame_tcm6-11291.pdf accessed 17 March 2009.
2 The ESRC REF defines research ethics as: 'the moral principles guiding research, from its inception through to completion and publication of results and beyond – for example, the curation of data and physical samples after the research has been published', *ibid.*, p. 7.

Selected Sources

Books

Adams, Rachel, and David Savran, eds, *The Masculinity Studies Reader* (New York: Wiley-Blackwell, 2002).

Aho, James, *The Politics of Righteousness: Idaho Christian Patriotism* (Seattle: University of Washington Press, 1990).

Atkinson, Paul, Amanda Coffey, and Sara Delamont, *Key Themes in Qualitative Research: Continuities and Changes* (Walnut Creek, CA: AltaMira Press, 2003).

Barry, Kathleen, *Female Sexual Slavery* (New York: Avon Books, 1984).

Bennis, W., E. Schein, D. Berlew, and F. Steele, *Interpersonal Dynamics: Essays and Readings on Human Interaction* (Homewood, IL: Dorsey, 1964).

Berg, Bruce L., *Qualitative Research Methods* (California: California State University Press, 2007).

——, *Qualitative Research Methods for the Social Sciences* (Boston: Allyn and Bacon, 2006).

Blee, Kathleen, *Inside Organized Racism: Women in the Hate Movement* (Berkeley: University of California Press, 2003).

Bouris, Erica, *Complex Political Victims* (Bloomfield, CT: Kumarian Press, 2007).

Buchanan, Cate, and Robert Muggah, *No Relief: Surveying the Effects of Gun Violence on Humanitarian and Development Personnel* (Geneva: Centre for Humanitarian Dialogue, 2005).

Burnet, Jennie E., *Genocide Lives in Us: Amplified Silence and the Politics of Memory in Rwanda* (University of North Carolina at Chapel Hill, Department of Anthropology, unpublished doctoral dissertation, 2005).

Burnett, John, *Where Soldiers Fear to Tread: A Relief Worker's Tale of Survival* (New York: Random House, 2005).

Carpenter, R. Charli, *'Innocent Women and Children': Gender, Norms and the Protection of Civilians* (Aldershot: Ashgate, 2006).

Churchill, Ward, *Struggle for the Land: Indigenous Resistance to Genocide, Ecocide, and Expropriation in Contemporary North America* (Monroe, ME: Common Courage Press, 1993).

Coffey, Rebecca, *Unspeakable Truths and Happy Endings: Human Cruelty and the New Trauma Therapy* (Maryland: The Sidran Press, 1998).

Cohen, Erik, *Thai Tourism Hill Tribes, Islands and Open-Ended Prostitution Collected Papers, Studies in Contemporary Thailand No. 4* (Thailand: White Lotus Press, 1996).

Cohen, Raymond, *Negotiating across Cultures: Communications Obstacles in International Diplomacy* (Washington DC: U.S. Institute of Peace Press, 1997).
Cunningham, Robert, and Yasin Sarayrah, *Wasta: The Hidden Force in Middle Eastern Society* (Westport, CT: Praeger, 1993).
Dallaire Roméo, *Shake hands with the devil* (New York: Carroll & Graf Publishers, 2004).
de Lame, Danielle, *A Hill Among a Thousand: Transformations and Ruptures in Rural Rwanda* (Helen Arnold, trans. Madison: University of Wisconsin Press, 2005).
de Silva, K.M., and S.W.R. Samarasinghe, *Peace Accords and Ethnic Conflict* (London and New York: Pinter Publishers, 1993).
Diamond, Sara, *Roads to Dominion: Right-Wing Movements and Political Power in the United States* (New York: Guilford Press, 1995).
Dyer, Joel, *Harvest of Rage: Why Oklahoma Is Only the Beginning* (Boulder: Westview, 1997).
Ellis, Carolyn, *Fisher Folk: Two Communities on Chesapeake Bay* (Lexington: University Press of Kentucky, 1986).
Emerson, Robert M., Rachel I. Fretz, and Linda L. Shaw, *Writing Ethnographic Fieldnotes* (Chicago: University of Chicago Press, 1995).
Emerson, Robert, ed., *Contemporary Field Research: Perspectives and Formulations* (Prospect Heights, IL: Waveland Press, 2001).
Esman, Milton, *Ethnic Politics* (Ithaca and London: Cornell University Press, 1994).
Faden, Ruth, and Tom Beauchamp, *A History and Theory of Informed Consent* (New York: Oxford University Press USA, 1986).
Fals Borda, Orlando, and Muhammad Rahman, *Action and Knowledge: Breaking the Monopoly with Participatory Action Research* (New York: Apex Press, 1991).
Feldman, Martha S., Jeannine Bell, and Michele Tracy Berger, *Gaining Access: A Practical and Theoretical Guide for Qualitative Researchers* (Walnut Creek, CA: AltaMira Press, 2003).
Ferber, Abby, *White Man Falling: Race, Gender, and White Supremacy* (Lanham, MD: Rowman and Littlefield, 2000).
Fielding, Nigel, *The National Front* (London: Routledge and Kegan Paul, 1981).
Flint, Colin, ed., *Spaces of Hate: Geographies of Discrimination and Intolerance in the U.S.A.* (New York: Routledge, 2003).
Flyvbjerg, Brent, *Making Social Science Matter: Why Social Enquiry Fails and How it Can Succeed Again* (Cambridge: Cambridge University Press, 2001).
Foucault, Michel, *Archaeology of Knowledge*, A.M. Sheridan Smith (trans.) (New York: Pantheon, 1982).
Gallaher, Carolyn, *After the Peace: Loyalist Paramilitaries in Post-Accord Northern Ireland* (Ithaca, NY: Cornell University Press, 2007).
——, *On the Fault Line: Race, Class, and the American Patriot Movement* (Lanham, MD: Rowman and Littlefield, 2003).
Geertz, Clifford, *Deep Play: Notes on a Balinese Cockfight* (Berkeley: University of California Press, 1979).
——, *The Interpretation of Cultures: Selected Essays* (New York: Basic Books, 2000).
Goffman, Erving, *On Fieldwork* (Prospect Heights, IL: Waveland Press, 2001).
——, *The Presentation of Self* (New York: Doubleday, 1959).
Gonzáles, Matilde, *Se Cambiá el Tiempo; Conflicto y Poder en Territorio K'iche' 1880–1996* (Guatemala: Asociación para el Avance de las Ciencias Sociales en Guatemala, 2002).

Gray, Fred, *The Tuskegee Syphilis Study: The Real Story and Beyond* (Montgomery and Louisville: New South Books, 2002).
Green, Linda, *Fear as a way of life* (New York: Columbia University Press, 1999).
Gurr, Ted Robert, and Barbara Harff, *Ethnic Conflict in World Politics* (Boulder: Westview Press, 1994).
Gurr, Ted Robert, *Why Men Rebel* (Princeton: Princeton University Press, 1970).
Hall, Edward T, *Beyond Culture* (New York: Anchor Books, 1989).
Hare, A. Paul, and Herbert H. Blumberg, *Dramaturgical Analysis of Social Interaction* (New York: Praeger, 1988).
Hatzfeld, Jean, *Dans le nu de la vie: Récits des marais rwandais* (Paris: Éditions du Seuil, 2000).
Hernan, Judith Lewis, *Trauma and Recovery: the aftermath of violence – from domestic abuse to political terror* (New York: Basic Books, 1992).
Hine, Christina, *Virtual Ethnography* (Thousand Oaks, CA: Sage, 2000).
hooks, bell, *Black Looks: Race and Representation* (Boston: South End Press, 1992).
——, *Feminist Theory from Margin to Center* (Boston: South End Press, 1984).
Humphreys, Laud, *Tearoom Trade: Impersonal Sex in Public Places* (Chicago: Aldine Publishing Company, 1968).
Ignatieff, Michael, *Blood and Belonging: Journeys into the New Nationalism* (New York: Viking Press, 1993).
Ignatiev, Noel, *How the Irish Became White* (New York: Routledge, 1995).
Kaldor, Mary, *New and Old Wars: Organized Violence in a Global Era* (Stanford: Stanford University Press, 1999).
Kalyvas, Stathis, *The Logic of Violence in Civil War* (Cambridge: Cambridge University Press, 2006).
Keen, David, *The Economic Functions of Violence in Civil Wars*, Adelphi Paper 320 (London: Oxford University Press and The International Institute for Strategic Studies, 1998).
Kennedy, George, and Daryl Moen, *What Good Is Journalism? How Reporters and Editors Are Saving America's Way of Life* (Columbia: University of Missouri Press, 2007).
Kenneth Cain, Heidi Postlewait and Andrew Thomson, *Emergency Sex and Other Desperate Measures: A True Story from Hell on Earth* (New York: Hyperion, 2004).
Lagnado, Lucette, and Sheila Dekel, *Children of the Flames: Dr. Josef Mengele and the Untold Story of the Twins of Auschwitz* (New York: Penguin, 1992).
Laqueur, Walter, *Guerrilla: A Historical and Critical Study* (London: Weidenfeld and Nicolson, 1977).
Lareau, Annette, and Jeffrey Shultz, *Journeys Through Ethnography: Realistic Accounts of Fieldwork* (Westview Press, 1996).
Levitas, Daniel, *The Terrorist Next Door: The Militia Movement and the Radical Right* (New York: Thomas Dunne Books, St. Martin's Press, 2002).
Livingstone, D., *The Geographical Tradition* (London: Blackwell, 1992).
Lofland, Lyn, John Lofland, David Snow, and Leon Anderson, *Analyzing Social Settings*, 4th edition (Wadsworth Publishing Company, 2006).
MacKinley, John, *Globalisation and Insurgency* (Oxford: Oxford University Press/ International Institute for Security Studies, 2002).
Maina Chris, and Edith Kibalama, eds, *Civil Society and the Struggle for a Better Rwanda. A Report of the Fact-finding Mission to Rwanda organised under the auspices of Kituo Cha Katiba* (Kampala: Fountain Publishers, 2006).

Malkki, Liisa, *Purity and Exile* (Chicago: University of Chicago Press, 1995).
Manz, Beatriz, *Paradise in Ashes: a Guatemalan journey of courage, terror and hope* (Berkeley: University of California Press, 2004).
——, *Refugees of a Hidden War: The aftermath of counterinsurgency in Guatemala* (Albany: State University of New York Press, 1988).
Marginson, Simon, and Mark Considine, *The Enterprise University Power, Governance and Reinvention in Australia* (Victoria, Australia: Cambridge University Press, 2000).
Mcguire, Patricia, *Doing Participatory Research: A Feminist Approach* (Amherst: University of Massachusetts, Center for International Education, 1987).
Mills, C. Wright, *The Power Elite* (New York: Oxford University Press, 1968).
Mitchell, Richard G., *Secrecy and Fieldwork* (Newbury Park: Sage, 1993).
Murray, Alison, *Pink Fitts* (Victoria: Monash University Press, 2001).
Ndayambajwe, Jean Damascène, *Le Génocide au Rwanda: Un analyse psychologique*, (Butare: Université Nationale du Rwanda/ Centre Universitaire de Santé Mentale, 2001).
Noddings, N., *Caring: A Feminine Approach to Ethics and Moral Education* (Berkeley: University of California Press, 1984).
Nordstrom, Caroline, *Shadows of War; Violence, Power and International Profiteering in the Twenty-First Century* (Berkeley: University of California Press, 2004).
O'Brien, Tim, *The Things They Carried* (New York: Penguin Press, 1990).
Odzer, Cleo, *Patpong Sisters: An American Women's View of the Bangkok Sex World* (New York: Blue Moon Books, 1994).
Olsen, Leanne, *A Cruel Paradise: Journals of an International Relief Worker* (Toronto: Insomniac Press, 2002).
Olson, Mancur, *The Logic of Collective Action* (Cambridge: Harvard University Press, 1965).
Overdulve, Christian M. *Apprendre la langue rwandaise* (The Hague/Paris: Mouton, 1975).
Payne, Leigh, *Unsettling accounts* (Durham: Duke University Press, 2008).
Phongpaichit, Pasuk, Sangsit Phiriyarangsan, and Nualnoi Treerat, *Guns, Girls, Gambling, Ganja: Thailand's Illegal Economy and Public Policy* (Chiang Mai, Thailand: Silkworm Books, 1998).
Pickering, Michael, *Stereotyping the Politics of Representation* (New York: Palgrave, 2001).
Popper, Karl, *Conjectures and Refutations: the Growth of Scientific Knowledge*, 4th ed. (London: Routledge and Kegan Paul, 1972).
——, *The Logic of Scientific Discovery* (New York: Basic Books, 1959).
Popper, *Objective Knowledge: an Evolutionary Approach* (Oxford: Clarendon Press, 1972).
——, Alessandro, *The Death of Luigi Trastulli and Other Stories* (Albany: State University of New York Press, 1991).
Pottier, Johan, *Re-Imagining Rwanda: Conflict, Survival and Disinformation in the late 20th Century* (Cambridge: Cambridge University Press, 2002).
Ratzel, Friedrich, *Anthropogeographie* (Stuttgart: J. Engelhorns Nachf, 1921).
Roediger, David, *Towards the Abolition of Whiteness* (New York: Verso, 1994).
Roht-Arriaza, Naomi, (ed.) *Impunity and Human Rights in International Law and Practice* (Oxford: Oxford University Press, 1995).

Rubin, Herbert, and Irene S. Rubin, *Qualitative Interviewing: The Art of Hearing Data* (London: Sage Publications, 2005).
Ruzibiza, Abdul Joshua, *Rwanda: L'histoire secrète* (Paris: Éditions du Panama, 2005).
Ryle, Gilbert, *The Concept of Mind* (Chicago: University of Chicago Press, 1949).
Saideman, Stephen, and Marie-Joëlle Zahar (eds), *Intra-State Conflict, Governments and Security: Dilemmas of Deterrence and Assurance* (London: Routledge, 2008).
Schram, Sanford, and Brian Caterino (eds), M*aking Political Science Matter: Debating Knowledge, Research, and Method* (New York: New York University Press, 2006).
Semple, Ellen Churchill, *American History and Its Geographic Conditions* (Boston: Houghton, Mifflin Co., 1903).
Shapiro, Ian, Rogers M. Smith, and Tarek E. Masoud, *Problems and Methods in the Study of Politics* (Cambridge: Cambridge University Press, 2004).
Shimamungu, Eugène, *Le Kinyarwanda: Initiation à une langue bantu*, (Paris: L'Harmattan, 1998).
Simons, Anna, *Networks of dissolution* (Boulder: Westview Press, 1995).
Singerman, Diane, *Avenues of Participation* (Princeton: Princeton University Press, 1995).
Smith, Linda Tuhiwai, *Decolonizing Methodologies: Research and Indigenous Peoples* (London: Zed Books, 1999).
Smith, Marc A., and Peter Kollock, *Communities in Cyberspace* (New York: Routledge, 1999).
Smith, N., *American Empire: Roosevelt's Geographer and the Prelude to Globalization* (Berkeley: University of California Press, 2003).
Snyder, Louis, *Encyclopedia of the Third Reich* (New York: Da Capo Press, 1994).
Sriram, Chandra Lekha, *Confronting past human rights violations: justice vs. peace in times of transition* (London: Frank Cass, 2004).
——, *Globalizing Justice for Mass Atrocities: A Revolution in Accountability* (London: Routledge, 2005).
——, *Peace as Governance: Power-sharing, Armed Groups, and Peace Negotiations* (London: Palgrave 2008).
Steinfatt, Thomas M, *Working at the Bar: Sex Work and Health Communication in Thailand* (Westport, CT: London: Ablex Publishing, 2002).
Stephen, Ryan, *Ethnic Conflict and International Relations* (Aldershot: Dartmouth, 1990).
Straus, Scott, *The Order of Genocide: Race, Power, and War in Rwanda* (Ithaca: Cornell University Press, 2006).
Sullivan, John, J. Pierson, and George Marcus, *Political Tolerance and American Democracy* (Chicago: University of Chicago Press, 1982).
Taylor, Peter, *Loyalists: War and Peace in Northern Ireland* (London: TV Books, 1999).
Tilly, Charles (ed.), *The Formation of National States in Western Europe* (Princeton: Princeton University Press).
Umutesi, Maria Beatrice, *Fuir ou mourir au Zaïre: Le vécu d'une réfugiée rwandaise* (Paris: L'Harmattan, 2000).
Warren, Kay B., *Indigenous movements and their critics: Pan-Maya activism in Guatemala* (Princeton: Princeton University Press, 1998).

Weaver, Gary, *Communication and Conflict: Readings in Intercultural Relations* (Boston, MA: Pearson, 2000).
Wolcott, Harry F., *Ethnography: A Way of Seeing* (Walnut Creek, CA: Altamira Press, 1999).
——, *The Art of Fieldwork* (Walnut Creek, CA: Altamira Press, 2005).
Wray, M., and A. Newitz, eds, *White Trash: Race and Class in America* (New York: Routledge, 1997).
Wright, Stuart, *Patriots, Politics, and the Oklahoma City Bombing*, (Cambridge: Cambridge University Press, 2007).
Yanow, Dvora, and Peregrine Schwartz-Shea (eds), *Interpretation and Method: Empirical Research Methods and the Interpretative Turn* (Armonk and London: M.E. Sharpe, 2006).
Zahar, Marie-Joëlle, *Fanatics Mercenaries Brigands ... and Politicians: Militia Decision-making and Civil Conflict Resolution* (Ph.D. Dissertation: Department of Political Science, McGill University, 2000).

Articles and book chapters

Abdelal, Rawi, Yoshiko M. Herrera, Alastair Iain Johnston, and Rose McDermott, "Identity as a Variable," *Perspectives on Politics* vol. 4, no. 4 (December 2006).
Adler, Patricia, and Peter Adler, "Observational Techniques," In P. A. Adler, P. Adler, N. K. Denzin and Y. S. Lincoln (eds), *Handbook of Qualitative Research* (Thousand Oaks, CA: Sage Publications, 1994).
Allen, Charlotte, "Spies Like Us: When Sociologists Deceive Their Subjects," *Lingua Franca* (November 1997).
Ansoms, An, "Striving for Growth, Bypassing the Poor? A Critical Review of Rwanda's Rural Sector Policies," *Journal of Modern African Studies* (forthcoming).
Askew, Marc, "City of Women, City of Foreign Men: Working Spaces and Re-Working Identities Among Female Sex Workers in Bangkok's Tourist Zone," *Singaporean Journal of Tropical Geography* vol.19, no. 2 (1998).
Bakonyi, Jutta, and Kirsti Stuvøy, "Violence and Social Order Beyond the State: Somalia & Angola," *Review of African Political Economy* vol. 32, no. 104 (2005).
Belousov, Konstantin, Tom Horlick-Jones, Michael Bloor, Yakov Gilinkskiy, Valentin Golbert, Yakov Kostikovsky, Michael Levi, and Dmitri Pentsov, "Any port in the storm: Fieldwork difficulties in dangerous and crisis-ridden settings," *Qualitative Research* vol. 7, no. 2 (2007).
Berdal, Mats, and David Keen, "Violence and Economic Agendas in Civil Wars: Some Policy Implications," *Millennium: Journal of International Studies* vol. 26, no. 3 (1997).
Bertini, Catherine A., "Protecting the Protectors," In Yael Danieli (eds), *Sharing the Front Lines and the Back Hills: International Protectors and Providers: Peacekeepers, Humanitarian Aid Workers and the Media in the Midst of Crisis* (New York: United Nations, 2002).
Beyoghlow, Kamal, "Lebanon's New Leaders: Militias in Politics," *Journal of South Asian and Middle Eastern Studies* vol. 12, no. 3 (1989).
Bourgois, Philippe, "Confronting Anthropological Ethics: Ethnographic Lessons from Central America," *Journal of Peace Research* vol. 27, no. 1 (1990).

Brainard, Jeffrey, "The Wrong Rules for Social Sciences?" *The Chronicle of Higher Education* (9 March 2001).

Brown, Stephen, "Quiet Diplomacy and Recurring 'Ethnic Clashes' in Kenya", in Chandra Lekha Sriram and Karin Wermester (eds), *From Promise to Practice: Strengthening UN Capacities for the Prevention of Violent Conflict* (Boulder: Lynne Rienner, 2003).

Burkle, Frederick M, "Complex Emergencies: An Introduction," *Prehospital and Disaster Medicine* vol. 16, no. 4 (2001).

Cahill, Caitlin,"Repositioning Ethical Commitments: Participatory Action Research as a Relational Praxis of Social Change," *ACMS: An International E-Journal for Critical Geographies* vol. 6, no. 3 (2007).

Christians, Clifford, "Ethics and Politics in Qualitative Research," In N. Denzin and Y. Lincoln (eds), *The Sage Handbook of Qualitative Research, 3rd Edition* (Thousand Oaks, CA.: Sage, 2005).

Coady, Tony, "Universities and the Ideals of Inquiry," In Tony Coady (ed.), *Why Universities Matter* (St Leonards, Australia: Allen & Unwin, 2000).

Collier, Paul, "Rebellion as a Quasi-Criminal Activity," *The Journal of Conflict Resolution* vol. 44, no. 6 (December 2000).

——, *"The Political Economy of Ethnicity,"* Paper prepared for the Annual World Bank Conference on Development Economics (Washington DC, 20–21 April 1998).

Cunningham, Robert, and Yasin Sarayrah, "Taming Wasta to Achieve Development," *Arab Studies Quarterly* vol. 16, no. 3 (1994).

Dean, John P., and William Foote Whyte, "How do you know if the informant is telling the truth?" in Lewis Anthony Dexter, ed., *Elite and Specialized Interviewing* (Evanston: Northwestern University Press 1970).

Denzin, Norman, and Yvonna Lincoln, "Introduction: The Discipline and Practice of Qualitative Research," In N. Denzin and Y. Lincoln (eds), *The Sage Handbook of Qualitative Research, 3rd Edition* (Thousand Oaks, CA: Sage, 2005).

——, "Preface," In N. Denzin and Y. Lincoln (eds), *The Sage Handbook of Qualitative Research, 3rd Edition* (Thousand Oaks, CA: Sage, 2005).

Duneier, Mitchell, "On the Evolution of Sidewalk," In R. M. Emerson (eds.), *Contemporary Field Research: Perspectives and Formulations* (Prospect Heights, IL: Waveland Press, 2001).

Eckstein, Harry, "On the Etiology of Internal Wars," in George A. Kelly and Clifford W. Brown Jr., eds, *Struggles in the State: Sources and Patterns of World Revolution*, (New York: Wiley, 1969).

Elbadawi, Ibrahim, and Nicholas Sambanis, "How Much War Will We See? Estimating the Incidence of Civil War in 161 Countries, 1960–99," *Journal of Conflict Resolution* vol. 46 (June 2002).

Ellis, Carolyn and Arthur Bochner, "Chapter 28: Autoethnography, Personal Narrative, Reflexity: Researcher as subject," in Norman K. Denzin and Yvonna S. Lincoln (eds.) *Handbook of qualitative research* 2nd edition. (Thousand Oaks, CA: Sage, 2000).

Emerson, R. M., and M. Pollner, "Constructing Participant/Observation Relations," In R. M. Emerson (ed.), *Contemporary Field Research: Perspectives and Formulations* (Prospect Heights, IL: Waveland Press, 2001).

Enloe, Cynthia, "All the Men are in the Militias, All the Women are Victims: The politics of masculinity and femininity in nationalist wars," in Lois Ann Lorentzen and Jennifer Turpin (eds.), *The Women and War Reader* (New York: New York University Press, 1998).

Evans, Michael Robert, "The Promises and Pitfalls of Ethnographic Research in International Communication Studies," In Mehdi Semati (ed.), *New Frontiers in International Communication Theory* (Lanham, MD: Rowman & Littlefield, 2004).

Evans, Peter, "The Role of Theory in Comparative Politics: A Symposium," *World Politics* vol. 48 (October 1995).

Fandy, Mamoun, "Information Technology, Trust, and Social Change in the Arab World," *The Middle East Journal* vol. 54, no. 3 (2000).

Fearon, James D., and David D. Laitin, "Ethnicity, Insurgency, and Civil War," *American Political Science Review* vol. 97, no. 1 (2003).

Fielding, Nigel, "Ethnography," In N. Gilbert (ed.), *Researching Social Life* (London: Sage, 1993).

——, "Mediating the Message: Affinity and Hostility in Research on Sensitive Topics," In C. Renzetti and R. Lee (eds), *Researching Sensitive Topics* (Newbury Park, CA: Sage, 1993).

Gans, Herbert J., "Participant Observation in the Era of Ethnography," *Journal of Contemporary Ethnography* vol. 28, no. 5 (1999).

Gibbs, S., "Post-War Social Reconstruction in Mozambique: Re-Framing Children's Experience of Trauma and Healing," *Disasters* vol. 18, no. 3 (1994).

Gleditsch, Nils Petter, Peter Wallensteen, Mikael Eriksson, Margareta Sollenberg and Håvard Strand, "Armed Conflict 1946–2001: A New Dataset," *Journal of Peace Research* vol. 39, no. 5 (2002).

Goodhand, Jonathan, "Research in Conflict Zones: Ethics and Accountability," *Forced Migration Review* vol. 8 (2000).

Heinz, Wolfgang S., "Review: Guerrillas, Political Violence, and the Peace Process in Colombia," *Latin American Research Review* vol. 24, no. 3 (1989).

Hills, Alice, "Warlords, militia and conflict in contemporary Africa: A re-examination of terms," *Small Wars and Insurgencies* vol. 8, no. 1 (1997).

Hirschkind, Lynn, "Redefining the "Field" in Fieldwork," *Ethnology* vol. 30, no. 3 (July 1991).

Howe, Benjamin Ryder, "Revolutionaries or Crooks?" *Foreign Policy* no. 122 (January–February 2001).

Hughes, Donna, "*Hiding in Plain Sight: a Practical Guide to Identifying Victims of Trafficking in the U.S.*" (2003), http://www.uri.edu/artsci/wms/Hughes/hiding_in_plain_sight.pdf.

——, "Men Create the Demand, Women Are the Supply," *feminista!*, vol. 4, no. 3, (2000).

Hutchings, Kate, and David Weir, "Understanding Networking in China and the Arab World: Lessons for International Managers," *Journal of European Industrial Training* vol. 30 no. 4 (2006).

Jacobsen, Karen, and Loren B. Landau, "The Dual Imperative of Refugee Research: Some Methodological and Ethical Considerations in Social Science Research and Forced Migration," *Disasters* vol. 27, no. 3 (2003).

Junas, Daniel, "The Rise of Citizen Militias: Angry White Guys with Guns," In C. Berlet (ed.), *Eyes Right! Challenging the Right Wing Backlash* (Boston: South End Press, 1995).

Kaldor, Mary, "Old Wars, Cold Wars, New Wars and the War on Terror," *International Politics* vol. 42 (2005).

Kalyvas, Stathis, "'New' and 'Old' Civil Wars: A Valid Distinction?" *World Politics* vol. 54 (October 2001).

——, "The Ontology of 'Political Violence': Action and Identity in Civil War," *Perspectives* vol. 1, no. 3 (September 2003).

——, "The Urban Bias in Research on Civil Wars,"*Security Studies* vol. 3, no. 3 (2004).

——, "Wanton and Senseless? The Logic of Massacres in Algeria," *Rationality and Society* vol.11, no. 3 (1999).

Kastberg, Arne Nils, "Risk and Protection for UNICEF Field Staff," In Yael Danieli (ed.), *Sharing the Front Lines and the Back Hills: International Protectors and Providers: Peacekeepers, Humanitarian Aid Workers and the Media in the Midst of Crisis* (New York: United Nations, 2002).

Kaufman, Stuart J., "Symbolic Politics or Rational Choice? Testing Theories of Extreme Ethnic Violence," *International Security* vol. 30, no. 4 (2006).

——, "Escaping the Symbolic Politics Trap: Reconciliation Initiatives and Conflict Resolution in Ethnic Wars," *Journal of Peace Research* vol. 43, no. 2 (2006).

King, Charles, "The Benefits of Ethnic War: Understanding Eurasia's Unrecognized States," *World Politics* vol. 53 (July 2001).

Langford, Peter, "The Rwandan Path to Genocide: The Genesis of the Capacity of the Rwandan Post-colonial State to Organise and Unleash a Project of Extermination," *Civil Wars* vol. 7, no. 1 (2005).

Le Billon, Philippe, "Angola's Political Economy of War: The role of oil and diamonds, 1975–2000," *African Affairs* vol. 100 (2001).

Lecocq, Baz, "Fieldwork Ain't Always Fun: Public and Hidden Discourses on Fieldwork," *History in Africa* vol. 29 (2002).

Leo, Richard, "Trial and Tribulations: Courts, Ethnography, and the Need for an Evidentiary Privilege for Academic Researchers," *The American Sociologist* vol. 26, no. 1 (1995).

Lewis, J. David, and Andrew Weigert, "Trust as a Social Reality," *Social Forces* vol. 63, no. 4 (1985).

Lichbach, Mark, "What Makes Rational Peasants Revolutionary? Dilemma, Paradox, and Irony in Peasant Collective Action," *World Politics* vol. 46, no. 3 (April 1994).

Löfving, Staffan, "Silence and the politics of representing rebellion: On the emergence of the neutral Maya in Guatemala," in Paul Richards, ed., *No peace no war: An anthropology of contemporary armed conflicts* (Athens: Ohio University Press, 2005).

MacGinty, Roger, "Ethno-National Conflict and Hate Crime," *American Behavioral Scientist* vol. 45, no. 4 (December 2001).

Malaquias, Assis, "Diamonds are a Guerrilla's Best Friend: The Impact of Illicit Wealth on Insurgency Strategy," *Third World Quarterly* vol. 22, no. 3 (June 2001).

Marginson, Simon, "Research as a Managed Economy: The Costs," In Tony Coady (eds.), *Why Universities Matter* (St Leonards, Australia: Allen & Unwin, 2000).

May, William, "Doing Ethics," *Social Problems* vol. 27, no. 3 (February 1980).

Miller, Seumas, "Academic Autonomy," In Tony Coady (ed.), *Why Universities Matter* (St Leonards, Australia: Allen & Unwin, 2000).

Mohamed, Ahmed A., and Hadia Hamdy, "The Stigma of Wasta: The Effect of Wasta on Perceived Competence and Morality," *Faculty of Management Technology Working Paper 5* (The German University in Cairo, 2008).

Molony, John, "Australian Universities Today," In Tony Coady (ed.), *Why Universities Matter* (St Leonards, Australia: Allen & Unwin, 2000).

Monk, Jan, and Susan Hanson, "On Not Excluding Half of the Human in Human Geography," *Professional Geographer* vol. 34, no. 1 (1982).
Morgan, Glenda, "Violence in Mozambique: Towards an Understanding of Renamo," *The Journal of Modern African Studies* vol. 28, no. 4 (December 1990).
Mueller, John, "The Banality of 'Ethnic War'," *International Security* vol. 25, no. 1 (Summer 2000).
Naylor, R.T., "The Insurgent Economy: Black Market Operations of Guerrilla Organizations," *Crime, Law and Social Change* vol. 20 (1993).
Newbury, David, and Catharine Newbury, "Review Essay: Bringing the Peasants Back In: Agrarian Themes in the Construction and Corrosion of Statist Historiography in Rwanda", *American Historical Review* vol. 105 (2000).
Olujic, Maria B., "The Croatian War Experience," in Carolyn Nordstrom and Antonius C.G.M. Robben, eds, *Fieldwork under fire* (Berkeley: University of California Press, 1995).
Paluck, Elizabeth Levy, "Reducing Intergroup Prejudice and Conflict Using the Media: A field experiment in Rwanda," *Journal of Personality and Social Psychology* (forthcoming).
Peet, Richard, "The Social Origins of Environmental Determinism," *Annals of the Association of American Geographers* vol. 75 (1985).
Peritore, N. Patrick, "Reflections on Dangerous Fieldwork," *The American Sociologist* (Winter 1990).
Posen, Barry R., "The Security Dilemma and Ethnic Conflict," in Michael Brown (ed.), Ethnic Conflict and International Security (Princeton: Princeton University Press, 1993).
Radsch, Courtney C., "Blogging in Egypt," *Reset: Dialogue on Civilization 103* (Rome: 2007), http://www.resetdoc.org.
———, "How Al Jazeera Is Challenging and Improving Egyptian Journalism," *Reset: Dialogue on Civilizations* (22 June, 2007), http://www.reset.org.
———, "Satellite Television in the Arab World," *Oxford Analytica* (22 April, 2008).
Raymond, Janice, "10 Reasons for Not Legalizing Prostitution," *The Coalition Against Trafficking in Women* (15 September 2003), http://action.web.ca/home/catw/readingroom.shtml?x=32972&AA_EX_Session = 7578.
Reyntjens, Filip, "Rwanda, Ten Years On: From Genocide to Dictatorship," *African Affairs* vol.103 (2004).
Rich, Paul B., "Warlords, State Fragmentation and the Dilemma of Humanitarian Intervention," *Small Wars and Insurgencies* vol. 10, no. 1 (1999).
Rupiya, Martin, "Historical Context: War and Peace in Mozambique," in Jeremy Armon, Dylan Hendrickson and Alex Vines (eds.), *The Mozambican Peace Process in Perspective*, special issue of *Accord – An International Review of Peace Initiatives* no. 3 (1998).
Sambanis, Nicholas, "What is Civil War: Conceptual and Empirical Complexities of an Operational Definition," *Journal of Conflict Resolution* vol. 48, no. 6 (December 2004).
Schooley, Kimberly Y., "Cultural Sovereignty, Islam, and Human Rights toward a Communitarian Revision," *Cumberland Law Review* no. 25 (1994).
Selim, Mohamed, "The Survival of a Nonstate Actor: The Foreign Policy of the Palestine Liberation Organization," in Bahgat Korany and Ali Hillal Dessouki, eds, *The Foreign Policies of Arab States* (Boulder: Westview Press, 1984).

Shafer, Jessica, "Guerrillas and Violence in the War in Mozambique: De-Socialization or Re-Socialization?" *African Affairs* vol. 100, no. 399 (2001).

Snider, Lewis, "The Lebanese Forces: Their Origins and Role in Lebanon's Politics," *Middle East Journal* vol. 38, no. 1 (1984).

——, "The Lebanese Forces: Wartime Origins and Political Significance," in Edward Azar et al., *The Emergence of a New Lebanon: Fantasy or Reality?* (New York: Praeger, 1984).

Sriram, Chandra Lekha, "Revolutions in Accountability: New Approaches to Past Abuses," *American University International Law Review* vol. 19, no. 2 (2004).

——, "Wrong-sizing international justice? The hybrid tribunal in Sierra Leone" *Fordham International Law Journal* vol. 29, no. 3 (2006).

——, "Dilemmas of accountability: politics, the military, and commissions of inquiry during an ongoing civil war: the Sri Lankan case," *Civil Wars* vol. 5, no. 2 (Summer 2002).

Stedman, Stephen John, "Spoiler Problems in Peace Processes," *International Security* vol. 22, no. 2 (Fall 1997).

Swinth, Robert L, "The Establishment of the Trust Relationship," *The Journal of Conflict Resolution* vol. 11, no. 3 (1967).

"Symposium: Methodological Foundations of the Study of International Conflict," *International Studies Quarterly* vol. 29 (1985) pp. 121–36.

Tanner, Samuel, "Saisir la violence de masse: Le nettoyage ethnique en Bosnie et l'apport d'une perspective locale et d'une approche de réseau,"; *Déviance et société* vol. 31, no. 3 (2007).

Theidon, Kimberly, "Gender in transition: Common sense, women, and war," *Journal of Human Rights* vol. 6 no. 4 (2007).

Turner, Mark, " 'We Are Helpers, Not Martyrs': UN Aid Workers Are Increasingly Becoming Targets in the War Zones They Try to Assist," *Financial Times*, (7 Oct. 2000).

Valentino, Benjamin, "Final Solutions: The Causes of Mass Killing and Genocide," *Security Studies* vol. 9, no. 3 (Spring 2000).

van den Hoonaard, Will C., "Is Research-Ethics Review a Moral Panic," *The Canadian Review of Sociology and Anthropology (Revue canadienne de sociologie et d'anthropologie)* vol. 38, no.1 (February 2001).

Waldorf, Lars, "Mass Justice for Mass Atrocity: Rethinking local justice as transitional justice," *Temple Law Review* vol. 79, no. 1 (2006).

Warren, Carol, "Gender and Fieldwork Relations," In Robert Emerson (ed.), *Contemporary Field Research: Perspectives and Formulations* (Prospect Heights, IL: Waveland Press, 2001).

Warwick, Donald, "Tearoom Trade: Means and Ends in Social Research," *The Hastings Center Studies* vol. 1, no. 1 (1973).

Weber, Max, "The Meaning of Ethical Neutrality," in Edward Shils and Henry Finch (trans.), *Methodology of the Social Sciences* (New York: The Free Press, 1949).

Wessells, M, and C. Monteiro, "Healing Wounds of War in Angola: A Community-Based Approach," In D. R. Donald, Andrew Dawes and Johann Louw (eds), *Addressing Childhood Adversity* (Cape Town: D. Philip, 2000).

Wolf, Charlotte, "Constructions of a Lynching," *Sociological Inquiry* vol. 62, no. 1 (1992).

Wood, Elisabeth, "The Ethical Challenges of Field Research in Conflict Zones," *Qualitative Sociology* (2006).

Zahar, Marie-Joëlle, "Protégés, Clients, Cannon Fodder: Civilians in the Calculus of Militias," *Managing Armed Conflicts in the Twenty-first Century*, a special issue of *International Peacekeeping* vol. 7, no. 4 (Winter 2001).

———, "Understanding the Violence of Insiders: Loyalty, Custodians of Peace, and the Sustainability of Conflict Settlement," in Edward Newman and Oliver Richmond (eds), *Spoilers and Peace Processes: Conflict Settlement and Devious Objectives* (Tokyo: United Nations University Press, 2006).

Zaharna, R. S., "Understanding Cultural Preferences of Arab Communication Patterns," *Public Relations Review* vol. 21, no. 3 (1995).

Reports and official documents

American Political Science Association, *A Guide to Professional Ethics in Political Science* (Second edition, revised 1998, reprinted 2004), available at http://www.apsanet.org/imgtest/ethicsguideweb.pdf

Anti-Defamation League, *The Execution of Timothy Mcveigh* (2001), http://www.adl.org/mcveigh/mcveigh_print.asp

Australian Government: National Health and Medical Research Council, *Media Releases 2002*, http://www.nhmrc.gov.au/news/media/rel102/index.htm.

Australian Government: National Health and Medical Research Council, *National Statement on Ethical Conduct in Research Involving Humans* (1999) http://www.nhmrc.gov.au/publications.

Australian National Government, *Joint NHMRC/AVCC Statement and Guidelines on Research Practice* (1997) http://www.nhmrc.gov.au/grants/policy/researchprac.htm

Brabant, Koenraad Van, *Operational Security Management in Violent Environments: A Field Manual for Aid Agencies* (London: Humanitarian Practice Network at the Overseas Development Institute, 2000), http://ngosecurity.googlepages.com/GPR8.pdf.

Campaign for the Right of Entry/Re-Entry to the Occupied Palestine Territory, http://www.righttoenter.ps.

Comisión para el Esclarecimiento Histórico, *Guatemala: Memoria del silencio* (Guatemala: UNOPS, 1999).

Davidson, Sara, *People in Aid Code of Best Practice in the Management and Support of Aid Personnel* (People In Aid, 1997), http://www.peopleinaid.org/code/.

DesForges, Alison, *Leave None to Tell the Story: Genocide in Rwanda* (New York: Human Rights Watch, 1999).

Duflo, Esther, *Field Experiments in Development*. (NBER Working Paper, 2006).

Economic and Social Research Council, *Research Ethics Framework* (not dated) at http://www.esrcsocietytoday.ac.uk/ESRCInfoCentre/Images/ESRC_Re_Ethics_Frame_tcm6-11291.pdf.

Economic and Social Research Council, *Research Ethics Framework* (Swindon), http://www.esrcsocietytoday.ac.uk/ESRCInfoCentre/Images/ESRC_Re_Ethics_Frame_tcm6-11291.pdf.

EU Commission, *Security of Relief Workers and Humanitarian Space* (Brussels: 1998), http://aei.pitt.edu/6712/.

Human Rights Watch, *Killings in Eastern Rwanda* No. 1 (2006).

Human Rights Watch, *Uprooting the Rural Poor in Rwanda* (London: Human Rights Watch, 2001).

254   Selected Sources

Humanrightsprofessionals.org, *Statement of Ethical Commitments of Human Rights Professionals* (University of Nottingham Human Rights Law Centre), http://www.humanrightsprofessionals.org/images/statement%20of%20ethical%20commitments_-nov%2028%202007_website.pdf.

ICRC, *Code of Conduct for the International Red Cross and Red Crescent Movement and Non-Governmental Organizations (NGOs) in Disaster Relief* (Geneva: ICRC, 1994).

——, *Seminar on the Security of Humanitarian Personnel in the Field for Non Governmental Organisations (NGOs)* (Geneva: ICRC, 1997).

Inter-Agency Standing Committee, *Consolidated Appeal Process Guidelines* (April 13, 1994), http://www.reliefweb.int/cap/CAPSWG/CAP_Policy_Document/Guidelines/CAPguid94.doc.

International Crisis Group, *Congo: Consolidating the Peace*, Africa Report No. 128 (2007).

——, *Consensual Democracy In Post-Genocide Rwanda. Evaluating the March 2001 District Elections.* Africa Report No. 34 (2001).

——, *Rwanda at the End of the Transition: A Necessary Political Liberalisation?* (Nairobi: ICG, 2002).

——, *The Congo's Transition Is Failing: Crisis in the Kivus*, Africa Report No. 91 (2005).

Mello, Siergio Vieira de, *Meeting of Special Rapporteurs/Representatives, Experts and Working Groups of the Special Procedures of the Commission on Human Rights* (Geneva: United Nations, 1999).

NHMRC/AVCC, *Joint Nhmrc/Avcc Statement and Guidelines on Research Practice* (1997), http://www.nhmrc.gov.au/funding/policy/researchprac.htm.

O'Neill, Mike, *Ask the Experts* (InterAction, 2000), http://www.interaction.org/library/detail.php?id=5476

Paluck, Elizabeth Levy, "Is it better not to talk? A field experiment on talk radio and ethnic relations in Eastern Democratic Republic of Congo" (Working Paper, Harvard University, 2007).

—— and Donald P. Green, "Deference, dissent, and dispute resolution: An experimental intervention using mass media to change norms and behavior in Rwanda" (Working Paper, Harvard University, 2008).

Perriello Tom, and Marieke Wierda, "The Special Court for Sierra Leone Under Scrutiny (March 2006), at http://www.ictj.org/static/Prosecutions/Sierra.study.pdf.

Potok, Mark, *Memories of 'Patriotism,'* The Southern Poverty Law Center's Intelligence Report 102 (2001) pp. 6–8.

Roberts, David Lloyd, *Staying Alive: Safety and Security Guidelines for Humanitarian Volunteers in Conflict Areas*, The International Committee of the Red Cross (revised 2005), http://www.reliefweb.int/rw/lib.nsf/db900sid/RURI-6LJUCY/$file/icrc-safety30jan.pdf.pdf?openelement.

Tangen, Lars, John Dyer, and Karl Julisson, *Stay Safe: Stay Safe – International Federation's Guide to a Safer Mission,* International Federation of the Red Cross (Mar 2008), http://www.reliefweb.int/rw/lib.nsf/db900sid/OCHA-7DBHYA/$file/113700-stay_safe_management-EN.pdf?openelement.

The List: The World's Top Social Networking Sites Foreign Policy (2008), accessed 12 April 2008, http://www.foreignpolicy.com/.

The School of International Service at American University, *American University's IRB Prescriptions,* http://www.american.edu/sis/irb/index.htm.

The State of the News Media 2007 (Washington, DC: Project for Excellence in Journalism, 2007), accessed 30 May 2008, http://www.stateofthenewsmedia.org/2007/.

UNDAC, *UN Security Structure* (2006), http://ochaonline.un.org/OchaLinkClick.aspx?link=ocha&DocId=1005295.

UNDPI, "2007 'One of the Deadliest Years' for United Nations Personnel, Staff Union Says; at Least 9 Peacekeepers, 33 Civilian Staff Members Killed During Year." In *Press Release ORG/1489* (New York: UNDPI, 2 January 2008).

UNIS, *Secretary-General Kofi Annan Promises Major Reform of UN Peacekeeping Calls on Member States to Provide Funds, Improve Decision-making* (23 August 2000).

UNIS, *Secretary-General, at Staff Security Summit, Urges States to Ratify Treaty on Safety of United Nations and Associated Personnel* (29 June 2001).

United Nations, *Security in the Field: Information for Staff Members of the United Nations System* (New York: Office of the United Nations Security Coordinator, UN, 1998), http://www.reliefweb.int/library/documents/security.pdf.

UNJLC, *United Nations Joint Logistics Centre Brief Description* (12 June 2006), http://www.unjlc.org/about/unjlc_brief_discription.

Index

abuse, protection against 25
abuses in medical studies 31
academic autonomy 25
academic independence 57
accent of research team 46
access
  in conflict zones 85
  to community 77–83
  to country 228
  to field site 74–77
  gaining 114–15
  to individuals 83–85
  modes of 78–79
  to participants 231–33
  to respondents 114–15
  security and 78–79
accompaniment 179
active conflict zones 79
age 83
American Political Science Association 58
Annan, Kofi 168, 191
anonymity
  of colleagues 51
  guarantees of 8, 13, 82
  of participants 14, 57, 58, 60, 62–63, 64, 67, 72, 81, 85, 86, 114, 229, 230, 232, 240
  of researcher 34
anonymized interviews 13, 62–63
Anti-Defamation League (ADL) 127
approach to dangerous subjects 138–40
Arab hospitality 100
Arab League 91, 102
Askew, Marc 28
audio recordings 238
Australia's Group of Eight (GO8)
  Human Research Ethics Committee 15, 21

Australian Vice Chancellors Committee (AVCC) Statement and Guidelines 24
autonomy of sex workers 23–24

Beauvoir, Simone de 22
behavioural measure, materials for 51
behavioural trust 73, 74, 78, 82, 85
belligerents 127–43
Belmont Report 25, 131, 132
bias 191
  of participants 45
  of readers 59
  of research assistants 81
  of researchers 109, 133, 193
  sources of 191
  state-centric 204
  urban 194
Blee, Kathleen 135, 136
blogging 13, 93–95, 101–4
Bosnian war 166, 191
boundaries 234
  ethical 75
  informants' 160, 234
  of researcher/participant relationship 39, 82
  researchers' 118
  of safety 228
  temporal 155
Brainard, Jeffrey 31
Braithwaite, Val 30, 33
bureaucratisation of higher education 32
business card 34, 101, 230

Charbonneau 34
Citizens for a Constitutional Kentucky (CCK) 127, 128
civil wars 200–201
Clausewitz, Carl von 199
clearance 58–59, 215, 240

ethical 21–35
  post-interview 65–66
  posthumous 59–61
clearance phase 59
codes of ethics and behaviour 8, 76
coercive elements 48
cognitive trust 72, 73, 74, 78, 81, 82, 83, 85
Cohen, Erik 24, 34
collegiality 59, 64–65
colonialism 136
Commission of the European
  Communities: *Security of Relief
  Workers and Humanitarian Space* 168
communal conflict, history of 170
community, access to 77–83
community duty 25
community trust 77
conduct in the field 213–25
confidentiality 57, 58–59, 72, 77, 83, 81–82, 85, 229, 232, 240
conflict of interest 230
conflict zones 74, 77, 79, 85
consent 28, 30
  informed 58, 72, 81, 82, 131–32, 138, 229, 230, 232, 240
  verbal 72
  written 63–64, 230, 232
consent forms 26, 30, 33–34, 138
constructivism 130
content analysis of texts 92
coping strategies 84
country, access to 228
creativeness 32
crime profile 171
crisis of representation 132, 133
critical ethics 132–34
critical model 143
critical paradigms 130, 134
critical race scholars 133
critical rationalism 192–93
cultural awareness 100–101
cultural taboos 78
culture of research 12
currency 228

data 51, 181–83, 233–35
  see meta-data
  relevance and validity of 233–35
Davidson, Sara 169
Dawkins Reform 34
Dawkins Report 31
Dayton Accords of 199 196
decentering 133
deception 151, 154

Democratic Republic of Congo 38–55
deniability 179
denial of entry 75
denials 10, 149, 153–55, 160
dialect of research team 46
digital networking 12–14
dignity of participants 31, 153, 166
disappearances 179–80
discomfort 229
distanced data collection 136
donors 58
draft sharing 59, 64–65
dramaturgical metaphor 9–12, 230
duty of the academic 25

e-mail 57, 66, 94–95, 173
Economic and Social Research Council 63
  Research Ethics Framework 58
economic dependency 28
economic factors, sex work and 24
economy/resource base and
  infrastructure 171
Egypt, access 94–95
Egyptian blogosphere 93
Egyptian hospitality 100
electronic copies of documents 238
Ellis, Carolyn 138
embellishment 10, 152–53
emergency sex 221
emotional trust 72–73, 74, 78, 81–83, 85
emotional truth 151, 153, 233
emotional wellbeing 237–38
empathy 135
employment test 46
Enloe, Cynthia 199
environmental determinism 132–33
escape plan 238
ethical clearance 21–35
ethical considerations 229–31
ethical gaps 134–38
ethnic background, trust and 83
ethnic identification 45–46, 47
ethnography 24, 26
evasions 149, 155–58, 160
exaggeration 10, 152–53
exculpatory evidence 140
expectations 134
expertise exchange 44, 50–53
Expresso Preprint 59
external factors, security environment
  and 170–71
external players, identification of 170
eye contact 128

Selected Sources

Facebook 12, 13, 95, 96–97, 102
fairness 134
false separation of the selves 214–15
feedback 50
feminist research 130, 133, 136
field site, access to 74–77
file sharing 12–14
filing as breach of confidentiality 61–64
focus groups 79, 92, 101
fog of war 182
Fordham International Law Journal 63
Foucault 194
funding 32

game theory 72
Geertz, Clifford 132
gender 22, 83, 99–100
gender balance of research teams 46
ghosts in the machine 40, 55
globalization 93
government surveillance 50
grand narrative 194
guarantees of anonymity 8
Guatemalan Commission for Historical Clarification: 'Memory of Silence' 182

harm minimization 2533, 229
hate groups 138–39
Havelhas, Ron 186
HERC 25
Hills, Alice 195
honesty 134
hospitality 100
hospitality, Egyptian 100
Hughes, Donna 21
human rights 26, 171
human rights monitors 58
human rights violations, protection against 25
human security *see* security
humanitarian aid workers 58

identification 44–48
 of participants 47–48
 of research project 44–45
identity 45, 57, 96–97
identity groups 43–44, 48
ideographic approaches to knowledge 192
illegal behaviour 139, 230
impartiality 194, 230
imperialism 136
implausibility 151
inappropriate questions 29

individuals, access to 83–85
information economy 77
informed consent 58, 72, 81, 82, 131–32, 138, 229, 230, 232, 240
inquisitiveness 32
Institutional Review Boards (IRBs) 8, 11, 14–16, 17, 21–35, 72, 130–32, 133, 134, 137–38, 143, 229, 230, 232
insurance 237
integrity of researchers 25
interference 116–21
internal threats, security environment and 170–71
Internally Displaced People (IDP) 183
International Centre for Ethnic Studies (ICES) 60
International Committee of the Red Cross (ICRC) 169
 Code of Conduct for the International Red Cross and Red Crescent Movement and Non-Governmental Organizations (NGOs) in Disaster Relief 169
 Stay Safe – International Federation's Guide to a Safer Mission 169
International Criminal Court (ICC) 183, 184
International Studies Association 59
Internet 57
interpretive and critical paradigms 130
interviewing 29, 92
 one-shot 160, 161
 questions, composition and translation of 51
 semi-structured 71, 79, 101
inventions 149, 151–53
invisibility of researcher 30
Irish Republican Army (IRA) 129
isnad 13, 92, 96

Kabila (Swahili for ethnicity) 48
Kaldor, Mary 198
Keen, David 198
Kentucky State Militia (KSM) 10, 127, 139, 140
knowledge and objectivity 192–94
Ku Klux Klan (KKK) 140

language 39, 99, 113
 of research team 46
latent conflict zones 79
law journals 57
Lebanon, access 94–95
Lecocq, Baz 194

legal institutions 170
legitimacy 195, 196
Leo, Richard 138
liberal activist bloggers 95
Liberation Tigers of Tamil Eelam
    (LTTE) 59–60, 61, 65–66
lies 154, 222–24
linguistic identity 46
literacy 30
lived experiences 23
Lomé Peace Accord 61
Loyalist paramilitaries, Northern
    Ireland 10, 141

managerial governance view 25
Marginson 32
Martín-Baró, Ignacio 179–80
Marxism 130
maximization of possible benefits 25
McKinlay, John 199
McVeigh, Timothy 127
meal as part of salary 51
medical protocol 31
Mengele, Joseph 130
meta-data 148–60, 235
Milgram, Stanley 24
militants 127–43
military developments 171
Miller, Seumas 25, 32
Milosevic, Slobodan 196
Ministry of Internal Security
    (MININTER) (Rwanda) 110, 118
Ministry of Local Government
    (MINALOC) (Rwanda) 110, 111, 113
mixed methods approach 71
mobile phone numbers 94–95
moral truth 153, 233
morale building, research team 49
motives, ulterior, of research subjects
    137–38
multiple interviews 160, 234
Murray 34
Muslim Brotherhood 95, 98, 99, 101,
    105
mutual trust 234

narrative research 73, 79
National Front 138
*National Health and Medical Research
    Council* (NHMRC) (Australia) 24, 25
    Media Releases 2002 30
    Principles of Ethical Conduct 31
    Strategic Plan for 1995–2004 31
    Statement and Guidelines 24

*National Statement on Ethical Conduct
    in Research Involving Humans*
    (NSECRIH) (Australia) 24, 30
    Research Merit and Safety, Section 1
        27
    Statement and Guidelines 26
National Thai Research Council 33
nationality 83, 97–99
natural disaster, probability of 171
Nazi concentration camps 130
neutrality 136
nomothetic approaches to knowledge
    192
non-governmental organizations
    (NGOs) 38–55, 231, 232
    best practice guides 169
    identification 44–45
    reputation 48
non-state actors 6, 194–95, 198, 204,
    206, 238
Norman, Sam Hinga 62
Nuremberg Code 131
Nuremberg Trials 24, 131

O'Brien, Tim 182
obedience/compliance experiment
    (Milgram) 24
objectivity 83, 136, 143, 191, 192–94
observation 92
Odzer, Cleo 24, 34
off-duty behaviour 217–19
Office of the United Nations Security
    Operations (UNSECOORD) 16, 168
one-shot interviews 160, 161
oral sources, credibility 151
ordres de mission 38, 48, 52
othering 22, 133
Overseas Development Administration
    (UK) 169
oversharing, dangers of 58–59

participant observation 71, 79, 82–83,
    92–94
participants, access to 231–33
participatory action research 134
participatory methods 79
patriarchal power relations 24
payment of interviewees 29, 54–55
peace as stability 202–3
peace education initiative 76
peacekeepers 167
People In Aid Code 169
performance indicators 31
permission

from authorities 231
to enter field 110–12
permissions process 23, 43, 48
persona, adopting 138–39, 234
personal ethical code, trust and 76
personal identity 238–39
personal questions, answering 221–24
personal relationships, off-duty 219–21
personal security (care of self) 165–74, 246–48
personal security plan 173
Peruvian truth commission 148
physical harm 229
physical security 48–49, 236–38
Pickering, Michael 21–22
political elites, identification of 170
Popper, Karl 193
population fractionalization 43–44, 45, 47, 50, 53
Positivism 192
post-interview clearance and academic integrity 65–66
postcolonial studies 130
posthumous clearance 59–61
power
in the field 136–37
relationships 133–34
of representation 140
power élite 22
preconceived ideas, avoiding 99, 235
prediction 192
premature web publication with attribution 64–65
prescriptive horizons 202–4
presence
in the field 54
of researcher, trust and 77
presuppositionist theories 194
primary local research assistant, value of 54
prison interviews 47, 118
privacy of respondents 81
privatization 93
professional conduct 25, 33, 216–17
Prostitution Act 1960 (Thailand) 27
prostitution/sex trafficking in Thailand 21–35
protection
of interlocutors 57
of justice 25
of vulnerable populations 132
pseudonyms 26
psychological distress 131
psychological harm 229
psychological security of research team 48–49
psychological truth 153, 233
publishing 240

queer theory 130, 133
question list 28, 33
questions, inappropriate 29
quid pro quo arrangement 134, 135, 137, 142–43

Radicals 127–43
rapport 135
rational action theory 29
rational choice methodologies 72
rationality 201–2
re-education 11, 108, 119, 120, 121, 235, 237
recruitment 112–14
relational trust 73
relationship
with NGO 52
personal, off-duty 219–21
power 133–34
quid pro quo relationship 137, 142–43
researcher/participant 39, 82
with researchers 51–52
relaxation 49
relevance of data 233–35
Relief and Rehabilitation Network 169
religion 83, 223, 224, 231, 236, 239
repellent informants 127–43
reprisals 161
reputation
of institution 15, 21–22, 30–32, 34
of journal 13
of NGO 45, 48
of researcher 137, 213, 214, 219, 221, 223, 231
research assistants 238
research collaborations 50–53
research ethics, evolution of 129–34
research grants 31
research honesty 25
research permit 111
Research Practice (1997) 24, 25–26
research proposal 227
research team leader, value of 54
resistance 83
respect for persons 1, 25, 31, 82, 84, 85, 101, 115, 117, 132, 160
Revolutionary United Front (RUF) 61–62
risk analysis 61

risk assessment 169–71, 173
risk disclosure 132
risk factor 21, 26
risk versus benefit analysis 14, 25, 26–29
romance, off-duty 219–21
rule of law 170
rumours 149–50, 160, 234, 239
Rwanda 38–55, 108–21
Rwandan Patriotic Front (RPF) 119

safety of interviewees 26
same-sex relationships 221, 222
Sankoh, Foday 62
Scarry, Elaine 181
scope of enquiry 197–200
scouting trip 26, 27, 28
security 44, 48–50, 227, 228
   of NGO 49–50
   of participants 57, 77–81
   as peace 203
   of the person 16–17
   and relevance of research 183–85
   research methods and 79–80
   silence and 178–81
   trust and 77–92
Security in the Field 168
security plan 237
security-seeking behaviour, impact on research 177–87
self-censorship 42
self-identify 44, 45–46
self-presentation 140
self-representation 141
Selim, Mohammed 195
semi-structured interviews 71, 79, 101
sensitivity, security and 80–81
separatist groups 139
Serrano, Jorge 178
sex, off-duty 219–21
sex workers in Thailand 21–35
sexual violence 46–47
Shopes, Linda 29
silences 149, 158–60
situational analysis 170, 173
snowballing 79, 80
social attributes 97
social networking 96–98
social risks 229–30
South African Truth and Reconciliation Commission 181–82
Special Court for Sierra Leone (SCSL) 62
speech, appropriate 48
Sri Lankan Monitoring Mission 66

Stanford Prison Experiment 24
state-centrism, integrity of fieldwork and 204–6
state control 42–43, 45, 47, 48, 50, 53
statistical analysis 92
Steinfatt, Thomas M. 28
stereotyping 21–22, 27–35, 133, 140
stigma 221–24
strategic ambiguities 159
stress management 168, 229
surveillance 116–21
surveys 71, 72–73, 160

taken-for-granted assumptions 29, 32, 33
Taylor, Charles 62
tearoom trade 131
testimony 181–83
textual analysis 92
therapist, interviewer as 115
thick descriptions 132
threat and vulnerability analysis 172–74
timing of research 227
Tiruchelvam, Dr Neelan 60–61
torture 182
translators 238
transnational activism 93
transparency 77, 82, 83
trauma 78, 181–83
triangulating different sources 151
true academic authority 30
Truman Institute 76
trust
   access in conflict zones 71–88
   after the fieldwork 86
   before fieldwork 85–86
   between the researcher and respondents 76
   definition 71–74
   during the fieldwork 86
   of participants 230, 232–33
Trust Fund for the Security of UN Personnel 168
trust period 73–74
Truth and Reconciliation Commission (TRC) 62
truth commissions 148
Tudjman, Franjo 196
Tum, Rigoberta Menchú 178
Tuskegee Syphilis Study 24, 130, 131, 132
Twitter 12, 102, 103

Ulster Volunteer Force (UVF) 129, 141, 142

undercover work 138–39, 234
United Nations Department of Safety and Security (UNDSS) 168
United Nations Security Council 62
university
  publications 32
  reputation 34
urban bias 194

validity of data 233–35
value-free inquiry 133
Van Brabant 172
  Mainstreaming the Organizational Management of Safety and Security 168–69
  Operational Security Management in Violent Environments 168
van den Hoonaard, Will 33, 34
verbal consent 63, 72
vice sharing 142
Vietnam War 166
violence 42, 44, 45, 47, 48, 50, 53
  state-sanctioned 170
violent and difficult situations 227–40

virtual ethnography 96
visas 75, 76, 104, 228
visionary pragmatism 136
vulnerability assessment 171–73
vulnerability, researcher 135–36

wasta 13, 92, 95
  virtual 96–98
Web posting, dangers of 59
Weber 194
Weblogs *see* blogs
webpage 13
welfare of interviewees 26
well being of participants 31
Willowbrook State School, New York 130–31, 132
Wright Mills, C. 22
writing up 240
written consent 63–64, 230, 232
written documents 238
written statement of research objectives 72, 232

youth survey 86–88

A library at your fingertips!

eBooks are electronic versions of printed books. You can store them on your PC/laptop or browse them online.

They have advantages for anyone needing rapid access to a wide variety of published, copyright information.

eBooks can help your research by enabling you to bookmark chapters, annotate text and use instant searches to find specific words or phrases. Several eBook files would fit on even a small laptop or PDA.

NEW: Save money by eSubscribing: cheap, online access to any eBook for as long as you need it.

Annual subscription packages

We now offer special low-cost bulk subscriptions to packages of eBooks in certain subject areas. These are available to libraries or to individuals.

For more information please contact webmaster.ebooks@tandf.co.uk

We're continually developing the eBook concept, so keep up to date by visiting the website.

www.eBookstore.tandf.co.uk

RELATED TITLE FROM ROUTLEDGE

CRITICAL THEORISTS AND INTERNATIONAL RELATIONS

Edited by **Jenny Edkins**, University of Aberystwyth
and **Nick Vaughan-Williams**, University of Exeter

Covering a broad range of approaches within critical theory including Marxism and post-Marxism, the Frankfurt School, hermeneutics, phenomenology, postcolonialism, feminism, queer theory, poststructuralism, pragmatism, scientific realism, deconstruction and psychoanalysis, this book provides students with a comprehensive and accessible introduction to 32 key critical theorists whose work has been influential in the field of international relations.

February 2009: 234x156: 368pp
Hb: 978-0-415-47465-8 **£75.00**   Pb: 978-0-415-47466-5 **£21.99**

Contents: Introduction *Jenny Edkins* and *Nick Vaughan-Williams* 1. Theodor Adorno *Columba Peoples* 2. Giorgio Agamben *Nick Vaughan-Williams* 3. Hannah Arendt *Patricia Owens* 4. Alain Badiou *Claudia Aradau* 5. Jean Baudrillard *François Debrix* 6. Simone de Beauvoir *Kimberly Hutchings* 7. Walter Benjamin *Angharad Closs Stephens* 8. Roy Bhaskar *Milja Kurki* 9. Pierre Bourdieu *Peter Jackson* 10. Judith Butler *Cristina Masters* 11. Gilles Deleuze *Robin Durie* 12. Jacques Derrida *Maja Zehfuss* 13. Franz Fanon *Himadeep Muppidi* 14. Michel Foucault *Andrew Neal* 15. Sigmund Freud *Vanessa Pupavac* 16. Antonio Gramsci *Mark Rupert* 17. Jürgen Habermas *Neta Crawford* 18. G.W.F. Hegel *Ritu Vij* 19. Martin Heidegger *Louiza Odysseos* 20. Immanuel Kant *Kimberly Hutchings* 21. Julia Kristeva *Vivienne Jabri* 22. Emmanuel Levinas *Elizabeth Dauphinee* 23. Karl Marx *Milja Kurki* 24. Jean-Luc Nancy *Martin Coward* 25. Friedrich Nietzsche *Robin Durie* 26. Jacques Rancière *Rens van Munster* 27. Richard Rorty *James Brassett* 28. Edward Said *Latha Varadarajan* 29. Carl Schmitt *Louiza Odysseos* and *Fabio Petito* 30. Gayatri Chakravorty Spivak *Catarina Kinnvall* 31. Paul Virilio *James Der Derian* 32. Slavoj Zizek *Diane Rubenstein*

'Edkins and Vaughan-Williams have produced a very helpful collection of introductions to the thinking of a wide variety of writers who have been influential in the critical analysis of international relations. This comprehensive set of accessible introductions helps the reader understand the core contributions of writers who have been seminal in the development of a critical account of international relations.'
– Professor Steve Smith, Vice-Chancellor, University of Exeter

'Global politics has provided an important context of critical theory. Yet its growing complexity has also called attention to the ongoing task of articulating and reflecting upon the roles of identity, power, order, and resistance in International Relations. *Critical Theorists and International Relations* is a splendid and much-needed volume that addresses and fills, in a truly original manner, this important niche. Providing comprehensive and authoritative analyses of the key critical theorists, this edited volume will continue to remind us of the ever-present need to wrestle harder with the contextual and overlapping meanings of critical theory in International Relations.'
– Steven C. Roach, Editor of Critical Theory and International Relations: A Reader

Available at all good bookshops
For ordering and further information please visit:

www.routledge.com/politics

RELATED TITLES FROM ROUTLEDGE

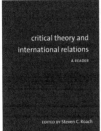

Critical Theory and International Relations: A Reader
Steven C. Roach

This innovative new Reader provides students, scholars, and practitioners with a comprehensive overview of essential works of critical theory and critical international relations (IR) theory, including the writings of Kant, Hegel, Marx, Nietzsche, Freud, Weber, Horkheimer, Adorno, Marcuse, Habermas, Linklater, and Honneth, among others.

Steven Roach frames each chapter showing the major tensions of four periods of the extension of critical theory into critical IR theory. This rich narrative, telling the story of how critical theory entered into international relations theory, seeks to deepen the reader's historical and sociological understanding of the emancipatory project of critical IR theory. Postmodernist and feminist texts are included to give context to the question of whether the discipline is in crisis or is working toward a cohesive and reflexive framework.

2006: 246x174: 424p
Hb: 978-0-415-95418-1 **£75.00** • Pb: 978-0-415-95419-8 **£21.99**

International Relations Theory for the Twenty-First Century: An Introduction
Martin Griffiths

International Relations Theory for the Twenty-First Century is the first comprehensive textbook to provide an overview of all the most important theories within international relations. Written by an international team of experts in the field, the book covers both traditional approaches, such as realism and liberal internationalism, as well as new developments such as constructivism, poststructuralism and postcolonialism.

The book's comprehensive coverage of IR theory makes it the ideal textbook for teachers and students who want an up-to-date survey of the rich variety of theoretical work and for readers with no prior exposure to the subject.

2007: 246x174: 200pp
Hb: 978-0-415-38075-1 **£70.00** • Pb: 978-0-415-38076-8 **£19.99** • ebook: 978-0-203-93903-1

International Relations Theory : A Critical Introduction
Cynthia Weber

This introduces students to the main theories in international relations. It explains and analyzes each theory, allowing students to understand and critically engage with the myths and assumptions behind them. Each theory is illustrated using the example of a popular film.

Key features of this textbook include:

- discussion of all the main theories: realism and neo-realism, idealism and neo-idealism, liberalism, constructivism, postmodernism, gender and globalization
- two new chapters on the 'clash of civilizations' and Hardt and Negri's Empire
- innovative use of narratives from films that students will be familiar with: Lord of the Flies, Independence Day, Wag the Dog, Fatal Attraction, The Truman Show, East is East and Memento
- an accessible and exciting writing style which is well-illustrated with film stills, boxed key concepts and guides to further reading.

This breakthrough textbook has been designed to unravel the complexities of international relations theory in a way that gives students a clearer idea of how the theories work, and of the myths associated with them.

2004: 246x174: 208pp
Hb: 978-0-415-34207-0 **£90.00** • Pb: 978-0-415-34208-7 **£19.99** • ebook: 978-0-203-48146-2

Available at all good bookshops
For ordering and further information please visit: **www.routledge.com/politics**